Jesus AND Mary

THE BLESSED MOTHER, THE HOLY SON AND HIS TEACHINGS OF THE WORD

JON KENNEDY, MA, JENNY SCHROEDEL AND REVEREND JOHN SCHROEDEL

JG
PRESS

Published by World Publications Group, Inc.
140 Laurel Street
East Bridgewater, MA 02333
www.wrldpub.com

Originally published as *The Everything® Jesus Book* and *The Everything® Mary Book*.

ISBN 10: 1-57215-749-6
ISBN 13: 978-1-57215-749-1

ISBN 10: 1-57215-751-8
ISBN 13: 978-1-57215-751-4

Printed and bound in the United States of America.

10 9 8 7 6 5 4 3 2 1

Contents

Jesus

Mary

Jesus

Top Ten Interesting Facts
You'll Learn About Jesus

1. Scholars generally agree that Jesus' life is better documented than that of any other figure of historical antiquity.

2. The church at large did not celebrate the birth of Jesus, Christmas, until between three and five centuries after the church's beginning.

3. The church does not teach that Jesus' date of birth was December 25.

4. Scholars have concluded that Jesus was born about five years earlier than the beginning of the current general calendar, or about 5 B.C.

5. After a replacement was found for Judas Iscariot, all but one of Jesus' closest disciples died martyrs' deaths after keeping the faith.

6. Jesus was circumcised as all Jewish males are, as part of their covenant with God.

7. Jesus was baptized by John the Baptist, who was his second cousin.

8. In most of the Christian world, Easter is known in the local language as the equivalent word for Passover.

9. What Jesus considered the best and worst prayers are only one sentence each.

10. Thousands of martyrdoms in the first three centuries of the church are generally considered the best evidence for the truthfulness of the Gospel and the biggest impetus for the church's growth.

Introduction

WHO WAS JESUS? What was the world that he was born into like? Who were his parents and ancestors? What did he teach? Who were his first followers, and how did they multiply in number to become the largest religious following in today's world?

What did Jesus mean when he told his followers they would be able to move a mountain? What did Jesus teach as necessary for salvation? Do his teachings contrast with—or complement—those of his apostles? How did we receive the Bible, and what causes orthodox Christians to believe it contains and is, in written form, the Word of God?

In today's more multicultural world, answers to such questions are no longer universally known, and with the competition of constantly increasing entertainment, educational, and information media, the Bible stories are not as widely taught to children, even if more Bibles are in the stores and in homes than ever before. Contemporary surveys of high-school-age and college-age young people have shown deep and widespread biblical illiteracy.

This book introduces Jesus from a slightly more distant perspective than that of the Bible by sharing some of the findings of Bible scholars, historians, archaeologists, and anthropologists on his life and times, his following in the church, and his impact on the world in the two millennia since his birth. The intention is to make this an easily accessible survey of Jesus, his life, his teachings, his historical impact, and more.

Chapters will give detailed accounts of the church in the first generation after Jesus ministered on earth, how persecution against Christians began and spread from Israel to the whole Roman Empire, how many of the martyrs died, and how they are considered the "seed of the church." Also looked at are the conversion of the Roman emperor Constantine and his influence on the church; and the church's influence on the emperor and, through him, on the succeeding emperors and the Roman Empire as a whole.

The Dark Ages, the Middle Ages, the Crusades, the Renaissance, the Age of Exploration, the Enlightenment, and the rise of modern democracies . . . all are surveyed in terms of their relationships with the story of Jesus, his life, and his world influence, and made easily accessible in this overview.

How is the church faring in today's generation? How big is the church in the United States, and in the world at large? How does it compare with other religions in size and the devotion of its followers? Has the Christian era peaked and started its decline, or is it poised for further growth in the world in generations to come? Who are the Catholics, Orthodox, Protestants, Modernists, and Evangelicals, and how do they relate to each other? How does the church fare alongside secular humanism in Europe, America, and the rest of the world?

Also included in this survey will be consideration of the Jesus of the future, as the Bible makes many references to the climax of history, the end of the world, the apocalypse, and the Second Coming of Jesus. What does the Bible say on these controversial topics, and what do the different churches say about those biblical teachings?

Throughout this work, references to "the traditional teaching" or "the tradition of the church" refer to the consensus of the united church before the great schism between Rome and Constantinople in 1054 (described in Chapter 11) and, especially, the defining documents and canons of the seven ecumenical councils that culminated in A.D. 787. References here to "the apostolic churches" mean those churches of the first millennium after Christ that claimed that all their bishops had been consecrated in an unbroken line of succession from the original apostles of the church (as described in Chapter 5). And consistent with this approach, though there are many theories among modern biblical scholars about the identity of the writers of the New Testament, especially Matthew and Luke, the references in this book refer to the author of Luke as "Luke," the author of Matthew as "Matthew," and so on, in the interest of simplification and clarity.

CHAPTER 1

Jesus of the Stable

If the widely cited claim that one-third of the world's population identifies itself as Christian is accurate, the story of Jesus' birth is most likely the best-known account of a birth in human history, and possibly even the best-known story ever told. Even those not literate enough to read for themselves are exposed to the story through Nativity scenes, pageants, readings, and carols accompanying Christmas celebrations around the world.

Humble Beginnings

The Gospel of Luke introduces the birth portion of Jesus' story in chapter 2:1–7. These verses describe his surroundings, suggest his purpose in coming, and provide the tenor of his story by beginning the human life of the Creator and King of the universe not in a palace but in a stable, probably built into a cave in the hillside, where no one would ever expect anything of great significance to occur.

discussion question

What is the origin of the word *Christmas*?
The early church's technical name of the day set aside for observance of Christ's birth is the Feast of the Nativity. Feasts are the resumption of a regular diet after a fast such as Advent, the forty-day fast preceding Christmas. The word *Christmas* comes from the English contraction of the Roman Catholic term "Christ's mass."

Some scholars believe Luke likely received his detailed account of the birth of Jesus directly from Mary, Jesus' mother. According to church tradition, Mary was early in her childbearing years at the time she became promised to Joseph, and she lived some years after Jesus' ascension into Heaven. Biblical scholars believe Luke's Gospel and the other three Gospels were written in the latter half of the first century after Jesus' birth.

Virgin Birth

A fundamental teaching of Christianity is that Mary was betrothed but had not consummated her marriage with Joseph when Jesus was born. Without this teaching, the claim that God was Jesus' father would be disbelieved. Luke says that "in the sixth month" the angel Gabriel was sent from God to Mary in Nazareth, a town in Galilee, a region of the Israel of that time northeast of Jerusalem, to tell her God the Father had chosen her to:

. . . bear a son, and shalt call his name JESUS. He shall be great, and shall be called the Son of the Highest: and the Lord God shall give unto him the throne of his father David: And he shall reign over the house of Jacob for ever; and of his kingdom there shall be no end.

Then said Mary unto the angel, How shall this be, seeing I know not a man? And the angel answered and said unto her, The Holy Ghost shall come upon thee, and the power of the Highest shall overshadow thee: therefore also that holy thing which shall be born of thee shall be called the Son of God . . . For with God nothing shall be impossible (Luke 2:31–35; 37).

Matthew's Gospel cites the virgin birth as a fulfillment of the prophecy of Isaiah, "Therefore, the Lord himself shall give you a sign: 'Behold, a virgin shall conceive, and bear a son, and shall call his name Emmanuel'" (Isaiah 7:14; Matthew 1:23).

fallacy

It's a widespread misconception that the "Immaculate Conception" is a technical term related to Jesus' virgin birth. The doctrine of the "Immaculate Conception," taught only by Roman Catholics among the Christian communions, refers not to the conception of Jesus in Mary's womb, but of Mary's in the womb of her mother. The Immaculate Conception reinforces Mary's sinlessness. The teaching became an official Catholic dogma in 1854.

God with Us

Emmanuel is a Hebrew phrase meaning "God with us." (El, the final syllable, is short for *Elohim*, a common Hebrew name for God that appears more than 2,500 times in the Old Testament.) Most Christian interpreters hold the prophecy of Isaiah as messianic and take it to refer to a specific child to be sent by God to save his people. Matthew, whose Gospel is tailored for Jewish readers, cites this verse from Isaiah as the first of many Old Testament prophecies he uses as evidence for the divinity and messianic mission of Jesus. Jesus, which is the name both Luke and Matthew say was given to Mary for her son, is from the Greek Iesous, which in turn comes from the Hebrew Jeshua (also written as Yeshua) or Joshua, all meaning "Yahweh is salvation."

Shepherds and Angels

One indication of the humble milieu into which Jesus was born is that initially no great or powerful people were told about one of the most important events thus far in human history. But shepherds, no doubt faithful Jewish people whose major yearning was the coming of their Messiah, were let in on the news by angels they saw singing Jesus' praise in the sky over the starlit hills where they were camped. Luke devotes what now amounts to ten verses of his Gospel to the shepherds' adoration of the Christ child (the original text was not broken into verses).

Though two Gospels record details about the birth of Jesus, and some recognition of Jesus' birth is recorded in historical documents as early as A.D. 200, the Nativity does not appear in church records as an official feast of the church until A.D. 566 or 567. The slow evolution of Christmas observance probably occurred mainly because early Christians thought that in the pagan Roman practice, "only sinners' birthdays were celebrated." The first generations of Christians celebrated Jesus' baptism, as well as the adoration of the Magi, as the events that revealed him as God with us. This now-lesser feast of the Magi is known and observed to this day as Epiphany (or, in Eastern Orthodoxy, Theophany), which falls twelve days after Christmas; this is the origin of the tradition of the twelve days of Christmas.

Kenosis (Self-Humbling)

Kenosis is a Greek term for self-emptying (*ekenosen*), or self-humbling. Though it refers specifically to the later work of Jesus in going to the Cross and giving himself over entirely to the will of the Father and the vulnerability of a human death, it also describes the humble circumstances of his birth and the gradual revelation of his godhead.

Theologians have debated whether Jesus gave up superhuman powers in this self-emptying, as some Protestant scholars have speculated, or whether he merely chose not to exercise them, as Catholic and Orthodox fathers maintain. Jesus' kenosis can also apply to his submission to the parental control of Mary and Joseph, whom he depended on and obeyed despite his divine nature.

Jesus' Family Tree

In Matthew's Gospel, Jesus' genealogy, or family tree, precedes the account of his birth to make the point that he was a direct descendant of Abraham, whom Paul described as the "father of the faithful" (Romans 4:11; "the father of all them that believe" in the King James version), and of David, the second king of Israel and the one most highly esteemed by the nation ever after, and the king most highly regarded by God Himself. The Gospel begins with "the book of the generation of Jesus Christ, the Son of David, the Son of Abraham." It was commonly believed among the Jewish people that the Messiah would be a member of the House of David, and would be born in Bethlehem of Judea.

factum

Some Eastern European Orthodox Christians celebrate Christmas thirteen days after Catholics, Protestants, and other Orthodox do, but do not date the holiday as falling on January 7. On their calendar (introduced by Julius Caesar in A.D. 45), December 25 falls 13 days later than in the Gregorian calendar (introduced by the Pope in 1582).

Whereas Matthew traces Jesus from Abraham through his stepfather Joseph, Luke traces him backward from Joseph all the way to Adam. This evidences the different primary audiences intended by the two Gospel writers:

the Jewish people in Matthew's case, who would have to see Jesus as a "Jew of the Jews," and Christians who weren't of Jewish origin in Luke's. Matthew emphasizes the royal bloodline, whereas Luke emphasizes his blood relationship with the whole race of humankind.

The Ancestors of God

The divine liturgy (worship service) attributed to fourth century Bishop St. John Chrysostom refers to the parents of Mary, in church tradition Joachim and Anna, as "the ancestors of God." Though of course the eternal God has no human forebears and cannot even be comprehended by human faculties, the church teaches that in the incarnation of the human Jesus, he is "very God of very God." For the same reason, to affirm the two natures of Christ, the fathers in the third ecumenical council, A.D. 431, called for the use of Theotokos, Greek for "God-bearer" or "Mother of God," to describe Mary and thus to underscore Jesus' fully human nature alongside his divinity. If Mary is God's mother, her parents are his grandparents or ancestors, though they all are fully human.

As mentioned previously, the genealogies of Matthew's and Luke's Gospels also trace the ancestors of Jesus. Among them are princes and kings (David, Solomon), but also ordinary people who played redemptive roles in the history of Israel, some of whom were not even ethnically Jewish (Rahab, Ruth). From this it is understood that the Gospel writers wanted to emphasize Jesus' relationship with the whole human race, "of the Jews first, and also of the Gentiles" as St. Paul repeatedly puts it.

Mary

After the shepherds came to adore Jesus in the stable, Luke says, "Mary kept all these things, and pondered them in her heart." This simple description has guided the church's impression and images of Mary since the beginning. Her traditional icon shows her holding her son. Though he is the size of an infant, he has the face of a man, which indicates his adult purpose for being born of Mary. Also in the icon she has her hand raised, pointing to him, indicating that he, not she, is the focus of the attention, not only of the icon viewers, but of human history.

discussion question

Why is Mary controversial?
Mary has been controversial, especially since the Reformation, because Protestants generally felt she got too much attention in Catholic piety, sometimes even calling Mariology "Mariolatry," or idolatry. Recently, however, some Protestants have begun asking how the angel Gabriel's prophecy that all generations will call Mary blessed is being fulfilled in their teaching and worship.

Roman Catholic teaching on Mary includes four dogmas: Mary's Immaculate Conception, which is seen as guarding her from original sin; Mary's sinlessness; Mary's perpetual virginity; and the Assumption (the ascension of her body to heaven directly after her death). Only one of these dogmas, Mary's perpetual virginity, is taught as dogma in the Eastern Orthodox Church. The Orthodox Church generally rejects the Immaculate Conception; most Orthodox believe in the Assumption but consider it not necessary to have a dogma about it, and though the Orthodox regard Mary as the most sinless natural human being ever, they feel it's not necessary to reiterate the issue of her sinlessness. As one Orthodox theologian puts it, some Orthodox writers have offered the opinion that during her lifetime, Mary probably did display some of the human foibles tracing to the fall, like impatience and anger. Protestants have a wide variety of opinions on Mary, as on most other theological issues, but in general they regard her role as a good mother to the Lord, but little else.

Joseph, the Betrothed, and James, the Lord's Brother

A Bible trivia question asks, "How many brothers and sisters—natural children of Joseph and Mary—did Jesus have?" The Bible doesn't say that Mary and Joseph had any "natural children," but the trivia question lists as its proof Mark 6:3: "Is this not the carpenter, the Son of Mary, and brother of

James, Joses, Judah, and Simon? And are not his sisters here with us?" On this basis the trivia game claims that Jesus had six or more "natural" siblings. The Roman Catholic and Orthodox churches have always held that Mary had no children with Joseph (as did Martin Luther and John Calvin, generally considered the founders of Protestantism); and that Mary remained a virgin all her life. In the ancient church, Joseph has always been referred to as "the betrothed" to emphasize that though he undertook Mary's and Jesus' protection, he and Mary never consummated their marriage.

A common interpretation of New Testament references to James as Jesus' brother is that Joseph, an older man when he was betrothed to Mary, had a previous wife, James' mother, who had died. The others mentioned by Mark may have been members of Joseph's close family as cousins, or could have been Joseph's offspring by his previous marriage. To refer to close relatives this way is not unusual, as occurred when Jesus, from the cross, referred to John the Apostle, who is believed by many scholars to have been Jesus' second cousin, as Mary's new son, meaning he was being charged with her care (John 19:26).

Has the Church Forgotten?

The ancient church claims that its tradition is reliable because the church was "there" from the beginning and never was lacking in rational sense, nor was it forgetful. The early church tradition says that Mary's "perpetual virginity" was prophesied in the Old Testament: "this gate shall be shut, it shall not be opened, and no man shall enter in by it; because the Lord, the God of Israel, has entered in by it. Therefore, it shall be shut" (Ezekiel 44:2).

That Joseph was considerably older than Mary is suggested by the fact that he had apparently died by the time of the crucifixion. That James was an older brother of Jesus, not a younger one, is evidenced by the fact that he came to believe in Jesus late in the Gospels' timeline. Some argue that younger siblings—including all the other five mentioned by Mark—would have attached themselves to an older brother of such charisma as Jesus from their childhood on, as younger siblings generally do. But although much is said about James, identified in early church records as the author of the epistle bearing his name in the New Testament, none of the other "brothers and sisters" mentioned in Mark are specifically kept in the church's tradition.

factum

In most of the world, Christmas is the most celebrated day every year. Solemn adult versions of the story are told in Gospel readings and recitations in candlelight services in Catholic, Orthodox, and Protestant churches, and children's versions are presented in pageants or plays, not only in churches but even in many non-Christian schools.

Jesus' Siblings

It's hard to imagine that the church would have forgotten those alleged stepsiblings, or that they would have had no role in the early church. Some say the offspring of Joseph and Mary after Jesus would have left a lineage that today would claim blood relationship with God. There has been considerable scholarly discussion concerning these siblings. According to Roman Catholic and Orthodox teaching, no woman whose womb had brought the very God into the world would have been used for any lesser purpose later. One theory, already mentioned, states that the siblings were stepsiblings or cousins who were already adults by the time Jesus was born. However, some scholars do believe that there is real New Testament evidence that the siblings of Jesus were his blood relatives, actual brothers and sisters.

The Star of Bethlehem

Planetariums often draw Christmas-season audiences by presenting programs built around theories about what the star of Bethlehem may have been if it was anything other than a story made up by some early disciples of Jesus. Amateur astronomer Susan S. Carroll, who has developed an extensive Web page about the star of Bethlehem, says that, although the star is mentioned only once in the Bible (in the Book of Matthew), it was likely "a genuine astronomical occurrence."

discussion question

Has Christmas always been celebrated in the United States?
No. Christmas was suppressed in Puritan New England and in Presbyterian Scotland as late as the nineteenth century. Both strict Puritans (later known as Congregationalists), in New England, and Presbyterian Covenanters in Scotland began as Calvinist denominations.

The science of astronomy studies observable events in the universe, and if the star came and went just for the Magi (the Greek word translated as "wise men" in the King James Version of Matthew's Gospel), there's nothing left to investigate or study. If we accept the ancient definition of astrology as "interpreting events in the heavens" rather than the contemporary meaning of "reading horoscopes," the Wise Men must have been astrologers, prescientific stargazers. In their era, before the advent of astronomy as a discrete science, they can be considered the closest thing then available to scientific observers of the heavens.

Astroarchaeology

Astroarchaeology, also known as archaeoastronomy, is the study of astronomy as it was practiced in ancient times, using archaeological evidence such as Stonehenge or the Great Pyramids of Egypt. Astroarchaeologist John Charles Webb, Jr., theorizes that the Magi were the only stargazers who could see (or "discern") the star of Bethlehem, because they found it through their ancient and advanced astrological knowledge (represented, for example, by the great pyramids of Egypt, Stonehenge, and other ancient evidences of astrological knowledge that have been lost to modern science).

Unlike most astronomers' speculations on what the star of Bethlehem was, Webb rules out an alignment of several planets, appearing as a great star, as the explanation. He claims that King Herod, undoubtedly served by stargazers of his own, seemed to be unaware of any special star when the Magi brought it to his attention. According to Webb's interpretation, there must have been a representation of the event visible in the heavens to the highly trained astrological eye, because Matthew says, "the star, which they saw in the east, went before them, till it came and stood over where the young child was" (Matthew 2:9b).

Year of Jesus' Birth

Webb's charting theorizes that the star appeared on March 2, in the year 5 B.C. Other scholars had long ago concluded that the calendars put the time of Christ's birth (A.D. 0) as about five years too late, based on historical evidence for the date of King Herod's death. Earlier attempts to establish the birthdate of Jesus had concluded that it most likely occurred in the spring, but the church—though not denying the evidence—rejected that date for the Nativity Feast because it would have been too close to Easter, or the Pascal Feast.

One reason the church may have chosen December 25 for the Nativity Feast is that it was the first day after the winter solstice on which the lengthening of days could be discerned. Thus, pagans celebrated it as the rebirth day of the sun. Some speculate that even long before there was an official widely observed Nativity Feast, Christians had begun reinterpreting the pagan "Sun Festival" in a Christian perspective as the birthday of the Sun of Righteousness, one of the prophetic names for the Messiah that appears in the Old Testament. As it is written in Malachi 4:2: "But unto you that fear my name shall the Sun of righteousness arise with healing in his wings; and ye shall go forth, and grow up as calves of the stall."

Visitors from the East

It's entirely consistent with their respective points of view that only Luke reports the visit of the shepherds to venerate the newborn Christ child, and only Matthew records the visit by the wise men. Luke's intended audience might have been more impressed to know that the child had been born and first worshipped under humble circumstances, whereas Matthew wanted to stress Jesus' divine royalty as a descendent of the house of David.

St. Matthew's recording of the visit by the "kings from the east" is consistent with his tracing of the royal lineage of Jesus. His Jewish audience would demand evidence of royal patronage or notice of the Messiah's birth. The

Magi were most likely from Persia and most likely followers of Zoroaster, known as "the king of the Magi" and the founder of what is widely thought to be the world's first monotheistic religion. The gifts the wise men brought were precious commodities, so they must have been wealthy, and even if there was only one wise man for each gift (which provides the theory that there were three of them), they most likely had a retinue providing security.

Matthew's account of the visit of the Magi is short and simple: "And when they were come into the house, they saw the young child with Mary his mother, and fell down, and worshipped him: and when they had opened their treasures, they presented unto him gifts; gold, and frankincense and myrrh" (Matthew 2:11).

symbolism

Gift giving was part of ancient feasts and celebrations, much like gifts today are given to newlyweds or graduates. Christmas gifts symbolize this universal practice and reflect the Gospel account that the Magi brought gifts of great value to the Child of Bethlehem. But pre-eminently, they recognize the Father's "indescribable gift" to us (2 Corinthians 9:15).

Scholars generally agree that the Magi arrived after the Christ child had been removed from the stable to a house, after the influx of taxpayers to Bethlehem had abated. They were most likely "kings" only in the sense that they had wealth and could move about freely in a dangerous environment. Indisputably, they are the first gentiles who worshipped Jesus.

An explanation of how the Magi found the star and the Messiah is provided by Moses in Deuteronomy, "if you shall seek the LORD your God, you shall find him; if you seek him with all your heart and with all your soul" (Deuteronomy 4:29); and the Prophet Jeremiah reiterated, "you shall seek me, and find me, when you shall search for me with all your heart," Jeremiah 29:13.

CHAPTER 2

The Silent Years

It's part of natural human curiosity to want more information on the "silent years" in Jesus' life—the years between the flight into Egypt and Jesus' baptism and the beginning of his public ministry. Neither the Bible nor church tradition provides much to go on. Beginning in the early years after Jesus' lifetime, many have offered theories and have written apocryphal accounts of the thirty years about which only a few biblical verses are available.

After the Birth

Luke's Gospel records the circumcision of Jesus on the eighth day after his birth, most likely in Bethlehem while Mary was recovering from her delivery, and before the wise men had come to worship him as recorded in Matthew. In Jewish tradition, male children were named at circumcision, and Luke reports that at Jesus' circumcision "his name was called JESUS, which was so named of the angel before he was conceived in the womb" (Luke 2:21).

discussion question

What is the "purification" that Mary had to undergo after the birth?
It was a Jewish tradition required of mothers after giving birth. Experts say the purification required Mary to stay indoors for forty days, and when it was accomplished, she was then able to make the five-mile walk (or ride by donkey) from Bethlehem to the Temple in Jerusalem for the presentation.

And without referring to the wise men; the threat of Herod and the infanticide he commanded; or the flight of Mary, Joseph, and Jesus into Egypt, in the very next verse (2:22) Luke begins the story of Jesus' presentation in the Temple in Jerusalem. The Magi might have arrived to worship Jesus just before the family journeyed to Jerusalem for the presentation, though this doesn't accord with the traditional (but arbitrary) dating of the Epiphany (as mentioned previously, an early Christian feast commemorating the worship of Jesus by the Wise Men, and Jesus' baptism) only twelve days after the Nativity.

If the Magi's adoration was only a short time before the presentation, by the time Herod realized the Magi had given him the slip, he was looking for newborns in the area of Bethlehem, but Jesus may have already been in Jerusalem. It may have been there that Joseph received the angel's warning to hide out in Egypt.

symbolism

Circumcision was widely practiced as a religious ritual in biblical times, including by the ancient Egyptians, as documented in artworks dating more than two thousand years B.C. Circumcision was given to Abraham as the sign and symbol of the covenant between him and his descendants with God (Genesis 17:1), and is still practiced as a religious requirement by the Jewish people.

The Presentation

Jesus' presentation, accompanied by a sacrifice of turtledoves or pigeons, as was traditional, was marked by the appearance of a devout man named Simeon who had been told by the Holy Spirit that he would live to see the Messiah. And Luke says Simeon took Jesus "up in his arms, and blessed God, and said, Lord, now lettest thou thy servant depart in peace, according to thy word: For mine eyes have seen thy salvation, Which thou hast prepared before the face of all people; A light to lighten the Gentiles, and the glory of thy people Israel" (Luke 2:28–31).

Simeon's speech prophesies both the reason Jesus came into the world (as the expected Messiah) and his passion (suffering) and death, which Simeon describes as piercing Mary's heart (Luke 2:35). This "Canticle of Simeon" (or the *Nunc Dimittis*, as it is called in the Roman Catholic Church, based on the first two words of the verse in Latin) was a prayer sung in the liturgies of the ancient church. It is still used in the regular evening services (vespers) of Eastern Orthodox Christians.

The Prophetess Anna

Luke's story of the presentation also includes a "prophetess," Anna, who had been a widow most of her life, and had been living in the Temple, praying and fasting and, like Simeon, waiting faithfully for the Messiah. "And she coming in that instant gave thanks likewise unto the Lord, and spake of him to all them that looked for redemption in Jerusalem" (Luke 2:38).

discussion question

What is the *synoptic problem*?
It is a theological term for the seeming discrepancies among the four Gospels: Matthew, Mark, Luke, and John. For example, Matthew records the visit of the Magi and Luke records the shepherds and angels coming to the stable, but each Gospel omits the opposite accounts.

Flight into Egypt

St. Matthew continues his parallel narrative after the Magi worshipped the baby Jesus (see Matthew 2:12–18). Angels directed the Magi not to return to Herod on their way back home, and also told Joseph to flee from Israel into Egypt to escape Herod's plot to thwart any challenge of his rule over Israel by an alleged newborn king, by having all baby boys under age two killed.

Legends and Apocryphal Traditions

Anne Rice's recent bestselling novel, *Christ the Lord: Out of Egypt*, may be the latest in a long history of fictitious attempts to imaginatively recreate the childhood of Jesus. Rice's story is told from the perspective of Jesus himself, at age seven, describing events that happen as he and his large extended family make their way from Egypt to Nazareth after the angel tells his stepfather Joseph that it's now safe for him to bring the child back to Israel.

Some reviewers claim that Rice got cues for her boy Jesus from *The Infancy Gospel of Thomas*, an apocryphal Gnostic text that has been traced back to A.D. 185, when Irenaeus, bishop of Lyon, cited it. This is the source of the famous myth of the child Jesus creating clay sparrows and giving them life, but it also shows him as petulant and vengeful toward those who cross him. *The Infancy Gospel* has no connection with Apostle Thomas of the New Testament, and students of its text say that its lack of knowledge about Jewish life of the first century discounts its claim to have been written by a follower of Jesus. The Infancy Gospel of Thomas says that Jesus arrived in

Egypt at age two, and after the angel gave the all clear, his family returned to Nazareth when he was seven.

Gnosis is a Greek word meaning "knowledge," but in the times of the early church, *Gnostics* referred to esoteric or hidden knowledge, which the Gnostics claimed to possess about Christ and his teachings. The Gnostics are also described as believing that matter is evil, and that therefore the goal of religion is to achieve a purely spiritual state. This contrasts with the orthodox Christian view, in which God himself took material form in the incarnation, and St. Paul's teaching that the material bodies of believers will play a vital part in their resurrection from the dead (1 Corinthians 15).

Why the Silence?

The New Testament's relative silence on the childhood and youth of Jesus is consistent with virtually all other biographies in the Bible. Jacob and Esau, Moses, Joseph, David, and Daniel are Old Testament figures whose early life is mentioned, but not with more than a few sentences.

As an infant, Moses was saved by Pharaoh's daughter after his mother and sister floated him in a reed basket on the Nile to hide him; the Egyptian Pharaoh had ordered all Hebrew babies killed. David killed a lion as a shepherd boy and killed Goliath using only a slingshot and five smooth stones before entering puberty, and was anointed as Israel's next king years before he reached manhood and the acceptance of his people. This is how the biblical stories of infancy, childhood, and youth unfold. Sketchy highlights are all that is given, in contrast to pagan and Gnostic writings that provide detailed accounts of childhood and youth.

factum

Joseph, the favorite among Jacob's twelve sons, was given the coat of many colors by his father and, because of jealousy over that favored treatment, his brothers sold him into slavery. When still in his youth, he resisted the seductions of his master's wife. And like Jesus, he saved his people, but temporally rather than eternally.

Jesus in the Koran

Interestingly, the Koran (also written Qur'an), written five to six centuries after the New Testament, has more descriptions of the childhood of Jesus than the New Testament. *The Catholic Encyclopedia* (1910) cites the Apocryphal writings (like *The Infancy Gospel of Thomas*) as the Koran's source.

The Koran affirms the virgin birth of Jesus to Mary and God's Spirit, and adds that as a baby he didn't require any teaching; he had access to all knowledge. It also refers to his making clay birds and giving them life. The Koran calls Jesus the only sinless man, but rejects his godhead, as taught in the Christian creeds and as he himself claimed. (See the Koran, Surah 3, 42–63; Surah 19 (Maryam), 16–50; Surah 4, 156–159; Surah 61, 6–9; Surah 3, 33–34, 38–39; Surah 5, 72–80.)

Settling in Galilee

Matthew's account continues by saying that an angel again appeared to Joseph to tell him Herod was dead and that it was now safe to return to Israel. Matthew also says the angel revealed that Herod Archelaus had succeeded his father, and that Joseph should take the family to Nazareth in Galilee rather than Judea (the region surrounding Jerusalem), "that it might be fulfilled which was spoken by the prophets, He shall be called a Nazarene" Matthew 2:23.

discussion question

What is the relationship of Mohammed to Christianity?
Mohammed was the prophet and founder of Islam; he was born in A.D. 570 in Mecca, the commercial and religious center of Arabia at the time. *The Catholic Encyclopedia* says that after meeting Christians and Jewish people during trade journeys, he brought monotheism to Arabia as a religious reform through the Koran, which he authored. He died in A.D. 633.

Luke relates that Nazareth had been the home city of Mary and Joseph before Jesus' birth, but it's understandable that the Holy Family may have been drawn to Jerusalem, their holy city and the center of all the action for the whole of Jewish history, knowing the promises the angels had given them regarding Jesus.

Teaching the Elders

Matthew's Gospel jumps from the Holy Family's arrival back in Nazareth to the adult ministry of John the Baptist, who is identified by Luke as Jesus' cousin, and the beginning of Jesus' public ministry. But Luke tells a few more salient facts about Jesus' formative years, saying "the child grew, and waxed strong in spirit, filled with wisdom: and the grace of God was upon him," Luke 2:40. He also reveals that the family annually went to Jerusalem for the feast of Passover and that, at age twelve, Jesus stayed behind in the Temple, teaching the teachers of the Temple, while Mary and Joseph began their return to Nazareth, assuming he was with other members of the extended family.

factum

Although people congregated in synagogues in various towns and cities to pray and study God's word, it was vital that devout Jewish people make regular pilgrimages to their Temple in Jerusalem, much the way Muslims of our time attempt to make at least one pilgrimage to Mecca in their lifetimes.

This is the closest the biblical biographies of Jesus come to the Apocryphal "petulant" boy God. But here he is precocious, not petulant, submitting to the discipline of his parents when they realized they had lost him and returned to the Temple to find him. This short passage suggests that the faithful from Galilee journeyed en masse to the great feast in Jerusalem. The procession provided security against robbers, company on the journey, and entertainment in the form of shared stories, impressions, and, no doubt, religious conversation and singing.

The Jewish World of Jesus' Childhood

From the beginning, the Jewish people were both a political (nation-forming) and a religious (God-fearing) entity. The nation was required, from the covenant between God and Abraham onward, to be a holy—that is, separated—people, not intermarrying or being otherwise corrupted by the pagan peoples around them, even those who ruled over them. As the Jewish wars and the destruction of the Temple later in the first century would demonstrate, the greatest crisis they ever faced was the Roman empire. It was in the height of this national crisis that Christ came. The Romans destroyed the Temple in A.D. 70, as part of their suppression of Jewish uprisings against Rome, and the Temple has never been restored. In Jesus' time the Temple in Jerusalem was the only lawful place where sacrifices were made for the atonement of the sins of the Jewish people, and where prescribed worship took place. And Jewish worship, without a Temple, has been incomplete ever since.

Josephus, a first-century historian from a priestly family of Jewish people, provides the best-preserved view of Jewish life, apart from the New Testament, in Jesus' time. He presents it as an era of much political upheaval, as some Jewish parties tried to mobilize revolts against Rome. At least five political groups existed in the Judaism of Jesus' lifetime: the Pharisees, Sadducees, Essenes, Zealots, and Samaritans.

Pharisees

The Pharisees were laymen who tried to preserve the Jewish faith through pious and legalistic practices, and although as a group they were strongly censured in Jesus' sermons, some of them were friends and supporters of Jesus and his disciples.

Sadducees

The Sadducees, the elite of the Jewish priesthood, tended toward less exact expressions of the faith than the Pharisees, and toward accommodating the political rulers of their time. They are described as denying the resurrection of the body, which is not specifically taught (only suggested) in the Old Testament, but which many Jewish people believed in at that time. Most of the historical information about the Sadducees, apart from the references in the New Testament, are from their critics, so historians describe them as hard to pin down.

discussion question

What is a Nazarite?
Nazarites were Jewish people who took temporary vows to abstain from wine or other strong drink, to refrain from cutting their hair, and to avoid touching the dead (see Numbers 6:2–21). They could complete their vows by performing ceremonial acts at the Temple. Acts records two instances of the Apostle Paul and others taking Nazarite vows (Acts 18:18, 21:23).

Essenes

Though Essenes are not mentioned in the New Testament, some believe that John the Baptist may have been an Essene before beginning his prophetic ministry. They are known from archaeological research (primarily from the Dead Sea Scrolls found at Qumran between 1947 and 1956) as a strict, almost monastic, sect of Jewish people who separated themselves from the Roman Empire, choosing to live in seclusion in the Sinai desert.

Zealots

Zealots were politicized Jewish people who advocated insurrection against Roman power. They were considered dangerous by the mainstream Jewish people of their time because they are thought to have tried to force the whole nation to join their rebellion, creating warlike conditions coming both from within and outside their ethnic and religious community.

Samaritans

Samaria, 35 miles north of Jerusalem and between Judea and Galilee (the region around Nazareth and bordering the Lake or Sea of Galilee), was home to another sect—Samaritans—claiming Jewish roots and faith, but not accepted by the Jerusalem establishment of that time, or any other Jewish establishment, since the nation had been taken captive by the Babylonians.

John, and Jesus' Baptism

Jesus' kinsman John, the son of Elizabeth and Zacharias (a priest in the family line of Abijah), became a highly visible symbol of the religious tumult of his and Jesus' generation by becoming a reclusive preacher of repentance in the deserts of Judea. Considered by Christians the last of the prophets of the Old Testament and the forerunner of Jesus and his New Testament, John is referred to in the Gospel of Mark as the fulfillment of Isaiah's prophecy, "I send my messenger before thy face, which shall prepare thy way before thee. The voice of one crying in the wilderness, Prepare ye the way of the Lord, make his paths straight" (Mark 1:2–3). John baptized those of his followers who wanted to purify their bodies to symbolize their repentance of spirit.

Of the Gospel accounts of Jesus' baptism by John, Matthew's is the most complete (see Matthew 3:5–17), creating a picture of Jerusalem, "and all Judaea, and all the region about Jordan" coming out to the Jordan River to be baptized by John. And when Jesus comes to John for baptism and John objects, saying, "I have need to be baptized of thee, and comest thou to me?" it is only Matthew's account that includes the detail, "And Jesus answering said unto him, Suffer it to be so now: for thus it becometh us to fulfil all righteousness."

The baptism of Jesus is the New Testament's most specific interplay of all three persons of the Trinity in one place and time. Jesus, the Son, is approved by the voice of the Father from heaven, and the Holy Spirit appears in the form of a dove above him.

CHAPTER 3

The Sermon on the Mount

After John baptized him, and the Father and the Holy Spirit proclaimed him, Jesus went into the surrounding wilderness to inaugurate his ministry by spending forty days and nights in prayer and fasting, and resisting the temptations of Satan. Following the baptism, John's Gospel segues directly to the calling of Jesus' first two disciples, and his ministry of healing and teaching the multitudes.

The Kingdom-of-God Lifestyle

By going into the wilderness to prepare for his public ministry, Jesus was following the example of the prophets and holy men and women of all the generations preceding him. This is probably why it is here, after Jesus had become an adult and been baptized in the presence of many witnesses, that Luke's Gospel veers off the narrative track to retrace his genealogy back to Adam, whom Luke calls "the Son of God," which Luke takes as foreshadowing the "second Adam" role Jesus had come to carry out. Matthew, Mark, and Luke all put Jesus' retreat to the wilderness immediately after his baptism, but John the Evangelist, in the fourth Gospel, tells a more personal, memoir-like account, describing events more in terms of his own impressions or what he was told, without trying to make them fit a sequential timeline.

Significance of the Wilderness

As mentioned previously, many of the prophets and other holy people performed important acts while in the wilderness. In the wilderness Moses met God in the burning bush and, atop Mount Sinai, talked with him and received The Law. Centuries earlier, Abraham had traversed the wilderness from Ur to the land of promise, and took his son, Isaac, into the wilderness to offer him up to God as a sacrifice. The nation of Israel spent forty years in the wilderness to get to the land God had promised to Abraham and his descendants forever. David the shepherd boy was tending sheep in the wilderness when he wrote the first Psalms. And it was John the Baptist—whom everyone in Jerusalem and all Judea came out to the wilderness to listen to and be baptized by—and the long line of prophets before him, that Jesus emulated in retreating to the desert before starting to preach.

Matthew and Luke have very similar versions of Jesus' retreat to the wilderness and his temptation by Satan, but Luke's version is a bit more detailed than the other Gospel accounts. Luke is the only Gospel writer who includes Jesus' reference to himself, in speaking to Satan, as "the Lord your God."

Satan uses possessions, the power to command vast lands or nations, even selected quotations from the Scriptures, to seduce, but the Word of the Lord can always best him. A widely held interpretation of this passage sees it as describing what believers go through following baptism, when they commit their lives to God. Temptation—testing—is part of the life of faith.

factum

The Apostle John, called the Beloved Apostle and the Evangelist, is not to be confused with John the Baptist. According to tradition the youngest of Jesus' twelve disciples, the Apostle John's is considered the last Gospel written, and also the most doctrinal or pedagogical of the four. He is thought to have been a leader of the church to the end of the first century.

Return to Galilee

After ending his fast and wilderness retreat, Jesus returned to Galilee (from the Judean desert near the Jordan River across from Jerusalem) to begin preaching and call his disciples. Galilee, more multicultural and less set in its doctrines than Judea, but home to numerous converts, was more likely ready to receive Jesus' message.

By now, many had heard that John the Baptist had been arrested by Herod, so the people may have been eager to hear a message like the one the baptizer was famous for. Also, since Jesus had been known in the region from his youth, it was possible that some young men there would be ready to follow him if he would only invite them. They were, and he did.

The First Called

John the Evangelist says that the first two followers of Jesus to commit to discipleship were initially followers of John the Baptist. "John, standing with some followers when Jesus walked by, said of him, 'Behold the Lamb of God!' And the two disciples heard him speak, and they followed Jesus" (John 1:35–37). One of these, John reports, was Andrew, and as the second is not named, it is believed that he was John himself, the author of the Gospel. Andrew then recruited his brother, Simon Peter, John reports, saying to Simon, "We have found the Messiah, which is, being interpreted, the Christ" (John 1: 41).

symbolism

John's calling Jesus "the Lamb of God" symbolized the Passover lamb, described in Exodus 12. God had ordered an angel to smite the firstborn of every family, man and beast, in Egypt, to force Pharaoh to release the Israelites from slavery. The angel passed over every house where his chosen people (the Jewish people) had sprinkled the blood of a Passover lamb on the doorway.

In this manner, Jesus gathered his first disciples. Luke gives additional background before the calling of the first disciples, indicating that Jesus had already begun preaching and becoming widely known in the region, first around Nazareth, and then in the north near the coast of the Sea of Galilee: "And came down to Capernaum, a city of Galilee, and taught them on the sabbath days. And they were astonished at his doctrine: for his word was with power" (Luke 4:31–32).

On the opposite end of the time spectrum from John's, the Gospel of Mark is believed by scholars to have been written first of the four evangels. Mark, though not an apostle like Matthew and John, is also believed to have been a close associate of the Apostle Peter, and some even believe his Gospel was composed under Peter's direction. Mark's is the shortest of the four Gospels, but much of its wording is repeated in one or more of the others.

Matthew provides a succinct transition from the call of the first disciples away from their profession as fishers, to fishers of men. See Matthew 4:23–25.

Jesus' actual teachings, considering the proportion of the Gospels they make up, are arguably the least known and least understood aspect of his ministry. The church in general has always said that Jesus' main teaching was that he was the Son of God, the Creator and Judge of the universe in the flesh. And, as C. S. Lewis so famously said in *Mere Christianity*, to make that claim, if it's not true, either indicates madness or a lie, and if either of those are true of him he couldn't possibly have been a "great moral teacher."

factum

Healing and miracles were marks of prophetic calling and ministry in Old Testament times, and the Gospels make it apparent that healings brought the multitudes out to see and hear Jesus. They were part of his ministry from the beginning, and they showed his power and his compassion toward the people he came to save.

The Beatitudes

Matthew's report of the Sermon on the Mount is the source of one of the most familiar teachings of Jesus, a poem that begins his sermon, known as *The Beatitudes*:

Blessed are the poor in spirit, for theirs is the kingdom of heaven.

Blessed are those who mourn, for they will be comforted.

Blessed are the meek, for they will inherit the earth.

Blessed are those who hunger and thirst for righteousness, for they will be filled.

Blessed are the merciful, for they will be shown mercy.

Blessed are the pure in heart, for they will see God.

Blessed are the peacemakers, for they will be called the sons of God.

Blessed are those who are persecuted for righteousness' sake, for theirs is the kingdom of heaven (Matthew 5:1–10).

The word *beatitude* is based on the Latin *beatus*, which refers to blissful happiness and, as used in religious context, implies the kind of bliss available only in being blessed or graced by God for attempting to please him. The theme of the beatitudes is humility, self-abasement, and being more other-oriented and Kingdom of God-oriented rather than self-oriented.

Hard Truths about the Kingdom of God

Jesus then says something unexpected that his hearers probably found difficult to accept, indicating that he was not there to incite revolution or the overthrow of any temporal power, but to teach and exemplify the Law of Moses (see Matthew 5:17–20). The wording suggests that Jesus' listeners may have been waiting for a new world order, a delivery from Rome's totalitarian oppression, but Jesus assures them near the beginning that he's no revolutionary or Zealot, though he advocates zeal toward the Kingdom-of-God lifestyle; in other words, fulfilling the commandments received by Moses and the prophets' teachings, for not a "jot or tittle" would be set aside.

discussion question

What is the difference between the "Kingdom Of God" and the "Kingdom Of Heaven"?
Scripture indicates that Jesus used the terms interchangeably. In Matthew 19:23 he states, "I tell you the truth, it is hard for a rich man to enter the kingdom of heaven," and in Matthew 19:24 he reiterates, "Again I tell you, it is easier for a camel to go through the eye of a needle than for a rich man to enter the kingdom of God."

In the original manuscripts, the word "jot" was "iota," one of the smallest Greek letters, and "tittle" (*keria* in Greek) was the apex of a letter. An iota was similar to our letter I, and the apexes of letters were tiny strokes. In other words, not the least appendage of the language of the law and the teachings of the prophets would be set aside or canceled out.

Jesus especially stresses that "anyone whoever shall teach men" to not keep the commandments will be regarded the lowest in the Kingdom. By citing the "righteousness" of the scribes (people who transcribed and continually studied the Torah) and Pharisees (the "strict constructionist" party of the Law of Moses), he urged his hearers to exceed the efforts to be (or appear) holy of the most conspicuous "holy classes" in the Holy City.

fallacy

The gospels teach that it was a common fallacy in the time of Jesus that the Messiah would be a political figure able to lead those waiting for him into a new secular kingdom safe from the pagan kingdoms surrounding them, and routinely taking them into various forms of captivity. Jesus' kingdom offers spiritual, not political, independence and lasting peace.

Jesus continues the sermon with warnings against holding anger or demeaning your brothers and calling them derogatory names, then emphasizes reconciliation with anyone in the community who may hold a grievance against you or against whom you hold a grievance: "if thou bring thy gift to the altar, and there rememberest that thy brother hath ought against thee; Leave there thy gift before the altar, and go thy way; first be reconciled to thy brother, and then come and offer thy gift" (Matthew 5:23, 24). This teaching referring to the altar in the Temple has generally been interpreted as being equally applicable to Christians taking Holy Communion or the Eucharist.

Obeying in Spirit

What comes next in his sermon is Jesus' interpretations of the spirit in which the commandments should be kept, and his teachings on adultery and divorce. In Matthew 5:30, Jesus states that it is better to cut off a hand that offends you rather than allow the whole body to be cast into Hell because of the sins of the hand. He continues, "It hath been said, Whosoever shall put away his wife, let him give her a writing of divorcement: But I say unto you, That whosoever shall put away his wife, saving for the cause of fornication, causeth her to commit adultery: and whosoever shall marry her that is divorced committeth adultery" (Matthew 5:31–32).

symbolism

The church has tried to apply Jesus' teachings on adultery and divorce to concrete rules or disciplines. But Jesus' teachings on these subjects can also be interpreted as metaphors or symbols of the relationship between God and his church. The church is God's bride, and when it fails to love him, it commits adultery. When it enters apostasy, as Jesus prophesies later in Matthew, it divorces him.

"Cutting off the hand and casting it away" is a metaphor for eliminating the source of temptation by excising it from one's life. And on marriage Jesus is advocating taking the extra step to make covenant relationships (marriages) work, just as earlier he emphasized that Kingdom-of-Heaven lifestyle requires going the extra mile to make peace with those who have grievances and to bear others' burdens.

Oaths Prohibited

The next section prohibits using oaths to establish your truthfulness. The church has generally interpreted this as pertaining to casual conversation, in which disciples are not to invoke God or something else holy to establish the reliability of their word, but the teaching is that it does not include formal situations in which an individual's word may not be good enough because his or her reputation is not known. "Let your yes be yes and your no, no" (Matthew 5:37) means that if you become known as a reliable and truthful person, you will not need to swear to everything. This is likely an extension, by Jesus, of the Old Testament's strict application of "you shall not take the name of the Lord your God in vain." The extension is, don't use any name in vain.

The generally accepted interpretation of the next paragraph, teaching his disciples not to use force to oppose evildoers, has been that it applies to individuals in one-to-one situations but not to civil authorities, who have social obligations to keep order (for example, a police officer cannot forgive a lawbreaker on the basis of his personal ethics, but must act on behalf of the government or the whole society). In other words, don't be a bully, and turn the other cheek rather than use violence, but keep civil order. St. Paul has more to say about this later in the New Testament.

Love Your Enemies

In Matthew 5:43–46, Jesus turns the "common-sense wisdom"—that we love our neighbors but hate our enemies—upside down: "But I say unto you, Love your enemies, bless them that curse you, do good to them that hate you, and pray for them which despitefully use you, and persecute you; That ye may be the children of your Father which is in heaven: for he maketh his sun to rise on the evil and on the good, and sendeth rain on the just and on the unjust.

"For if ye love them which love you, what reward have ye? do not even the publicans the same?" (Matthew 5:44–46). Jesus acknowledges that it is very easy to love those who are already your friends and who love you in return. Here Jesus is asking his followers to undertake the much more difficult task of loving those who they would not naturally be inclined to love, and who do not love them.

Jesus' reminder that God's rain falls on both the just and the unjust could be extended to natural disasters: his hurricanes, tsunamis, and earthquakes befall the good and the evil both, and they are not meant as judgments of anyone's merit. Jesus then wraps up the first portion of his sermon with the simple, easier-said-than-done rule: "be perfect even as your Father in heaven is perfect" (Matthew 5:48).

Prayer for the Glory of God

The next section of the sermon teaches that alms must be given secretly, not openly for recognition; prayer is to be between you and God, not out in public for the notice of others; and "when you pray, do not use vain repetitions, as the heathen do, for they think that they shall be heard for their much speaking. Do not be like them, for your Father knows what you need before you ask him," (Matthew 6:7, 8). In other words, be confident that God hears prayer. And though he later teaches that persistence in prayer is a good thing, he is here condemning insincere, vain repetition (or babble) for its own sake. Then Jesus goes on to give the multitude his famous exemplary prayer, known as the Lord's Prayer or the "Our Father."

Forgiving others their debts or trespasses as God forgives ours is an extension of many of the previously stated precepts Jesus is preaching. In this context he interprets it by illustrating his own meaning: reach out and love someone who, by your standards, is unlovable, and you'll begin approaching the Kingdom-of-God lifestyle. "Lead us not into temptation" refers to the kinds of temptation he had just recently withstood from Satan; that part of the prayer could be rephrased as "Father, don't test us beyond our spiritual strength to withstand." And the threefold conclusion of the prayer is a reminder that the glory is not to be ours, but to be reflected back to God and that all is to be undertaken, and prayed for, for his sake, not our own.

After Jesus recites the Lord's Prayer he returns to the earlier theme: don't do your spiritual obligations for show, but for the Father only, applying the point this time to fasting. Then follows one of the most famous passages in the sermon: "Lay up your treasure in heaven, where neither moth nor rust corrupt and where thieves do not break in to steal. For where your treasure is, there will your heart be also," (Matthew 6: 20–21).

factum

It's a recurring theme of Jesus' teaching that doing things for show or to impress others is hypocrisy, and that this is a sure shortcut to failure in the spiritual life. "Judge not" is a key to overcoming superior attitudes that lead to a great fall.

Exhortations to Holiness

The conclusion of the sermon comes in Matthew 7, the highlights of which include do not judge, that you not be judged, and with what standards you use to judge shall be used by God when he judges you. Jesus tells his listeners, don't try to pull a "mote," or tiny splinter, out of another person's eye before first removing the "beam" or post from your own eye. In other words, don't be a hypocrite.

Jesus tells his listeners not to give holy things to dogs or cast pearls to swine. Then he says, "Ask, and it shall be given you; seek, and ye shall find; knock, and it shall be opened unto you: For every one that asketh receiveth; and he that seeketh findeth; and to him that knocketh it shall be opened. Or what man is there of you, whom if his son ask bread, will he give him a stone? Or if he ask a fish, will he give him a serpent?" (Matthew 7:7–10). Here he is reiterating the Old Testament teaching that anyone who truly seeks the Lord will surely find him, for God wants to give his best to his children.

He also compares good trees and their good fruits with corrupt trees that produce evil fruit; "wherefore by their fruits ye shall know them" (7:20). Jesus ends the sermon with the parable of the man who built his house on a rock and it withstood the ravages of life's storms, and the man who built his house on the sand and it was quickly demolished by the wind. He ends by saying that those who hear his sayings and act accordingly are like the wise man, and those who hear but fail to act accordingly are the foolish ones.

Jesus' Authority and the New Covenant

Matthew writes that when Jesus had ended these sayings, the people were astonished at his teaching, for he taught them as one having authority, and not as the scribes. All of the true prophets, including John the Baptist, also taught as though they were speaking the very words of God, because telling the truth with boldness was the mark and the sign of a prophet.

Though it has only been partially revealed thus far, the point of Jesus' authoritative speaking is that he was there to impart, and even to personify, a whole new covenant between God and his people. From Law to Grace is the general theme of the New Testament and the life of Jesus Christ. By setting out the necessity of fulfilling the Old Covenant (the Law) in the Sermon on the Mount, Jesus is setting the stage for disclosing the new grounds on which his believers will meet God.

discussion question

What was meant by "taught as one having authority"? One commentator says the scribes taught by invoking various theories and experts, but refusing to take a position themselves, whereas his followers saw Jesus as speaking as though he was, himself, authoritative about the Kingdom of Heaven and the requirements to fulfill the law and the teachings of the prophets.

CHAPTER 4

Jesus the Miracle Worker

The matter-of-fact way in which the Gospels treat the healing aspects of Jesus' ministry suggests that Jesus' listeners expected healing power from someone who offered a prophetic ministry and who could be the Messiah. The church teaches traditionally that holiness and godly authority are bound up with power over physical infirmities. In other words, spiritual perfection overrides natural limitations. In a time when medicines were primitive, what is now generally called faith healing was a major treatment for all ailments.

A Leper Cleansed

The first healing specifically described in Matthew's Gospel is the cleansing of a leper who worshipped Jesus and said that if Jesus chose to do so, he could make him clean. "Uncleanness" was the Law's way of describing those with leprosy. Jesus replied, "I will be thou clean" while touching him (something prohibited in the Law of Moses, Leviticus 7:21). And immediately the man was "cleansed" of the leprous spots over his body. Thus Jesus demonstrates—immediately after sermonizing that the smallest letter of the Law of Moses should not be abrogated but must be fulfilled—that he is the Lord of the Law, not its slave.

factum

Though it is widely believed that the healings were done mainly to demonstrate his messianic claims and to verify his teaching, Jesus performed many healings upon his arrival in Galilee, before choosing his first disciples and giving his most important teaching sermon.

Though Jesus had access to all power, the power he is demonstrating here is similar to powers earlier prophets also used. His attitude here in the early days of his ministry is "come and see." And as the passage says, large crowds chose to go along, wanting to see more wonders and hear more encouraging words. Anyone who advocated the Golden Rule, as Jesus did, could not avoid the imperative to use any power he had to help those humbly asking for help. Compassion and mercy were the keystones of his ministry, not optional virtues.

Paralysis Reversed

The second healing Jesus accomplished was the reversal of paralysis that, in the King James translation, is called palsy. As Jesus entered the city of Capernaum, a centurion (an officer in the Roman legion) approached him and told him his servant lay sick at home with paralysis. When Jesus offered to go to the officer's home to heal the afflicted man, "the centurion answered and said, Lord, I am not worthy that thou shouldest come under my roof: but speak the word only, and my servant shall be healed." To this, the gospel says, Jesus, "marvelled, and said to them that followed, Verily I say unto you, I have not found so great faith, no, not in Israel." Read the whole account in Matthew 8:5–13.

discussion question

What do the churches make of Jesus' unqualified acceptance of the centurion?
The preponderance of church teaching has interpreted Jesus' not questioning or judging the centurion's military occupation, as part of the oppressing Roman army, as evidence that Jesus was not advocating pacifism. The personal and interpersonal peace he advocated and offered was qualitatively different from peace among factions and nation-states.

The centurion, a Roman military officer who commanded over a hundred men, was a gentile, the first since the Wise Men to recognize Jesus for who he was. Galilee is said to have been home to many such non-Jewish seekers after God, but Jesus is prophesying when he says this gentile is prefiguring multitudes of others who will eventually follow him, while most of the Jewish multitudes ("children of the kingdom") will turn aside. His saying that "I have not found so great faith in Israel" refers to the centurion's humility by opening with "I am not worthy."

A Second Paralytic Healed

A second account of a paralytic being healed also takes place in Capernaum, the city that Jesus chose as his headquarters while ministering in Galilee (see Matthew 9:1–8). This time, it was the crowd that marveled at Jesus' words, because instead of telling the man to rise and walk, he said, "your sins are forgiven." And scribes (scholars in the Old Testament teachings) who were there murmured that he had blasphemed by presuming to forgive sins, which power belongs to God only.

symbolism

> As mentioned previously, healings in prophetic ministries like Jesus' were symbolic of godliness on the part of the healer. To accusers who said Jesus healed through satanic powers or black arts, he retorted that Satan cannot cast out Satan; the tree is known by its fruits. He used healings of human afflictions to demonstrate his power to heal the sickness we all suffer unto death, sin.

In the accounts in Mark's and Luke's Gospels, this event is even more dramatic; it's added that because of the crowds, the paralytic's friends lowered him down through an opening they made in the roof of the house to get to Jesus. The presence of scribes on the scene of his healings suggests that Jesus' fame had become so significant that the scribes felt they had to check up on him by lurking around the fringes to get whatever goods they could get on him.

Sins Forgiven

Knowing what the public's reaction would be, Jesus reveals that he used the phrase, "your sins are forgiven" intentionally to get his mission noticed, to inaugurate the kind of controversy that was bound to follow, and to get people wondering, what manner of man, prophet, or messiah is this? And Jesus lets the people know that he can read the thoughts of their hearts even though they had not uttered them.

Infirmities Alleviated

Healings of varied infirmities are next described, beginning with the healing of Simon Peter's mother-in-law of fever, described in Matthew 8:14–15. The

Bible records thirty-eight specific healings and miracles, as well as numerous healings mentioned only in general terms (for example, Matthew 4:24).

▼ HEALINGS AND MIRACLES IN THE GOSPELS

Event	Matthew	Mark	Luke	John
Feeding of the five thousand	14:13–21	6:34–44	9:11–17	6:2–14
Walking on water	14:22–33	6:47–51		6:16–21
Gentile's daughter exorcised of demons	15:22–28	7:24–30		
Deaf-mute healed		7:32–37		
Feeding of the four thousand	15:32–38	8:1–9		
Blind man healed at Bethsaida		8:22–26		
The transfiguration	17:1–8	9:1–8	9:28–36	
Demon-possessed boy exorcized	17:14–21	9:17–29	9:37–42	
Shekel taken from a fish's mouth to pay tax	17:24–27			
Blind man healed		10:46–52	18:35–43	9:1–38
Many crippled, blind, and mute healed	15:30–31		7:21–22	
Woman healed on the Sabbath			13:10–17	
Resurrection of Lazarus				11:1–44
Man with dropsy healed on the Sabbath			14:1–6	
Ten lepers cleansed			17:11–19	
Two blind men healed at Jericho	20:29–34	10:46–52	18:35–43	
Fig tree cursed to not bear fruit	21:18–22	11:12–14		
Ear of High Priest's servant restored	*	*	22:49–51	*
Resurrection	28:1–10	16:1–8	24:1–12	20:1–18
Ascension		16:19–20	24:50–53	

*All four Gospels record the ear being severed; only Luke reports it being restored.

In the healing of the leper, Jesus used touch; in the healing of the centurion's paralytic servant, he used only his word. Jesus uses touch again to heal Peter's mother-in-law. Later, a woman is healed by simply touching the hem of his robe as he passes. In each case, the faith of the ones healed is the key.

Mastery over the Weather

One of the most dramatic accounts of a miraculous event in Jesus' early ministry is the calming of a storm on the lake where his first disciples were fishing. The disciples were frightened of the storm and begged Jesus to save them (see Matthew 8:23–27).

factum

Geographers say that the Lake of Galilee is highly susceptible to sudden strong storms, as the mountainous terrain around it causes extreme changes in high and low barometric pressure. These changes produce winds that blow down onto the lake, making it treacherous to anyone in a small craft of the type used by fishermen of the time.

Some interpreters have proposed that not only did Jesus subdue the storm; he also may have summoned it in the first place to give the disciples an unforgettable teachable moment. Though this account is presented in the Gospels as a real event, it has parable-like aspects that many have cited: when believers or the church are "tempest tossed," Jesus is only a prayer away.

Feeding the Five Thousand

The feeding of the 5,000 is the only miracle Jesus performed before his followers that is recorded in all four Gospels (see John's account in John 6:2–13).

The disciple Andrew seems to have become familiar enough with Jesus' modus operandi to be hoping against hope that the five barley loaves and two small fishes might be used to feed the multitude. Some interpreters say the 5,000 "men" does not include a large population of women and children who would have also been fed. And one commentator has been quoted as saying the miracle wasn't all it has been thought to be; perhaps they were just five very large loaves and two big fishes.

Walking on Water

Jesus walking on water is reported by the Gospels of Matthew, Mark, and John, but Matthew is the only one who tells of Peter's joining him on the lake's surface (see Matthew 14:22–33). It seems apparent that Jesus wanted to test and to strengthen his disciples' faith when, as Matthew records, he sent them across the lake before him. Peter's faith has long and often been characterized as the most impetuous of all the disciples, which is demonstrated here, but it could also be called the most robust, as he was willing to test his own limits. And Jesus' invitation to him to join him on the water can be seen as symbolizing his desire that his disciples become more like him by being willing to try previously impossible feats, through growing faith.

Feeding of the Four Thousand

Matthew's and Mark's Gospels both record this second mass feeding miracle just a few paragraphs after describing the feeding of the 5,000 (see Mark 8:1–10). This miracle was performed on the other side of the lake from the first, where most of the residents were gentiles. And Matthew specifies in his account that this time there were 4,000 men, plus women and children. The large crowds who were attracted to Jesus and experienced his miracles no doubt made up the core of early members of the church, which spread quickly after Pentecost, as will be discussed in Chapter 9.

Exorcising Demons

Jesus and his disciples again crossed the Lake of Galilee for Jesus' next demonstration of power, this time over demonic spirits. Matthew 8:28–34 tells the story of their visit to the Gergesenes on the eastern shore of the Lake of Galilee. There, Jesus and his companions met two men possessed by "fierce devils" who lived in a cave. Jesus cast out the demons, who asked permission to go into a herd of swine that was feeding nearby. Jesus granted their request, but the swine leapt off a cliff into the lake, and drowned. The people in the city who came out to meet him were more angry than impressed. It was the economic effect of losing the swine, not the personal salvation or the healing of mental disease or demon possession, that mattered most to the Gergesenes, and their feelings led them to reject Jesus and his miraculous works. Swine were unclean to Jewish people, but keeping the animals was without doubt a livelihood to their gentile keepers. What effect the death of the swine had on the demons isn't specified, but it seems apparent that they were no longer able to work in that locale.

Power of God, or Power of Satan?

Matthew 12:22–29 gives another account of Jesus casting out a demon, this time from a blind and mute man. The people witnessing the miracle were amazed, but Matthew says that when "the Pharisees" heard of it, they accused Jesus of casting out demons by the power of "Beelzebub the prince of the devils." Jesus replies with the logical syllogism that a house divided against itself cannot stand, so how could the prince of devils be interested in casting out devils?

Luke relates that after appointing the twelve disciples (which is discussed in more detail in Chapter 5), Jesus had appointed a second level of disciples, "the seventy," whom he commissioned to go out and preach, heal, and cast out demons in his name (see Luke 10:17–22). When they return rejoicing in their power over demons, Jesus tells them that he witnessed Satan being cast out of heaven "like lightning," and that it would be better for them to rejoice that they are accounted worthy of the kingdom of heaven rather than in their power over evil spirits, and that they can withstand scorpion stings and venomous snakebites without harm. Literal-minded snake handlers have interpreted the previous passage as suggesting that the faithful should take up venomous snakes to prove they have received the power of the Holy Spirit. But such demonstrations seem counter to the spirit in which Jesus performed his miracles, and also seem to contradict the statement "rejoice not in your power but in having your names being written down in heaven."

discussion question

What is the unforgivable sin?
Jesus gave a solemn warning in Matthew 12: "blasphemy against the Holy Spirit shall not be forgiven" In the story of Jesus casting out a demon from a blind and mute man, the "offense against the Holy Spirit" is attributing the Spirit's works to Satan, which Jesus is saying is what these Pharisees have done.

Miracles vs. Stunts

Jesus' works of power or miracles are not publicity stunts, as shown by his frequent injunctions that the recipients of healing not broadcast that he has healed them. Moreover, any attempt to demonstrate God's power would seem to prove more vanity and pride on the claimant's part, rather than holiness and power. Though later disciples and holy followers of Christ are able to survive venomous snakebites (as in Acts 28:3–7), the metaphor here is that despite the tremendous power of Satan and his minions, Jesus' followers have greater power to overcome them.

Water into Wine

The Apostle John describes Jesus' turning water into wine in the wedding in Cana as the beginning of his miracles (see John 2:1–11). When the host of the wedding ran out of wine, Jesus' mother, Mary, told him of their plight. He objected, "Woman, what have I to do with thee? mine hour is not yet come," but undeterred, she told the servants to do whatever he said, and Jesus told them to fill six stone water pots, holding two or three firkins each, with water. That done, he then directed them to take some of the contents of the water pots to the governor of the feast, who, in turn, sent some to the bridegroom. Usually, everyone sets out the best wine in the beginning, with the poorer quality beverage saved for later, he declared, but this time the best has been kept for last; the water had turned into wine of the best quality.

Many have observed that God is always turning water, in the form of rainfall and irrigation, into wine by nature's turning the juice of grapes into wine. But the creator of the grape can bypass a few steps to make it happen more expeditiously when necessary.

Some take Jesus' words in response to Mary's request as suggesting a distancing between himself and his mother. But considering that he fulfilled her request exactly as she made it, by providing wine for the wedding, the whole miracle can be seen as a reward of Mary's faith. In that, she becomes the first of the believers in Jesus to bring about a miraculous event through her requests. And by seeing how Mary's faith was rewarded, the other disciples realized they could call forth similar power over nature, and by doing so confirm their faith.

Resurrections

Resurrections from the dead are rare in the Bible, even in the ministry of Jesus, who is described as restoring life to three whose loved ones sought his intervention. Though he became incarnate in order to be the resurrection and the life (John 11:25) it is apparent that even his earthly adoptive father Joseph had passed away and was not restored to life before Jesus launched his ministry. And the three who returned under his ministration from the other side of the veil between life and death still faced the penalty of sin.

The First Resurrection

The first resurrection performed by Jesus is recounted in all three of the synoptic Gospels, Matthew, Mark, and Luke. Matthew 9:18–27 records the event. A certain ruler (identified by both Mark and Luke as Jairus, a ruler of the synagogue) told Jesus that his daughter was already dead, but that if he were to lay his hand on her she would revive. Jesus and his disciples joined the man on the way to his home. On the way, "a woman diseased with an issue of blood twelve years" touched the hem of Jesus' robe, believing that act would heal her. Sensing the power go out of him, Jesus turned to her and said "Daughter, be of good comfort; thy faith hath made thee whole."

On arriving at the ruler's house, minstrels were already playing mourning music, but Jesus said the maid was only sleeping, which elicited macabre laughter from the mourners. But Jesus "went in, took her by the hand, and the maid arose." On his way out of the neighborhood, Jesus was importuned by two blind men seeking healing.

Second Resurrection

The second resurrection is recounted only in Luke 7:11–17. As Jesus and his disciples approached the gate of Nain, a town in Galilee south of Nazareth, they met a funeral party carrying a dead man on a bier, his widowed mother mourning with many townspeople. Jesus "had compassion on her, and said unto her, Weep not. And he came and touched the bier: and they that bare him stood still. And he said, Young man, I say unto thee, Arise. And he that was dead sat up, and began to speak. And he delivered him to his mother." This miracle so impressed the witnesses that its word spread as far as Judea, the region around Jerusalem, beyond Samaria from Galilee and Nain.

Resurrection of Lazarus

The final resurrection miracle performed by Jesus was the raising of his friend Lazarus, which immediately preceded Jesus' passion week, which will be taken up in Chapter 8.

These "temporary" resurrections all pale beside the resurrection of Jesus himself, in which he returned from the grave in a totally renewed, "spiritual body," which was permanent and indestructible (see 1 Corinthians 15). These resurrections demonstrate the power of the Creator and the Lord of Life but those who witnessed these miraculous events had seen little compared to the resurrection to come.

Blindness Cured

Several incidences of blindness being cured are recounted in the Gospels. The most illuminating one is given in the Gospel of John, Chapter 9. The whole chapter tells the story of a man who had been born blind but was restored to sight by Jesus, who made clay of dust and spittle, put it on the man's eyes, and directed him to wash his eyes in the pool of Siloam, which he did, receiving his sight.

The account of this miracle affirms several significant bits of good news (the meaning of "Gospel"). First, the Jewish teaching affirmed by Jesus, by the blind man who regained his sight, and even by the Pharisees trying to prove Jesus was healing through satanic power, was an established tradition: that a measure of spiritual purification was a prerequisite of wonder-working power. Second, those who think themselves able to see are blind (deluded), and those who consider themselves lacking insight ("poor in spirit") are given sight. Those who have their own light have no need from the Light of the World that Jesus came to bring and to be.

discussion question

How does Jesus' healing relate to Moses?
Though the Pharisees who opposed Jesus professed to be followers of Moses, not "this fellow," all of the healings of Jesus are typified in the ministry of Moses in the wilderness journey from Egypt to the Promised Land, where God called himself "Yahweh, Rapha," the Lord your healer.

Through Moses, God promised, conditionally, not to bring sicknesses on the Israelites. "If you will diligently listen to the voice of the LORD your God and will do what is right in his sight, and will hear to his commandments and keep all his statutes, I will put none of these diseases upon you that I have brought upon the Egyptians: for I am the LORD who heals you" (Exodus 15:26).

CHAPTER 5

Choosing the Twelve

After Jesus recruited as disciples John, the son of Zebedee, and Andrew, (with help from John the Baptist, whose disciples they had first been), Andrew recruited his bother Simon Peter, and John's brother James was quickly added. To this initial core of four disciples, eight more were added to become the Twelve, ordained as the inner circle, the ones to whom Jesus would entrust the full disclosure of the Gospel of the Kingdom and, later on, the establishment of his church.

Fishermen Made Fishers of Men

Matthew 4:18–22 recounts the famous story of Jesus choosing his disciples: Jesus saw the brothers Simon Peter and Andrew, and said, "Follow me, and I will make you fishers of men." Next he called brothers James and John, the sons of Zebedee, likewise. They all answered the call without hesitating. Mark's account is virtually the same, but it is preceded with a reference to Jesus being spurred by the arrest of John the Baptist to declare the time right for the introduction of the Gospel of the Kingdom.

Difference in Perspective

The difference between Matthew's and Mark's accounts, and that of John's Gospel (as given in Chapter 3, which begins with John's and Andrew's call from the very side of John the Baptist), reflects a difference in perspective between John and Peter. John was there, on the scene and, most likely being the youngest of the fishermen, was probably more strongly impressed by all the new events and the incredible charisma of John the Baptist and Jesus. Peter, many believe, told his story the way he remembered it in Mark's presence, and Matthew may have got his outline of details from Mark's account.

factum

In *Fox's Book of Martyrs* (1563), John Fox refers to James and John, the sons of Zebedee, as relatives of Jesus "for [their] mother Salome was cousin-german to the Virgin Mary." Cousin-german is an old English term for first or full cousin, a child of your uncle or aunt.

Neither Matthew nor Mark was on the scene when Jesus called the fishermen. This is not to say it didn't happen; only that it happened a little later than when Simon Peter and Andrew were first tapped to be followers of Jesus. The first "call" may have been understood by brothers Andrew and Simon Peter as a one-time short enlistment, maybe for one evening event, but when Jesus came to their boat to call them again, it finally sank in that he was calling them to a permanent change of life. They would still continue fishing for a livelihood, as other events already discussed (like Jesus walking on the water to join them on their fishing vessel) confirm, but that kind of fishing would be—from this call onward—their secondary vocation. Both sets of brothers (Simon Peter and Andrew; James and John) now had a higher calling.

The Third Calling and the Other Eight

The synoptic Gospels Matthew, Mark, and Luke all have similar versions of the selection of the Twelve to the higher calling of apostles. The four first called to be followers are still listed as the first four disciples, but it's clear that the additional eight now being ordained for special ministry were considered from a larger pool of followers, most of whom may have followed Jesus during his ministry and even on into the beginning of the church. It's instructive that with all his power and knowledge, Jesus still spent a whole night in prayer—what later monastics call a vigil—seeking the Father's direction on the choosing of the Twelve. This choosing of the Twelve for apostleship is the basis for the ordination processes followed by most Christian communions and denominations today.

discussion question

What have the modern churches learned from Jesus' discipleship process?
Many ministries have discipleship programs concentrating on cementing loyalty to the ministry by having senior and junior ministers spend great amounts of time in one-to-one interaction. Some of the world's largest congregations are built on a cell model, in which tiny groups are instructed by intensive fellowship and training.

The word *apostle*, from the Greek *apostello*, means "sent" or "sent out." At this point, the Twelve are not yet ready to be sent out, but they have now been put on what today's generation might call a fast track leading to the mission field. Their "ministry graduate school"—theological seminary—was the most intensive 24/7 crash course the church has ever known.

Mark 3:14–15 adds that Jesus ordained twelve apostles to be with him, so that he might send them out to preach, and empower them to heal infirmities and cast out demons. Matthew 10:1 specifies that Jesus gave them power to cast out unclean spirits and to heal all kinds of disease.

Simon Peter

Called "the rock" by Jesus (Cephas or Kephas, in Aramaic) and commonly known as Peter (from Petros, the Greek equivalent of Cephas), Simon (also called Simeon) Bar-jona (son of Jona) is the first-named apostle and was the first to declare that Jesus was "the Christ, the Son of the living God." To that dramatic confession, Jesus gave a response that has been controversial for much of the church's next two millennia: "Blessed are you, Simon Bar-jona, for flesh and blood have not revealed this to you, but my Father who is in heaven. And I say also to you, you are Peter, and upon this rock I will build my church; and the gates of hell shall not prevail against it. And I will give to you the keys of the kingdom of heaven so that whatever you shall bind on earth shall be bound in heaven and whatever you shall loose on earth shall be loosed in heaven" (Matthew 16:16–19).

factum

Catholic scholar J. Macrory suggests that Mark was Peter's interpreter in Rome in the latter days of Peter's ministry and life. Having heard all of Peter's memories many times, Mark felt compelled to write them down after Peter's death as the first written Gospel. Peter was born in Bethsaida, on the Lake of Galilee, where, it's reported, the house he lived in is still preserved beneath a church.

The Catholic and Orthodox Churches have held that, from the beginning, Jesus' choice to lead his church was Peter. But Peter received the strongest rebuke from his Master of any disciple, in response to Peter's protesting to Jesus foretelling the fate he would suffer from the leaders of the Temple. "Get behind me, Satan," Jesus tells him. "You are an offence to me, for you don't prefer the things of God but those of man" (Matthew 16:23). As with the incident of Peter's wanting to join Jesus on the surface of the lake, his impetuosity got ahead of his better judgment. But the most critical moment in Peter's time under Jesus' teaching is found in Luke 5:3–10 where, in response to Jesus performing a miracle by filling their nets with fish, Peter "fell down at Jesus' knees, saying, Depart from me; for I am a sinful man, O Lord." But Jesus replied, "Fear not; from henceforth thou shalt catch men."

In this moment Peter's humbling was complete, and his redemption had been won. The lesson could not have been more transparent. Compared with fishing for men, fishing Lake Galilee is no big thing.

discussion question

What is "the Petrine office"?
The Roman papacy is also known as "the Petrine office," or the office of Peter as first Bishop of Rome. According to Catholic theologians, the Roman Papacy has authority over all other church leaders. The Orthodox churches agree that Peter was bishop of Rome and, as Rome was the center of the empire, that office was first to receive honor, but it does not have ruling authority over other leaders of the church.

John

The younger son of Zebedee and Salome (called Mary Salome by some Bible scholars) and the brother of James the Greater calls himself the disciple "Jesus loved" (John 13:23) and is generally called "the beloved disciple." As previously mentioned, he is also called John the Evangelist because he is the writer of the fourth Gospel ("Evangelium" in Latin), and he also is believed to be the author of three short New Testament epistles (1–3 John) and the Apocalypse, or Book of Revelation.

Luke's account of the raising of Jairus' daughter from the dead says John was one of the three members of Jesus' inner circle: "he did not allow any man to go with him, except Peter, James, and John." At several other key moments in Jesus' ministry (as will be shown) these were the only disciples invited as witnesses.

The New Testament records James as the first apostle to die (martyred by King Herod Agrippa I in A.D. 44, Acts 12:2). The Catholic and Orthodox tradition, also affirmed by the Protestant author John Fox in his *Book of Martyrs*, indicates that his brother John was the last of the Twelve to die, having ministered, by one account, for sixty-eight years after the Passion of Jesus. A Roman Catholic source puts his death in about A.D. 100, and a Greek Orthodox one puts it at A.D. 104.

Andrew and James

Simon Peter's brother, Andrew Bar-jona, was first a disciple of John the Baptist, who was with John the Beloved when John the Baptist said of Jesus, "behold the Lamb of God." With John the Beloved, Andrew immediately began following Jesus. He rushed to tell Simon that they had found the Messiah, and later it was he who told Jesus that a boy in the crowd of 5,000 had five barley loaves and two small fishes. Andrew, thought to be a common name at the time, is Andreia, in Greek, meaning manly boldness or valor.

symbolism

Baptism symbolizes washing, bathing, and new life. The Apostle Paul calls it being buried with Jesus and being raised in newness of life (Romans 6:4). Churches and theologians disagree about baptism's power to affect new life (baptismal regeneration). But all say it symbolizes desire to receive new life and identify with Christ and that, unaccompanied by sincere faith, it effects nothing.

James the Greater, son of Zebedee and Salome and brother of John the Beloved, was a fisherman on the Lake of Galilee on his father's ship. He is said to have been dubbed "the Greater" to distinguish him from the other James among the Twelve, called "James the Less," possibly because the latter was of shorter height. Jesus referred to both of the sons of Zebedee as Boanerges, "sons of thunder" (Mark 3:17). James is *Yakob* in Hebrew and *Iakobos* in New Testament Greek.

The fact that James' mother, Salome, is believed to have been the cousin of the Virgin Mary may be pertinent to James and John being included in Jesus' inner circle, and also connected to a plea and Mark's Gospels, to "Grant that these my two sons may sit, the one on thy right hand, and the other on the left, in thy kingdom."

Jesus asked if the Apostles were prepared to drink from his cup and partake in his baptism, which they agreed they were. Then he replied that the decision was not his, but his Father's, to make. Drinking from his cup and participating in Jesus' baptism, the Apostles shared in the suffering and death he would be required to endure.

Philip and Nathanael Bartholomew

Apostle Philip is listed fifth in the three lists of Apostles in the synoptic Gospels. Like John and Andrew he was also an earlier follower of John the Baptist. After Jesus asked Philip to follow him, Philip recruited Nathanael (John 1:43–51). A Jewish man from Galilee, Philip's Greek name is taken by some to have been given in honor of Philip the Tetrarch, who had been credited with making positive reforms in Philip's family's area under his administration.

Nathanael is thought by many to be another name for Bartholomew, his full name being Nathanael Bar-tholomew, meaning Son of Tolmai. John's Gospel identifies Nathanael as a friend of Philip, but all three of the other lists of disciples pair Philip and Bartholomew, omitting the name Nathanael. Bartholomew is likely his more formal name.

John also attributes a widely quoted line from the New Testament as coming from Nathanael, a reply to Philip's telling him that they have found the prophesied Messiah, Jesus of Nazareth: "Can there any good thing come out of Nazareth?" But after meeting Jesus and hearing him call Nathanael "an Israelite indeed, in whom is no guile!" because Jesus had earlier noticed him under a fig tree (possibly praying), Nathanael was so impressed that he exclaimed, "Rabbi, thou art the Son of God; thou art the King of Israel."

Thomas

Although there is a persistent history of claims that Thomas was the apostle to India, and there is a Mar Thoma Church (St. Thomas Church) there that claims him as its founder, very little hard historical evidence is available about Thomas beyond his mention in the lists of apostles in the synoptic Gospels, four anecdotes in John's Gospel in which he plays key parts, and the "doubting Thomas" sequence in John 20, which will be taken up in Chapter 9.

John's Gospel gives its first brief look at Thomas in Chapter 11, where Thomas responds to Jesus' sorrow about the death of Lazarus: "Then Thomas, who is called Didymus, said to his fellow disciples, 'Let us also go, that we may die with him.'" Though less specific than Peter's and Nathanael's confessions ("truly you are the Son of God"), this displays deep faith in Thomas, who puts his fate entirely in the Master's hands.

John's next glimpse of Thomas comes in another well-known passage on Jesus' divinity and his way of salvation, chapter 14:1–7. Jesus describes his intention of creating "many mansions" in his Father's house for his disciples, and says they know where he goes and how. But Thomas interrupts to say, "Lord, we know not whither thou goest; and how can we know the way?" To which Jesus replies that he is the way, the truth and the life; no man comes to the Father except by him. This is probably the most specific declaration in the Bible by Jesus of being the exclusive way of eternal salvation.

fallacy

There is much Gnostic apocryphal literature bearing Thomas' name (including *The Infancy Gospel of Thomas*), and some of it purports to be his biography. However, the claim in one of these accounts that he was the twin brother of Jesus himself indicates that the Apostle Thomas is most likely not the author of these documents.

Matthew, Also Known as Levi

Matthew, also known as Levi, despite being author of the Gospel bearing his name, is mentioned only four times in the New Testament, excluding the lists of the apostles. His call to discipleship, however, is described in more personal terms than that of the others in the latter half of the lists. In his own Gospel, that event is described in these words: "And as he went out, he saw a man named Matthew sitting at the receipt of custom, and he said to him, 'Follow me.' And he arose, and followed him" (Matthew 9:9).

Matthew seems to be too humble to mention his own parts played among the followers of Jesus, because while his Gospel alludes to their going into a house for a dinner, it is only in Luke's Gospel that we are told that Matthew (Levi) made a great feast "at his own house" for Jesus and his disciples, with many other publicans being invited to join in (Luke 5:29). And the reaction among the scribes and Pharisees to this event turned it into a significant teachable moment in Jesus' ministry. They accuse him, to put it in modern parlance, of partying with his disciples too much for a holy man of God. To which Jesus replied, "Can ye make the children of the bridechamber fast, while the bride-groom is with them? But the days will come, when the bridegroom shall be taken away from them, and then shall they fast in those days." Here Jesus is previewing the understanding of the church as bride of Christ, which he will make clearer toward the end of his time with his disciples. His eating and drinking with people considered vulgar and unholy by the pillars of religious society is consistent with his being born among farm animals and being worshipped by shepherds rather than introduced with fanfare and splendor in the Temple.

factum

Matthew was labeled a publican (public tax collector), and for that the Pharisees, who held all publicans in contempt, despised him. This may be why Jesus recruited him, to show that none is beyond the reach of the Father's grace, and that man's superficial standards for judging are not God's standards.

James the Less, Thaddeus, and Simon of Canaan

As previously mentioned, James, the son of Alphaeus, as Matthew and Luke identify him (Matthew 10:3, Luke 6:15, and Acts 1:13) is better known as James the Less to distinguish him from James, the son of Zebedee, or James the Greater. The Less, or Minor, can mean in Latin either smaller of stature or younger. Though there are many opinions about the various Jameses in the New Testament, the consensus seems to be that there were four principal ones: James, the brother of the Lord (described earlier as the son of Joseph by a previous marriage), who was the first bishop of Jerusalem and the author of the Epistle of James; the two apostles named James (Greater and Less); and James, the son of Cleopas and another Mary (Mark 15:40, Luke 24:10). Some Roman Catholic writers conflate James, the brother of the Lord, with James, the son of Cleopas.

Thaddeus

The Apostle Thaddeus is also known as Jude, Judas the brother of James, and "not Iscariot" (Luke 6:16 and John 14:22), and Lebbaeus (Matthew 10:3, which calls him "Lebbaeus, whose surname was Thaddeus." Mark 3:18 refers to him simply as Thaddeus). His speaking is recorded only once in the New Testament when, in John 14:23, he asks Jesus, "Lord, how is it that you will manifest yourself to us and not to the world?"

Simon of Canaan

Also called Simon Zelotes, Simon the Zealous or Simon the Zealot, Simon of Canaan is believed by some to have been the bridegroom at the wedding in Cana where Jesus turned water into wine. Though some believe he was a member of the party known as the Zealots who advocated violent overthrow of the Roman oppressors in Israel, a Roman Catholic source says the better reading of Zelotes is "Zealous," as in zealous for the faith and Jewish teachings.

As Jesus early dispelled any hopes some may have had that he would lead a revolution, it is likely that if Simon was ever a member of the Zealots, he was converted into a zealous apostle of his newfound Lord. An apocryphal *Acts of Simon and Judas* (Thaddeus) maintains that after the establishment of the church Simon and Thaddeus preached the Gospel in Persia.

symbolism

The Roman Catholic Church assigns symbols to each apostle. Those associated with Simon the Zealous are a saw (by which tradition says he was martyred by being cut in two) and a book. A scroll and a key represent Simon Peter. Peter's brother Andrew is represented by a decussate cross, the type on which he was crucified.

Judas Iscariot

The only one of the Apostles set off by himself in the lists is Judas Iscariot, who is traditionally remembered as the betrayer (Matthew 10:4; Mark 3:19; Luke 6:16) who sold his Master for thirty pieces of silver (Matthew 26:15). Iscariot is said to refer to his birthplace, Iscariot being a Hebrew phrase "man from [the town of] Kerioth or Carioth." Judas is the Greek form of the Hebrew Judah.

John's Gospel in Chapter 6 describes a point at which many of Jesus' disciples abandoned him. "Will you also go away?" Jesus asked the Twelve. To which Simon Peter answered, "Lord, to whom shall we go? You have the words of eternal life and we believe, and are certain, that you are the Christ, the Son of the living God." In reply, Jesus, speaking of Judas Iscariot, said, "Have I not chosen you twelve, one of whom is a devil?"

Matthew's account says that Judas, after realizing how wrong he had been in setting up his Master for crucifixion through betraying him into the hands of the Temple leaders, first threw away the pieces of silver he'd been paid in the Temple, then hanged himself in despair. The Temple leaders used the silver to buy a potter's field to "bury strangers in" (Matthew 27:3–7).

But Peter, in a sermon quoted by Luke in Acts 1:18, says that "this man purchased a field with the reward of iniquity and, falling headlong, he burst asunder in the midst, and all his bowels gushed out." Catholic writer W. H.

Kent suggests that by returning the pieces of silver to the Temple leaders, Judas "indirectly" paid for the field that Matthew says the Temple leaders bought for use as the potter's field.

CHAPTER 6

Parables and Other Teachings

In addition to his sermons, Jesus is famous for another kind of teaching: the telling of stories with moral points, called parables, the general theme of which is the Kingdom of God and how to attain it. The Gospels record approximately four dozen parables, depending on how you calculate the overlap among the accounts. Several parables also appear in the Sermon on the Mount. Another type of teaching Jesus used, as recorded in the Gospels, is prophecy, which can be described as "foretelling while forth-telling."

Hidden Wisdom

Matthew's Gospel says "Jesus spoke to the multitudes in parables; and didn't speak to them without a parable, in order to fulfill the saying of the prophet, 'I will open my mouth in parables; I will utter things that have been kept secret from the foundation of the world'" (Matthew 13:34–35, referencing Psalm 78:2).

It seems obvious from Jesus' teaching that he is pacing himself. Usually, he seems to be trying to avoid an argument by posing propositions as riddles or in ambiguous wording so detractors will have a hard time pinning him down through accusations. But at other times, he speaks directly, as if to confront his detractors, even by reading their negative thoughts and disclosing his power to do so (as was shown in Chapter 4).

discussion question

Why are the parables' meanings not always clear?
The parables have a sense about them that they will be understood better after Jesus' listeners have the whole picture. This may have led to the academic discipline of systematic theology or dogmatics; Jesus instilled in his listeners a need that resounds even now: to comprehend the big picture of God's plan for his world and its capstone, the human community.

Some of his parables, short of being stories, are simple similes, like "The Parable of the Treasure Hidden in a Field," that requires only one verse in Matthew: "Again, the kingdom of heaven can be likened to treasure hidden in a field which, when a man found it, kept to himself and, in joy, went out and sold all he had to buy" (Matthew 13:44). The moral is that anyone finding how to attain the Kingdom of Heaven should put aside anything necessary in order to do it.

Mysteries of the Kingdom

When Jesus' disciples asked him about why he spoke in parables, he replied, "It is given to you to know the mysteries of the kingdom" but to those among the crowds gathering to hear him teach who reject him and his Kingdom, "it has not been given . . . I speak to them in parables because they do not see when seeing, and do not understand when hearing" (see Matthew 13:10–17, Mark 4:10–12, and Luke 8:9–10). This information is sandwiched between each of the evangelists' recitation of Jesus' Parable of the Sower and his explanation to the disciples of its meaning.

As with most events in his ministry, Jesus' parables are ordered in different sequences from one Gospel to the next, and some appear in some Gospels, or in only one, but not in all, as the following table illustrates.

▼ **PARABLES IN THE GOSPELS**

The Parable of	Matthew	Mark	Luke	John
12. Kingdom compared to a mustard seed	13:31,32	4:30–32	13:18,19	
13. Leavening yeast	13:33		13:20,21	
14. Treasure hidden in field	13:44			
15. Pearl of great price	13:45, 46			
16. Both good and bad fish caught in the net	13:47–50			
17. Scribe like a householder	13:52			
18. The lost sheep and the 99	18:12–14		15:3–7	
19. Forgiven servant who doesn't forgive	18:23–35			
20. Hired laborers for vineyard	20:1–16			
21. Sons and the father's will	21:28–32			
22. Guests for wedding feast	22:2–14		14:16–24	
23. Wise and foolish virgins	25:1–13			
24. Talents	25:14–30		19:11–27	
25. Debtors and forgiveness			7:41–43	
26. The Good Samaritan			10:30–37	
27. Friend in need persists			11:5–13	

28. The foolish rich farmer			12:16–21	
29. Watching servants			12:35–40	
30. Servants unprepared for master's return	24:45–51		12:42–48	
31. Barren fig tree spared			13:6–9	
32. The shepherd and sheep				10:1–30
33. Highest and lowest seats			14:7–11	
34. The cost of building and of making war			14:25–35	
35. Lost drachma coin			15:8–10	
36. The prodigal son			15:11–32	
37. Scheming manager			16:1–13	
38. Rich man and Lazarus			16:19–31	
39. Unworthy servants			17:7–10	
40. The widow's persistence			18:1–8	
41. The prayers of a Pharisee and a tax collector			18:9–14	
42. The vine and the branches				15:1–27

The Sower

Luke's version of the parable of the sower who sowed seeds on varied soils is the most concise of the three takes on it in the New Testament. Asked by the disciples to explain the parable's meaning, Jesus said the seed is the word of God, those by the wayside are those who hear; the devil comes and takes away the word out of their hearts.

The seeds that land on rock and have no roots are those who hear and receive the word of God, but do not follow it. And the seed that fell among thorns represents listeners who, when they hear, get choked with cares, riches, and pleasures of this life, and bring no fruit to perfection; in other words; they don't attain the Kingdom of God. The seed that falls on the good ground represents those who, hearing the word, keep it, and bear fruit through persevering.

symbolism

Bringing "fruit to perfection" is presented here as the key to attaining the Kingdom of God, and it is won only by struggling for it and persevering in the place where the believer takes root.

The Good Samaritan

Though the Good Samaritan is one of the best known and widely preached parables in Jesus' repertory, it appears only in Luke's Gospel, where Jesus gives it in answer to a question meant to ensnare him when "a certain lawyer" asked him what he would have to do to inherit eternal life. When Jesus asked him how he reads the Law on that question, the man replied, "Thou shalt love the Lord thy God with all thy heart, and with all thy soul, and with all thy strength, and with all thy mind; and thy neighbour as thyself." But, he asked when Jesus concurred, "who is my neighbor?"

The Spirit of the Law

Jesus replied by telling the story of a man traveling on the road to Jericho being attacked, stripped, robbed, and left injured on the roadside. A priest and a Levite going that way saw him lying in great pain but passed by without offering aid. But a Samaritan, a member of the untouchable class in the midst of Israel, seeing the man, stopped, dressed his wounds, put him on his donkey and took him to an inn for additional treatment and time to recuperate, telling the innkeeper he would take care of any additional charges that might be accrued the next time he passed that way. The road from Jerusalem to Jericho, though ancient and long traveled, was notoriously dangerous both by the terrain it crossed through treacherous passes, and because of highwaymen like those who beset the victim in Jesus' story.

The priest and Levite fell short of the spirit of the Law. The Samaritan, a member of a sect that claimed to be Jewish but was shunned because they were considered apostate by the orthodox, showed more of the Law's spirit than its representative main advocates in Israel.

The Woman at the Well

John writes that in order to return to Galilee from Judea (from the area of Jerusalem to that of Nazareth and Capernaum) Jesus "had to go through Samaria." And there he stopped at a well, a center of community life, to rest and get a drink while his disciples went into town to get something for lunch, it being around the sixth hour, which in the way of reckoning in that era meant noon, or about six hours after daybreak.

Jesus didn't have anything to use to draw water from the well, so he waited until a woman from town approached to get her household water, and asked her for a drink. She was taken aback: "How is it that you, a Jew, ask me for a drink, seeing I am a woman of Samaria and the Jews have no dealings with the Samaritans?" To this, Jesus replied that if she knew who it was who was asking, she would be asking him for a drink which, once drunk, would quench her thirst forever. And he also revealed that he knew her very heart by describing her sinful past, though they had not met before.

factum

So powerful was Jesus' Good Samaritan parable that, even in today's parlance, a Good Samaritan refers to a stranger who offers help to someone in need. The origins of the Samaritan ethnic and religious minority in Israel have been studied for centuries. DNA tests made on what remains of ethnic Samaritans show that their genetic lines go back to both Jewish and Assyrian ancestors.

The Samaritan woman at the well was so amazed at what Jesus said that she ran to bring the men of her household to meet him, something that the disciples were scandalized to see when they returned. (Presumably it was okay to buy food from the Samaritans, but not to be sociable with them.)

Jesus' radical departure from the customs of his generation is in line with his eating with publicans and touching lepers to heal them.

The Rich Farmer

The parable of the prosperous farmer who tried to plan his life without taking into account God's will for it seems—compared with the story of the Good Samaritan—more like an imaginative story than an account of actual events. Like the Samaritan story, it was offered in response to a question from a man who approached Jesus to ask something of him. Luke 12:13–21 has the account. The request this time was, "Master, speak to my brother, that he divide the inheritance with me." Jesus replied that he was not a judge between people. And he warned, "beware of covetousness . . . a man's life doesn't consist in abundance of things and possessions."

Then he told the story of the farmer who had such a good harvest he had to build bigger barns to make room for storing it. He told himself he had enough goods "laid up for many years" so it was time to eat, drink, and be merry. "But God said unto him, Thou fool, this night thy soul shall be required of thee." And Jesus concluded, "so is he who lays up treasure for himself and is not rich toward God."

As Psalms 14:1 and 53:1 say, "The fool has said in his heart, There is no God." Jesus is saying that anyone who doesn't realize his accountability to God is a fool.

The Great Supper

As he sat with his disciples at mealtime, Jesus told the story of a man who put on a dinner party but could not find people to share it with him (see Luke 14:15–24). Everyone he invited to the dinner started making excuses, and when none on his guest list accepted, he told his servant, "Go out quickly into the streets and lanes of the city, and bring in hither the poor, and the maimed, and the halt, and the blind." This done, the servant said there was still room and food for more, so the host told him to go out in the street and "compel" anyone who would join them to come and fill the house. And those on the guest list who had refused to come would not be allowed to partake of his feast, he said.

This parable shows how God invites everyone to his house, but only those poor enough in spirit to realize they need his generosity will receive it and, as a result, only they will be awarded a place at his banquet. Nothing takes precedence over an invitation from the Lord, though it is human nature to say, when distracted by the busyness of every day, "Please excuse me this time."

The Talents

Both Matthew and Luke recount Jesus' parable of the talents (a talent in this context is a large amount of money), though the two versions of the parable vary somewhat in the details. Matthew 25:14–30 probably provides the text of more sermons, and therefore Matthew's version of the parable is more familiar than Luke's version. In it, Jesus likens the kingdom of heaven to a man traveling to a far country. He called his servants to him to entrust his assets to them, giving five talents to one, two talents to a second, and one to a third.

fallacy

The church taught for centuries that Jesus prohibited lending at interest. Though Jesus isn't advocating market investing and speculation, this parable has more recently been used to support lending and investing at interest, which, over the centuries, has virtually obliterated the earlier church teaching that charging interest on loans or paying dividends on investments constitute the sin of usury.

The first two servants managed to double their assets on the master's behalf, but the third buried his share of the money. When the master returned after a long time and reckoned with them, he said "well done thou good and faithful servant" to each of those people who doubled their funds and promised to entrust them both to many more assets in the future.

But when the third servant boasted that he had not lost his talent but buried it to keep it safe, the master said, "Thou wicked and slothful servant, thou knewest that I reap where I sowed not, and gather where I have not strawed: thou oughtest therefore to have put my money to the exchangers, and then at my coming I should have received mine own with usury. Take therefore the talent from him, and give it unto him which hath ten talents. For unto every one that hath shall be given, and he shall have abundance: but from him that hath not shall be taken away even that which he hath."

Though many sermon illustrations have rung interpretations on this parable related to financial stewardship and wise investment, as well as making the most of the "talents" God has given you, the parable's weight is directed to faith and grace. To the person who has faith, God will give more, and to the one who lacks trust and obedience, God will not give faith or grace to believe, so even his doubts will harden into disbelief.

The Pharisee and the Tax Collector

The parable of the Pharisee and the publican, or tax collector, has influenced the church's understanding of prayer and the state of the heart in which prayer originates. Luke 18:9–14 provides the only account of this parable, introducing it as being intended for "certain who trusted in themselves and their own righteousness, and despised others." A Pharisee and a publican went to the Temple to pray. The Pharisee prayed, "God, I thank thee that I am not as other men are, extortioners, unjust, adulterers, or even like this publican. I fast twice in the week, I give tithes of all that I possess. And the publican, standing afar off, would not lift up so much as his eyes unto heaven, but smote upon his breast, saying, God be merciful to me a sinner." Jesus concludes that "this man went down to his house justified rather than the other: for every one that exalteth himself shall be abased; and he that humbleth himself shall be exalted."

The publican's prayer, slightly altered as "Lord have mercy on me a sinner," is the basis of the Jesus Prayer, which is the subject of one of the most widely read books of the modern era, the nineteenth-century Russian anonymous novel (or what some believe is a nonfiction biographical account),

The Way of the Pilgrim, and also is a focal point in J. D. Salinger's novel, *Franny and Zooey*. The most common enlarged version of the Jesus Prayer is, "Lord Jesus Christ, Son of God, have mercy on me a sinner."

factum

In *The Way of the Pilgrim*, the protagonist tours Czarist Russia asking spiritual people how it's possible to "pray without ceasing," as recommended in 1 Thessalonians 5:17. The Pilgrim discovers the Jesus Prayer and the technique monastics used for centuries, internalizing the Jesus Prayer as a continuous state of prayer at an almost subconscious level referred to as praying from the heart.

Also of interest in this short parable is the insight it provides into the spiritual practices of pious first-century Jewish people, such as two days of fasting each week. And Jesus' summation, "he who humbles himself shall be exalted" is considered a keystone of the spiritual life, words to live by as an antidote to the first deadly sin of pride.

The Prodigal Son

Alongside the parable of the Good Samaritan, the story of the Prodigal Son is another of the best-known parables of Jesus, and as a story it has the most fully developed characters, motivations, settings, plot, resolution, and emotional impact. Some lists of Jesus' parables refer to it as the parable of the two sons, because of the contrast drawn between two of the three central characters. Reminiscent of the stories of Cain and Abel, and Jacob and Esau in Genesis, the story has served as inspiration for some of the great works of literature, including Shakespeare's *The Merchant of Venice*, John Steinbeck's *East of Eden*, and for movies including *Legends of the Fall* and *Boogie Nights*.

The Child Who Rebels

Like the Good Samaritan, only Luke recounts the parable of the Prodigal Son. In current speech, a prodigal son refers primarily to any child who rebels and becomes a new kind of person, especially if he or she openly rejects father and family and later returns with his tail between his legs. But Jesus' parable contrasts the rebellious son who leaves with a good and loyal son, who stays.

After asking for his inheritance from his father early to leave and make his own way in the world, the younger, rebellious son spirals from liberation into debauchery until eventually, broke and jobless, he ends up tending a herd of pigs for the privilege of being able to eat any of the pigs' food they miss.

Nothing would seem more demeaning to a good Jewish son than to have fallen so far. Finally, in desperation, the younger son sees the error of his ways, and returns home to offer to take a job as one of the household servants, just to be able to live on the family's farm again. The father, seeing him approaching "from afar," welcomes him with great fanfare by running to embrace him and order that he be given new clothes, a ring, and a feast featuring the family's fatted calf as the entrée. "For this my son was dead, and is alive again," the father says, "he was lost, and is found. And they began to be merry."

Sibling Rivalry

Everyone was overjoyed . . . except for the older, loyal, son who realized that if his rebellious brother is again taken back into the family, part of the inheritance he was expecting to receive is going to be diminished by the portion the brother has already squandered. "And he said to his father, 'All these many years I have served you, and I have never disobeyed your commandment. Yet you never gave me a kid [a young goat], so I might make merry with my friends. But as soon as this son came back who devoured your substance with harlots, you have killed the fatted calf for him."

The father's response is one of the most dramatic and touching in the New Testament:

"Son, you are always with me, and all that I have is yours. It was proper that we should make merry and be glad, for this your brother was dead, and is alive again; was lost, and is found"(see Luke 15:11–32).

Prophetic Teachings

Prophecy is central to the ministry and the life of Jesus, as the Apostle Matthew, especially, documents in his Gospel. Not only does Matthew cite scores of passages from the prophets from centuries before Jesus' birth to support his messianic claims, but also he emphasizes, more than any other New Testament writer, the prophetic utterances of Jesus himself concerning the future of the church and the world. Matthew describes Jesus' teachings as peppered with prophecies about his own suffering, crucifixion, and resurrection, as well as allusions to the future of the church, like his reaction to Peter's confession that Jesus truly was the Son of God ("on this rock I will build my church," Matthew 16:18), and the sending of the Holy Spirit to be the church's Comforter.

Prophecies in Matthew

It is widely known that the Book of Revelation (also called The Apocalypse) is the major prophetic book in the New Testament, especially when it comes to things that are widely believed as not yet fulfilled. But it's not as well known that Jesus gave long-term prophecies that occupy much of two chapters of Matthew's Gospel. The first prophecy is his prediction that the Temple of Jerusalem would be destroyed: "There shall not be left here one stone upon another, none that shall not be thrown down" (Matthew 24:2). This was fulfilled in A.D. 70, less than forty years after he said it. Some scholars claim the "prophecy" proves that Matthew's Gospel was written after the event.

The action in Chapter 24 of Matthew takes places at the Mount of Olives, where Jesus and the disciples retreated to get away from the crowds, and it seems that the disciples were in a mood to hear more prophecy. "Tell us, when shall these things be?" they asked. "And what shall be the sign of your coming and of the end of the world?"

Jesus replied:

Beware so no one deceives you. Many shall come in my name, saying, I am Christ; and shall deceive many. And you shall hear of wars and rumors of wars; don't let that trouble you, for all these things must come to pass, but the end is not yet. Nation shall rise against nation, and kingdom against kingdom; there shall be famines, pestilences, and earthquakes in various places. All these are the beginning of sorrows. Then they shall deliver you up to affliction and shall kill you. And you will be hated of all nations for my name's sake (Matthew 24:4–9).

Past or Future

Traditional church interpretations of these prophecies see them as referring to things that will take place when Jerusalem and the Temple are destroyed by Rome in A.D. 70, still the future when Jesus was speaking. Matthew indicates these lengthy prophecies of Jesus were given just two days before the Passover that culminated in his betrayal and crucifixion, making these the last teachings the disciples received from him.

factum

Mark's Gospel has a shorter passage, in Chapter 13, with parallels to chapters 24 and 25 in Matthew. Luke also recounts much of the same scenario, but more briefly, in Chapter 21, with this dramatic climax: "When these things start to occur, look up and lift your heads to see that your redemption draws near" (Luke 21:28).

These passages predict many attempts to deceive the church and pull it away from its first love to Jesus (many Bible scholars refer to this deception as the apostasy), the great tribulation, and "the abomination of desolation" of the Temple, followed by "the end." In this section, many Protestants believe, he speaks of taking his faithful away from the tribulation through "the rapture" (though that word does not appear, it has been applied to the predicted mysterious "taking" of many of his followers).

CHAPTER 7

His Following Multiplies

In the apostolic churches the woman at the well in the parable of the Good Samaritan is known as St. Photini, meaning "the enlightened one." Tradition holds that she traveled to far parts of the Roman Empire to evangelize pagans. None of this is mentioned in the New Testament, and historical documentation is sparse, but Photini is representative of multitudes of early converts, largely unknown, whose names have been lost but who surely must have existed in order for the church to grow as quickly as it did.

Mary Magdalene

From the New Testament itself, it seems safe to say that Mary Magdalene was the leading woman convert and follower of Jesus. She is mentioned in only twelve verses in the Gospels—three times in Matthew (27:56 and 61, and 28:1), four in Mark (15:40 and 47; 16:1 and 9), two in Luke (8:2 and 24:10), and three in John (19:25; 20:1 and 18)—but these suggest a zeal for the Kingdom and a special love for Jesus, who healed her.

Delivered from Demons

Luke is the only evangelist who establishes Mary Magdalene's background and conversion: "He went throughout every city and village, preaching and showing the good news of the kingdom of God, with the company of the twelve [apostles] and certain women who had been healed of evil spirits and infirmities: Mary called Magdalene, out of whom seven demons were cast; Joanna, the wife of Chuza, Herod's steward, and Susanna, and many others, who ministered to him of their substance" (Luke 8:2–8).

This passage suggests that such women may have been Jesus' and the other disciples' major financial supporters, or at least that they contributed by getting meals and other essential support, a bit of historical trivia that can easily be missed in a casual reading of Luke's Gospel. It's likely that Jesus' and the disciples' having women as part of their retinue was something of a scandal in that time, as well.

Not a Prostitute

Pope Gregory the Great referred in a sermon in A.D. 591 to Mary Magdalene as a converted prostitute, conflating into one person Mary of Magdala (from which Magdalene is derived), Mary of Bethany, and an unnamed woman in Luke 7:37, called "a sinner," who, like Mary of Bethany, anointed Jesus' feet.

Much of the contemporary fascination with Mary Magdalene is rooted in Gnostic gospels, including a Gnostic *Gospel of Mary*, purportedly written by Mary Magdalene, only fragments of which have survived. That apocryphal gospel pits Mary against Simon Peter and the male disciples, and claims that the men, out of jealousy over Mary's closeness to Jesus, conspired to exclude her from a position of recognized leadership in the church. Traditional Christian scholars, however, recognize only the twelve apostles mentioned in the New Testament.

fallacy

There is no support for the claim that Mary Magdalene was a prostitute in the New Testament or in the Orthodox Church tradition, and in 1969 the Vatican amended its documents to represent the two women as separate persons. The image persists, however, and was perpetuated in the 1973 rock musical *Jesus Christ Superstar*, where Mary Magdalene is presented as a would-be lover of Jesus.

The New Testament does not hide Mary Magdalene's central role in first discovering Jesus' empty tomb and meeting the resurrected Christ in the garden. On the contrary, Mark and Luke state that the disciples did not believe Mary's report about Jesus' rising from the dead. Mark says, "Now when Jesus had risen early the first day of the week, he appeared first to Mary Magdalene, out of whom he had cast seven demons. And she went and told them who had been with him, as they mourned and wept. And they, when they had heard that he was alive and had been seen by her, did not believe it" (Mark 16:9–11). And Luke's statement of the disciples' disbelief is even more pointed: "It was Mary Magdalene, and Joanna, and Mary the mother of James, and other women who were with them, who told these things to the apostles. And their words seemed to them as idle tales, and they did not believe them" (Luke 24:10–11).

Joanna and Susanna

Joanna is mentioned only one more time in the New Testament, again in Luke's Gospel, when she is one of the women who goes to the sepulcher on the morning of the Resurrection with Mary Magdalene, and is with her when she reports the news of the empty tomb to the disciples. Though Susanna is not mentioned again, in Orthodox tradition she was with the others who followed Jesus from Galilee to Judea, and was a witness to the Crucifixion and

Resurrection. Both women are called saints in the Orthodox churches, and both are cited by advocates of the ordination of women to the priesthood as examples of early women leaders in the church who were considered on par with the apostles.

The Greek tradition says that Mary Magdalene became a companion of Mary, the Mother of Jesus, and lived with her in her latter years in Ephesus, in Asia Minor (modern Turkey). Gregory of Tours (538–594), in his time the highest-ranking churchman in Gaul (modern France) supports the claim that Mary spent her later years in Ephesus, and makes no claim that she lived in Gaul. But a strong French Catholic tradition holds that Mary Magdalene spent her later life in Marseilles, France, where she was instrumental in evangelizing Provence.

discussion question

What are saints?
Protestants consider all followers of Jesus saints, citing the Apostle Paul, who called believers "saints," and Protestants have no canonization process. In Roman Catholicism, exceptionally holy people are declared saints through lengthy examination by church courts. In Orthodoxy, popular acclaim and veneration of a holy example can lead to canonization. Moreover, many uncanonized persons are considered saints.

Lazarus, Mary, and Martha

John 11:5 describes Lazarus, Mary, and Martha of Bethany as close friends of Jesus. Luke is probably referring to this same Martha and Mary when he records a visit of Jesus and his disciples: "as they went, he entered into a certain village and a woman named Martha received him into her house. And she had a sister, Mary, who also sat at Jesus' feet, and heard his word. But Martha, encumbered with the work of serving their guests, came to him and said, 'Lord, do you not care that my sister has left me to serve alone? Ask her to help me.' But Jesus replied, 'Martha, Martha, you care and are troubled about many things. But one thing is needful, and Mary has chosen that good thing, which will not be taken away from her.'"

Mary had found the only thing really needed in life, the top priority: loving and serving her savior. The next encounter with Martha and Mary is recorded in John's Gospel, in Chapter 11, where an emissary of the sisters tells Jesus that Lazarus, "he whom you love, is sick." But Jesus says the sickness "is not unto death but for God's glory" and he stays on in Jerusalem several days longer. His disciples, meanwhile, urge him to return to Judea because the opposition to him in Jerusalem is getting intense.

Lazarus Asleep

"Our friend Lazarus is sleeping," he replies "but I'm going to awake him from his sleep." The disciples replied, "Lord, if he's asleep, he'll do well." But Jesus was speaking of his death, though they thought he had meant taking rest in sleep. Then said Jesus plainly, "Lazarus is dead. And I am glad for your sakes that I was not there, so that you may be caused to believe. Now, let us go unto him" (John 11:3–15). Jesus is making certain that the disciples know that he waited before going to Lazarus to demonstrate his power over death. And this miracle will seal Jesus' fate with his enemies in Jerusalem who seek to have him put to death.

Martha and Mary Speak to Jesus

When they arrived at Bethany, only about two miles from Jerusalem, they were told that Lazarus had been in the tomb for four days already, and when Martha met Jesus on his arrival, she said, "Lord, if you had been here, my brother would not have died. But I know that even now, whatever you will ask of God, God will give it to you." To which Jesus replied, "Your brother shall rise again."

Martha said, "I know that he shall rise again in the resurrection at the last day." But Jesus replied, "I am the resurrection and the life. Whoever believes in me, though he is dead, shall yet live. And whoever lives and believes in me shall never die. Do you believe this?"

"Yes, Lord," Martha replied. "I believe that you are the Christ, the Son of God, who should come into the world." And having said this, Martha left and called Mary, her sister, privately, saying, "The Master is here and calls for you."

factum

Traditionally, these events are considered to have taken place on the Sabbath before the Crucifixion. This Saturday, the day before Palm Sunday, is a prelude to Holy Week in Orthodoxy, where it is called Lazarus Saturday.

Jesus is taken to the tomb of Lazarus, and seeing that his friend is dead, he weeps for him and his skeptical followers are impressed, saying, "See how he loved him." He orders the stone sealing Lazarus' grave removed, and after praying, "'Father, I thank you that you have heard me. I know that you always hear me, but because of the people who stand by I said it, so they may believe that you have sent me.' And when he had spoken, he cried with a loud voice, 'Lazarus, come forth.' And he who was dead came forth, bound hand and foot with grave clothes and his face bound with a napkin. Jesus said to them, 'Loose him, and let him go.'"

The next day, six days before Passover, Jesus goes to a dinner hosted in his honor by Simon of Bethany, a leper whom he had healed. And when Jesus' enemies saw Lazarus there with Jesus, they added Lazarus to their list of people to kill to end Jesus' claims to being the Messiah, and the human Son of the Eternal God.

It was at the dinner at Simon of Bethany's house that Mary of Bethany anointed Jesus' head with oil and washed his feet with her tears and precious perfume. This is considered an indication of Mary's consummate faith in Jesus, and her recognition of what the disciples were refusing to receive, that his death was near.

Roman Catholic tradition says that Lazarus was shipped out of Israel and became the first bishop of Marseilles, in what is now France. Orthodoxy records him as the first bishop of Kition, Cyprus, and commemorates him each year on the Saturday before Palm Sunday. The tradition also says that Mary and Martha lived with him in Cyprus and spent the rest of their lives there. The ancient liturgical hymns describe Lazarus' resurrection as a preview of the general resurrection of the believers in Christ.

Zaccheus

The story of Zaccheus is known by every Sunday school child who has sung the chorus about the "wee little man" who climbed the sycamore tree to see Jesus pass by because he was too short to see over the taller people in the crowd around him. Those who don't recall the chorus can find the whole record in Luke's Gospel, 19:1–10. The Gospel says he was both rich and the chief among the publicans. Because of his short stature, he ran ahead of the parade accompanying Jesus' procession through Jericho, to climb the tree to get a good look at this much-talked-about preacher of the Kingdom. "And when Jesus came to the place, he looked up, and saw him, and said unto him, Zaccheus, make haste, and come down; for today I must abide at thy house."

Zacchaeus seems to have been looking for approval from a religious figure, because Luke says he "made haste" to come down and joyfully received Jesus and took him to his home. Some were scandalized that, again, a publican was being treated as worthy of God's grace. But Zaccheus was so impressed and moved that he said "the half of my goods I give to the poor; and if I have taken anything from any man by false accusation, I restore him fourfold."

And Jesus said unto him, "This day is salvation come to this house, for he also is a son of Abraham. For the Son of man is come to seek and to save that which was lost."

fallacy

The women described earlier as supporters of Jesus' ministry are like Zaccheus in that they are all affluent disciples. According to Jesus, it is the love of riches, or making them an end in themselves, that gets in the way of sanctification.

Though, in another incident, Jesus called upon a rich young man to give all that he had to the poor in order to gain the Kingdom of God (Luke 18:18–23), he made no such demand on Zaccheus. Knowing the hearts of both men, Jesus understood that his wealth would be an impediment to the rich young man, but that Zaccheus had already become poor in spirit, meaning he was aware of the vacuity of his riches. In other words, Zaccheus understood that his wealth was meaningful only if used to make the lot of less fortunate better.

Joseph of Arimathea

Joseph of Arimathea is also an affluent follower of Jesus. And though he is mentioned in all four Gospels, each names him only one time, and in each case it is to mention that it was he who asked Pilate for permission to remove Jesus' body from the cross and bury it in his own private sepulcher.

Mark calls Joseph "an honorable counselor" (meaning, most likely, a lawyer); Luke calls him a Jew who was waiting for the Kingdom of God, and John says he was a secret disciple of Jesus "for fear of the Jews," meaning the Temple leaders who sought to destroy Jesus, of course, not all Jewish people. Catholic writer Francis E. Gigot says that there's evidence that he was a member of the Sanhedrin, the ruling council of the Jewish people, which would shed light on his access to Pilate.

Extra-biblical Texts

But unlike Zaccheus, for whom no extra-biblical legend is found, there is more nonbiblical legend about Joseph of Arimathea than in the Gospels. One text attributes to apocryphal sources a legend that the Apostle Philip led Lazarus, Mary Magdalene, Joseph of Arimathea, and others to Marseilles, in Gaul, and thence Philip and Joseph continued north, over the English Channel, to what was then the Roman province of Britain.

Joseph might have been a trader in metals, a business that may have taken him to Britain even before the crucifixion of Jesus. Even the Arthurian myth includes a passage saying that Joseph of Arimathea arrived in Britain in the middle of the first century A.D.

Nicodemus

Nicodemus is mentioned in connection with Joseph of Arimathea's request to take the body of Jesus. He, too, is identified as a rich member of Israel's Sanhedrin, and a Pharisee, and is the man who came to Jesus by night and asked him the often-cited question, "How can a man be born when he is old? Can he enter the second time into his mother's womb, and be born?" (John 3:4). This was his response to Jesus telling him, "Truly, truly, I say to you, unless a man is born again, he cannot see the kingdom of God."

The *Catholic Encyclopedia* of 1911 says that in his night visit to Jesus, Nicodemus "[was] a learned and intelligent believer, but timid and not easily initiated into the mysteries of the new faith. He next appears (John 7:50–51) in the Sanhedrin, offering a word in defense of the accused Galilean; and we may infer from this passage that he embraced the truth as soon as it was fully made known to him. He is mentioned finally in John 19:39, where he is shown co-operating with Joseph of Arimathea in the embalming and burial of Jesus."

The latter passage in John says Nicodemus "brought a mixture of myrrh and aloes weighing about a hundred pounds" to the burial, which would indicate a rather serious commitment. An Orthodox source contrasts Nicodemus' courage in openly taking the body of Jesus when the apostles had all gone into hiding, and calls the hundred pounds of myrrh and aloes "a symbolic number exalting the dignity of Christ as King."

factum

A later apocryphal *Gospel of Nicodemus* is considered orthodox (in the sense that it doesn't counter the general teachings of the church), but it is believed to have been first published centuries after the church's beginning, and after Nicodemus's lifetime.

The Seventy

Luke is the only evangelist who records the appointment of seventy disciples by Jesus, saying that he "sent them two and two before his face into every city and place, which he himself planned to visit" (Luke 10:1). The Seventy could be compared with the "advance teams" that visited America preceding the arrival of John Wesley and George Whitfield and the Great Awakening (a widespread revival of religious fervor) in the eighteenth century, and the public relations-trained specialists who Billy Graham used in his crusade days, and others like him still do.

The Seventy were to prepare the cities for the coming of the Master, who ordered them to travel shoeless, not stop to kibitz on the way, take no personal effects along, and accept hospitality wherever they could find it.

Eusebius' Reference

Eusebius, c. A.D. 260–341, the bishop of Caesarea and the father of church history, says that he knew of no comprehensive list of the Seventy, but he lists Barnabas, Cephas, Sosthenes (later bishop of Caesarea), Matthias, Thaddeus, and "the Lord's brother" James among those commonly believed to have been among them.

Some manuscripts render the figure of this second flank of disciples as seventy-two rather than seventy, and St. Jerome chose the seventy-two figure for his Vulgate translation of the Bible into Latin. Many prefer seventy, however, as it comports well with other uses of seventy as a significant figure in biblical history, such as Moses' appointing seventy leaders of the twelve tribes of Israel, the Psalmist proclaiming the lifespan of a man as three score and ten, the seventy nations of the world established after the flood of Noah, and the requirement to forgive adversaries "seventy times seven."

Barnabas

Among those listed by Eusebius, the most prominent is Barnabas, a native of Cyprus and a member of the Jewish tribe of Levi, the priestly tribe. Some believe he may have met Paul before the latter's conversion (when Barnabas was known as Joseph, and Paul was known as Saul), when they both studied under Gamaliel, the best-known Jewish teacher of their generation.

The disciples renamed Joseph Barnabas, meaning "son of consolation," in recognition of his gift of healing hurting hearts. He joined Paul after the latter's conversion, and they traveled widely together but parted company when Paul did not want to include Barnabas' cousin, Mark, as an additional team member, though the three men later worked together after the initial rift. Tradition says that Barnabas was the first disciple to take the Gospel to Rome, but he was martyred in his native Cyprus and was buried by Mark in Salamis.

Titus

Another prominent member of the Seventy, Titus was also highly educated (in Greek philosophy), but upon reading the Prophet Isaiah began looking for more information and traveled with some fellow natives of Crete to Jerusalem. Here he became a convert to Jesus and, later, an esteemed companion of Paul, by whom he was baptized. Paul refers to him in epistles as a son (Titus 1:4) and a brother (2 Corinthians 12:18). Titus is believed to have been a witness to Paul's martyrdom by beheading in Rome, and to have returned to Crete to serve as the bishop there for the rest of his life.

Partial lists of lesser-known members of the Seventy have included Tychicus (referred to in Acts and several times in Paul's epistles); Aristarchus, who became bishop of Apamea, Syria, and is mentioned by Paul (Philemon 24), as a "fellow laborer"; and Simeon (see Matthew 13:55 and Mark 6:3), a son of Cleopas and a nephew of Joseph, Jesus' stepfather, and therefore a full cousin of James, "the Lord's brother."

Mark

John, as he was known in Hebrew, had Marcus added to his name and is known more commonly as Mark, the writer of the second Gospel in the New Testament. He is also known as the son of a prominent woman follower of Jesus, as a friend of Simon Peter in Jerusalem, and as the cousin of Barnabas.

Though an early source says that Mark was not himself a follower of Jesus (joining the apostles later), others feel the source is mistaken. Some believe that Mark is alluding to himself in his Gospel, 14:51–52, when soldiers come to Gethsemane in the night to arrest Jesus: "And there followed him a certain young man, having a linen cloth thrown around his naked body; and when the young men laid hold on him he left the linen cloth and fled from them naked."

discussion question

What is Mark's connection with Simon Peter?
Mark is believed to have been Peter's interpreter in Rome. From that experience, having often heard Peter's accounts of the life of Jesus, he wrote his Gospel, which many believe to have been written first of the four.

Luke

As the author of a Gospel and the book of Acts, Luke is one of the most significant of the early church evangelists who were not among the Twelve, yet little historical data survives about him other than a few references to him in Paul's writing, which describes him as a "dear and beloved physician." Catholic scholars have concluded that he was born in Antioch and was born a Greek, not a Jew, both of which facts seem to explain the partiality to gentiles and the city of Antioch that appears in his writings.

factum

Reading between the lines in Luke's writings, referencing things that show knowledge both medical and nautical, some speculate that he may have worked as a shipboard physician, sailing the Mediterranean Sea.

The origin of Luke's faith in Christ is not recorded. An ancient source speculates that he was a companion of Cleopas on the walk to Emmaus on the evening after the Resurrection. However, Luke's knowledge of the Septuagint (the Jewish Bible translated into Greek, which was the widely circulated version of the Bible in the first century) suggests that he may have been a convert to Judaism, though he could have also studied the Jewish Bible through his association with Paul and other apostles.

Luke's association with Paul is introduced in Acts 16:8–12, which relates Paul's "Macedonian call" to take the Gospel to Asia, and where the narrative point of view becomes the second-person "we," rather than the more distanced third-person reporting style before this point. Though Luke's method of gathering the information on the life and ministry of Christ is less dramatic than Mark's method, the introduction to his Gospel is fairly specific about his method and his purpose: "Forasmuch as many have taken in hand to set forth in order a declaration of those things which are most surely believed among us, Even as they delivered them unto us, which from the beginning were eyewitnesses, and ministers of the word; It seemed good to me also, having had perfect understanding of all things from the very first, to write unto thee in order, most excellent Theophilus, That thou mightest know the certainty of those things, wherein thou hast been instructed" (Luke 1:1–4).

discussion question

Who was Theophilus?
There is some debate over whether the Theophilus Luke addresses is a real person or a figure he invents to represent the faithful, since the Greek term Theophilus means "lover of God."

Though Luke's esteemed mentor Paul was not a disciple during Jesus' ministry, he received a divine revelation in the form of a vision set in heaven itself, which may have revealed facts and intentions of the Gospel that the eyewitnesses at the time missed or tended to ignore. Without seeming to boast, Luke is establishing his credentials as a scholar, saying that he has set out to establish all that could be learned about Jesus and the Gospel.

There is also a hint in this introductory passage that Luke was an eyewitness, "having had perfect understanding of all things from the very first." But this could mean "from the very first hearing about them." His stress that his account is "in order" suggests that he believes the events he describes are in the chronological sequence in which they happened, something that is missing from Mark's Gospel.

CHAPTER 8

From Triumph to the Cross

The raising of Lazarus in Bethany so impressed Jesus' followers and the public that it led to Jesus' triumphal entry into Jerusalem a day or two later, and a week of preaching in the Temple. But both Lazarus' raising and his triumphal entry fueled growing opposition to Jesus among most of the Temple leaders, and culminated in his being arrested on a charge of blasphemy, scourged, and executed on a cross. His enemies used his claim of divinity as proof he blasphemed their God and insulted their religion.

The Transfiguration

The Transfiguration comes at the climax of Jesus' public ministry. Just after speaking to his disciples about his coming death at the hands of his enemies in Jerusalem, Jesus led the inner core of the Twelve—Peter, James, and John—from the town of Caesarea Philippi (miles to the north from the Lake of Galilee) up a high mountain. And there he was transfigured before their eyes; his facial look changed, he literally glowed with white light, and his clothes turned as white as snow. Moses, representing the Law, and Elijah ("Elias" in Greek), representing the Prophets, joined him. The disciples could hear the three discussing Jesus' impending arrest and suffering.

And while Jesus, Moses, and Elijah were speaking, a dark cloud settled down over the mountaintop, and a voice thundered from the cloud, "This is my beloved Son; hear him." Mark says that the disciples were terrified by the transcendent vision, and Peter characteristically offered to build tabernacles over the spots where the three men had sat glowing. Matthew and Mark say that after the cloud dispersed, Moses and Elijah were gone as suddenly as they appeared.

As they started down the mountain, Jesus commanded that they speak nothing about this "until the Son of Man has risen from the dead," a new conception to the disciples that they speculated about. After they regained their courage, the disciples asked Jesus specifically, "Why do the Scribes say that Elijah would come before the Messiah and declare his coming?"

John the Baptist Was Elijah

Jesus said Elijah, in fact, was to come first, and restore all things written about the Son of man, and that Jesus must suffer many things, and be put to death. "But I say to you, Elijah did indeed come, and they did to him whatever they liked, as it was written of him" (Mark 9:12–13). Matthew, only, adds, "Then the disciples understood that he was speaking to them of John the Baptist" (Matthew 17:13).

Matthew also says earlier in his Gospel, quoting Jesus: "Truly I say to you, among those born of women not a greater one has come than John the Baptist, notwithstanding he who is least in the kingdom of heaven is greater than he." Jesus continued, "For all the prophets and the law prophesied before John. And if you will receive it, this is Elijah, who was to come. Let him who has ears to hear, hear" (Matthew 11:13–15).

discussion question

What does Jesus say about the use of violence?
Matthew quotes Jesus as saying, "from the days of John the Baptist until now the kingdom of heaven has suffered violence, and the violent take it by force." This "violence" refers to forcing oneself to do the right thing, to keep the faith despite all opposition. It is a spiritual, not physical, violence.

John the Baptist Was Not Elijah

But elsewhere the Apostle John, one of the three disciples who witnessed the Transfiguration and participated in the discussion with Jesus while they descended the mountain, says of John the Baptist: "this is the record of what John [the Baptist] did when the Jews sent priests and Levites from Jerusalem to ask him, 'Who are you?' And he did not deny; but confessed, 'I am not the Christ.' And they asked him, 'Then who? Are you Elijah?' And he said, 'I am not.'" And when they pressed him, John the Baptist said, "I am the voice of one crying in the wilderness, 'Make straight the way of the Lord, as said the prophet Elijah'" (see John 1:19–21).

symbolism

Jesus' Transfiguration to a being of light reconfirmed his divinity claims—as "true light of true light," as the Nicene Creed puts it. It also revealed John the Baptist was at a higher level than Jesus' disciples, for he now says no prophet ever surpassed him, and that all the prophets formed a succession that led to his appearance.

The explanation of the apparent contradiction between Jesus' words and John the Baptist's is found in the angel's appearance to the father of John the Baptist, as recorded in Luke's Gospel: "your wife Elisabeth shall bear a son who you shall name John. . . . And he shall go before him in the spirit and power of Elijah, to turn the hearts of the fathers to the children, and the disobedient to the wisdom of the just; to get the people ready for the Lord" (see Luke 1:13–17).

The Disciples' Wondering

Those who asked John if he "was" Elijah were trying to see if he would claim to be a reincarnation, something the Old Testament prohibits believing in. He was not Elijah reincarnated, but he was Elijah come back "in spirit and power." This is what Jesus meant when he qualified his affirmation of John as Elijah with "if you will receive it, this is Elijah." Jesus' cryptic statement about taking the kingdom of heaven by violence "and the violent take it by force," has been interpreted traditionally as referring to John's heroic asceticism, "neither eating or drinking" (fasting and abstaining from strong drink).

Lazarus Saturday

The early Catholic Church observed the Saturday before Palm Sunday as Lazarus Saturday, a preview of the resurrection of believers before the last day of judgment. As mentioned previously, the Orthodox Church still observes this day. As was seen in the section on Lazarus in Chapter 7, Jesus' followers saw Lazarus' rising from the dead after four days in the grave as an amazing wonder. This phenomenon, coupled with the plotting of those seeking to silence Jesus by having him put to death, got greater Jerusalem in a buzz just a few days before the beginning of the greatest feast of Judaism's liturgical year, Passover.

After Lazarus rose from the tomb, to impede the growth of the Jesus movement, Jesus' enemies added him to their list of those to be put to death. And later, whether the same evening or the next, Lazarus and Jesus attended a dinner in Bethany put on by Jesus' friend Simon, a leper. The morning after that dinner, Jesus and his companions started making their way to Jerusalem. Jesus sent two of the disciples to "Go into the village, and . . . find an ass tied, and a colt with her. Loose them and bring them to me. And if any man asks about it say, 'The Lord needs them,' and he will let them be taken." And the disciples went and did what Jesus commanded (see Matthew 21:1–6).

discussion question

What is liturgical worship?
Liturgical worship, unlike freeform worship, is a service of prayer led by the clergy following a script, with choir and congregational responses. Both the Temple in Jerusalem and the synagogues followed liturgies, drawing mainly from the Psalms and other prayers from the Torah, which the first churches adapted to their services. Liturgy means "the people's work."

Triumphal Entry (Palm Sunday)

John's Gospel (12:10) says "the chief priests consulted that they might put Lazarus also to death" because his resurrection had caused another wave of people to believe in Jesus. And the next day, the people heard that Jesus was coming to Jerusalem from Bethany, so they "took branches of palm trees" and met him, crying "Hosanna, blessed is the King of Israel who comes in the name of the Lord." And those who had witnessed Lazarus' coming out of the grave "bore witness. . . .For this cause the people also met him, for that they heard that he had done this miracle."

The Pharisees began to think that their efforts to dissuade the people from following Jesus were coming to nothing, saying among themselves, "the world is gone after him." John then interjects that "certain Greeks among them" came up to worship and asked Philip, knowing him to be from Bethsaida of Galilee, how they could meet Jesus. So Philip told Andrew, and they together went and told Jesus. "And Jesus answered them, saying, 'The hour is come, that the Son of man should be glorified'" (John 12:23).

factum

Based on John's Gospel, most Bible scholars agree that this is the third Passover recorded in the Gospel accounts of Jesus' ministry, indicating the end of his ministry's third year, though some dispute that number. Regardless of how many years he and the disciples ministered together, there is no doubt that this was the last Passover they observed together on earth.

Matthew says, "when he came into Jerusalem, all the city was moved, saying, 'Who is this?' And the multitude said, 'This is Jesus the prophet of Nazareth of Galilee'" (Matthew 21:10–11).

The reference to the Greeks who wanted to see Jesus, the crowds coming out to welcome Jesus with palms, the cries of Hosanna, and (as Matthew and Luke add) the people putting down their garments on Jesus' path as a virtual carpet to follow into the city paint a picture of the festive air that filled the Jewish capital city before the holiday.

Jesus Glorified

All three synoptic Gospel writers—Matthew, Mark, and Luke—specify that the triumphal procession brought Jesus all the way to the Temple, and there children and other followers continued worshipping him, incurring the wrath of the chief priests and Temple leaders. But despite this, Luke says Jesus continued preaching in the Temple every day that first Holy Week.

Only John's Gospel describes Jesus' glorification as the climax of his triumphal entry. After saying he was going to die, like a "corn of wheat" that falls into the ground and dies to be raised up and yield fruit, Jesus prayed, "'Father, save me from this hour: but for this cause came I unto this hour. Father, glorify thy name.' Then came a voice from heaven, saying, I have both glorified it, and will glorify it again. The people that stood by and heard it said that it thundered: others said, An angel spake to him. Jesus answered, This voice came not because of me, but for your sakes. Now is the judgment of this world: now shall the prince of this world be cast out" (John 12:23–31).

The grain-of-wheat simile refers to the body being buried and decaying, so that the resurrection body can rise from it as a spiritual body.

Moneychangers Routed

Later on this first Holy Week, Jesus threw the moneychangers out of the Temple, saying they had turned his house into a "den of thieves." He spent the night after that event back in Bethany, and on the way back to the Temple the next morning, he looked in the branches of a fig tree along the way for some breakfast fruit, and finding it barren, "said to it, 'Let no fruit grow on you ever again,' at which the fig tree immediately withered away. And when the disciples saw that, they marveled, 'How soon is the fig tree withered away!' Jesus answered to them, 'Truly I say to you, if you have faith, and doubt not, you shall not only do this that was done to the fig tree but also if you shall say to this mountain, "Be moved and be cast into the sea," it shall be done'" (Matthew 21:19–21).

Interpreters often see the fig tree as representing the Jewish established leaders, who, that week, would reject him and be quickly replaced in God's reckoning by his church. And if that's so, some propose that the mountain represents the pagan Roman Empire that would fall from its pinnacle of power in Rome, to be recreated under Christ's dominion in Byzantium. The word that the apostles and their successors had to say to "move the mountain" was the good news of the Gospel.

factum

Some theologians call Jesus' week of preaching in the Temple and throwing out the moneychangers his "occupation of the Temple." Josephus, the Jewish historian, says that Pharisees in the Temple asked the people to throw lemons at him and his followers to expel them.

Also that week, the Temple priests tested Jesus with questions like "under whose authority do you teach these things," to which he replied, "tell me first whether John the Baptist and his baptism were from God," which they refused to answer, knowing John was revered by the multitude who considered him a prophet from God. So Jesus didn't answer their questions, either.

Crowd Pleaser

But Jesus continued teaching the multitudes at the Temple that week (in the courtyard areas inside the walls, but under the sky), with the people waiting for their Passover feast and basking under the power of the master teacher.

Matthew recorded one of Jesus' most controversial teachings:

"Did ye never read in the scriptures, The stone which the builders rejected, the same is become the head of the corner: this is the Lord's doing, and it is marvellous in our eyes? Therefore say I unto you, The kingdom of God shall be taken from you, and given to a nation bringing forth the fruits thereof. And whosoever shall fall on this stone shall be broken: but on whomsoever it shall fall, it will grind him to powder." And when the chief priests and Pharisees had heard his parables, they perceived that he spake of them. But when they sought to lay hands on him, they feared the multitude, because they took him for a prophet (Matthew 21:42–46).

In exasperation, the Pharisees conspired to take him, and found their opportunity in his one skeptical disciple, Judas Iscariot. John 13:21–30 begins the account of Judas' betrayal at the Last Supper, when Jesus hosted his disciples in one last and everlastingly significant meal somewhere in Jerusalem. There Jesus cryptically revealed that Judas would give him into his enemies' hands. After the meal ended, Judas slipped out to the Temple and sold the chief priests and Pharisees the information about where Jesus might be found later that night. In exchange for this information, Judas gained another thirty pieces of silver for the disciples' treasury.

Good Friday

After Judas left the room where Jesus and the other disciples were finishing their supper, John says Jesus took advantage of their last, fleeting, sociable moments together to teach more truths: "A new commandment I give you, that you love one another as I have loved you, so should you also love one another. By this shall all men know that you are my disciples, if you love one another" (John 13:34–35).

"And when they had sung a hymn, they went out into the Mount of Olives," Matthew says. The mood is tired and drowsy after the supper, and the disciples' voices are clear but seem distant or ethereal as they walk in the dark out of the city to the place called Gethsemane. Holy Land geographers describe Gethsemane as an area in "the Kidron gully," a narrow valley or arroyo (as they are called in the American southwest, Spanish for "dry creek") that runs adjacent to the Mount of Olives and continues out of the city all the way to the Dead Sea.

factum

Gethsemane is now the site of many Jewish, Christian, and Muslim cemeteries. Perhaps there were burial grounds there then, too, which may be the origin of the place being called "the garden of Gethsemane," even though it is barren, rocky, and desert-like. But there were also olive trees, including some that botanists believe were already a thousand years old by the first Good Friday.

Though it was still Thursday night when they left the room where the Last Supper took place (as the Jewish calendar reckons one day to the next from sunset to sunset), it was already Good Friday. And though the Passion of the Christ is mainly thought of in terms of his trial before Pilate in the morning, along with the whippings by the Roman arresting officers, and Jesus carrying his own cross out to Golgotha, another view is that the real Passion was the final hours he spent that night with his disciples praying in Gethsemane.

The Passion of Christ

Jesus' "dark night of the soul" is, like the Transfiguration, recounted in all three synoptic Gospels, with an especially detailed listing of his Gethsemane prayers in John's Gospel. As at the Transfiguration, Jesus invites only his three core apostles—Peter and the sons of Zebedee, James and John—to share it with him. But what a contrast this night is with the night he and his core disciples went up the Mount of the Transfiguration. Then he was filled with light and met Moses and Elijah, and his three closest disciples were terrified by the display of God's power.

On this night, Jesus "began to be sorrowful and very heavy and said to them, 'My soul is overly full of sorrow, even unto death. Wait here and watch with me.' And he went a little farther, fell on his face, and prayed, 'O my Father, if it can possibly be, let this cup pass from me. Nevertheless, not my will, but yours be done.' And he came back to the disciples and found them sleeping" (see Matthew 26:37–40).

Jesus' Vigil

Matthew's and Mark's Gospels repeat this pattern three times and end it with Jesus rousing his vigil-breaking disciples because his betrayer and the mob have arrived. Luke adds these most dramatic details: after Jesus prays "'nevertheless, not my will but yours be done,' an angel appeared to him from heaven, strengthening him. And being in agony he prayed more earnestly, and his sweat was, as it were, great drops of blood falling down to the ground. And when he rose up from prayer he came to his disciples, whom he found sleeping for sorrow, and said to them, 'Why do you sleep? Rise and pray, lest you fall into temptation'" (Luke 22:43–46).

Jesus Leaves His Disciples

Jesus, with Peter, James, and John, met up again with the other disciples just as the mob organized by the chief priests of the Temple came looking for him. Judas came along "with a great multitude carrying swords and staves," and kissed Jesus on the cheek to let the officers know whom to arrest. Jesus asked who they were looking for. "Jesus of Nazareth," they replied, and he told them, "I am he." He asked why they had to come looking for him with swords and staves when he had been preaching daily in the Temple. Peter, agitated, cut off the ear of the High Priest's servant, but Jesus quickly healed the wound and told his followers not to take up swords in his defense.

The Crucifixion

The story of Jesus' trial before Pilate, his transportation to Herod, the attempts of both political leaders to wash their hands of the matter of "Jesus the accused blasphemer," his scourging, the long trudge to Golgotha, and the crucifixion is so well known that most people can recite the main points.

discussion question

Why did Jesus entrust Mary to John?
As the beloved disciple, John was the closest thing Jesus had to a full brother. From the cross, Jesus beheld John, kinsman of Mary and himself, and his mother standing by, and said, "Mother, behold your son," and to John, "behold your mother." It was Jesus' last will and testament.

The mob from the Temple bound Jesus, and after consulting among the Temple leaders, took him to the palace of the Roman governor, Pilate. The disciples slunk to the background. Peter warmed his hands over a fire behind the palace, and, when asked if he hadn't been with Jesus, denied it, three times. And when the rooster crowed, it reminded him of his protestation the previous evening that he would never deny his Lord and Master. Then he wept.

All four Gospels tell the crucifixion sequence. Read John's account in John 18:16–37. John warrants to all who read his Gospel that he witnessed it all by his own eyes, and has written in his own words, "that you might believe."

The Resurrection

All four Gospels tell the story of the resurrection of Jesus, with John's being much more detailed than the others. The accounts vary in details, differing according to the perspective of the source who told it to the evangelists. (John's account varies from the others' because he was a Gospel writer who was also an eyewitness.) But the main outline is that at dawn following the Sabbath, myrrh-bearing women made their way to the tomb where Jesus had been interred, sealed by a huge stone.

When they got near, they saw the stone rolled away, and an angel glowing like lightning greeted them and told them Jesus was not there, but had risen as he had foretold. The angel also said they should tell the Eleven (Judas having hanged himself after realizing the gravity of his sin in betraying his Lord), and should return to Galilee, where he would come to them.

Some skeptics point out that the resurrection and its aftermath get fewer verses in the Gospels than many other events, including the crucifixion, to suggest that this may be an addition to the story of Jesus appended later. The church's traditional answer to this doubt is two-fold. First, Jesus' resurrection was foretold many times in the other sections of the Gospels; the prophesies about Jesus' life and passion were fulfilled when he arose. And second, the raising of Jesus was the precursor of the raising of his other, larger, body, the church, which was the point of all of his stories or events.

The Ascension and Great Commission

Jesus made appearances among his disciples for forty days after the resurrection, the first day being celebrated by the church as Easter or Pascha (Greek for Passover) and the last, Ascension Day. According to St. Paul in his first epistle to the church in Corinth, probably written earlier than any of the Gospels, Jesus also appeared in his resurrection body to a congregation of "five hundred brethren" at one time (1 Corinthians 15:6).

Matthew's and Mark's Gospels record the "Great Commission" as the last instruction Jesus gave his followers. Matthew ends with this rendering: "Then the eleven disciples went away to Galilee, to a mountain Jesus had appointed to meet them. And when they saw him, they worshipped him: but some doubted. And Jesus spoke to them, saying, "All power is given to me in heaven and in earth. Go, therefore, and teach all nations, baptizing them in the name of the Father, and of the Son, and of the Holy Spirit, teaching them to observe all that I have commanded you. And, lo, I am with you always, even to the end of the world. Amen" (See Matthew 28:16–20). Mark and Luke add that after that teaching he rose up out of their presence into heaven.

factum

John records a miracle he performed, bringing many large fish into the disciples' nets, and Jesus also "restored" Peter to leadership among the disciples by giving him three opportunities to rescind his three-times denial on the morning before the crucifixion. Peter's blessing came at a price; Jesus also predicted the persecution and violent death he would face years later.

CHAPTER 9

The Acts and Paul

Dating from about four or five decades after the Ascension (A.D. 75–85), Acts is the earliest conscious attempt to chronicle the history of the fledgling and struggling church. The book is divided mainly between the leadership of Peter in the beginning, and of Paul later on. It also follows the companions of Peter and Paul and their interaction with other apostles when Luke was an eyewitness, or when others told him their stories.

Acts of the Apostles

From its beginning, it's apparent that the Book of Acts is a continuation of the Gospel of Luke. The writing style in Acts will strike any reader of Luke's Gospel as familiar. He opens with a one-sentence thesis statement:

> *The former treatise have I made, O Theophilus, of all that Jesus began both to do and teach, until the day in which he was taken up, after that he through the Holy Ghost had given commandments unto the apostles he had chosen: To whom also he shewed himself alive after his passion by many infallible proofs, being seen of them forty days, and speaking of the things pertaining to the kingdom of God, and, being assembled together with them, commanded them that they should not depart from Jerusalem, but wait for the promise of the Father, which, saith he, ye have heard of me (Acts 1:1–4).*

The "former treatise" is the Gospel that Luke also addressed to Theophilus, whether that is an actual person or a collective name for all the lovers of God (as mentioned previously, the literal translation of Theophilus) likely to read his books. Note the King James Version's use of "passion" as Luke's word for the suffering and death of Jesus, if any wonder about the origin of that term. Also note that the forty days' sojourn of Jesus with his disciples after the resurrection compares with the forty days he was tested by Satan in the wilderness before beginning his ministry. What the disciples were to wait for in Jerusalem was the coming of the Holy Spirit and the official birthing of the Church of Christ at Pentecost.

Unlike Matthew and Mark, Luke didn't include the Great Commission in his Gospel, but recaps it at the beginning of Acts as a transition to Pentecost. "You shall receive power when the Holy Spirit comes upon you. And you will witness to me in Jerusalem and in all Judea, Samaria, and to the end of the earth" (see Acts 1:8). Luke also elaborates a bit on the Ascension: "And when he had spoken these things, while they watched, he was taken up. And a cloud received him out of their sight. And while they stood gazing toward heaven as he went up, two men in white apparel stood by them and said, 'Men of Galilee, why do you stand gazing up into heaven? This same Jesus who has been taken up from you into heaven shall come in like manner as you have seen him go into heaven'" (Acts 1:9).

Christian Pentecost

Luke says that when the fiftieth day after Passover had fully come, the disciples were all gathered in one place, waiting as the Lord had instructed. Then there was a sound like a rushing strong wind coming into the house and the room they occupied. And they saw "tongues" of fire, one hovering over the head of each person in the room. They began speaking in other languages "as the Spirit gave them utterance." The people who were crowded into Jerusalem for the Pentecost feast, after hearing the noise of the wind at that place and of the people speaking in tongues, gathered around them and "marveled" at what they saw, people who were of all one dialect speaking in many different languages. The account says that "Parthians, Medes, Elamites, dwellers in Mesopotamia, and in Judea, Cappadocia in Pontus, and Asia, Phrygia, and Pamphylia in Egypt, and in the parts of Libya about Cyrene, and foreigners from Rome, Jews and proselytes, Cretes, and Arabs" all heard their own languages coming from these Galilean Christians.

factum

Moses instituted Pentecost to end the Passover season, fifty days after Passover Sabbath. Originally the "feast of the harvest of first fruits," the name used by Greek-speaking Jewish people (*pentekonta* being fifty in Greek) was common in the first century. These Jewish Christians continued to worship in the Temple and observe holy days, fasts, and hours of prayer (see Acts 3:1).

Many marveled, Luke said, but some mocked, attributing the miracle of the tongues to "new wine." Peter answered, "these are not drunk, as you suppose, as it is only the third hour of the day," or 9 A.M. Then Peter began a sermon, fulfilling the prophecy that when the Spirit came on the disciples they would receive power to witness for Jesus and his Gospel to all nations. Luke records Peter's sermon, the first evangelistic sermon in Christian history, in Acts 2: 16–24. Peter then showed how the prophesies concerning the Christ (Messiah) as the descendant of David the great king, pertained to Jesus. And then Peter showed those who wanted to repent how to be saved (see Acts 2:36–47).

The First Megachurch

Not only was a megachurch, as congregations of several thousand members are called today, reportedly founded in Jerusalem on Pentecost, but most likely dozens, possibly scores, of churches were created by members of the crowd who were in Jerusalem for the feast, heard Peter's sermon, were baptized, and returned home to tell the news to friends and relatives. Presumably, those with the gift of tongues that day were interpreting Peter's words in all the languages represented.

Memories Still Fresh

Many of these people had been in Jerusalem for Passover just more than fifty days earlier and had seen Jesus being hailed on what Christians now call Palm Sunday, his preaching in the Temple, and his being crucified, and it's likely his passion was a topic of conversation at the time. The seed that had been planted had sprung up and already was having its first fruits, on this the festival of the first fruits of harvest. Not only would Passover become the most important feast in the new church (as Easter is called in most non-English-speaking churches), Pentecost would also be adopted from Judaism to be commemorated everywhere Christians established congregations and received the Holy Spirit.

The New Church

The leadership Jesus had assigned to Peter, and that Peter had partially assumed when traveling with Jesus and the Twelve, was quickly confirmed at Pentecost. And the next time we see Peter in Acts, his acts are even more impressive. While walking into the Temple with John for the prayers of the ninth hour (3 P.M.), he is accosted by a lame beggar asking for alms. Peter utters the famous line, "Silver and gold have I none; but such as I have give I thee. In the name of Jesus Christ of Nazareth, rise up and walk." And the man not only makes an effort to get up, he also leaps and runs around the Temple porch, calling out like a man who has just met his Savior.

Such is the ruckus the healed man stirs up that a large crowd gathers around him, Peter, and John, asking how the man they had known as a lame beggar all his life was now whole and praising God.

Church Growth

Peter's response is similar to the one he made at the feast when the Holy Spirit had given the disciples the gift of tongues. He tells them the Jesus they had crucified is living again, and he is the one God had promised through all the prophets and had even said would be persecuted by those he came to redeem, "all the prophets from Samuel and those that follow after, as many as have spoken, have likewise foretold of these days. You are the children of the prophets, and of the covenant God made with our fathers. For he said to Abraham, 'And in your seed shall all the peoples of the earth be blessed.' Unto you first God, having raised up his Son Jesus, sent him to bless you, in turning away every one of you from his iniquities" (see Acts 3:24–26).

Then, Luke says, the rulers of the Temple sent the captain of the temple (a high-ranking official charged with maintaining order in the temple precinct), who arrested Peter, John, and the man healed from lameness, and put them in a cell for the night. But even despite this, "many who heard the word believed;" and this time, "the number of the men who believed was about five thousand."

Witnessing to their Enemies

The next morning the chief priests and leaders of the Temple put Peter and John "in their midst" and asked them, "by what power, or by what name, have you done this?" And Peter, Luke says, "filled by the Holy Spirit," started witnessing to these same men who had delivered Jesus to Pilate for crucifixion: "Let it be known to all of you and to all the people of Israel that by the name of Jesus Christ of Nazareth, whom you crucified, who God raised from the dead, even by him does this man stand here before you whole. This is the stone that was set aside as nothing by you builders, and has become the head of the corner. Neither is there salvation in any other: for there is no other name under heaven given among men, whereby we must be saved." (See Acts 4:10–12.)

discussion question

What was behind the apostles' new "holy boldness"? Though Peter had addressed the lame man with what seems to be doubt about his own power to cure him, the man's healing was a miracle that confirmed that power and pushed the mushrooming church from 3,000 new members the first day to 8,000 the next, and similar miracles followed everywhere the apostles went, with even more growth occurring with every new event.

Free Speech Prohibited

The accusers marveled at Peter's and John's boldness and, consulting among themselves, privately admitted that a verifiable miracle had been performed by the accused on the formerly lame man. And fearing repercussions if they punished Peter and John, they commanded them not to speak any longer in Jesus' name. But again the lead apostles were fearless: "Whether it's right in the sight of God to obey you more than God, you can judge. But we cannot do other than speak the things we have seen and heard." So after the accusers had further threatened the apostles, they let them go (see Acts 4:19–21). Peter's fame spread so much that people tried to position themselves in line with his shadow, thinking that being touched by his shadow would heal them.

Solomon's Porch

The apostles continued to preach in Solomon's Porch (inside the Temple walls), to the great displeasure of the Temple rulers, so much so that the rulers eventually threw the apostles back into the Temple jail cell. But while the apostles were incarcerated, an angel released them, and told them to return to Solomon's Porch early the next morning and continue teaching the Word as they had been.

After they continued teaching, they were taken before the council, and when the council was about to punish them, a Pharisee and "learned teacher," Gamaliel, rose to the apostles' defense, concluding, "If this is of men, it will come to nothing, but if it is from God, we can do nothing to stop it." So the council agreed to ignore the apostles a while longer, and they continued to teach in the Temple.

factum

Gamaliel was a teacher of Saul, who became Paul; and Joseph, who became Barnabas. Historians say Gamaliel was a son of Simeon and a grandson of the famous Rabbi Hillel, whose teachings are still widely used in Jewish synagogues.

Throughout this growth period, Luke inserts facts about the internal working of the new church. The newly baptized shared among themselves their property and a common purse, for example, and Luke describes the need of some members for more personal ministry and help, for which reason the apostles appointed the first deacons. Among the deacons, the first named is Stephen, "a man full of faith and of the Holy Spirit."

The First Martyr

Stephen is described as doing many miracles, but because his zeal attracted opposition in several of the synagogues, his opponents conspired to have him executed by stoning, thus making him the first martyr of the church: "They threw him outside the city and stoned him: and the witnesses laid down their clothes at a young man's feet, whose name was Saul" (Luke 7:58).

Writing after the fact, of course, here Luke foreshadows the rise of Saul/Paul by noting his presence at the stoning of Stephen. For although Luke records in the first chapter of Acts the replacement of Judas Iscariot by casting lots among names of disciples close to but not part of the Twelve, God seemed to have another apostle in mind to round out the select core of the founding church. Saul, converted from persecutor of the church and ranking "official" witness to Stephen's martyrdom, becomes the Apostle Paul in the second portion of Acts, and the main influence on the direction the church would now take, away from Jerusalem.

Stephen's sermon occupies the whole seventeenth chapter of Acts and shows the same kind of power from the Holy Spirit as Peter's sermons. It may have been because Stephen spoke in a less central location when he testified of the resurrected Christ and where converts were not yet numerous that he was executed, while Peter and John were able to escape that fate.

From Persecutor to Apostle Extraordinaire

Luke said that Saul was consenting to Stephen's death. And, he adds, there was a great persecution against the church at Jerusalem, and all the Christians, except the apostles, scattered throughout the regions of Judea and Samaria. Devout men buried Stephen, "and made great lamentation over him." As for Saul, he made havoc of the church, entering into individual houses and arresting men and women and committing them to prison (see Luke 8:1–3).

The persecution in Jerusalem, by scattering the less-active apostles and converts, affected the rapid growth of the church in outlying areas. For example, Philip preached in Samaria and found the people ready to receive his message.

discussion question

What did Jesus teach were the worst and the best prayers?
The worst was "Thank you, God, that I am not like this sinner"; the best, "Lord have mercy on me, a sinner."

God directed Philip to go into the Gaza desert beyond Jerusalem, where he found a high-ranking Ethiopian sitting in a chariot reading the Prophet Isaiah. So Philip approached him and preached the Word by way of the prophesies in Isaiah and forthwith baptized him into the faith. Sub-Saharan Ethiopia is by all historical evidence one of the first distant countries to receive the Gospel, its evangelization probably inaugurated by this early convert.

Saul's Conversion

Saul asked the high priest of the Temple to give him a letter of introduction to synagogues in Damascus, Iturea (as it was called in the Roman Empire, Syria in modern times), so that he could have Jewish converts to Christ there arrested and returned to Jerusalem (a long journey) for trial.

But on the way to Damascus, a bright light blinded Saul, and he heard a heavenly voice that identified its speaker as Jesus, "whom you persecute." Saul's companions heard the voice but saw no source for it, and when Saul's eyes were reopened, he found himself sightless and had to have his companions guide him on to Damascus, leading him by the hand.

A disciple of the Lord in Damascus, Ananias, one of those no doubt Saul wished to persecute, had a vision from the Lord telling him to seek out Saul on the "Street called Straight" and heal his blindness. But Ananias told the Lord he had already heard of the letters Saul had received from the high priest to persecute Damascus' Christians. "Go on your way," the Lord replied, "for he has been chosen by me to carry my name to the Gentiles, and kings, and the children of Israel, for I will show him how great things he must suffer for my name's sake" (see Acts 9:15–16).

Paul Proves His Conversion

Like Ananias, the Christians in Damascus were reluctant to receive Saul, their persecutor. But when he began preaching in the synagogues and making converts, the Christians were soon convinced of his true conversion, and the people who opposed the converts became Paul's enemies and tried to arrest him.

He escaped by being lowered out the city wall in a basket by night, and returned to Jerusalem to join the apostles. But he was again rebuffed because they feared him, until his old acquaintance from student days under Gamaliel, Barnabas, was convinced and took Paul to vouch for him before the apostles.

After Paul began openly preaching the Word of Jesus in Jerusalem, he became targeted for death, and when he was secretly shipped back to his hometown of Tarsus, Luke says there was a time of peace for the churches in Judea, Samaria, and Galilee. In the meantime Peter's ministry continued to flourish, and he healed a paralytic, and raised Tabitha, also called Dorcas, from the dead at Joppa.

An Angel Visits a Gentile

Cornelius, a god-fearing gentile and devout centurion (a Roman military officer with command of a hundred men), was visited in Caesarea by an angel, who told him to call Peter from Joppa and invite him to visit Cornelius at his home. At the same time, Peter had a vision in which the Lord told him to eat animals considered unclean under Jewish dietary law, which God was showing him being lowered from the sky on a sheet.

factum

Although it looks like a contradiction in terms, the phrase "Jewish Christian" is not an oxymoron. Jewish Christians were people who believed in Jesus, but continued to follow the Laws of Moses and to observe the Jewish rituals and holy days. This term is used to describe the followers of Jesus in the early days of the Christian movement, before Christians began to be expelled from Jewish temples (some time in the A.D. 80s).

Cornelius' invitation was waiting for Peter when he came out of his vision-trance, and after a four-day journey, he arrived in Caesarea where he met a "large company" waiting for him in Cornelius' house. And he said, "You know it is an unlawful for a Jewish man to keep company or come to one of another nationality, but God has shown me that I should not call any man common or unclean. Therefore, I came to you without hesitation, as soon as I was sent for. I ask therefore for what intent you have sent for me?"

And after Cornelius explained his visitation from the angel, Peter preached Christ to the people at the house, many of whom received the Holy Spirit as Peter spoke, the gentiles even demonstrating the gift of tongues to the astonishment of those "of the circumcision." After he finished, Peter baptized those who believed in Christ, again to the astonishment of the Jewish Christians.

A Turning Point

This was a great turning point for the church, as for the first time the disciples started preaching to gentiles who had not first become Jewish through proselytism and circumcision. But it did not become "official" church practice until a council, called among the apostles in Jerusalem, debated and decided that circumcision was not necessary to become a Christian. They put their finding in a letter to Barnabas and Paul at the church in Antioch, about 300 miles from Jerusalem. When Judas, Barnabas, and Silas, the disciples appointed to take the letter to Antioch, got to their destination and presented the letter to the large congregation gathered there, the congregation rejoiced (Acts 15:28–31).

discussion question

Why does the church emphasize sexual purity?
One source of this policy is the apostles' letter to Barnabas and Paul and the church in Antioch, which said, "it seemed good to the Holy Spirit, and to us, to lay upon you no greater burden than these necessary things: That you abstain from meats offered to idols, from blood and from things strangled, and from fornication. If you keep yourselves from these you shall do well. Fare ye well."

First Church Council Teaching

This decision that a person did not have to be circumcised to become a Christian created a permanent separation of Christians with the Old Testament ceremonial and moral laws. Christians are not required to keep Jewish ceremonial laws (including circumcision, abstaining from "unclean meats" like pork and shellfish, mixing meat and dairy foods, and many other rules given under Moses), while they are still held to the moral laws of Moses.

Born Out of Time

Most of the rest of the book of Acts is coverage of Paul's three missionary journeys. In 1 Corinthians 15:8, Paul recites the evidence for Jesus' resurrection, citing the many eyewitnesses who saw him after his death, and adds, "And last of all he was seen by me also, as one born out of due time." This is more than an expression of regret that he was "born too late" to have been in the first group named as apostles. It's closer to Paul's confession elsewhere that he is the least of the apostles, and the chief of sinners.

Some of this humility may be repentance for the role Paul played in the stoning of Stephen and the persecution of the church before his conversion, but more likely it is Paul's adoption of the Beatitudes discussed in Chapter 3, in other words, taking on the self-effacing meekness that puts oneself last in order that Christ can come first.

But in other cases Paul boasts of his sufferings for Christ and of his apostleship. As an apostle he became one of the key leaders of the first-generation church, despite not having been there when the original Twelve were chosen, or when Judas Iscariot's official successor was chosen by lot.

The First Foreign Missionary and Itinerant Preacher

Paul made three major missionary journeys that Luke covers between chapters 13 and 28 of Acts. The first, described in Acts 13 and 14, took Paul and Barnabas from Antioch in Cilicia (in modern-day Syria), to Antioch in Pisidia (modern-day Turkey), by way of Seleucia; Salamis, and Paphos, Cyprus; and Perga and back via Iconium, Lystra, Derbe, and Attalia.

discussion question

What is an itinerant preacher?
Paul preached in one place for a while, and went on to another. Thus he became the first itinerant preacher (in other words, a traveling preacher). This job title was common in American colonial and frontier times, where congregations were too small to support full-time ministers, and parishioners were so scattered that constant travel was often a central item of a preacher's job description.

The second missionary journey, during A.D. 49–52, is covered in Acts 15–18. It took Paul and Silas from Jerusalem to Antioch, Derbe, Lystra, Troas, Neapolis, Philippi, Amphipolis, Apollonia, Thessalonica, Berea, Athens, Corinth, Cenchreae, Ephesus, and Caesarea. The third journey, from A.D. 53 to 57, is recorded in Acts 18:23 through 21:16. In it, Paul went from Antioch to Ephesus, Thessalonica, Corinth, Philippi, and Toras, and back by way of Assos, Mitylene, Miletus, Tyre, and Caesarea to Jerusalem.

Paul's epistle to the church in Rome, Romans, is especially theological, often described as the inspiration for most major renewal periods in church history from St. Augustine on. Hebrews, also, is highly doctrinal, but its authorship has been disputed, as its style seems Paul-like, but its language and tone do not quite sound like his.

Paul's Interpretation of the Gospel

Paul expounds on grace and its free provision by Christ, and emphasizes the emancipation of the Christian from "the law" so forcefully that he is sometimes thought to have been at odds with Jesus' emphasis on the fulfillment, rather than the abrogation, of the law. But the apparent contradiction is resolved in Romans 15:13: "May the God of hope fill you with all joy and peace in believing, so that you may abound in hope by the power of the Holy Spirit." Paul consistently teaches that one should be willing to suffer for one's testimony to the Gospel by resisting temptation and not yielding to coercive attempts to force disobedience to Christ (as the Roman persecutors of the early church did, overtly and persistently). But he says it is "all joy and peace" (Romans 15:13) to be freed from sin, and in that freedom there is no "law," no sense of coercion, because the desire to do what Christ requires wells up from the willing heart that he has given second birth.

factum

Paul wrote more books of the New Testament than any other early church leader, though Luke's two books may contain as many words as Paul's. Twelve of the twenty-eight books are his epistles, if Hebrews is not counted. And his epistles are the foundation of most orthodox Christian theological study, as they speak to specific problems congregations faced.

The Epistles to Timothy and Titus

Timothy was a steadfast follower of Paul and a leader in the Thessalonian and Corinthian churches. Being young, he was besieged by teachers of various innovations in the young church's doctrine, and Paul may have written his epistles as much to bolster Timothy's positions as to teach him things he didn't already know. It's a safe assumption that a congregation of that generation would have been willing to settle many disputes with just a word on the subject from an apostle of Paul's stature.

fallacy

It's a myth that Paul himself chose to "take over" the fledgling Jesus movement. Jesus told Ananias in his vision, "Saul has been chosen by me to carry my name to the Gentiles, and kings, and the children of Israel, and I will show him how great things he must suffer for my name's sake."

Titus was a gentile convert of Paul who worked with Paul and Barnabas at Antioch and journeyed with them to Jerusalem, where the Twelve agreed that he did not have to be circumcised to become a church leader. Paul used him as his emissary to the church in Corinth and wrote to him about overseeing the church in which he was Paul's personal representative (but not, yet, a bishop himself). In the conclusion of this letter Paul asks Titus to meet him in Nicopolis.

Pharisee to Martyr

Sources outside the New Testament record Paul's death as an execution under orders from Nero in Rome somewhere between A.D. 64 and 67. From Paul's studying under Gamaliel to be a Pharisee, he became what many believe is the most important founder of the Christian religion other than Jesus Christ himself. Many commentators have expressed the opinion that the fledgling church may have faded out had Paul not come along and solidified its doctrines, reached and supported scores of struggling congregations, and written many of its most closely reasoned documents.

CHAPTER 10

The Church, the Body of Christ

After Luke's history, spanning roughly the first thirty years of church history, the work of Josephus, who chronicled Roman and Jewish history about the same time the New Testament was being written, is the first external historical documentation of Jesus' life and impact. Ignatius, the bishop of Antioch who was a child in the time of Jesus, and Eusebius, the bishop of Caesarea in Palestine in the time of Constantine the Great, were the next recorders of some aspects of church history.

The Early Jesus Movement

Apart from the New Testament itself, the best historical documentation of Jesus' life and influence, and of the infant church surviving from ancient times, comes from Flavius Josephus, A.D. 37–101, a historian in the courts of several Roman emperors. Though Josephus was Jewish and of a priestly lineage, some Jewish people have considered him suspect because he tried to sustain a middle ground between paganism and orthodox Judaism. But since Josephus' writings date from the same period as the writing of the New Testament, historians generally consider them the most reliable general records of those times. His writings deal widely with Israel, Judah, Palestine, Rome, and (briefly) the new sect called Christians. Josephus' main description of Jesus and the church is this passage, from a section on Herod the Great from his twenty-volume work, *Jewish Antiquities* (Book XVIII):

> *About this time lived Jesus, a man full of wisdom, if indeed one may call him a man. For he was the doer of incredible things, and the teacher of such as gladly received the truth. He thus attracted to himself many Jewish people and many of the Gentiles. He was the Christ. On the accusation of the leading men of our people, Pilate condemned him to death upon the cross; nevertheless, those who had previously loved him still remained faithful to him. For on the third day he again appeared to them living, just as, in addition to a thousand other marvelous things, prophets sent by God had foretold. And to the present day the race of those who call themselves Christians after him has not ceased.*

Josephus' *Jewish Antiquities* recapitulates the Torah and tries to tell the whole history of the Jewish people, from which the excerpt just provided about Jesus and the church, is just one paragraph.

It is curious that Josephus wrote so positively about Jesus and the Christians, as Christianity was considered an illegal religion in Rome at the time, and was opposed by the Jewish establishment. Some scholars believe his positive treatment of Jesus came not from him, but from additions made by later Christian editors.

factum

Josephus wrote in Greek, the language of scholarship in the era of the emperors under whom he served (Vespasian, Titus, Domitian, and Trajan). His works were translated in the common language of the empire at the time, Latin, and were widely read and circulated throughout the churches.

Missions to Pagan Rome and the Gentiles

The Roman Empire of the time of Jesus and the early church dates from the Roman emperor Octavian's reorganization of the Roman Republic in 31 B.C. Octavian added Egypt to the collection of territories, like Greece and what is now called the Middle East, that were part of the previous Roman Republic.

discussion question

What does "fullness of time" mean?
Many biblical commentators have suggested that the Apostle Paul, in referring to his era as "the fullness of time" in which God chose to send the Messiah and establish his church, was suggesting that the Roman Empire was the right place at the right time for the Gospel (see Galatians 4:4 and Hebrews 1:2).

Octavian became Caesar Augustus, the first Roman emperor and the one still in power when Jesus was born, as recorded in Luke's Gospel: "there went out a decree from Caesar Augustus, that the entire world should be taxed" (Luke 2:1). Augustus was the most powerful world ruler since Alexander the Great, who had conquered the known world (from Europe to India) 300 years earlier.

Like Greece four centuries earlier, Rome was devoutly pagan, with mythological deities renamed and resized to fit the Roman ethos from their earlier Grecian reigns, and a cult of the emperor as the divine lord. Pertinent to the church's growth is a look at the social conditions paganism fostered, which the population increasingly rejected as inhumane or morally defective as the Christian minority grew.

factum

The New Testament did not exist at this early date. Epistles like Paul's, Peter's, and John's, and individual Gospels and Acts appeared one by one and were sent around congregations. Reading aloud from these, as well as Old Testament passages, was part of worship in the early church, which was modeled after worship in the Jewish Temple and synagogues.

The early Christians' charity and compassion for their neighbors commended the Gospel to large segments of the population. One writer observes that when a plague decimated the population of the empire early in the church's history, the only people caring for both their own families and their neighbors, rather than running from the infectious population centers, were the Christians.

Paul's Definition of Apostle

Most of Paul's thirteen epistles begin by establishing his credentials as an apostle, specifically as the apostle to the gentiles (ironically, as he was trained as a Pharisee, an especially strict group among orthodox Jews). Paul claims he became an apostle through the will of God. In his first epistle to the church in Corinth, he explains the importance of his apostolicity most completely: "Am I not an apostle? Am I not free? Have I not seen Jesus Christ our Lord? Are not you my work in the Lord? If I am not an apostle to others, still without doubt I am one to you, for you are the seal of my apostleship in the Lord" (see 1 Corinthians 9:1–2).

Missionary

The word *apostle* means "sent one," a synonym for "missionary." Yet from Jesus' way of selecting and commissioning the Twelve (as discussed in Chapter 5), he was using the word *apostle* as an office apart from and above others in the church. And Paul in Corinthians reinforces this meaning and undoubtedly elevated its understanding to the early church. Moreover, his words, which follow, leave little doubt that he considered the apostolic office the church's highest after the Ascension of its Founder and Head:

"And God has set some in the church, first apostles, secondarily prophets, thirdly teachers, after that miracles, then gifts of healings, helps, governments, diversities of tongues. Are all apostles? Are all prophets? Are all teachers? Are all workers of miracles?" (1 Corinthians 12:28–29).

Apostolicity the Seal

Even Protestants who broke from authoritarian church hierarchies in the Reformation considered being an apostle the seal of God, as referred to earlier in the formula, "Apostolicity was the norm of canonicity," meaning that when the New Testament books were collected in one volume and given the church's seal as the Word of God, those written by apostles or companions of apostles were in, and the many other books of the time that dealt with Jesus and early church leaders were out.

Though the twenty-seven books that now make up the New Testament were all written, according to tradition, by A.D. 100, they were not declared to be the official New Testament until near the end of the fourth century. In one way, it is remarkable it took so long for the church fathers to recognize their New Testament as the Word of God. The New Testament itself constantly cites the Old Testament as the church fathers knew it in its widely circulated version in their generation, The Septuagint (a Greek version of the Old Testament dating from the third century B.C.).

Paul, for example, writes to Timothy: "From childhood you have known the holy scriptures, which are able to make you wise unto salvation through faith in Christ Jesus. All scripture is given by inspiration of God and is profitable for doctrine, for reproof, for correction, for instruction in righteousness in order that the man of God may be perfect, thoroughly equipped to all good works" (see 2 Timothy 3:15–17).

discussion question

Who canonized the New Testament?
In 382, a council in Rome, not an ecumenical one (an ecumenical one would have delegates from all corners of the known church with which its conveners had communion), agreed that the twenty-seven books that are now considered the New Testament were the only ones to be included.

Persecutions Multiply

The success of the church in its first generation, having established congregations from Ethiopia in Africa to India in Asia, and to Rome, Gaul, and Britain in Europe, unfortunately led others to persecute Christians. Some early Christians escaped the persecutions recorded in Acts with the martyrdom of Stephen and the scattering of the Jerusalem flock, only to find themselves persecuted in the pagan Roman empire. The people of the Roman empire initially thought this new Jewish sect curious, then bizarre, then fair game for use in sports spectacles in their coliseums, and, finally, a threat, as their growth in numbers and unflagging loyalty to Christ made Jesus more beloved and worshipped by more people than the current Caesar.

The Book of Martyrs

John Fox (or Foxe), 1517–1587, a brilliant English scholar, and master of biblical languages and history of the early church, compiled the most definitive study of the persecution of Christians under the Caesars between Nero and Constantine (A.D. 54–313). Also containing chapters on later persecutions of Christians, the book is described by James Miller Dodds thus: "After the Bible itself, no book so profoundly influenced early Protestant sentiment as the *Book of Martyrs*. Even in our time it is still a living force."

Fox begins with the crucifixion of Jesus, followed by the martyrdom of Stephen, adding to the details in Acts that Stephen's time of death is believed to have been the Passover following the crucifixion, and that "about 2,000" suffered martyrdom during this persecution in Judea.

The Second Martyr

"The next martyr we meet with, according to St. Luke in the History of the Apostles' Acts," Fox writes, "was James the son of Zebedee, the elder brother of John . . . ten years after the death of Stephen, [James'] martyrdom took place; for no sooner had Herod Agrippa been appointed governor of Judea than . . . he raised a sharp persecution against the Christians . . . by striking at their leaders.

"Thus did the first apostolic martyr cheerfully and resolutely receive that cup, which he had told our Savior he was ready to drink. Timon and Parmenas suffered martyrdom about the same time; one at Philippi and the other in Macedonia" in A.D. 44.

Fifteen Others

Fox records another fifteen apostles and disciples who died as martyrs:

- Philip "suffered martyrdom at Heliopolis, in Phrygia. He was scourged, thrown into prison, and afterwards crucified, A.D. 54."
- Matthew was martyred in Ethiopia, "slain with a halberd in the city of Nadabah, A.D. 60." (A halberd is an ax with a long, pointed spike.)
- James, the Lord's brother and bishop of the church in Jerusalem, "at the age of ninety-four was beaten and stoned . . . and finally had his brains dashed out."
- Matthias, elected to succeed Judas Iscariot, "was stoned at Jerusalem and beheaded."
- Andrew, Simon Peter's brother, "on his arrival at Edessa, was taken and crucified on a cross, the two ends of which were fixed transversely in the ground. Hence the derivation of the term, St. Andrew's Cross."
- Mark, companion of Peter and author of the Gospel bearing his name, "was dragged to pieces by the people of Alexandria . . . ending his life."
- Peter, bishop of Rome, was crucified upside down, because he thought he was unworthy to be crucified in the same way as the Lord.

- Paul died at the hands of Nero's soldiers, who "came and led him out of the city to the place of execution, where he, after making his prayers, gave his neck to the sword."
- Jude, author of the epistle bearing his name and "the brother of James, and commonly called Thaddeus, was crucified at Edessa, A.D. 72."
- Bartholomew, said to have translated the Gospel of Matthew into an Indian language and to have preached it there, was "cruelly beaten and then crucified."
- Thomas, the twin famous for doubting Jesus' resurrection, "preached the Gospel in Parthia and India, where exciting the rage of the pagan priests, he was martyred by being thrust through with a spear."
- Luke, author of the Gospel bearing his name and of Acts, "is supposed to have been hanged on an olive tree, by idolatrous priests of Greece."
- Simon "Zelotes, preached the Gospel in Mauritania, Africa, and even in Britain, in which latter country he was crucified, A.D. 74."
- John was cast into a cauldron of boiling oil, but miraculously escaped without injury. He was the only apostle who escaped a violent death.
- The death of Barnabas, one of the Seventy, erstwhile companion of Paul, "is supposed to have taken place about A.D. 73."

John Fox summarizes the list of the martyrdoms of the church's first generation of leaders with: "notwithstanding all these continual persecutions and horrible punishments, the church daily increased, deeply rooted in the doctrine of the apostles and of men apostolical, and watered plenteously with the blood of saints."

discussion question

Why was John the only apostle allowed a natural death?
The Bible doesn't say, but some relate it to his being Jesus' "beloved disciple." His being entrusted with the care of Jesus' mother from the Cross, some speculate, led to a relatively peaceful life as an earthly reward for that. Ironically, John's brother James was the first apostle who was also a martyr.

The Ten Persecutions

Fox documents ten waves of persecutions in Imperial Rome.

NERO (ROMAN EMPEROR A.D. 54–68)

Nero ordered Rome burned, and it was in flames for nine days, killing thousands. Afterward he blamed the fire on the Christians and started persecuting them. "Nero even refined upon cruelty, and contrived all manner of punishments for the Christians that the most infernal imagination could design. In particular, he had some sewed up in skins of wild beasts, and then worried by dogs until they expired; and others dressed in shirts made stiff with wax, fixed to axletrees, and set on fire in his gardens, in order to illuminate them. This persecution was general throughout the whole Roman Empire; but it rather increased than diminished the spirit of Christianity. In the course of it, St. Paul and St. Peter were martyred." Fox mentions that Nero martyred members of "the Seventy," including Erastus, Aristarchus, Trophimus, Joseph Barsabas, and Ananias, bishop of Damascus.

DOMITIAN (ROMAN EMPEROR A.D. 81–96)

Fox describes emperor Domitian as "naturally inclined to cruelty," having executed his own brother and some members of the Roman Senate, "some through malice and others to confiscate their estates." Under his rule, many Romans turned in their Christian neighbors for persecution and martyrdom. Paul's coworker Timothy, bishop of Ephesus, was among the many martyrs from this period.

TRAJAN (ROMAN EMPEROR A.D. 98–117)

Fox says that under Trajan's reign, "Pliny the Second, a man learned and famous, seeing the lamentable slaughter of Christians, and moved to pity, wrote to Trajan, certifying him that there were many thousands of them daily put to death, of which none did anything contrary to the Roman laws worthy of persecution."

fallacy

Many have the impression that Protestants deny that Peter was ever the Bishop of Rome, but Fox includes the martyrdom of Ignatius as occurring under Trajan. Himself an early Protestant reformer, Fox affirms the tradition that Ignatius was second bishop of Antioch, after Peter had moved to the same position in Rome.

Trajan was succeeded by Adrian. "About this time Alexander, bishop of Rome, with his two deacons, were martyred; as were Quirinus and Hernes, with their families; Zenon, a Roman nobleman, and about ten thousand other Christians."

But when Adrian died in A.D. 138, he was succeeded by Antoninus Pius, "one of the most amiable monarchs who ever reigned, and who stayed the persecutions against the Christians."

MARCUS AURELIUS ANTONINUS (ROMAN EMPEROR A.D. 161–180)

Marcus Aurelius instigated the fourth wave of persecutions. Polycarp, bishop of Smyrna and a father of the church, is one of the most famous martyrs of this period. When guards came to arrest him, he prepared a feast for them and asked them for an hour in which to pray, and his prayer was so fervent that "his guards repented that they had been instrumental in taking him. He was, however, carried before the proconsul, condemned, and burnt in the market place." Fox also reports that especially harsh persecution flared up in Lyon, France, at this time.

SEVERUS (ROMAN EMPEROR A.D. 193–211)

Though Fox says that Severus was inclined to relieve the persecutions, the people at this time had come to fear the Christians because of the explosive growth in the churches, so they pressured the government to have the older laws against the Christians enforced. "Tertullian," Fox says, "who lived in this age, informs us that if the Christians had collectively withdrawn themselves from the Roman territories, the empire would have been greatly depopulated." Fox lists scores of martyrs in Rome, Africa, and Lyon during this period, including that of the celebrated bishop of Lyon, Irenaeus, a father of the church and author of a book considered a classic in Christian literature, *Against Heresies*.

MAXIMINUS THRAX (ROMAN EMPEROR A.D. 235–238)

During this sixth wave of persecution, some of the martyrs were members of the Roman Senate, as the church continued to make inroads in the society and culture of Rome. Fox writes, "During this persecution, raised by Maximinus, numberless Christians were slain without trial, and buried indiscriminately in heaps, sometimes fifty or sixty being cast into a pit together, without the least decency. When the tyrant Maximinus died in A.D. 238, he was succeeded by Gordian, during whose reign, and that of his successor Philip, the church was free from persecution for the space of more than ten years."

DECIUS (ROMAN EMPEROR A.D. 249–251)

Decius, who hated Philip (who was rumored to be a Christian), again turned up the campaign against the church. By now, the pagan temples were being abandoned and churches were bulging, but, Fox reports, factions were beginning to appear in the church as well. The rack, which stretched the bodies of the victims before they were beheaded, was put into use at this time.

VALERIAN (ROMAN EMPEROR A.D. 253–260)

The eighth persecution began in A.D. 257 and continued for three and a half months. "The martyrs that fell in this persecution were innumerable, and their tortures and deaths as various and painful." During this time the government ordered the execution of the clergy in Rome. "In Africa the persecution raged with peculiar violence; many thousands received the crown of martyrdom, among whom" was Cyprian, bishop of Carthage. "At Utica . . . three hundred Christians were, by the orders of the proconsul, placed round a burning limekiln. A pan of coals and incense being prepared, they were commanded either to sacrifice to Jupiter, or to be thrown into the kiln. Unanimously refusing, they bravely jumped into the pit."

Diocletian (Roman Emperor a.d. 284–305)

The ninth wave of persecutions began with Aurelian (Roman Emperor a.d. 270–275), and was continued by Diocletian, his successor. Under Diocletian, the most severe campaign against the Christians began with an imperial order to destroy all churches and their Scriptures. "The persecution became general in all the Roman provinces, particularly in the east; and as it lasted ten years it is impossible to ascertain the numbers martyred, or to enumerate the various modes of martyrdom. Racks, scourges, swords, daggers, crosses, poison, and famine, were made use of . . . to dispatch the Christians."

After the executions "became tiresome," some of the provincial governors petitioned for relief, and the executions were changed to bodily mutilations and other means of making the lives of the Christians miserable. "The persecution of Diocletian began particularly to rage in a.d. 304, when many Christians were put to cruel tortures and the most painful and ignominious deaths."

Constantius and Galerius

Diocletian was succeeded by Constantius (Roman Emperor a.d. 305–306) and Galerius (Roman Emperor a.d. 305–311), who divided the empire into two provinces: eastern (ruled by Galerius) and western (ruled by Constantius). In the east Galerius continued the persecutions just as severely, while in the west Constantius was much more benign and tolerant of the Christians.

Miracles Continue

The church of the imperial era considered the martyrs to be instant saints, inheritors of the Kingdom of Heaven by virtue of earning the martyr's crown. And as the persecutions spread and Christians told their stories everywhere, martyrdom seemed to take on some appeal, as though it were a shortcut to eternal bliss. Whether the persecutions culminated in execution or "only" physical tortures or mutilations, they were means of grace that set the suffering Christians of this era apart from their neighbors, who didn't have to suffer.

Accounts of miracles like the deliverance of St. John the Beloved from a cauldron of oil continued, and most hagiographies (biographies of saints) of the period are full of similar reports. But in most cases the martyrs may have stayed their execution by a miracle, only to be killed soon after by another method, usually beheading.

Fox Recounts Miracles

Fox's *Book of Martyrs* recounts several notable miracles of this type. "Some of the restless northern nations having risen in arms against Rome, the emperor marched to encounter them. He was, however, drawn into an ambuscade, and dreaded the loss of his whole army. Enveloped with mountains, surrounded by enemies, and perishing with thirst, the pagan deities were invoked in vain; when the men belonging to the militine, or thundering legion, who were all Christians, were commanded to call upon their God for help.

"A miraculous deliverance immediately ensued; a prodigious quantity of rain fell, which, being caught by the men, and filling their dykes, afforded a sudden and astonishing relief. It appears that the storm which miraculously flashed in the face of the enemy so intimidated them, that part deserted to the Roman army; the rest were defeated, and the revolted provinces entirely recovered."

Lions in the Coliseum

Another account of miracles is typical of wonders seen when Christians were being executed by lions in the Coliseum:

"Blandina, on the day when she and her three other champions were first brought into the amphitheater, was suspended on a piece of wood fixed in the ground, and exposed as food for the wild beasts; at which time, by her earnest prayers, she encouraged others. But none of the wild beasts would touch her, so that she was remanded to prison.

"When she was again brought out for the third and last time, she was accompanied by Ponticus, a youth of fifteen, and the constancy of their faith so enraged the multitude that neither the sex of the one nor the youth of the other were respected, being

exposed to all manner of punishments and tortures. Being strengthened by Blandina, he persevered unto death; and she, after enduring all the torments heretofore mentioned, was at length slain with the sword."

Presbyters, Bishops, and Martyrs

As described previously, the office of apostle was considered a conduit of the will and word of God from the heavenly realm to the congregations on earth. The office of apostle was so important that the apostolic church developed the doctrine of apostolic succession as a standard for ordaining bishops.

discussion question

What is a bishop?
Bishops (*episcopos* in Greek), comparable in rank to high priests of the Jewish Temple, were the senior pastors in the church's multiple congregations in metropolitan areas. This is why metropolitan is another name for bishop in Eastern Orthodoxy. *Priest*, an old English rendering of the Greek word *presbyter*, or minister, is comparable to the priests of the Jewish Temple.

The idea of apostolic succession is simple: Catholic and Orthodox teaching claims that all of the bishops were appointed first by an apostle, as in the case of Timothy, who was appointed bishop of the church in Ephesus by Paul. Most metropolitan sees of the ancient church trace their bishops from the beginning of the church, as in Antioch, where, as mentioned earlier, Simon Peter is traditionally recorded as the first, and Ignatius the second, having succeeded in Antioch while Peter was still overseeing the congregations in Rome. After this first generation, all subsequent bishops, to be considered legitimate in the whole church, were appointed by bishops that had been selected by apostles.

The same Ignatius, writing just before his martyrdom in A.D. 107, says "your bishop presides in the place of God." But although the bishops of the ancient churches, including the Anglicans, claim to be successors of the apostles, they do not to claim to have been given the direct communication channels from God the original apostles had. Though they were often godly and holy men, and many of them worked wonders in their time, the bishops of the early church also confessed to being sinners, and less than infallible.

To be a bishop in the pre-Constantinian Roman empire, as Fox's *Book of Martyrs* indicates, was often a sentence of death, especially in Rome, where the first martyr in another wave of persecution mentioned by Fox is often "the bishop of Rome."

CHAPTER 11

The Jesus of History

The martyrdom of thousands in the first three centuries of the church who were willing to face death rather than burn incense to Caesar or a pagan idol, is the strongest evidence for the truth of the claims of the New Testament. Men who had recently been afraid to be seen with Jesus when he hung on the cross on Golgotha were willing to bet their very lives on the conviction that he was raised from the dead and that his victory had procured their own hope for life beyond death.

Western History Begins with Him

Though there has been effort for some years to redefine the western calendar as divided between B.C.E. (before common era) and C.E. (common era) rather than B.C. (before Christ) and A.D. (Anno Domini, or year of our Lord), there can still be little doubt about the dividing line between the "before" and "after"; it is the approximate birth of Jesus, the God whose incarnation marks, for Christians, the watershed between lost and found, between law and grace, old and new, the world that was perishing and the world being renewed.

The Calendar Is Established

In western civilization, all history is anchored to this event. However, although the general sense is that A.D. 1 was Jesus' first birthday, in the Roman empire of the caesars the calendar was restarted every time a new emperor was installed. Dionysius Exiguus (translated as Dennis the Small) changed the Julian calendar's revision method, under direction of the Latin side of the church, in the sixth century. As this was long before the Gregorian calendar was introduced in 1582, but also long after Christianity was recognized as a religion tolerated by the Roman Empire in 313, Dionysius Exiguus' calendar had to be redacted back into historical records.

discussion question

How accurate were Dionysius Exiguus' calculations?
Later scholarship found that the death of Herod the Great had taken place about five years earlier than Dionysius Exiguus' year 1, so his calendar is about five years off (since Herod was ruling when Jesus was born, according to Matthew's Gospel).

Dionysius Exiguus' calendar reform was the first time Jesus' estimated year of birth was officially fixed as the permanent beginning of the new era, though by that time many historians had already been referring to it as the great watershed of history.

Some Unconvinced

Despite the biblical evidence confirming Jesus and his ministry, some still dispute whether there ever was such a person as Jesus of Nazareth who preached his own advent as the Jewish Messiah. And since the Enlightenment (1700s), there have been theologians who feel the Bible is unreliable, so their duty is to strip off the religious testimony about Jesus and research the historical evidence about him to determine the elusive truth.

The Historical Jesus Debates

Since 1985, much mainstream media coverage of Christianity has focused on the work of the Jesus Seminar, a group of scholars convened by the Westar Institute, a nonprofit "educational institute dedicated to the advancement of religious literacy." The purpose of the Jesus Seminar is described as being to "renew the quest of the historical Jesus and to report the results of its research to more than a handful of gospel specialists."

This purpose assumes that the historical figure of Jesus has eluded popular, and much of scholarly, comprehension. The Institute's intention of making its research known to the general public, rather than just the academic community, is promoted through its public-relations efforts. This PR has helped the Institute gain a PBS network series, much coverage on major television network news programs, where religion is seldom considered news, and exposure in major newspapers and magazines throughout the United States.

Operating Assumption

At its meetings, the Seminar fellows present scholarly papers on aspects of the biblical and historical record on Jesus' words and acts, and vote on whether the papers fit the Jesus that their historical approach has caused them to believe in.

Critics of the Seminar say that "voting on whether something is true or false" may seem silly, but it is one way of producing (or some might say, creating) a consensus across a spectrum of religion experts. And it is in accord with the Enlightenment approach to human governance, which relies on the will of the majority to determine policy on social programs and goals.

Higher Critics

For example, an early theory proposed and widely accepted in academic and liberal religious circles was that the Old Testament books traditionally attributed to Moses (Genesis, Exodus, Leviticus, Numbers, and Deuteronomy) were actually the work of a variety of authors adapting much older oral traditions. Among that movement's higher critics were the following four scholars.

DANIEL SCHLEIERMACHER

Daniel Ernst Schleiermacher (German, 1768–1834), called the father of modern or liberal theology, taught that Christianity should be viewed as an entirely new religion, not an extension or enlargement of Judaism. He believed that Hellenizing (Greek philosophical) influences on the New Testament books obscured the real Gospel Christ represented.

fallacy

Though "criticism" may suggest conceit or arrogance (to the extent that the critic is judging what is critiqued), "higher criticism" was not applied to modernist biblical text research out of arrogance, but to differentiate it from "lower criticism." Lower criticism examined the minutiae of the texts, getting close to find tiny clues; higher criticism examines the whole picture.

ADOLPH HARNACK

Adolph Harnack (born in Livonia, now Estonia, taught mostly in Germany, 1851–1930), one of the most influential liberal professors of religion, taught that in the Reformation, Protestantism had begun to get rid of the "husks" of Christianity as handed down by Rome to get to the kernel of its true message, and should continue the process of winnowing out more. He believed most of the accretions to "true Christianity" could be traced to the fourth century, when Christianity became an officially tolerated religion of the Empire, and shortly afterward, when it became the favored one, it was syncretized with classical Greek philosophy. Most importantly, he taught that the New Testament (produced, he thought, much later than the church claims) was overlaid with these Greek lines of thought that had to be stripped away to reveal the true or historical Jesus.

ALBERT SCHWEITZER

Albert Schweitzer (German, 1875–1965) held that Jesus was an eccentric Jewish Messiah figure and argued in the dissertation for his medical doctorate that Jesus probably would not have been considered mad in the time in which he lived because of the apocalyptic fervor of that generation, but might have been insane by modern psychiatric criteria. The most famous of the higher critics, by virtue of winning the Nobel Peace Prize in 1952 (for promoting the brotherhood of nations), he was a missionary physician in what was then French Equatorial Africa, and famous for a "reverence for life" that included avoidance of accidentally killing insects while walking through the mission compound.

RUDOLF BULTMANN

Rudolf Karl Bultmann (German, 1884–1976), though a student of Karl Barth (Swiss, 1886–1968), rejected Barth's call to accept the full text of Scripture "including the myth" portions of it. Bultmann called Martin Heidegger's existential philosophy a "profane" version of the biblical view of man, and he is considered the most influential modern demythologizing (or scientific) theologian of his generation.

Modern Approach

Though this approach to study of the Scriptures is relatively recent, one Roman Catholic source from almost a century ago found an early foreshadowing of it in the biblical studies produced by Theodore of Mopsuestia, 350–428, an orthodox bishop of Syrian birth whose "exegetical tendencies [demonstrated] an almost exclusively grammatical-historical and realistic explanation of the text." Though Theodore did not venture unorthodox conclusions, his method presaged that of the post-Enlightenment humanist theologians who wanted to make Bible teaching more compatible with modern science.

Though Roman Catholic, Eastern Orthodox, and evangelical Protestant communions generally reject or discount higher critical hypotheses and premises, they are widely considered to have had decimating impact on Christian numbers throughout Europe (even in Catholic strongholds) and to have greatly weakened most American Protestant denominations, though those seem to have been supplanted by new evangelical replacements that thrive as mainline denominations wither. Chapter 17 will take up this phenomenon in more detail.

The Edict of Milan

Many contemporary liberals in Christian higher education and denominations consider the fourth century the time when the early Jesus movement went wrong, and there has been a strong current of thought among even conservative Protestants (as suggested by Harnack, as mentioned earlier in this chapter) that considers that period one of defection from the original substance of Christianity into a new hierarchical institution.

But it was not until the fourth century that the church began to emerge from generation after generation of persecution and martyrdom from all quarters, and was able to worship above ground in buildings that could openly display Christian signs and symbols.

Praying for Guidance

Eusebius, the church historian, says that Constantine felt his military strength insufficient to ensure victory, so he decided to turn to God, but seeing the "downfall of those who turned to idols," he pondered what God to pray to for help, and concluded that "his father's God" had been faithful when others failed.

When he prayed this God to reveal his identity to him, Eusebius says, "a most marvelous sign appeared to him from heaven, the account of which it might have been hard to believe had it been related by any other person, but the victorious emperor himself long afterwards declared it to the writer of this history. . . . He said that about noon, when the day was already beginning to decline, he saw with his own eyes the trophy of a cross of light in the heavens, above the sun, and bearing the inscription, Conquer by this. At this sight he himself was struck with amazement, and his whole army also. . . witnessed the miracle," (Eusebius' *Life of Constantine*).

The victory that followed this vision in 312 led Constantine to liberate the Christians of the empire in 313 by issuing the Edict of Milan jointly with his co-emperor of the Eastern Tetrarchy, Licinius. In 311, Emperor Galerius had issued an indulgence to the Christians of the empire, stating that if they would pray for him and the empire he would ensure their safety in their homes.

Ensuring Religious Freedom

But the Edict of Milan went considerably farther, the main provisions of which were "to remove all conditions whatsoever, which were . . . formerly given to you officially, concerning the Christians and now any one of these who wishes to observe Christian religion may do so freely and openly." The Edict of Milan also promised to return to anyone property confiscated by the government because they were Christians "without payment or any claim of recompense and without any kind of fraud or deception." Promising the same protections to other religions represented in the empire for the sake of peace, the Edict of Milan also promised the return of "those places in which they were accustomed to assemble, but also other property, namely the churches, belonging to them as a corporation and not as individuals."

Though many later historical references to Constantine question the genuineness of his conversion based, in part, on his deferring baptism until the end of his life, both the Roman Catholic and Eastern Orthodox, following the witness of his contemporary bishop, Eusebius, consider him a genuine believer, and the Orthodox, especially, revere him as a saint. His saint's day is commemorated, along with that of his mother, Helena, who converted after her son and traveled the empire establishing churches and researching sites of biblical significance.

The Edict of Milan has been a model for religious toleration by governments from its issuance by Constantine and Licinius, especially in the republican nations descended from the Roman Empire in most of Europe and the Americas.

fallacy

Though it has been a widespread opinion that Constantine made Christianity the official religion of the Roman empire, this is not the case. The Edict of Milan made Christianity a legal religion, no longer subject to persecution. It was under Theodosius I (A.D. 379–395) that Christianity was elevated to the preferred religion and paganism was dismantled.

Adjusting to Success

Success always extracts its price. Even discounting the claims of some Protestants (which the most influential sixteenth-century Reformers, Luther and Calvin, did not make) that the church had lost its way by the end of the fourth century, many scholars agree that some of its success in becoming the empire's favored religion cost it some of its previous innocence and holy zeal. For example, one bishop is said to have considered Emperor Constantine an "angelic being," who would rule in some capacity alongside or under Jesus in the Kingdom of Heaven.

But that was not an opinion the emperor himself claimed or that most Christians shared. Constantine made reforms that demonstrated the seriousness of his newfound profession of faith in Jesus. For example, for the first time in Roman law the abduction of girls was criminalized; divorce was made more difficult; Sunday was elevated to equality with pagan feasts; and Christian Passover (Easter in English-speaking countries) was declared a holiday. Constantine also encouraged owners of slaves to emancipate them.

Martyrdom Missed

But the loss that was most widely felt throughout the church of the empire, surprisingly to anyone with modern priorities and values, was the loss of martyrdom. By 313, the call to sacrifice one's own life or that of a loved one to the Jesus movement had occurred for nearly three centuries. The "opportunity" to be a victim came to be seen as its own reward, and many instances are recorded of "collateral martyrs" coming forward, when someone they loved was about to be sacrificed, and boldly proclaiming, "I stand with Jesus, too!"

Those devout believers who most regretted the loss of such opportunities became founders of the monastic movement. Following the footsteps and example of John the Baptist, the prophets of the previous covenant, and of Jesus himself, they sought the desert and lives of ascetic struggle. The ascetic life was a substitute form of martyrdom, of sacrificing normal life for the life centered, in every moment, in Christ. It was not ever considered an escape from life, but rather the removal of the distractions of the world that keep believers from staying in constant communion with the Lord.

Monasticism Begins

Post-New Testament monasticism began in the very first generation after the Edict of Milan, in the Egyptian desert by Anthony the Great (Antony in Greek), c. 252–357. His biographer, St. Athanasius, indicates early monasticism was then much different than the way most Western people may encounter it at beautiful, prosperous-looking, campus–like monastery and convent settings. The early monasteries were in poor and bare quarters, often caves in the desert hills, and Spartan huts.

Within a century, accounts were circulated of pilgrims going to visit monks in Egypt and finding communities, sometimes numbering thousands, who had rejected secular life. But despite the comparative austerity of primitive monasticism, Anthony was typical of all Orthodox and Catholic monks from the beginning until now, in renouncing property and a sex life (not to say all succeed, of course). And although Anthony started out alone, and therefore had no vow of obedience to other ascetics, within a short time he had been joined by other faithful who were required to choose obedience to their spiritual father and the rules that his experience in the life produced.

Monasticism is from the Greek *monos*, meaning alone. Though most monastics from early times have worked at tasks from agriculture to copying manuscripts to creating items for sale to the public, their main task is continual prayer, with those employed learning how to pray even while doing other tasks. From the time of Anthony they have also ministered to the faithful by giving spiritual counsel and instruction to pilgrims and the brothers and sisters in their communities less advanced in their journeys.

Early Heresies, Councils, and Defections

A profound price of the church's success was that security from persecution gave greater leeway for controversies to develop that led into factions that developed and that caused the propagation of heresies. But a benefit of having an emperor who professed to believe in Christianity was that the church was able to call an ecumenical (churchwide) council to debate the controversies and propound an orthodox position.

Gnosticism

Gnosticism was already extant when the church began, in the time of the Book of Acts. In general, Gnosticism believes in "secret knowledge," which is akin to and sometimes overlaps occultism. It is dualistic, meaning it believes in virtually equal good and evil divinities, and that the good divinity rules the spirit, and the evil, the material realm. Orthodox Christianity professes, conversely, that in becoming a man in the form of Jesus Christ, God took on material form, and that in this, all of his creation was blessed and to be appreciated, not rejected. Some claim that despite Gnosticism's early origin, its best-known representation is in Dan Brown's contemporary novel, *The Da Vinci Code*.

factum

Many attribute the early church's development of baptismal creeds (one of which may be an early form of the Apostles' Creed) that summarize basic differences of Christian teaching versus Gnostic teachings, as a factor in the decline of early-church Gnosticism.

Considering all the persecution of Christians in the church's first three centuries, the numbers of Gnostics were diminished by the fourth century, though there have been small groups of them throughout modern history. New Age philosophy, which had a resurgence in the late 1960s and 1970s, is widely considered a revival of Gnosticism, as was the emergence of theosophy (religious philosophy based on mystical insight into the divine), and other attempts to introduce Asian dualism (yin and yang) in western forms earlier in the nineteenth and twentieth centuries.

Though much of Gnostic writing is prescientific, some of its source material has been used in some of the "scientific" or humanist approaches to Christianity advocated by form criticism (analyzing the literary forms of biblical passages) and evolutionary theology.

Montanism

Montanus presented himself as a prophet from Phrygia, a province of Asia Minor (now Turkey) in the mid to late second century. He and his female disciples, prophetesses Prisca (Priscilla in English) and Maximillia, predicted an apocalypse in their time and claimed superiority over the church because they claimed to have received revelations directly from God. The Montanists taught that a convert who fell away from baptismal vows or beliefs could not be restored, though the church taught that repentance was always efficacious for any who lost the light and later returned to it.

Though the bishops of the church at the time counseled their followers to flee from persecution, Montanus and his followers advocated seeking out persecution. Part of the success of the sect was its tendency to exaggerate teachings that many others in the church also held, and eventually to dogmatize about their exaggerations. Orthodox believers in Asia Minor met in councils, and, after examining the Montanist teachings, condemned them and excommunicated their proponents. The sect died out, except in the immediate area of its origin, when its self-styled prophets died.

Manichaeism

Founded by Persian seer Mani in the third century, Manichaeism blended elements of all known religions at the time, especially Gnosticism, Christianity, and Zoroastrianism, under a strongly dualist umbrella. Mani is actually a title (something like "light king"), not a name, the name of the founder having been lost through the general use of his title. Mani claimed to have received a revelation from an angel of God at age twelve, and to have been told to wait another twelve years before launching his public ministry. This he did with this preamble: "As once Buddha came to India, Zoroaster to

Persia, and Jesus to the lands of the West, so came in the present time this prophecy through me, the Mani, to the land of Babylonia."

The sect is believed to have practiced forms of baptism and Eucharist. A Catholic source says that it's clear that Mani intended a convergence between his teachings and those of Christianity, which may have been the chief religion in Mesopotamia at the time he lived.

discussion question

What was the Paraclete?
Mani claimed to be the "Paraclete" or "Comforter" Jesus had foretold. Orthodox Christianity has held, since the time recorded in Luke's Book of Acts, that the Paraclete was the Holy Spirit revealed and received at Pentecost (see Acts 2).

Mani is said to have rejected all of the Old Testament and adapted parts of the New Testament to suit his doctrines. In his dualism he regarded Jesus of Nazareth a fiction, and the true Jesus to be a personification of light. Like Gnosticism, Manichaeism taught that salvation comes through intellectual knowledge, and that ignorance is sin.

The sect spread rapidly beyond Babylon (or Mesopotamia) to India and other territories east of Persia, and throughout the Roman Empire, despite the persecution of its followers. In the Christian world, its strongest following was in Egypt, though it also had strong followings in Italy and seems to have penetrated to southern France, to the west of Rome, and to Bulgaria in the east.

Augustine (A.D. 354–430), the seminal theologian of the early church era among Roman Catholics and Protestants, and the bishop of Hippo on the North African coast (now Algeria), wrote against the Manicheans and described the extent of their heretical influence.

Donatism

After the persecutions of Emperor Diocletian described earlier, Donatus, a bishop of Carthage in North Africa (now Tunisia), refused to reinstate those who had renounced their baptisms to avoid martyrdom. He and other bishops he influenced said the sacraments of such "apostates" were invalid. He refused priests and bishops permission to serve sacraments in their sees, and also forbade their parishioners to receive sacraments from such when traveling. A council in Arles, France, called by Emperor Constantine in 314 (just a year after his Edict of Milan) condemned the Donatists' refusal to forgive the repentant former apostates.

The Donatists refused to accept the council's decision and seceded from the rest of the church. Most of the churches in North Africa sided with the Donatists until Augustine's writing against the heresy won the majority back.

Arianism

The most important heresy and controversy in the early church was Arianism, as it forced the church to define the Trinity and hold its first Ecumenical Council. Arius (256–336), a priest in Alexandria, Egypt, taught that Christ, though divine, was not coeternal with God the Father, and was therefore inferior to him. His teaching was originally offered as an alternative to a less widespread heresy, Sabellianism or modalism, which held that the three persons of the Trinity were merely different modes of God's appearing or interacting, or roles he was using with his creation.

Arianism became popular in the church, and for some time it seemed to have won more support than the Trinitarians (who believed that the Father, Son, and Holy Ghost of the Trinity were equal parts of one Godhead), whose cause was most eloquently argued by Athanasius, also an Alexandrian, ordained a priest a little after Arius. Emperor Constantine called the first Ecumenical Council of the church in Nicea, just outside Constantinople, in 325 to settle the controversy. Athanasius accompanied Alexander, the bishop of Alexandria, a Trinitarian and the council's president, to the Council, and Athanasius emerged as the most persuasive speaker for the Trinitarian side.

The Council adopted Athanasius' position, and issued the original form of the Nicene Creed to define it. Though the Council had spoken, Arius' defenders continued campaigning against the Trinitarian position and persuaded Constantine to grant amnesty to the Arians who had been exiled after the Council and, instead, to exile Athanasius. By A.D. 360, another debate had broken out over the divinity of the Holy Spirit. After Constantine's death in 337, his successors were less interested in Christianity than he had been, until the succession of Theodosius I the Great in 378. He convened the second Ecumenical Council in Constantinople in 381 to finally settle the Arian/Trinitarian debates and to ratify the first Ecumenical Council.

Pelagianism

Pelagius, a monk who lived in Rome in the fifth century, taught that Adam's sin was not transferred to all human beings, and that salvation through works (in other words, keeping of the Old Testament Law) was possible without the work of Christ. Little is known about Pelagius, but Augustine said he lived a long time in Rome before he was excommunicated and exiled. Several regional church councils condemned his teachings, and the Ecumenical Council of Epheus ratified those condemnations in 431.

factum

Semipelagianism (a later movement in churches not condemned in church councils) teaches that human beings can seek God by their own efforts without prevenient (preparatory or leading) grace from God.

Nestorianism

Nestor, appointed patriarch of Constantinople by Theodosius II in 428, opposed the use of the term *Theotokos* to describe Mary, the Mother of Jesus. *Theotokos* is Greek, meaning "God-bearer," and is usually rendered as "Mother of God" in English. Nestor's point was that while God was the Father of Jesus' divinity, Mary was the mother of only his humanity. This idea, however, separates Jesus into two distinct persons, which orthodox Christianity rejects. The Council of Ephesus was called in 431 to settle the controversy. The Council ruled that the Nicene Creed presupposes Mary's motherhood of both the divine and human natures (not persons) of Jesus by affirming that no separation is possible between his godhead and his manhood.

Division of the Roman Empire

Emperor Diocletian, who ruled from A.D. 284 to 305, divided the administration of Rome into four areas ruled by four caesars. Though the scheme was never completely successful because of rivalries among the caesars, it led to the division of the empire into two major and eventually permanent divisions. When Constantine gained control of the eastern major region (as well as the western one, which he originally ruled), he moved his capital from Rome to his own new city in the east, Byzantium, renamed Constantinople, which was on the strait between the Black Sea and the Sea of Marmara that demarks the border between Europe and Asia. Constantinople was, at that time, in the territory of ancient Greece, and is now in Turkey.

fallacy

Though many social commentators have claimed that civilizations seldom survive three or four centuries (the approximate lifespan of ancient Greece and of the western Roman Empire), historians sympathetic to the eastern Roman Empire contend that it actually improved after four centuries and continued intact for fully a thousand years. The eastern Roman Empire and its churches had no "dark ages."

Under Theodosius I, who ascended Constantine's throne after him, the division became officially permanent. But while the west, administered from Rome, got weaker and was overrun by Germanic tribes, the eastern empire, which always called itself "the Roman empire" but which those in Rome have called "the Byzantine Empire," thrived and continued to be generally stable for a millennium after Constantine.

Greek became the language of the eastern empire, with Latin continuing as the official tongue in the west. Eventually, this division led to a division of the Catholic Church, between western (Latin) under the supreme magisterium of the bishop of Rome, and eastern (Greek) Christendom that continued under a pluralism of bishops of equal power throughout the far-flung empire.

The Great Schism

The secession of the North African churches over their Donatism was a minor and relatively short-lived schism in the catholic and apostolic churches. A more serious and thus-far permanent schism, however, was the defection of the Coptic Orthodox and the Armenian Apostolic Church (referred to as the "Oriental Orthodox" churches) after the Ecumenical Council of Chalcedon, which condemned monophysitism.

factum

Monophysitism refers to belief in only one nature in Jesus, which both Armenian and Coptic churches don't hold. Committees of the Oriental and Eastern Orthodox churches have reached agreement that the schism between them is based on semantic rather than substantive issues, though they have failed to re-enter into communion.

Considered by the churches more tragic, because of the hundreds of millions of believers it involves, is the Great Schism between the Latin churches (Roman Catholic) under the bishop of Rome, and the Greek churches (Eastern Orthodox), whose ecumenical patriarch (archbishop) is in Constantinople (now officially Istanbul). Eastern Orthodoxy includes the Greek and Russian Orthodox, and many other autonomous and national churches like the Romanian, Ukrainian, Serbian, Antiochian, Bulgarian, and Carpatho-Russian Orthodox.

The Great Schism culminated with the serving of excommunication letters between the pope of Rome and the ecumenical patriarch in 1054, and has been exacerbated by doctrinal disputes such as the *filioque* (Roman Catholic doctrine that states the Holy Ghost proceeds from the Son as well as from the Father) and papal authority. Most historians say that it had been in the making for centuries, from the time the Roman Empire was divided, and most educated people on both sides no longer spoke both official languages.

Since the Schism, the Latin Crusaders' sacking of Constantinople in 1204 and certain innovations in Catholic dogma have exacerbated the conflict. In the other direction, Pope John Paul II apologized for the atrocity of the Crusaders, and both sides have rescinded their excommunications of the other. The main doctrinal issues between the communions now are papal authority, the filioque, the immaculate conception of Mary, purgatory, and indulgences.

The Reformation

The third significant schism was the breaking away of the evangelical and reformed churches under Luther and Calvin in the sixteenth century. There is a case for saying the Reformation brought long-overdue corrections and renewal, both in the churches that originated from it and, by reacting to it (as in the Council of Trent, 1545–1563, the major event in what is called the Counter-Reformation), in the Roman Catholic communion. A more complete account of the roots of the Reformation is found in Chapter 13.

The leaders of the Reformation—Luther, Calvin, Zwingli, Cranmer, and others—set out to reform the one Catholic Church they knew, not to create new churches, or what came to be called denominations. But they set in motion a process that led to that end, and continues to produce new denominations to fit every taste in doctrine, liturgy, polity, and ecclesiology.

CHAPTER 12

Salvation

More than 175 passages in the New Testament refer to salvation, being saved, and to Jesus as the Savior. Even the Old Testament may be called a testament of salvation, because its dominant themes are the deliverance (salvation) of Israel and specific Israelites from various captivities and the anticipation of the Messiah. But what is meant in the New Testament by salvation and, specifically, the salvation that Jesus came to bring and that the churches offer?

What Must I Do to Be Saved?

"'What must I do to be saved?' the jailer of Phillipi asked his inmates Paul the Apostle and Silas (Acts 16:30). "'Believe in the Lord Jesus Christ,'" Paul and Silas answered, "'and you and your whole household will be saved.' And they spoke to him and to all in his house the word of the Lord, and the same hour of the night the jailer washed the wounds of Paul's and Silas' scourging. And immediately he and all his household were baptized."

Paul's Definition of Salvation

Paul's take on what salvation means is deliverance from sin, both from the consequences, or the "wages of sin," which is death (Romans 6:23), and from the power or attraction of sin over the person saved. Salvation from sin was the most holy act in the Jewish calendar, when people asked forgiveness of God at Yom Kippur, the Day of Atonement. As Charles Haddon Spurgeon, probably the most highly esteemed Baptist preacher in history, said, salvation includes "the delivery of our soul from all those propensities to evil which now so strongly predominate in us."

Not an Evangelical Franchise

"Being saved" is well known to be a priority in the evangelical churches like Spurgeon's Baptists, the Wesleyans (evangelical Methodists, Holiness, and Pentecostal denominations), and many other denominations and non-denominational churches, but many Protestants are unaware of the high priority the need for salvation also has in Catholic, Orthodox, traditional Anglo-Catholic (Church of England), and Lutheran teaching, prayers, Scripture readings, and liturgies. Catholics are taught to pray the prayer of contrition every day. It says:

O my God, I am heartily sorry for having offended Thee, and I detest all my sins, because I dread the loss of heaven and the pains of hell; but most of all because they offend Thee, my God, Who are all good and deserving of all my love. I firmly resolve, with the help of Thy grace, to confess my sins, to do penance, and to amend my life. Amen.

The Orthodox ask salvation from their sins in the Trisagion (thrice holy) prayers that are part of both the morning and evening prayers all faithful make, and which also are part of every Orthodox worship service (as excerpted here):

Glory to you O Lord, glory to you. O heavenly King, O Comforter, the Spirit of Truth, who are in all places and fill all things, Treasury of good things and the Giver of life, come and abide in us, cleanse us from every stain, and save our souls, O Good One.

There are differences in the interpretations by various Christian communions of how salvation is effected, but the goal of salvation, and salvation's being a consequence of faith through grace are generally agreed on.
Teachings on salvation are complicated by questions like these:

- Is salvation a once-and-for-all "event," or a gradual transformation?
- What conditions, if any, are attached to being saved or receiving salvation?
- Can salvation be lost?
- What must those "saved" do after receiving salvation to keep it?
- Are "the saved" incapable of sinning again?
- Can a person be "saved," lost again, and saved again? (And, perhaps, again and again?)
- Can a person be baptized more than once?

Such questions and the way they are answered have launched numerous denominations and factions within Christendom, ever since the Donatist heresy arose (see Chapter 11).

Believing: *Sola Fide*

"Only believe, only believe," says an old evangelistic hymn by Paul Rader. Then the hymn paraphrases the angel's words to Mary prior to Jesus' conception, "with God nothing shall be impossible." The hymn's words reflect the five principles, or the "five solas" of the Protestant Reformation: Sola Scriptura, Solus Christus, Sola Gratia, Sola Fide, and Soli Deo Gloria; which translate to: Only Scripture, Only Christ, Only Grace, Only Faith, and Glory Only to God.

Sola Fide, only faith, is a core teaching that all Protestants traditionally affirm. The reformers, stung by corruption in the church (especially in the sale of indulgences), used this teaching to highlight that the only thing efficacious for salvation is faith. Works of the law, whether of the Old Testament or the rules of the church, are not enough.

factum

Indulgences are release from sin in return for donations to the Catholic Church. In Martin Luther's time (1483–1546), the Catholic Church sold indulgences to raise funds for the building of St. Peter's Basilica in Rome. Indulgences are not permissions to sin, though many have thought they are. Though no longer technically sold, indulgences are still given, especially to large donors to Catholic institutions.

The proponents of Sola Fide didn't want to discount works of the law (being moral, for example), or imply that obedience to Christ (a form of keeping the law) wasn't necessary, but the law was not the means of salvation. Again, faith through grace from God (the "free gift," to use a favorite redundancy of evangelists) is the sole efficacious way of salvation.

Fundamentals Only

Many preachers and teachers have, however, taught that everything beyond "only faith" can actually get in the way of salvation. At this point they part company with most Catholics, Orthodox, and more traditional Protestants, including most contemporary evangelicals.

Many call this emphasis on belief "fundamentalism," which means, in this case, "fundamentals only." Jesus certainly taught much more than "only believe," as did the apostles and the church from its beginning, though believing is the necessary first step toward getting on the way to salvation.

Once Saved, Always Saved

Many Protestants, like Luther, Calvin, and Zwingli especially, have taught that salvation is a once-and-for-all event (some calling it "once saved, always saved" or "the security of the believers"). However, even most of the people who believe salvation is a one-time event have allowed that a person can be misled to think he or she has been saved, only to fall back into sin again later (or seem to fall back, if the person was never saved in the first place) and, in some cases, be saved again, this time for real.

Catholics, Orthodox, and Wesleyans (followers of the teachings of the great Protestant revivalist John Wesley), emphasizing Jesus' repeated words, "he who endures to the end shall be saved," generally teach that calling oneself saved is presumptuous. Orthodox writers like to put it, "I have been saved; I am being saved, and, God willing, I will be saved," referring to the need to "endure," or, as Calvin famously rendered that word, "persevere."

Sacraments

The Christian sacraments are the (traditionally seven) rites instituted by Jesus and mentioned in the New Testament that confer sanctifying grace on the faithful. The seven sacraments of Catholicism are baptism, confirmation, the Eucharist, penance and restoration, anointing of the sick, holy orders (ordination to the ministry), and matrimony. The Eastern Orthodox Church has the same seven, though some of them are defined slightly differently, and the Eastern Church also teaches that anything exhibiting the presence of God (described in the Trisagion Prayer as being "in all places and filling all things") can be considered sacramental, or holy.

Though fundamentalist Protestants generally reject the notion of sacraments, one of the most famous fundamentalists, Dr. Bob Jones, is often quoted as having preached, "all ground is holy ground," which raises the question whether fundamentalist objections to "sacraments" are mainly semantic, since most Baptists and many other "Bible" church members refer to communion and baptism not as "sacraments" but as "ordinances."

Overlaps and Differences

What Catholics call confirmation, the Orthodox call chrismation, and what Catholics refer to as penance and restoration is referred to in Orthodoxy as repentance. Protestants, understandably, with their hundreds (some say their tens of thousands) of denominations, have many divergent views on sacraments. Virtually all practice baptism, and communion or the Eucharist (which means "thanksgiving"), also called "the Lord's Supper."

symbolism

Symbols are said to mean something different in Eastern and Western perception. In the Eastern Churches, symbols are not figurative but are actually essential to the thing symbolized. So, for example, Orthodox believers consider Christ the true symbol of God, while actually being God himself. Western believers think of symbols of Christ as "tokens" or "suggestive" ornaments, like the *Ichthus* (fish) symbol.

In a recent book of dialogues between Orthodox and Reformed (Calvinist) theologians, the Reformed writer agreed that the two communions could find agreement on the Eucharist and baptism. Calvin (the founding father of the Reformed and Presbyterian Churches) spoke of the sacraments of communion and baptism as "means of grace." Lutherans, likewise, are in virtual agreement with Catholics and Orthodox about the two main sacraments. Neither Lutherans nor the Orthodox use the Catholic term "transubstantiation" for the miraculous change of the bread and wine into the body and blood of Christ, but neither do either of them consider the term a stumbling block.

Sacraments Not Enough

Though earlier teachings may have been widely interpreted as holding that Catholics, the Orthodox, or both believe the sacraments are efficacious for salvation by themselves, the teachings of both communions now clearly state that without underlying faith on the part of the recipients, the sacraments do nothing in terms of achieving salvation. On the other hand, in virtually all of the sacramental liturgies, the salvific (or saving) work of Jesus Christ is so plainly presented that anyone hearing and sincerely believing the words could find saving faith through them.

The use of the word *ordinance* rather than *sacrament* by some evangelicals is sometimes explained as stemming from their rejection of any "means" of grace. A look at some of their documents on the issue shows that they take communion because Jesus mandated it, not because it does them any good in terms of achieving salvation. Though they may call the communion a "symbol," they distance themselves from the use of that word as understood in more traditional churches.

Not Always Literalists

Though evangelicals usually claim to take the Scriptures literally, they sometimes reject a literal (and usually even a spiritual) interpretation of Jesus' words, as when he instituted communion at the Last Supper, he said, "this is my body, this is my blood." They likewise do not take literally "baptism for the remission of sins" in Mark 1:4 and Acts 2:38, or Acts 22:16, which describes baptism as "washing away your sins." The best explanation of communion they have is that it "memorializes" Jesus' shedding his blood and having his body broken for those who believe in him.

factum

In much of the evangelical tradition, baptism is performed primarily for a "testimony" to the world that the believer (either an adult or a youth having achieved the "age of accountability") has come to saving faith in Christ and therefore wants to follow him into this symbolic act (some shudder at calling it either a "rite" or a "ritual").

But across the Protestant spectrum, some consider baptism a sacrament, some see it as the very means of salvation (as in "baptismal regeneration"), and many see it as merely following orders. Many (Lutherans, Anglicans, Presbyterians, Methodists) practice infant baptism, as do Catholics and the Orthodox. All of the infant-baptizing Protestants administer the water by sprinkling or pouring, as Catholics do. The Orthodox, uniquely, immerse infants, and they also immerse any adults converting who have not previously been baptized or have been baptized in a non-Trinitarian church (one that does not adhere to the doctrine of the Trinity).

Works of Righteousness

Paul writes to Titus, "Not by works of righteousness that we have done, but according to his mercy he saved us by the washing of regeneration and by the renewing of the Holy Spirit" (Titus 3:5). Many consider this text a summary of Paul's theology: not by works, but by grace, are we saved. Here "works" is defined as keeping the laws of the Old Testament, and sometimes it is interpreted in preaching as also referring to good works like social programs, alms-giving, and standing up for justice.

One can hardly read Paul without concluding that salvation comes not by works, but, conversely, that works can even get in the way of what is needed for salvation by giving false hope to those doing and depending on their works. Paul's Gospel is bad news to those who think their good deeds will get them into heaven. "All our righteousness is as filthy rags," Isaiah the prophet says, as though anticipating Paul (Isaiah 64:6).

Faith Without Works Is Dead

Nevertheless, James writes, "faith without works is dead" (James 2:17 and 20). Indeed, James adds, "Yes, a man may say, 'you have faith and I have works; show me your faith without your works and I will show you my faith by my works'" (2:18) and even, "a man is justified by works, and not by faith only." Having already written in the margin of his Bible the word *alone* next to Paul's "a man is justified by faith without the deeds of the law," (Romans 3:28, compare Romans 5:1 and Galatians 3:24). Martin Luther was sorely vexed by James's epistle and labeled it "an epistle of straw" or "a right strawy epistle," depending on how you translate his German.

James explains that Abraham demonstrated his faith by taking Isaac to the mountain to sacrifice him to God as God had ordered, his work thus proving his faith. All of James's "works" fall under obedience to God and his Christ. The apostolic church has traditionally advocated works or, as discussed in Chapter 10, "violence," or force, to "take" the Kingdom of God. This work—*ascesis*—is prayer, bolstered by fasting and more prayer, known as keeping vigil or praying all through the night. Fasting is also accompanied by alms-giving or giving help to the poor, but the alms-giving without the faith demonstrated in prayer with fasting is not advocated as a good work.

Sanctification or Divinization

Catholics, traditional Protestants, and the Orthodox alike profess that salvation is primarily a relationship with God through Christ. Though there is much tongue-wagging about "a personal relationship with Jesus," a formula most often uttered by American evangelicals, no genuine Christian prayer life exists without connecting in prayer with God through the God-man, Jesus Christ, the only mediator between Creator and created, Eternal and temporal, the Sinless and the sinful.

discussion question

What is *intercession*?
Though Catholics and the Orthodox refer to saints as "interceding for us," they mean nothing more by that intercession than an evangelical means when calling the prayer circle to ask it to "intercede with God on our behalf."

Divine Nature

Athanasius, the saint described in Chapter 11 as leading the opposition to the heresy of Arianism, wrote that God "gave himself to us through his Spirit. By the participation of the Spirit, we become communicants in the divine nature. . . . For this reason, those in whom the Spirit dwells are divinized." Athanasius is referring to the Apostle Peter's second epistle: "By his divine power [he] has given to us all things needed for life and godliness, through the knowledge of him who has called us to glory and virtue, by which are given to us very great and precious promises that by these you may be participants in the divine nature, having escaped the corrupting lusts of the world" (see 2 Peter 1:3, 4).

Divinization, as Athanasius called it, is more commonly known as *theosis*. Theosis is the goal of salvation in Orthodoxy, and is also taught but not widely known in Catholicism. It means that the human nature is intended to be united with the divine nature in heaven, through what Protestants call sanctification and the Orthodox call theoria, the process of becoming holy.

Theosis

The most famous summary of the doctrine, also from Athanasius, is, "The Son of God became man that we might become God." Orthodox theologians say that theosis takes believers in Christ beyond the perfection of Adam and Eve before the Fall and on to what Adam and Eve were intended to attain, had they obeyed God.

Several passages in the Old Testament refer to the judges of Israel as "gods": "You shall not revile the gods nor curse the ruler of your people" (Exodus 22:28); "God stands in the congregation of the mighty; he judges among the gods. . . . I have said, 'You are gods; and all of you are children of the most High. But you shall die like men, and fall like one of the princes,'" (Psalms 82:1, 6–7). Jesus refers to these passages when he says, "Is it not written in your law, I said, 'You are gods?'" (John 10:34).

Immortal Creatures

C. S. Lewis affirmed this aspect of salvation in *Mere Christianity* when he said any of us can become "immortal creatures" whom God calls "gods." In all cases, this "divinization" is distinct from pantheism and far eastern religions, which believe that eventually we become one with the totality of the universe, or "god." Nor is it similar to "progressive divinization" as taught in Mormonism, in which human beings become part of the godhead. But as "immortal creatures," we will be Lords over worlds Christ has gone ahead to the Kingdom of Heaven to prepare for us.

The Great Awakenings

The Reformation may be seen as a Christian adaptation to the Renaissance and the introduction of Renaissance humanism into the ekklesia, to use a term religion writers occasionally employ to refer to "the church" in its essence, without images of an organized superstructure.

The Methodist Movement

The Enlightenment is about the dawn of the modern scientific age, but its radical effect on common Europeans and especially the American colonists, and on western Christendom, was its experiments in popular self-government. The new ideas in human democracy caught fire, and a new fervor broke out in American intellectual, pastor, and theologian Jonathan Edwards, in England's John and Charles Wesley, who started the movement called Methodism, and in their colleague John Whitfield. Methodism brought revivals in England, Wales, and, through the travels of the Wesleys and Whitfield to America, to the colonies that were moving toward a revolution.

Methodism was an even bigger success in America, and the Great Awakening also awoke a small dormant movement called the Baptists, who were influenced a little by Europe's and Pennsylvania's Anabaptists (from whom they took their approach to baptism), and much more by the Congregational and Presbyterian Calvinists of New England and New Jersey (from whom they adopted most of their theology and social theory).

Baptists Multiply

The Baptists soon eclipsed even the Methodists. They quickly seemed to be the form of Protestantism best suited by the fledgling American people, and they have remained so ever since, by this generation outnumbering all of the other American Protestant denominations combined. Except for Princeton's Jonathan Edwards, the Great Awakening seemed to affect the grassroots population both widely and deeply, but the intelligentsia very little. After the creation of the Baptists and Methodists (both of which communions grew by millions of members), the movement's main innovation was the Sunday school.

Starting in the 1730s, the Great Awakening was a force through the American Revolution, and continued being one into the nineteenth century. And no sooner had its strength begun to wane than a Second Great Awakening began in the 1820s.

The Second Great Awakening

Though the first Great Awakening seemed sociologically oriented to the frontier and the widespread rural population of the late colonial and Revolutionary periods, the second was most influential in New England (where it was a reaction to deism and Unitarianism), and in Western New York, which was the home of the Chautauqua Campgrounds that spawned a nation-wide revival camp meeting movement. The Second Great Awakening also heavily influenced religious life in Appalachia, where a new burgeoning Protestant movement began that produced the Christian Churches and Disciples of Christ, which became one of the country's largest denominations.

factum

The Latter Day Saints, or Mormons, started in the same period as the Second Great Awakening. Like the founders of the Disciples and Churches of Christ, their founders thought they provided an alternative to the proliferation of denominations, and didn't want to be thought of as spawning new ones. The Mormons do not accept orthodox Christian creeds.

The Third Great Awakening

A third Great Awakening, starting in the 1880s, seemed oriented to the burgeoning cities of the United States, especially Chicago. It brought another wave of fervor across the continent, though it was strongest among women and helped launch the suffrage and prohibition movements. This revival period was the time of evangelist Billy Sunday and political leader William Jennings Bryan.

The Salvation Army, brought to the United States from England, and the YMCA, also an import from England, were taking hold in the cities with the support of Dwight L. Moody (1837–1899), Billy Sunday (1862–1935), and other evangelicals. Moody bridged the gap between the Second and Third Great Awakenings and made a lasting impact in New England and especially Chicago, where the Moody Bible Institute, Moody Press, and Moody Broadcasting continue to flourish.

Born Again

Born again as a term for salvation seems to have entered the Christian lexicon through the Wesleyan revivals in the United States, and the term underwent permutations with each wave of revival. For example, Wesley called it the "new birth." A 1911 encyclopedia of Catholicism defines baptism as "the sacrament by which we are born again of water and the Holy Ghost, that is, by which we receive in a new and spiritual life, the dignity of adoption as sons of God and heirs of God's kingdom."

discussion question

Who was Billy Sunday?
Billy Sunday was famous as a baseball player, and was a heavy drinker when he attended a revival meeting at Chicago's Pacific Garden Mission. After attending several times, he was "born again" during the Third Awakening. His previous affinity for alcohol may have contributed to his becoming a major force behind Prohibition.

Probably the greatest recognition for the "born again" name for salvation occurred in the 1970s, when a revival called the Jesus Movement or Jesus People Movement swept American campuses and other youth-culture enclaves, and when Jimmy Carter, while running successfully for President, declared that he was a born again Christian. In 1976, Charles W. Colson, former chief counsel in the Nixon White House and a convert after being indicted on charges related to Watergate, wrote a book entitled *Born Again*. The next year Billy Graham published *How to Be Born Again*.

CHAPTER 13

Christian Culture

In Revelation, John describes a vision of a city of gold, "And the city had no need of the sun or of the moon to shine in it, for the glory of God lit it and the Lamb is the light of it." Then John continues: "The nations of those who are saved shall walk in the light of the Lamb and the kings of the earth will bring their glory and honor to it." John is trying to show that believing in and following Jesus changes every aspect of life.

Biblical Culture

The Old Testament illustrates that Israel is—and has been since Abraham received the covenant establishing it—a culture, a social matrix of transmitted values, behaviors, beliefs, and institutions. In certain times and under certain conditions, Israel has also been a religion and a nation, but even when it was only one or neither of those, and through all the dispersions of the Jewish people, Israel has always been a culture.

Over the millennia, some of the Jewish people became atheists, agnostics, or secular humanists, but Jewish culture survived and continues to endure. Though life in Jesus is much more than culture and religion, the church has tried to instill a similar sense of culture and the place religion plays in it.

Further consideration of the Old Testament leads readers to conclude that Jewish culture was important to God. He purposely established it, and intended its continuation for his purposes of having a testimony among the nations of the world, and, pre-eminently, as a vehicle or medium through which to give the world his Son, its Savior. His covenants were everlasting, and their lasting depended on their being handed down through a stable social milieu, a culture.

Culture Matters

As Jesus said, God, who created Adam from the dust, could have raised up descendants of Abraham from the stones (Matthew 3:9, Luke 3:8); he could have sent his son into any society and historical setting, but he did not. He sent him to these people, this time, this place. Culture mattered, as the recitation of Joseph's genealogy in Luke's and Matthew's Gospels, along with Matthew's constant citation of Old Testament prophecies to Israel, underscores. This culture was not just accidental, but the result of a mandate God gave to Israel's ancestors, as recorded in Genesis 1:26–28.

Some find fault with the fourth century developments in the Roman Empire—Constantine's conversion and his participation in the church, and his attempt to accommodate Jesus' teachings to secular government. Culture is messy, and many people think religion should not be messy, so they try to divorce religion from culture and keep religion internal. Or, as the radical Anabaptists (the Amish) do, they keep religion within the extended family and their likeminded neighbors, and allow only as much interaction with "the world" as is necessary for survival.

discussion question

Who are the Anabaptists?
Anabaptists (the Greek name means "rebaptizers") is the generic name for the descendents of the "radical Reformation" in sixteenth century Holland and Germany. Their most visible branch is the Amish, who eschew modern conveniences, but other Pennsylvania Dutch (actually "Deutsch," meaning German) are part of this pacifist movement, including the Mennonites, the Church of the Brethren, and the (German-descended) Brethren Churches.

But such separatists are not the only Christians who eschew participation in the larger culture. Many others reject the dominion role described in Genesis 1:26–28 ("and let them have dominion . . . over all the earth") and which is confirmed by example through Israel throughout the Old Testament and in the testimony of the Fathers of the Church in its first three centuries.

The Christian Empire

The Roman Empire continued in the east for more than a millennium after Constantine, mindful of its Christian mandate. Sometimes that "Christian mind" was stronger, at other times weaker, but it was never absent. In 1453, its last bastion of the Roman Empire fell to the Muslim Ottomans after centuries of being threatened and whittled down from its original domain of Asia Minor, the Middle East, and Northern Africa to a territorial remnant around Constantinople.

This culturally Christian empire had extended its influence into the Balkans and Russia through missionary outreach, and the Russian empire that eventually emerged proudly proclaimed itself the Christian successor of Constantine's Rome. But Edward Gibbon (1737–1794), author of *The History of the Decline and Fall of the Roman Empire*, taking clues from the church in Rome and European xenophobia about Byzantium, dismissed the Eastern Empire as a thousand years of decline, a notion that still influences European attitudes toward followers of Jesus taking leadership in human cultures.

Church Traditions

Jewish culture and its products were always tied to the religion, transmitted through the Law and the covenants that the ethnic nation had from and with God. The Temple and synagogues, feasts, fasts, dietary restrictions and proscriptions, attachment to the "land of promise," and attitudes toward travel and pilgrimage all were part of the religion.

Likewise, Catholic countries exhibit cultural distinctiveness, reflecting national histories, myths, and achievements. Protestant countries tend to reflect fewer accoutrements of religion, as the Reformation stripped away most of the saints and their feast days and the attendant myths, leaving different kinds of art and literature.

Orthodox Art

Orthodox countries also reflect variations in their values and emphases compared with Latin-formed cultures. For example, art in the Catholic west tends toward lushness, realism, passion, and sensuality, whereas Orthodox artists try to reflect the Orthodox emphasis on dispassion, holiness, ascesis, and spiritual truths. Western critics often call Orthodox art "primitive," to which the Orthodox reply that there's a message behind their methods in art. It's not that they haven't noticed the third dimension and how to paint using perspective, for example; they have generally chosen not to.

Catholic Magisteria

Perhaps the biggest influence church traditions have on national and regional cultures, however, stems more from assumptions and intangible values of the respective churches than their outward policies and practices. For example, the magisterial role of the pope and bishops of the Catholic Church tends to give it a more authoritarian demeanor than the Orthodox and Protestant Churches, who have nothing quite like it.

Though *magisterial* means only "teaching," in Catholicism the interpretation of Scriptures is the sole province of the magisterium (the authority of the Catholic Church to teach religious truth). The magisterium's interpretation is capable of being considered infallible, a claim that the Orthodox would reserve only for ecumenical councils, and even then a condition of finality is the acceptance of Council findings by the laity of the church at large.

Christian Art and Science

A worldview based on Jesus and his teachings, and the mandate to adapt the religion to the cultural environment as necessary, have influenced the arts and scientific research and discovery since the early church. One of the divergences early Christians took from their Jewish predecessors was opening their culture for representational depictions in art, whereas Jewish orthodoxy said all images violated the commandment to avoid graven images.

But during the building of the Tabernacle that served as a mobile precursor to the Temple, not long after giving Moses the Commandments, God mandated the creation of images of cherubim to grace the altar. Exodus 25:18 says these images were to face the mercy seat and describes how they should appear.

Graven Images

Though Orthodoxy has generally eschewed (but not absolutely prohibited) statues, still under the influence of the Second Commandment, Eusebius (referred to previously) reported that the first known statue of Jesus was put up in Caesarea-Philippi by a woman Jesus had healed of a hemorrhage.

factum

Church historian Eusebius noted the existence of images of Peter and Paul, though he personally declined to provide an image of Jesus to the wife of a caesar who requested one, citing biblical restrictions. Some early churches forbade images, but historians say they spread quickly nevertheless.

Statues, paintings, and mosaics were common in pagan Rome, and early converts may have made their artwork before they knew that Jewish law prohibited them and that some Christians frowned on them. But eventually the church declared that images of Jesus and saints were permitted because, in Jesus' incarnation as God, he made himself visible to man for the first time.

Icons

By the seventh Ecumenical Council in the eighth century, icons had become widespread, but so had opposition to them. The Council determined that icons were proper aids to worship, but that any veneration given before them was to the saint depicted, not the painting itself.

A tract by St. John of Damascus, "On Holy Images," best stated this position. He said that not all images are idols, and not all veneration is worship; for example, the veneration soldiers on the battlefield give when kissing photographs of their wives and children is not religious devotion.

discussion question

What is Hagia Sophia?
The Great Church, as it was originally called, was built in Constantinople by Constantine, and was so named because it was larger than the other churches of the time. Rebuilt by Justinian in A.D. 537, it still remains one of the largest and oldest domed *buildings* in the world. It was eventually renamed Hagia Sophia, or the Holy Wisdom (of Christ).

Architecture

The church's first major contribution to artistic expression was in architecture, especially the architecture of church buildings. Influenced by the Jewish tradition of having an elaborate Temple in Jerusalem, and imposing synagogues in major cities inhabited by Jewish people in Roman times, once Christians were free to start raising their own temples, they wanted them to represent their devotion to God, as well as to wear well in daily use.

Early churches imitated the Imperial basilicas (large public buildings) of the Roman Empire, and many of the first ones built after the end of the persecutions were made for the church by Constantine and his mother, Helena.

At its peak, 80 priests, 150 deacons, 40 deaconesses, 60 subdeacons, 160 readers, 25 chanters, and 75 doorkeepers served the Great Church in Constantinople. In 1204, Catholic Crusaders pillaged the church and also sacked the city.

St. Peter's Basilica

Emperor Constantine ordered construction of the original St. Peter's Basilica in Rome, completed in A.D. 349, on the site where Peter had been buried in A.D. 64. During the removal of the papacy to France (1305–1378), the basilica fell into disrepair, and was replaced by a restored and larger church mandated by Popes Nicholas V and Julius II. The architect of the restored church, Donato Bramante, was succeeded in 1547 by Michelangelo, who died two years before its completion in 1626.

In the same period, most of the rulers, abbots (heads of monasteries), and bishops of Europe supported the construction of elaborate cathedrals, each city trying to outdo the next. Many of these, called Gothic in architectural style, are still in use, and are generally regarded as great treasures of human culture in the western world. St. Patrick's in Manhattan, Grace Cathedral in San Francisco, and the National Cathedral in Washington are examples of cathedrals built in the United States in the Gothic style.

symbolism

Ottoman Turkish Sultan Mehmet the Conqueror took Constan-tinople in 1453, and converted Hagia Sophia into an imperial mosque. Later, the Muslim Turks turned it into a museum, as it is to the current time, the best-preserved relic and symbol of the Byzantine Roman Empire.

Papal Art Patrons

Popes of Rome were among the world's main art patrons from antiquity until the eighteenth century, so the Vatican houses many of Europe's most valuable artworks, including Michelangelo's frescoes on the ceiling of the Sistine Chapel, and his *Last Judgment* on a chapel wall. Also found in the Sistine Chapel are works by Renaissance artists Botticelli, Domenico Ghirlandaio, Pinturicchio, and Luca Signorelli. Among other prized Vatican art treasures is a jewel-encrusted cross that was commissioned in the sixth century by Byzantine Emperor Justin II as a gift for the pope.

The Crusades

The 500 years after the fall of Rome to the Germanic Vandals is often thought of as Europe's Dark Ages. The period from about A.D. 476 to 1000, the Dark Ages originally referred to the lack of Latin literature produced in the period. Later, the term Dark Ages was expanded to cover a dearth of cultural advances in general. The Middle Ages refers to the period between the Dark Ages and the Renaissance (400 to 500 years later); some Renaissance writers called the Renaissance the modern age.

The most historically memorable though highly debated phenomenon of the Middle Ages was the crusades, military campaigns carried on in the name of Jesus and under the banner of his cross, under papal sanction, from the eleventh through thirteenth centuries. The first of these was launched in 1095 by Pope Urban, inspired by a letter from Emperor Alexius Comnenus in Constantinople to Robert, Count of Flanders, asking for aid to stop the persecution of pilgrims to the Holy Land by Muslims who were conquering more and more of the empire.

Crusaders Take Jerusalem

Count Robert forwarded the letter to the pope, who used it to raise an army to travel to the Holy Land and take Jerusalem and the Holy Land back from the Muslims. An army of both knights and peasants traveled over land and sea to reach Jerusalem, took it in 1099, and established a Kingdom of Jerusalem ostensibly under patronage of Jesus Christ, their professed High King.

The crusades arose from pietistic fervor that swept Europe at this time coupled with a desire of thousands of people to make radical changes in their poor and drab lives. The First Crusade was also boosted by its proximity to the change of millennia, and events in the heavens, including the appearance of a comet and a meteor shower.

A dozen or more crusades followed in this period, depending on how they are counted (some are considered subcrusades of larger or earlier ones), but nine are identified by number. As a whole, the crusades can be called the most clearly defined holy war in Christian history, in the sense that the crusaders—mainly uneducated peasants—considered themselves defenders of the sovereignty of Jesus Christ against a newer competing religious movement.

Papal Superiority

A subtext of the holy war was gaining papal superiority over the Orthodox churches in the east, which was temporarily achieved by the sacking of Constantinople in 1204 during the Fourth Crusade. Byzantine ruler Michael VIII Palaeologus recaptured Constantinople in 1261.

Only the First Crusade succeeded at achieving its goal, gaining control of Jerusalem. The general view of history, including that of the modern Catholic Church, is that the crusades were a misapplication of religious zeal, trying to win infidels in a way that was against the teachings of Jesus.

Rise of the Universities

Europe's first universities grew out of motivation to apply the teachings of Jesus and the Bible's cultural mandate to all of life. The first university began in the Italian city of Bologna in 1119. The University of Paris also began before 1200, though a specific year is not available, and Oxford University also has no clear date of origin, but claims it grew rapidly beginning in 1167, when King Henry II banned English students from going to the University of Paris.

Two other Italian universities date from the same period: Siena began in 1203, and Vincenza, 1204. Cambridge dates its beginning from 1209. The universities (the word is Latin for "corporation") were seen as providing higher educational opportunities to sons of the expanding merchant class.

Though still related to the churches and providing a Christian worldview, the universities provided the first higher education for secular vocations, the only educational institutions in most of Europe before then being monasteries. Though monasteries fostered and extended literacy, their main charter was not imparting specialized knowledge.

Secular university studies required something else that was not readily available in the world at that time: nonreligious books. Texts were handwritten by experts, who left them in stationers' stores, where the student, or someone he hired, could go and copy them by hand.

Enhancing the Christian life and worldview was also the main impetus for the beginning of a revolution in publishing. Though some books (especially Bibles) were circulated in Europe prior to the invention of the printing press by using a single block of hand-carved characters for each page, movable type and the printing press for using it were invented by Johann Gutenberg in the 1450s. His first book created after introducing the printing press was the Bible.

factum

Thomas Cahill, in *How the Irish Saved Civilization*, claims that Ireland, after St. Patrick, became the first European bastion for monasticism. After the Dark Ages began, the Irish monks copied the literature of the time and exported books and sent monks of intellectual strength to the continent, and probably as far as Russia, to help keep learning alive in an otherwise dark era.

The Renaissance

The Renaissance, a period of expanding knowledge in the arts and sciences, is considered to be a bridge from the Middle Ages to the modern era. Beginning in Italy in the fourteenth century, it spread to northern Europe in the late fifteenth century. The word means "rebirth" in its Italian form (*rinascenza*) and in its French and English form.

The first person many historians identify as embodying the Renaissance spirit is poet Dante Alighieri (Florence, 1265–1321), famous for *The Divine Comedy*, a volume containing three books including his best-known work, *The Inferno*, an allegorical tour of hell and a Christian classic.

Dark Ages

Petrarch (full name Francesco Petrarca; 1304–1374), educated in the law but more interested in literature and writing, is considered, with Dante, a major early figure in the Renaissance and the father of the term "Dark Ages" to describe the period after the fall of Rome. He was named the first poet laureate of Rome since antiquity, and also worked as a diplomat.

During the Renaissance, new breakthroughs also occurred in architecture and, most notably, in sculpture and painting. Some believe that much of the innovation was spurred by the patronage of the De Medicis of Florence, whose money inspired new heights of creativity. Probably the most famous Florentine painter, among many, is Leonardo da Vinci, whose *Last Supper* and *Mona Lisa* are known everywhere. Besides his paintings, he was also an accomplished architect, anatomist, and inventor.

English Renaissance

In England, the Elizabethan-era Renaissance produced William Shakespeare, John Milton, Christopher Marlowe, and Edmund Spenser, all writers and playwrights. Albert Durer, Pieter Bruegels, and van Eycks are also Renaissance painters who worked in the northern European Renaissance.

In science, the Renaissance was led by Kepler, Galileo, Nicolaus Copernicus, Sir Francis Bacon, and Isaac Newton.

Cracks in the West's Christian Culture

Though often studied as separate phenomena, many historians consider the Protestant Reformation an extension of the Renaissance spirit into religion. The most common date for the beginning of the Reformation is October 31,

1517, when Martin Luther posted a challenge to debate on the door of All Saints' Church in Wittenberg, Germany, in the form of ninety-five theses or propositions.

Luther

Martin Luther (1483–1546) was a pious Augustinian monk who became dissatisfied with corruption in the Catholic Church, especially the sale of indulgences to raise funds for the building of St. Peter's Basilica. His father wanted him to study law, but a brush with death turned him to the monastery, where his superior sent him back to academic life to prepare for the priesthood. He was such a quick study that four years later, with a doctorate of theology, he joined the faculty of the University of Wittenberg as a professor of theology.

Becoming immersed in study of the Bible, Luther quickly came to question Catholic interpretations of certain biblical teachings, including repentance/penance, righteousness, justification by faith, and grace. His challenge to debate the sale of indulgences ("The Ninety-five Theses") was quickly printed using the newly introduced printing press, and circulated throughout Germany within two weeks of their posting.

Invitation to Rome

Counter-challenged by the pope to come to Rome, Luther, fearing treachery, resisted and, further examining his claims, replied by challenging the pope's authority and the papal office as it existed at the time. As the gap between his views and the pope's demands widened, his writings were being disseminated throughout Europe, and throngs of students were traveling to Wittenberg to hear him directly.

On June 15, 1520, the pope warned Luther that he risked excommunication if he didn't recant 41 points in his writings. The following year, the emperor of the Holy Roman Empire banned Luther's writings and declared him an outlaw and a heretic before the Diet (legislature) of (the city of) Worms.

factum

On his return trip from Worms, Luther was abducted and taken to Wartburg Castle in Eisenach, but it was a friendly kidnapping carried out by his protector, Frederick the Wise. He was kept in the castle in voluntary exile for a year, and during that time received and responded to correspondence from people stirred by his reform doctrines.

Demands for Reforms Spread

Meanwhile, the Reformation had begun, with throngs of people demanding church reforms, including an end to masses conducted for private individuals, an end to the magisterial role of church hierarchs, and the removal of images from churches. The rest, as they say, is history, as about half of the population of Germany followed Luther into the newly organized Evangelical Church.

Calvin

John Calvin (in French, Jean Chauvin, 1509–1564), eight years old when Luther posted his ninety-five theses, studied law and humanities at the University of Paris. He was summoned to Geneva by Swiss reformer William Farel and there, except for a three-year preaching stint in Strasburg, he lived for the rest of his life. Not as outgoing as Luther, Calvin's main influence was through his writings, especially his *Institutes of the Christian Religion*, which he first wrote at age twenty-six and revised and reissued three times over the next twenty-five years.

Calvinism

Calvinism spread widely and became the dominant variety of Christian theology in Scotland (as the Presbyterian Church), the Netherlands (the Reformed Church), parts of Germany (Reformed), France (Huguenots), Hungary (Reformed), and Poland. The early settlers (in other words, the

Puritans and Pilgrims) of the American colonies that eventually became the United States were mostly Calvinists. The Puritans and Pilgrims later became known as Congregationalists, Dutch Reformed emigrants settled in New York and New Jersey, and Scots-Irish Presbyterians came to New Jersey, Pennsylvania, and south through Appalachia. Additional seminal figures in the Reformation were:

- **Thomas Cranmer**, Archbishop of the English Catholic Church when it transformed itself into the Church of England under Henry VIII. He consulted with both Luther and Calvin and leaned more strongly toward Calvin's theology.
- **John Knox**, the fiery reformer of Scotland who visited Calvin in Switzerland and adapted Calvin's theology to the Scottish temperament. The Reformation took Scotland like a firestorm, with Presbyterianism adopted by the Parliament as the established church of Scotland.
- **Ulrich Zwingli**, reformer of the church in Switzerland, beginning in Zurich. Half of Switzerland's ten cantons followed him and Luther into the Reformation; the other half remained Catholic. The cantons went to battle over their disagreement, and Zwingli was killed in battle.
- **Menno Simons**, a Dutch Catholic priest who became a critic of the church, and eventually led a group of dissenters, known as Anabaptists, to leave. Having become convinced infant baptism was unacceptable, they became rebaptized as adults, which is the source of the name. Simons also advocated pacifism and withdrawal from the world, including politics. Mennonites, Amish, and German Brethren see him as one of their source teachers.

The Age of Exploration

Probably the aspect of the Renaissance that affected more lives in Europe than any other, except the Reformation, was the increase in worldwide exploration, especially across the Atlantic Ocean. Christopher Columbus' "discovery" of the Americas in 1492 led to an era of increased trade and economic growth, and the development of new missions to take Jesus to "unreached peoples." The potato, introduced from Peru where it was a dietary staple, is credited as making it possible for the average European family to feed more members better than they could before. That led to a population explosion in some countries, including England and Wales.

Taking the Gospel of Jesus Christ to new peoples was a major impetus in settling the New World. According to *Christian History* magazine, Columbus himself was "a very devout Catholic who observed all the fasts of the church and prayed regularly. His very name Christopher . . . means Christ-bearer." He named the first land he claimed San Salvador, (Holy Savior), and dedicated it with a prayer "that thy holy Names may be proclaimed in this second part of the earth."

CHAPTER 14

Modernity

Historians have different opinions of life in medieval Europe; some think it was unbearably difficult, and others think that despite the poverty of most people, there was generally a high level of satisfaction with life during the whole medieval period. Regardless of which assessment is more accurate, once the Renaissance and liberated thinking appeared, there was no going back.

The Rise of Skepticism

Skepticism is as human a condition as curiosity or longing. The New Testament's most famous example of it is the Apostle Thomas' doubt when confronted with the testimony of his fellow disciples that Jesus had risen from the grave and visited them. When the other disciples told him "We have seen the Lord," Thomas replied, "Unless I see in his hands the print of the nails and put my finger into them, and put my hand into his side, I will not believe it."

Zachariah Struck Dumb

John the Baptist's father, Zachariah, when visited by an angel telling him his prayer for a child had been answered, and that Elizabeth, his wife, would give birth to John, "who shall turn many of Israel to their God," was incredulous. "How can I believe such a thing?" Zachariah exclaimed. "I am an old man and my wife well up in years."

The angel answered, "I am Gabriel who stand in the presence of God, and I have been sent to give you these glad tidings. For not believing, you shall be struck dumb and not able to speak until the day these things come to pass" (see Luke 1:18–20). The Gospel says Zachariah was unable to speak until John was born and it was time for him to name the infant.

Abraham Laughed

In the same way, even Abraham, the "Father of the Faithful," had a skeptical side. "God said to Abraham, 'As for Sarai your wife, do no longer call her Sarai, but her name shall be Sarah. And I will bless her and give you a son also by her. Yes, I will bless her, and she shall be a mother of nations; kings of people shall be descended from her.'

"Abraham fell upon his face, laughing, and thinking in his heart, 'Shall a child be born to one who is a hundred years old, and shall Sarah, who is ninety years old, bear?' And Abraham said to God, 'O that Ishmael [Abraham's son by his concubine] might live for you!' But God replied, 'Sarah your wife shall indeed bear you a son, and you shall name him Isaac, and I will establish with him and with his seed after him an everlasting covenant'" (Genesis 17:15–19).

fallacy

Some think God is an unyielding taskmaster, but in these instances he recognizes human skepticism as part of fallen nature, and throughout his dealings with his people, he encourages their questions and transparent reservations, and is willing to negotiate. But also in the cases reviewed in this section, there is a prior commitment to faith and a prior relationship with God.

Accepting Miracles

All three of these doubters wanted to believe but seemed afraid to accept that such wonders could happen. When God approached with gifts of miracles, he wanted belief and gratitude. The attitude of a father who brought a speechless child to Jesus for healing seems to be one God wants all to have. "Jesus said to him, 'If you can believe, all things are possible to him who believes.' And the father of the child, not hesitating, cried with tears, 'Lord, I believe; help my unbelief'" (Mark 9:23–24). And Jesus healed the child.

The Enlightenment Begins

The Enlightenment was the first serious challenge of the Lordship of Jesus over western culture. Historians often approach it as having been a response, primarily, against the Spanish Inquisition, a reign of terror in the name of Jesus that turned many against the church and from identifying with Jesus as Lord.

Spanish Inquisition

In its root meaning, "inquisition" means nothing more than an inquiry into teachings that contradict dogma within the Catholic Church, or an inquiry in territories where Catholicism was the established church. But in its popular usage, an inquisition denotes an era of persecution of non-

Catholic people, mainly in Spain, Peru, and Mexico, from 1497 until 1836, when it was officially ended, though the last execution of a heretic in Spain occurred ten years earlier.

Spanish King Ferdinand (who, with Queen Isabella, sponsored Columbus' explorations) petitioned the Vatican to authorize an Inquisition, which Pope Sixtus IV opposed, but was persuaded through political maneuvering to permit. Experts disagree about how many people were put to death for dissenting from Catholic doctrine. Historians range in their estimates from several thousand to well over 100,000.

There is also wide disagreement about the role torture played in the punishments and confessions, with some claiming it was severe and widespread, while defenders of the church say few instances of torture, and those "not lasting longer than 15 minutes," can be validated from the historical records. The Inquisition remains the most damaging charge ever laid against Catholicism and, by extension, against Christians in general. Although there is nothing comparable to the Inquisition in Orthodoxy or Protestantism, it is sometimes compared with the Salem witch trials in the seventeenth century.

Witch Trials

Outside Catholicism, the only thing comparable to the Inquisitions in post-medieval Christendom is the Salem (Massachusetts) witch trials in 1692. The Salem trials contrast with the Inquisition in that they were carried out by a town and its church, which, being Congregational, was not contractually connected to any other church, communion, or denomination. The persecution lasted nearly a year, with twenty-five executions by burning, and the jailing of several scores of other suspects.

At the end of the Salem persecutions, highly respected Boston Congregational pastor Increase Mather published a plea that there be no more such trials, saying, "It were better that Ten Suspected Witches should escape, than that the Innocent Person should be Condemned." The statement became a widely quoted slogan that some historians believe inspired the United States constitutional provision that the accused are presumed innocent until proven guilty.

Prominent Enlightenment Thinkers

The Enlightenment, considered as a frame of mind tending toward "modernism" and secular humanism, extends from the Renaissance through the seventeenth century. Some of its main players are sketched here, in chronological order by date of birth.

Rene Descartes (French, 1596–1650)

Considered by some the father of modern philosophy and of modern mathematics, Descartes was the founder of analytic geometry and Cartesian philosophy. He is credited with giving the natural sciences their first philosophical framework. Though the Vatican put his works on the "Index of Prohibited Books," he claims in *Meditations* to have proven the existence of a benevolent God. *Cogito ergo sum*, I think therefore I am, is his succinct summary of his philosophy.

Blaise Pascal (France, 1623–1662)

A mathematical genius, Pascal was a child prodigy, and, though he sometimes lived a worldly life, he died an orthodox believer in Jesus Christ. He is most famous as the father of probability theory, which is essential to actuarial research and economics. He also wrote a brilliant critique of casuistry (the use of deceptive reasoning), calling it a Jesuit system for justifying moral laxity. Though the Pope condemned the book, he later ordered an end to laxness in church standards. At the time of his death at age thirty-nine, Pascal was working on a theological apologetic, published posthumously, as *Pensees*, which Will Durant, in *The Story of Civilization*, calls "the most eloquent book in French prose."

John Locke (England, 1632–1704)

The philosopher who introduced the Lockean social contract, from which the American colonies' Declaration of Independence got its phrase "consent of the governed," he is widely regarded by historians as the philosopher most influential to American thinking through at least the nineteenth century. Brought up a Puritan, he studied and advocated religious toleration, and later joined the Church of England and supported latitudinarianism, a theological openness to many points of view, which later became known as "broad church" policy and led to the Anglican tolerance of later times. Though considered a major influence on modern political liberalism, which some people feel doesn't promote religion, Locke taught that because governments have a vested interest in their citizens keeping their promises, and because there is no moral constraint to be honest other than religious scruples, governments may promote religion.

Sir Isaac Newton (England, 1643–1727)

A major figure of the English Renaissance, and considered by many the most ingenious thinker in history, Newton is best known for his discovery of gravity and as the inventor of calculus. A bridge from the Renaissance to the Enlightenment, he is often cited for his Christian orthodoxy, with quotations like: "I have a fundamental belief in the Bible as the Word of God, written by those who were inspired. I study the Bible daily." Like some of the founding fathers of the United States, however, some maintain that he had "deist leanings" despite the seeming orthodoxy of some writings. He wrote an essay about the Trinity that was sent to John Locke but has never been published. He is said to have scientifically calculated the crucifixion of Jesus as occurring on April 3, 33.

factum

During the French Revolution, churches were confiscated, and their priests were required to make a vow of loyalty to the state. In the Napoleonic Republican era that followed the Revolution, the Vatican condemned Napoleon, and in response he invaded Rome.

Voltaire (French, pen name of François-Marie Arouet, 1694–1778)

A poet, playwright, author, social commentator, and defender of civil liberties and freedom of religion before either were available in France, Voltaire's most famous work is *Candide*, which ridicules orthodox views of

God in the wake of an earthquake that leveled Lisbon and was followed by a tsunami and fire. His major contribution to the Enlightenment may have been his outspoken agnosticism, which in old age hardened into atheism, by encouraging many more timid skeptics to declare themselves. One of his most famous quotations is: "One hundred years from my day there will not be a Bible in the earth except one that is looked upon by an antiquarian curiosity seeker."

Jean-Jacques Rousseau (French-Swiss, 1712–1778)

A writer, political theorist, musician, and philosopher, Rousseau's writings influenced the development of socialism and nationalism, and of the French Revolution. Having grown up in Geneva reading *Plutarch's Lives* and Calvinist theology, after entering into a liaison with a French lover, he converted to Catholicism. He later fathered five children by a second lover and put the children in a foundling home at birth, saying they would fare better growing up in an orphanage than in his home. His most famous philosophical kernel is that human nature is corrupted by society, and his major tome is *The Social Contract,* which claims, among other things, that true disciples of Jesus would make poor citizens, an opinion that won him condemnation in both his Catholic and Calvinist home cities, Paris and Geneva, respectively.

Thomas Paine (English, American, 1737–1808)

As the author of *The Age of Reason*, Paine, of the American founding fathers, is the most representative of the Enlightenment mindset. On meeting Benjamin Franklin in London at age thirty-five, Franklin suggested he move to the colonies, which invitation Paine accepted, moving to Philadelphia in 1774, just two years before the creation of the Declaration of Independence and the launch of the American Revolutionary War. Considered an archetypical liberal, Paine supported universal public education, social security, a graduated income tax, and a guaranteed minimum wage, all generations before they came about. His tract *Common Sense*, supporting independence of the colonies from England, was widely read and influenced much of the free population of the colonies at the time, including George Washington. As a Deist, Paine weighs-in against organized religion in *The Age of Reason*: "I do not believe in the creed professed by the Jewish church, by the

Roman church, by the Greek church, by the Turkish church, by the Protestant church, nor by any church that I know of. My own mind is my own church. All national institutions of churches, whether Jewish, Christian, or Turkish, appear to me no other than human inventions set up to terrify and enslave mankind, and monopolize power and profit."

Secular Humanism

Paine's declaration, "My own mind is my own church," a profession of the rationalism, or the reason he refers to in his title *The Age of Reason*, has also been called a confession of secular humanist faith. Most Christian critics believe that secular humanism, though the term is not found that early, derives from the predominant Enlightenment worldview. Though Paine begins his treatise with a statement of faith in "one God," his only admitted way to perceive that God is his own reason. In other words, his god is of his own creation.

symbolism

A BBC analysis of French secularism was occasioned by controversy over Muslim girls wanting to wear headscarves to school, against state rules, as symbols of their religion. Christian philosophers critical of France's turn to secularism often cite the guillotine as the main symbol of their Revolution and their invasion, under Napoleon, of most of Europe in the next generation.

Thomas Paine went to France after the American Revolution to encourage the anti-monarchy forces there (and it was while he was in Paris that he wrote *The Age of Reason*), and he found a receptive audience for his views. Generally, the French Enlightenment thinkers considered the church an impediment to the Revolution's goals of "liberty, equality, and fraternity."

Napoleon worked out a concord with the Vatican that brought the churches under the state, a radical reversal of the medieval practice in which states were under the church. In 1905, France passed a separation of church and state law that has been interpreted as making public schools religion-free zones.

The Protestant Ascendancy

Most of the early colonists in what became the original thirteen American states were professors of faith in Jesus as Calvinists. Many Lutherans, Quakers, and Anabaptists from Germany, Holland, and England also were among the colonies' earliest immigrants, especially to Pennsylvania. Even in the latest national census, persons of German descent were found to still be the most populous ethnic group in Pennsylvania, with Scots-Irish (mostly Protestant) a close second.

The original immigrants to New England—Pilgrims and Puritans—were fleeing England for greater religious freedom in the New World, as were the Quakers and Anabaptists who colonized Pennsylvania. The Dutch Reformed who first settled New York and overflowed in large numbers into New Jersey were primarily entrepreneurs rather than religious refugees. The Presbyterians who dominated New Jersey, Pennsylvania, and Delaware were mainly northern Irish seeking better opportunities for advancement in life, as Presbyterianism was the religion favored by their British rulers in Ireland at the time.

factum

All of the American colonies except Maryland—which was founded through a land grant to an Irish Catholic aristocrat, Cecil Calvert, Second Lord Baltimore—had established churches. But as the colonies grew and began competing for new settlers, they downplayed their religious preferences, and by the time of the American Revolution, the established church was no longer a significant issue.

Members of the Church of England dominated the southern colonies such as Virginia, the Carolinas, and Georgia, with noticeable numbers of Huguenot refugees from France in South Carolina, and Moravian refugees (descended from the ministry of reformer Jan Hus in Moravia, in what is now the Czech Republic) in Salem (now Winston-Salem) in North Carolina. An earlier sizable colony of Moravians had also been established earlier in Bethlehem and Nazareth, Pennsylvania.

Most of the early settlers of America, refugees from countries where the Catholic Church dominated, strongly feared Catholic immigration or, at the least, Catholic domination of their towns. Many towns and localities barred Catholic churches by either tacit or explicit measures through the nineteenth century, and some such towns were still known as Protestant towns well into the twentieth century.

Anti-Catholic Sentiments

There are reports of a Catholic church being burned down by disgruntled Protestants in New York in 1831, and of Protestant-Catholic riots in Philadelphia claiming thirteen lives in 1844. A political party campaigning as the American Party in 1854, which elected governors in Massachusetts and Delaware, and got Millard Fillmore on the presidential ticket, asked prospective party members to pledge to "elect to all offices of Honor, Profit, or Trust, no one but native born citizens of America, of this Country to the exclusion of all Foreigners, and to all Roman Catholics, whether they be of native or Foreign Birth, regardless of all party predilections whatever."

Another gauge of anti-Catholic sentiments is the historical record of the American Protective Association, sometimes wrongly called the American Protestant Association (APA). Founded in 1887 in Clinton, Iowa, the APA is said to have drawn membership largely from the Masons, who at that time did not admit Catholics (though it's debated whether the Vatican permitted Catholics to join quasi-religious Masonic organizations).

An APA Oath

An oath required of APA candidates for membership said, in part: "I do most solemnly promise and swear that I will always, to the utmost of my ability, labor, plead and wage a continuous warfare against ignorance and fanaticism; that I will use my utmost power to strike the shackles and chains of blind obedience to the Roman Catholic church from the hampered and bound consciences of a priest-ridden and church-oppressed people; that I will never allow any one, a member of the Roman Catholic church, to become a member of this order . . . to promote the interest of all Protestants everywhere in the world that I may be; that I will not employ a Roman Catholic in any capacity if I can procure the services of a Protestant." Though most American Protestants may have been ignorant of the APA and its oath, such attitudes were still widely found during the campaign for the presidency of John F. Kennedy in 1960. That campaign, in fact, may have been a turning point in the decline of such attitudes. As the first nation on earth to have a pluralistic but Protestant-dominated population enjoying freedom of religion, it's understandable that despite the changes of the modern age, American Protestants would only reluctantly welcome change.

Protestant Power

At the time of the American Revolution, the population was 98 percent Protestant. And in 1900, Protestants of English, Scots, Irish, German, and Dutch background comprised 55 percent of the population, with national immigration laws favoring immigration from similar ethnic backgrounds well into the twentieth century.

symbolism

To the current era, the United States is considered a country controlled by Protestants, with that religious group dominant in every branch of federal government and most state governments as well. Even in 2005, the media considered it newsworthy that the U.S. Supreme Count had its first Catholic and non-Protestant majority among the nine justices.

Under the gentle husbandry of the American Protestant mainstream, Protestantism has also grown exponentially in the Third World in the past generation. According to recent statistics, there are 1.1 billion Roman Catholics and over 800 million Protestants, Independents, and Anglicans worldwide, which is approximately four times the 218 million Eastern Orthodox worldwide. Considering that up to now, in this consideration of Jesus' world impact, the Orthodox have received second-place attention after Catholics, this signals a significant turning point in the history of the Jesus movement.

CHAPTER 15

The "Christian" Century

It's hard to imagine that the twentieth century may be seen as the "Christian" century, the first or best representative of the church giving of itself for the world. The church did not win over the world through its appealing words and strategies of evangelism so that the world gave up its strife and self-serving and -aggrandizing attitudes. The century of Hitler, Stalin, Mao, Pol Pot, Slobodan Milosevic, and Saddam Hussein wasn't quite the breakthrough for the Kingdom Come many hoped for.

Higher Criticism

The Christian world may have had reasons for optimism as the nineteenth century faded into the twentieth. Great Britain was the empire on which the sun never set, and its monarch, Queen Victoria, was the most influential one since Henry VIII made England Protestant (and she was far better loved). Also, Queen Victoria was, by multiple testimonies, a devout believer in Jesus who prayed for her world and how to best serve it.

One of her granddaughters, Alexandra, arguably even more pious and sincere in her devotion to Jesus, was married to the ruler of the second-largest empire at the time, Russia, which still thought of itself as Holy Russia. Even if Alexandra's German cousin Kaiser Wilhelm II (also a grandchild of Queen Victoria) may have sometimes seemed a bit of a loose cannon, what were the odds of his upsetting the whole world?

Breakthroughs

In the world professing to belong to Jesus, and the churches, there was enthusiasm about the breakthroughs of the nineteenth century, especially in biblical scholarship, an academic domain that higher criticism had already turned upside down in Germany and the rest of European academe. Around 1900, biblical scholarship was beginning to influence the pulpit speech of Protestant America, the sleeping giant, still isolated from European intrigues and happily ignorant of just about anything Asian.

factum

By 1910, one researcher claims, up to 25 percent of American clergy looked positively on the higher criticism that claimed to disprove the miracles claimed in Scripture by using scientific assumptions and techniques of literary scholarship.

Nineteenth-century higher criticism revolved around the Graf-Wellhausen documentary hypothesis propounded by German biblical scholars Julius Wellhausen (1844–1918) and Karl Heinrich Graf (1815–1869). The hypothesis is that the Pentateuch, the first five books of the Bible, were not written by one author, Moses, as held in tradition, but by a collection of unknown sources whom Graf and Wellhausen named J, E, D, and P.

Christianity Without Jesus

Robert Anderson, author of *The Bible and Criticism*, wrote that higher criticism "directly challenges the authority of the Lord Jesus Christ as a teacher; for one of the few undisputed facts in this controversy is that our Lord accredited the books of Moses as having divine authority." He was referring to John 5:46, which has Jesus saying, "Had you believed Moses, you would have believed me, for he wrote of me." If the author of the first five books of the Bible wasn't Moses, but four authors, Jesus' authority is undermined.

As another critic of higher criticism put it, if John 5:46 and many other references to Moses in Jesus' teaching are not factual, either he was himself misled or he was misleading his hearers, but "in either case the Blessed One is dethroned." Wherever higher criticism has been influential, faith and churches have atrophied.

Missions in Crisis

Missionary outreach is considered by all branches of Christendom to be a response to Jesus' commission in Matthew 28:19, "Go and teach all nations, and baptize them." The history of planned missionary outreach to faraway lands by the church begins with St. Paul's accepting the call described in Acts 16:9–10: "And a vision appeared to Paul in the night. There stood a man from Macedonia who asked, 'Come over into Macedonia and help us.' And after he had seen the vision, immediately we endeavored to go to Macedonia, convinced that the Lord had called us to preach the gospel to them."

Some historians believe that the first intentional missionary after the early church period was Patrick (A.D. 387?–493). Having been kidnapped as a youth on the west coast of Britain or Wales, he was a slave in Ireland for seven years. After escaping, he spent twelve years as a monk living in France where, like Paul, he saw a vision "of the children from Focluth, by the

Western sea, who cried to him: 'O holy youth, come back to Erin, and walk among us once more.'"

discussion question

Did early missions succeed?
Throughout the first generation of the church, missionary travels like Paul's and Thomas' were common and far-reaching. Partially because of them, the church was being built in Europe, the Levant (roughly "the Holy Land," and to all points east, into India), and Africa.

Apostle to Ireland

Appointed bishop of Ireland, where a church barely existed at the time, his mission was so successful that virtually the entire island nation converted from paganism to Christianity in his lifetime. He is considered the apostle to Ireland (the title used since the original apostles were only for missionaries who converted whole peoples), and is the first of Ireland's patron saints, along with St. Columba and St. Bridgid.

The next most notable missionaries in church history were Cyril and Methodius, brothers and priests who were called when living at a monastery on the Bosphorous to minister to the Slavs. The language of the Slavs had no written form at that time, so they created an alphabet for it based on the Greek alphabet.

Colonizing efforts of Roman Catholic countries like Spain and Portugal in Central and South America included missionaries who taught Christianity to the indigenous peoples. Such missionary work is dramatically depicted in the 1986 feature film *The Mission*. Many Americans are aware of the missionizing work of Junipero Serra, the Franciscan priest who had twenty-one missions constructed, each a day's journey apart from the next one, along the path called El Camino Real in California, stretching hundreds of miles.

factum

All four of California's largest cities, San Diego, Los Angeles, San Jose, and San Francisco, as well as many of its smaller ones, have grown up around Junipero Serra's missions and take their names from them.

Mission to Alaska

The most famous Russian Orthodox mission is that of Innocent of Alaska (Fr. John Veniaminov, 1797–1879), who brought the gospel from Irkutsk, Russia, to what was then Russia's territory in North America, Alaska. Like many other missionaries, he learned the local dialects (six of them), translated portions of the Bible into those languages, and created the first written version of the languages to do so. The Alaskan churches eventually sent out their own missionaries, reaching as far south as what is now Fort Ross, north of San Francisco, in California.

In the modern era, one of the most important developments was the organizing of the Mission Society by Anglican, Presbyterian, and independent church clergy and laity in London in 1794, "to spread the knowledge of Christ among heathen and other unenlightened nations." Its first outreach was Tahiti in the South Seas in 1796, and it expanded to North America and South Africa. Renamed the London Mission Society in 1818, it later sent missionaries to Russia, Greece, Malta, and the Jewish population in London. Other nineteenth-century lands it served include China, Southeast Asia, India, the Pacific, Madagascar, Central and Southern Africa, Australia, and the islands of the Caribbean.

American Board for Foreign Missions

A similar endeavor began in the United States with the American Board of Commissioners for Foreign Missions (ABCFM), organized in 1810 as a nondenominational, voluntary association not controlled by any denominational body. The ABCFM was responsible for most American Protestant overseas missionary efforts through the Civil War period. It considered its first priority, however, the settling and Christianizing of the expanding continental United States.

factum

Estimates are that by 1900, some 5,000 American missionaries were taking "their version of the gospel of Protestantism and American civilization" to far reaches of the planet. By this time, denominational mission boards, rather than the previous interdenominational board, were sending out most of the missionaries. A century later, the number of American foreign missionaries is about 40,000.

From the late 1870s on, there was some debate over whether—or how much—preaching of "civilization," as defined by American Protestants, was part of the missionary calling, and whether civilizing or Americanizing indigenous peoples along with missionizing them, was part of the missions charter. The dominant view is that missionaries should Americanize indigenous people, in part because raising funds to support missions becomes easier when it is seen as being both patriotic (or serving national interests) and a way to save souls. The issues of whether certain countries persecute American missionaries abroad, as well as whether foreign countries welcome missionaries, have long influenced the foreign-policy stances of some members of the United States Congress.

American Protestant Vision

Foreign missionary ventures from early times produced an American Protestant alternative to the hagiographical books and legends from the church in the centuries of Roman persecution. Books about foreign lands and the sacrifices made by missionaries, and books often about their lives in general, were widely read and served to broaden the perspectives about the world of many Americans. Even today, icons of foreign missionaries, in the form of color glossy photos, grace the foyers or vestibules of thousands of American evangelical churches.

By 1900, about 60 percent of the foreign missionaries going from the United States to foreign fields were women, many of them unmarried field workers, and the others wives of male missionaries who generally worked alongside their husbands.

symbolism

Foreign missions were considered symbolically romantic in a classical sense, going beyond the normal calling of all Christians to live for Jesus, and the missions gave women a chance to devote their lives to ministry in an era when almost no denominations ordained women to pastoral ministries.

The World Missionary Conference in Edinburgh, Scotland, in 1910 drew 1,200 participants from denominations and mission agencies around the world. Chaired by an American Methodist lay leader, John Mott, it laid the groundwork for the ecumenical movement and the formation of the World Council of Churches in 1948.

The Ecumenical Movement

In the early church, ecumenical councils were called, usually by the emperor, to sort though disparate views about issues like the Trinity; whether Jesus Christ was two persons or had two natures, and how they were defined and related to each other; and so on.

The following is a list of the councils that had representatives from both the Western (Latin) church and the Eastern (Greek) church, their locations, and their findings:

- **Nicea, 325.** Called by Emperor Constantine, with 318 bishops attending, to settle the Arian teaching, which denied the eternal consubstantial existence of the Son with the Father (see Chapter 11). The result was the first ecumenical creed, an incomplete version of the Nicene Creed, and the first creedal definition of the Trinity.

- **Constantinople, 381.** Called by Emperor Theodosius the Great, with 150 bishops attending, to further define the Holy Spirit. Produced the final version of the Nicene Creed.

- **Ephesus, Asia Minor, 431.** Called by Emperor Theodosius II, grandson of Theodosius the Great, with 200 bishops attending, to settle the Nestorian claim that Mary gave birth to a divine man but not the eternal Logos (Word of God). It defined Christ as the Incarnate Word of God, and Mary as Theotokos (God-bearer).

- **Chalcedon, Asia Minor, 451.** Called by Emperor Marcian, with 630 bishops attending, to settle the monophysite controversy (the belief that Christ has a single nature that is both human and divine). It defined Christ as Perfect God and Perfect Man in One Person.

- **Constantinople II, 553.** Called by Emperor Justinian the Great, with 165 bishops attending, to settle Nestorian and Eutychian (the belief that Christ is solely divine and does not have a human nature) heresies (see Chapter 11). Further defined the two natures of Christ and condemned certain Nestorian writings.

- **Constantinople III, 680.** Called by Emperor Constantine IV, with 170 bishops attending, to settle the monothelite controversy. Affirmed that though Jesus had two natures, he had only one (divine) will.

- **Quinisext Council (Trullo), Constantinople, 692.** Held in the Imperial Palace under the Trullo Dome, it ratified acts of the previous two councils, with no new agenda.

- **Nicea, Asia Minor, 787.** Held under Empress Irene, with 367 bishops attending, to settle the iconoclastic controversy (to determine whether icons should be displayed). Ruled that the holy icons should be exhibited.

Twentieth-century Ecumenism

The ecumenical movement of the twentieth century, rather than debating heresies, considers heresy an outdated concept of no use to an evolving church. Instead, it studies ways to overcome doctrinal differences in the church bodies that participate in it. Though originally intended to create one communion out of many (or, critics claimed, one world church), it has met with little success in that direction. Mainline Protestants now organize and administer the ecumenical movement.

Since the movement began in 1948, the mainline Congregational Church has merged with the Hungarian Reformed Church in America and the Evangelical and Reformed Church to become the United Church of Christ, the Methodist Church has merged with the Evangelical United Brethren Church to become the United Methodist Church, the United Presbyterian Church has merged with the Presbyterian Church (US) to become the Presbyterian Church (USA), and three mainline Lutheran churches have merged to become the Evangelical Lutheran Church of America, ELCA.

The main agencies for the ecumenical movement are the World Council of Churches, and the National Council of Churches of the USA. Based in Geneva, Switzerland, the WCC numbers 340 denominations, including most of the Orthodox Churches, which say they are there only to be witnesses to believers in Christ from other communions. They do not participate in ecumenical communion services or plan to merge into any evolving church.

discussion question

Has the contemporary ecumenical movement been successful?
Though ten denominations have merged to become four since the movement began, many more small Protestant denominations (including new breakaways from the Methodist and Presbyterian bodies that merged) have been started, and the independent church movement has exploded.

Catholicism and the World Council of Churches

The Vatican sends observer-participants to WCC conferences, but the Catholic Church has not officially become a member denomination. The Pontifical Council for Promoting Christian Unity at the Vatican sends twelve members to the Faith and Order Commission of the World Council as full members.

The National Council of Churches in the USA is composed of thirty-five member denominations and Orthodox jurisdictions, and is the United States affiliate to the World Council of Churches. Its major projects have included publishing the revised standard version and the new revised standard version of the Bible, and an annual *Yearbook of American and Canadian Churches* that attempts to give comprehensive statistical data on churches regardless of their affiliation with the Council.

Twentieth-century Fundamentalism

Since the hostage crises in Iran during the Carter Administration (1977–1981), the major American news media have used the term fundamentalist as if it were synonymous with Islamic terrorists and conservative Christians, especially those conservative Christians active in political campaigns. Even before its reassignment to Muslims, fundamentalist had gone from its original use as a self-applied label used by orthodox Protestants in the mainstream, especially Presbyterian faculty members at Princeton Theological Seminary in the 1920s, to an epithet for TV evangelists, snake handlers, and tent-show faith healers.

The leading light of the earlier group was J. Gresham Machen, who had been on the Princeton faculty for twenty-three years. When Princeton Theological Seminary reorganized along more liberal lines, he left it to form Westminster Presbyterian Seminary in Philadelphia in 1929.

When the denomination's mission board refused to stop support for liberal missionaries, he established an independent mission board to support only missionaries that orthodox Presbyterians would feel comfortable supporting. The denomination ordered members of the independent board to resign from it or be stripped of their ordination. He and other members refused to resign and, facing being defrocked, started a new denomination, the Orthodox Presbyterian Church.

After graduating from Johns Hopkins University and Princeton Theological Seminary himself, Machen had studied in Germany for a year with one of the leading proponents of the higher critical approach to biblical studies, Wilhelm Hermann, at Marburg. In correspondence, he relates that this was a great crisis of faith, because although Hermann disbelieved most of what orthodox Christians consider essential, his faith seemed so radiant that Machen found it magnetic, almost entrancing. By contrast, he said that one of his professors at seminary, B. B. Warfield, revered for his orthodox theology, was "a very heartless, selfish, domineering sort of man."

The Fundamentals

A decade before Machen became the leader of the early Protestant fundamentalists, an anthology of ninety articles about the essential doctrines of Christian orthodoxy appeared in a twelve-volume set of paperback books titled *The Fundamentals*. Intended for use by pastors and church leaders to understand the issues that were very controversial in many churches by that time, some three million copies of the booklets were circulated throughout the United States. Some of the titles and authors are:

The History of the Higher Criticism, by Canon Dyson Hague, M.A.
The Mosaic Authorship of the Pentateuch, by Prof. Geo. Frederick
    Wright, D.D., LL.D.
Fallacies of the Higher Criticism, by Prof. Franklin Johnson, D.D., LL.D.
Old Testament Criticism and New Testament Christianity, by Prof. W.H.
    Griffith Thomas
Science and Christian Faith, by Rev. Prof. James Orr, D.D.
My Personal Experience with the Higher Criticism, by Prof. J.J. Reeve

These monographs were republished in a four-volume set in 1993, and they are now available online (see Appendix A: Web Resources, and Appendix B: Bibliography). The main focus of the writings these monograms critiqued was the findings of biblical criticism.

New Evangelicalism

The movement that is now positioned in the American media as the leading force in American religion, evangelicalism, fronted for a half century by evangelist Billy Graham, *Christianity Today* magazine, and longer by Baylor University, Wheaton College, Calvin College, and scores of other similar colleges and seminaries, descends directly from the fundamentalists of the beginning of the Christian century. Seeing the writing on the wall (see Daniel 5) that "fundamentalist" was going to be a hard designation to live with, they intentionally recast themselves as the "new evangelicals" and eventually, just evangelicals. The subject of evangelicals will be taken up further in Chapter 17.

Vatican II

Another major development of the twentieth century is Vatican II, the Second Vatican Ecumenical Council, opened in 1962 by Pope John XXIII and closed in 1965 by Pope Paul VI. The Council may be misnamed as "ecumenical," in the sense that only Roman Catholics had voting privileges in it. But it certainly was ecumenical in the sense that the reforms it instituted made the Catholic Church much more accessible by all other orthodox Christians and conservative members of other religions, especially the other monotheistic ones, Judaism and Islam. "Accessible" here means comprehensible, easier to find common ground with, and open.

Liberal Catholic Hopes

Liberal Catholics are generally perceived in Christian periodicals and Web sites as having had higher hopes for the reforms to come from the Council than actually appeared (especially women priests and an end to the celibacy requirement for priests). Conservative Catholics and confessing Protestants are generally pleased, especially in the way Vatican II has been interpreted in the administrations of Pope John Paul II and Pope Benedict XVI.

Protestants who may have visited Catholic services in pre-Vatican II days but not since are often amazed at how different they have become. Though the magisterium felt that folk masses went too far in the early years after the Council, restraints they put in effect in the intervening years have made Catholic masses almost as visitor friendly as typical evangelical services.

Biblical Support

Almost as radical as the decisions of the Council, probably because it is the most hands-on medium of the Council's reforms that the average person can get access to, is the revised Catholic Catechism, published in 1992 by Pope John Paul II. A catechism is a compendium of the teachings of a religion, with answers to just about any question a person might raise, from church teachings on birth control and homosexuality, to the seven deadly sins and seven virtues.

symbolism

Catholic use of hymns by Martin Luther and Charles Wesley is now common in masses—even Billy Graham's theme, "How Great Thou Art"—as well as praise songs of the type seen in most evangelical and mainline churches trying to appeal to young worshippers. The use of these songs may be the most pointed symbolical proof of the Roman church's hopes for reconciliation or reunion with Protestants.

From a church that, its own scholars admit, hardly ever cited scripture in its literature before Vatican II, the new Catechism makes profuse use of proof texts. And a feature that the Eastern Orthodox appreciate is the liberal use throughout the catechism of citations of church fathers and the ecumenical councils of the early church.

Pope John Paul II and Mother Teresa

Possibly more important to the Catholicism of the twentieth century and to the relations of the Catholic Church to Christians of other communions are the persons of the late Pope John Paul II and Mother Teresa. Before their sojourns were over, the joke was, the main thing, maybe the only thing, Protestants, Orthodox, and Catholics had in common was appreciation for the author and lay theologian C. S. Lewis. But John Paul and Mother Teresa are a level even higher, embodying holiness besides great wisdom and insight into the human spirit. Billy Graham calls the late Pope "unquestionably the most influential voice for morality and peace in the world during the last 100 years," a sentiment shared by the last Soviet leader, Mikhail Gorbachev, who called him, "the highest moral authority on earth."

factum

President George W. Bush remarked of Pope John Paul II, "One journalist, after hearing the new Pope's first blessing in St. Peter's Square wired back to his editors: 'This is not a pope from Poland, this is a pope from Galilee.'"

Likewise, Mother Teresa was so inspiring that a lifelong agnostic journalist and church dissenter, Malcolm Muggeridge, who chose to write a biography of her (*Something Beautiful for God*) and was able to get personal time with her, became a Catholic and spent his latter years writing Christian apologetics. Often her own words reveal her better than those of her admirers. For example, "I once picked up a woman from a garbage dump and she was burning with fever; she was in her last days and her only lament was: 'My son did this to me.' I begged her: You must forgive your son. In a moment of madness, when he was not himself, he did a thing he regrets. Be a mother to him, forgive him. It took me a long time to make her say: 'I forgive my son.' Just before she died in my arms, she was able to say that with a real forgiveness. She was not concerned that she was dying. The breaking of the heart was that her son did not want her. This is something you and I can understand."

CHAPTER 16

Meanwhile, in the East

Most Americans' impression of Eastern Orthodoxy likely comes from gold-leafed onion-domed churches, clergy traveling in cassocks and wearing untrimmed beards, and metropolitans in what seem to be Russian versions of the top hat. To many Americans, such images may invoke the most foreign and distant subculture imaginable. Even the Orthodox observance of Christmas doesn't coincide with the American celebration, many think. And what, they might wonder, does this religion have to do with Jesus and Christianity?

Byzantium: The Orthodox Empire

Paul writes in 1 Corinthians 1:12–13 that he has heard about dissention in the Corinthian Church, that some were following one teaching, one faction were disciples of another teacher, some were Paul's disciples, and some were claiming to be only Jesus' followers. "Is Christ divided," Paul inquires. Likewise, critics of the churches have been known to ask over the millennium since the split between the Latin West and the Greek East, "Is Jesus divided? Is his body split?" And with the Reformation they now ask, "Has he been splintered into not two, but now scores and hundreds of factions and pretenders to the claim of being his true body?"

Is the Catholic body his real expression? Did the Reformation recover what Jesus meant—and what he left of his body—to the world two millennia after his earthly life and sacrifice? Or has the Orthodox representation of Jesus followed the course most faithfully? Is diversity in unity the real key to Jesus? Is the church, the body of Christ, somehow mystically present in all these and more efforts to find and serve him? Such questions can only whet our appetites in this survey, but in raising them we can hope for new insights on these issues.

Byzantium has been discussed in other contexts several times earlier, but now takes center stage in an examination of its particular expression of the Jesus movement. Byzantium, from the name of the village that was built up into the city of Constantinople in the fourth century, is being used here to refer to both the Roman empire in the configuration it took almost a thousand miles east of Rome, and for the ethos of Eastern Orthodoxy, the variation of Christianity that had Greek rather than Latin as its mother tongue.

Historian Eusebius (see Chapter 7) reports that after seeing the vision of a cross in the sky before a crucial battle near Verona, northern Italy, in A.D. 312, Emperor Constantine described it to his colleagues and ordered its likeness rendered in precious metals and gems and raised, accompanied with a banner adorned by the first two letters of the Greek form of "Christ," X and P, (chi, written as X, for "ch," and rho, written as P, for what in the western alphabet is "r"), as well as portraits of himself and his children. Called a labarum, he had it duplicated repeatedly and appointed that it precede his armies into battle.

symbolism

The symbol that Constantine ordered to lead his armies is still used in Orthodox and Roman Catholic religious processions. Called a labarum, it is also often called the chi-rho or a Christogram. Some believe Constantine's labarum was the first time a cross was used to symbolize Christianity.

Constantine the Great

Constantine's vision came in two parts, the appearance of a cross in front of the sun as he marched with his troops in daylight, and in a dream where he was told to conquer under that symbol. Eusebius also records that after his vision sank in, Constantine asked his counselors to explain the religion of the Christians to him.

fallacy

Some sectarian teachers have accused Constantine of corrupting Christianity, merging church and state, or both, thus interrupting the progress of the true faith. Most historians say this claim is unsupported. And most Bible scholars (Catholic, Orthodox, and Protestant) say such actions would have contradicted Jesus' words, "the gates of hell shall not prevail" against the church.

Another historian, Lactanius, an earlier Christian convert and writer of apologetics for his new religion, having been persecuted under Constantine's predecessor Diocletian, was taken under Constantine's wing. He became a tutor of the emperor's son, and probably was one of Constantine's teachers of Christianity. It is thought, however, that Lactanius was not well taught in Christian beliefs, as his apologetic works show little knowledge of the Bible.

Later in life, it is reliably reported, the emperor preferred the company of bishops of the church, and the emperor's active role in addressing the Arian heresy controversy indicates that he was fascinated by discussions of Christian theology or doctrines.

Classical Rome, like Greece, its model, used paganism as what modern sociologists and political scientists call civil religion, the glue that holds the society together. It's possible that the pagan gods of either Greece or Rome were not taken very seriously by the people or the leaders, all considering them mythological, but there is much evidence that the leaders wanted the gods respected and to be called upon to bless their enterprises.

factum

Lord John Julius Norwich ranks Constantine fourth in world influence after Jesus, Buddha, and Mohammed. Constantine's most important decisions include making Christianity a tolerated religion of Rome, and establishing his capital at Byzantium, renamed Constantinople.

The creation of pagan gods accords with the recognition, universal among human cultures, of a spiritual dimension native to mankind: If we want god(s), then such realities must precede our very existence. Plato and Aristotle taught variations on this motif, suggesting that even before pagan people heard of Christ, they were being prepared to look for their savior.

Civil Religion

There is some indication that Constantine consciously chose Christianity as his empire's new civil religion in part because it was growing rapidly despite the extreme measures his predecessors employed to stop it, and in part because when he understood it, regardless of the depth of his faith, it made more sense, and seemed more effective at promoting public welfare, than pagan mythology.

So Constantine was the first world ruler who had to deal with the separation and the interplay between the dominant religion and state or national life, and he was the first to endorse Christianity as his state's leading civil religion. That he may have chosen Christianity out of political motives, as some have written, is not in itself evidence of nefarious motives. Nor does it discount his sincerity, the authenticity of his vision, or his eventual choosing baptism into the church near the end of his life. When something is the right thing to do, it's usually the best choice for a variety of reasons and motivations.

fallacy

Though many think Constantine intended to move to Byzantium, there's no definite reason why he moved his capital from Rome. The eastern region of the empire was the last portion he controlled, so he likely wanted more direct presence there to consolidate his political power. Historians believe he didn't mean to make "New Rome" the only capital; it became that by default.

Constantine's "Control"

Some claim that the fact that Constantine sponsored the Council of Nicea proves that he ran the church, but the fact that controversies like the Arian heresy raged back and forth for decades discounts such claims. The church had no dictator. Bishops at the time were equal and independent, deferential but not required to answer to a synod or the bishop of Rome, and they were scattered from Britain to the Holy Land and Africa.

Though many heresies are recorded as being held from time to time by early bishops, none of the bishops are on record as claiming to have been pressured to conform their teachings to ones Constantine may have wanted to promote. The fact that Constantine was on the side of the heretic Arius for most of the bishops' lives, and that the church still prevailed against Arius, is overwhelming evidence that Constantine did not dictate to the church, as often claimed.

Orthodoxy's Different Take on Salvation

All traditional Christian communions teach that salvation is being in a relationship with the personal God through Jesus, and that salvation is made possible by faith through God's grace. But there are varied interpretations on the teaching of the Apostle Paul that God has highly exalted Jesus and "given him a name which is above every name, that at the name of Jesus every knee should bow, of things in heaven, and things in earth, and things under the earth, and that every tongue should confess that Jesus Christ is Lord, to the glory of God the Father. Wherefore . . . work out your own salvation with fear and trembling" (Philippians 2:9–12).

Why does Paul, the champion of salvation by grace (the gift of God), and whose writings are often used to counter any suggestion of "working" to earn or get grace, exhort his readers in Philippi to "work out your own salvation"? Some might propose that he means this only in the sense of "live out your lives as saved people," but the counter to that idea is that Paul does not waste words or embellish, and is always careful to teach the straight truth, mindful of the dangers of being ambiguous. When he says "work out your own salvation" he means it all.

Keep the Faith

The Orthodox take is that he is referring to the fact that, being under house arrest in Rome, he might not be visiting the Philippians again. They might have found it relatively easy to keep on keeping on when an actual apostle was among them, but the Orthodox feel he is saying, "You're on your own. I'm not around to pick you up and brush you off when you fall. Take care of the gift you've received without my help. You've been saved by faith; now save yourselves by not failing to guard it." In other words, though Jesus is the only savior in the sense of having eternal life that no one else has or can give, Paul might save some just by being around to protect them, to pick up on their lapses in enthusiasm, their starting to backslide. But they can also save themselves in his absence if they will heed his words. They have to work at it. Again, when writing to Timothy, his young bishop over the flock in Ephesus, he tells him to "Study to show yourself approved to God, a workman who need not be ashamed, rightly dividing the word of truth" (2 Timothy 2:15). Even bishops have to work at it.

discussion question

What does the "work" consist of?
The context provided answers the question. "Every knee—the knee of every thing in heaven, and of every thing in earth, and of every thing under the earth" should be subjected to the Lord Jesus. Conversation, thoughts, vocations, avocations, friends, lifestyle, use of money, use of leisure time . . . every thing must be made worthy of God's approval.

Being saved is not just a bath in the baptistery; it's constantly working on not getting dirty again. The Orthodox emphasis on this idea, which is not as readily found in the western churches, is what was cited in Chapter 12 as divinization or theosis, which means saving more and more of the person until all of the person is in Christ and therefore is maximally partaking of the divine nature.

Salvation Past, Present, and Future

So for the Orthodox, salvation is past (been there), present (doing it), and future (going farther). Some part of the person has already been changed by grace and sealed in baptism, some is still being remodeled by faith, and some will be revealed as still needing work as grace abounds or becomes more visible in the saved person's life.

A second difference in the understanding of salvation is the purpose of the atonement. Though the Orthodox do not take issue with the traditional biblical references used by western theologians in support of their doctrine of penal substitutionary atonement derived from Augustine of Hippo (such passages as Isaiah 53:6–10; Romans 1:18; 3:22–5; 5:8–9; 2 Corinthians 5:21; Galatians 3:13; Hebrews 9:11–28; 1 Peter 3:18; and 1 John 4:10), Orthodox fathers have never emphasized the penal aspect, which sometimes gets presented as God the Father angrily punishing his Son on the cross to get vengeance for human sin (some have even called it "divine parental child abuse"). God's love and Jesus' love, not the vengeful wrath of any person of the Trinity, sent Jesus to the cross for humanity's sins, in the Orthodox emphasis.

Salvation from Death

A third difference in the understanding of salvation between western and eastern Christendom, linked to the second difference, is the emphasis on what salvation is from. In western teaching it is often expressed as salvation from sin, but Orthodox teachers more generally emphasize the salvation from the effect (or wages) of sin, which is death. Salvation is centered more in the resurrection, and victory over death, than on the atonement of Jesus wrought on the Cross, which was the means to the victorious end. This is not to say Orthodoxy minimizes the work of Jesus on the cross or the atoning sacrifice of Jesus as Lamb of God (language that is part of every Eucharistic offering in the Orthodox church), but that the main emphasis is the paschal (Easter) morning rather than the Good Friday afternoon.

Orthodoxy does not charge St. Augustine of heresy in his different emphases; he is regarded a saint of the preschism church by Orthodoxy as well as by Catholicism. Orthodox opinion does think Augustine's atonement emphasis has been exaggerated in the works of Luther and Calvin and in some attempts to popularize these views, and considers these other perceptions a somewhat inferior understanding of the core meaning of salvation.

Between Constantine and Czar Nicholas II

How did the Jesus movement fare after Constantine the Great? After his death in 337, Constantine's sons governed the empire, with Constantine II in the west; Constantius II in Constantinople; and the youngest, Constans, in the central prefecture, composed of Italy, Africa, and Illyricum. Challenges to the brothers' rule from outside pretenders eventually left Constantius II (the namesake of Constantine's father) the sole ruler of the empire.

Constantius II was strongly Arian in his Christian preferences, resisting the first draft of the Nicene Creed, but also attempted to enforce reforms based on Christian doctrines, like outlawing magic and dismantling pagan temples. One account says that he called a church council in A.D. 360 (which is not recognized by the surviving church) to issue a revised, Arian, creed.

And apparently, after visiting Rome and seeing the continued splendor of that city's pagan temples, he lost his enthusiasm for dismantling them. His reign from 337 until his death in 361 is one of the longest of any Roman emperor.

Constantius II was succeeded by Julian the Apostate, a cousin of Constantius as the son of a half brother of Constantine. One of his first acts after succeeding Constantius II was declaring his strong commitment to paganism, and he began disenfranchising the Christians and undoing their gains since Constantine's edict of toleration. He died just two years after Constantius II, in a battle with Persians on a canal between the Tigris and the Euphrates rivers.

factum

Emperor Valentinian was a Christian supporter of the orthodox (or Nicene) Christians and a supporter of absolute religious freedom, while Valens was an Arian who persecuted the Nicean party, as well as pagans.

Jovian (Flavius Iovianus in Latin, c. 332–364) was a soldier and a Christian the army selected to succeed Julian, but he ruled less than a year, dying from an accidental asphyxiation. Valentinian, who the army also chose, ruled for eleven years in the west (from Milan and cities in Gaul), and after his succession appointed his brother Valens to rule the east from Constantinople.

Valentinian was succeeded by his son, Gratian, at nineteen years of age. He, in turn, appointed Theodosius I to rule the east on the death of his uncle Valens in A.D. 379. Under Gratian, who was counseled by Bishop Ambrose of Milan (the first bishop so popular that he could be seen as a threat to the government), pagan practices were curtailed and orthodox Christianity dominated the entire empire for the first time.

Rebel generals assassinated Gratian in 383, after which Theodosius I, ruling in Constantinople, emerged as the most powerful Caesar. He also turned out to be the last emperor of the entire empire, east and west, was the one to declare Christianity the state religion, and called the First Council of Constantinople in A.D. 381 to ratify the First Ecumenical Council, fine-tune the Nicene Creed, and finally settle the Arian controversies.

The Eastern Empire, though marked as the unified empire had been by ups and downs, expansions and contractions, continued for another millennium, until the fall of Constantinople under Constantine XI to Ottoman Sultan Mehmed II in 1453. While the pope of Rome became the figurehead successor of the western caesars (as the primary focal point for western European cultural integration and progress), the Eastern Orthodox Church, under its equal and independent bishops (though not officially separate from its western counterparts until 1054), continued to make spiritual progress.

discussion question

When did Rome fall?
Visigoths sacked Rome in A.D. 410 under Alaric, and the fall of the Western Roman Empire was underway. The empire ended officially when Odoacer, a German tribal chieftain, deposed Romulus Augustus in A.D. 476.

Second-Longest Surviving Empire

The Byzantine or, more properly, the Eastern Roman Empire, under Orthodox influence and tutelage, is one of the longest-lasting empires in world history. If it is considered as the successor of the Roman Empire (as most historians would), the Roman Empire lasted just twenty years fewer than the Chinese Empire founded in 221 B.C. by Qin Shi Huangdi, which lasted until 1279.

The leader of the Bulgarian Empire claimed the title czar (also spelled tsar and tzar), meaning caesar, when it had a victory over the "Byzantine" Empire in A.D. 913. Ivan IV of Russia also appropriated it for himself in 1547, and some Russian Orthodox promote the claim that Russia succeeded Byzantium as the next embodiment of the spirit of the Roman Empire. This claim may be an attempt to promote the patriarch of Moscow, the leader of the world's largest Orthodox church, as the rightful Orthodox hierarch deserving the place of highest honor among Orthodox bishops, but as long as the Russian Orthodox remain in communion with the ecumenical patriarch in Istanbul, they can't press that case very far. And there's little evidence to support Moscow's claim that, since the rise and fall of the Soviet Union, it has the largest membership in the Orthodox world.

Piety of Nicholas II

The biographies of the last czar of Russia, Nicholas II (who was executed with his family in Yekaterinburg by the Bolsheviks), leave little doubt that he was a successor in the tradition of religious Byzantine emperors. His biographers say he and his czarina Alexandra were pious Orthodox believers, and that he was motivated because of his convictions to abdicate his throne, believing it was the best thing for his people when the Communists overthrew his government.

Icons, Saints, and Monasticism

For Orthodox believers, the church's witness to Christ through the lives of its saints and martyrs, and the consistent teaching of its fathers and preaching of its pastors are of utmost importance. Saints and martyrs overlap in the church's teaching, as to be a true martyr for confessing Christ is to be a saint. Thousands were martyred in the early church, and probably millions more saints were made in the twentieth-century church during the reigns of Stalin, Hitler, and other dictators.

Saints are considered to be icons of Christ in Orthodoxy, an understanding that is related to the Orthodox teaching on theosis, or believers struggling with their passions to become partakers of the divine nature. Saints, perfected people, are windows to heaven and images of Jesus. And icons (wood and paint representations of saints) are windows to the saints, which in turn open on to the presence of the Lord.

fallacy

Though Orthodox worshippers appear to venerate or even worship icons, they are taught that the veneration is only to that which the icons represent, in other words the saints depicted, and that the saints in turn are depictions or representations of God in Jesus Christ.

Saints, though gone to glory, are not dead but living, as Jesus said regarding the meaning of the resurrection: "Have you not read what God said to you, 'I am the God of Abraham, the God of Isaac, and the God of Jacob?' God is not the God of the dead, but of the living" (Matthew 22:31–32).

Monasticism, as a school in which to train the passions or re-educate human nature to divine ends, is also seen in Orthodoxy as integral to making saints. Though most monks and nuns are not thought of as achieving the level of perfection that leads to talk of sainthood, most of those who do achieve that level of retraining, apart from those suffering physical martyrdom, are men and women who take up the monastic life.

discussion question

Who was St. Seraphim of Sarov?
St. Seraphim of Sarov (1759-1833) has been an inspiration to thousands who chose the pursuit of theosis. The purpose of life, he taught, was to acquire the Holy Spirit. "Acquire the Holy Spirit, and thousands around you will acquire salvation" was his answer to how to best become a witness for the Gospel.

There are still many Orthodox monasteries in Russia (most of the ones now in use have been rehabilitated after the fall of the Communists), Greece,

Romania, and even a few in Great Britain and the United States. The oldest one that has been in existence from ancient times is St. Catherine's Monastery in the Sinai Peninsula between Egypt and the Holy Land, which was begun in the fifth century A.D. with support of Emperor Justinian. The most famous center of Orthodox monasticism is Mount Athos, a rugged peninsula that juts into the sea near Thessaloniki in northern Greece. It is the home of scores of large monastic communities, most of which are accessible only by boat from the sea and, once off the boat, by footpaths.

The Jesus Prayer

The Way of the Pilgrim is a story, now available in paperback book form, by an anonymous writer. In 1884, the abbot of St. Michael's Monastery at Kazan found the story in the possession of a monk at Mt. Athos. The tale is set in Russia before 1861. The story tells of a wandering man looking for a way to pray without ceasing, as the Apostle Paul teaches in 1 Thessalonians 5:17.

Eventually, the pilgrim finds a monk who counsels him that, according to the teaching in *The Philakalia* (*The Love of Good Things*, a four-volume work of teachings on how to pursue the spiritual life, by fathers of the church), the way to achieve this state of spiritual advance is by reciting the Jesus Prayer continually. The Jesus prayer is, "Lord Jesus Christ, Son of God, have mercy on me, a sinner."

factum

Advocates of the prayer recommend using variations for praying for others, such as, "Lord have mercy on dear Patricia, who is ill with the flu," or, "Raymond who is struggling with anger," without judgmentally calling anyone else a sinner.

In *The Way of the Pilgrim*, the young man is told to start by reciting the prayer 3,000 times a day, using a knotted prayer rope to keep count of his total. Eventually, he says he was counseled to move his total repetitions per day up to 20,000.

Eastern Christianity Missionizing the West

In *Becoming Orthodox*, Father Peter Gillquist tells the story of a nationwide fellowship of evangelicals, whose leaders had begun as staff members of Campus Crusade for Christ in the 1960s, setting out to find the most perfect expression of the church they could. Though some of them were already ordained as Presbyterian or Baptist, or had backgrounds with charismatic and other traditionally conservative evangelical churches, the more they searched, the less satisfied they became. Eventually, they decided to form their own denomination, and trying as best they could to make it conform to all the New Testament had to say about the early church, they launched another Protestant church.

But eventually someone noticed that the church they'd come up with was similar to the Orthodox Church, which they hadn't even considered in their initial search, so foreign to them was the idea. And on that realization, they went back to the source documents and found some additional changes that made their church look even more like the Orthodox Church.

discussion question

Do the Orthodox set out to convert members of other communions?
Orthodoxy officially does not proselytize, and the Orthodox jurisdictions (the largest are the Orthodox Church of America, the Greek Orthodox Archdiocese of North America, and the Antiochian Orthodox Archdiocese) would not say they're out looking for converts from other communions. However, many books like Fr. Peter Gillquist's indirectly support that end.

Finally, they merged their fellowship of nearly 2,000 believers across the country into an established Orthodox jurisdiction in communion with the ecumenical patriarch in Constantinople. But theirs is only a small portion of a similar pattern of long-time Protestants, and some Catholics, converting to Orthodoxy in the United States, and, to some extent, in Great Britain. Over half of all the Orthodox priests in the United States now are converts from other faith communities, and the movement continues.

CHAPTER 17

Evangelicalism

Evangelicalism has been a major force in American society since before the representatives of the thirteen original states declared themselves a nation at the Continental Congress in 1776. By that time, the First Great Awakening, or first nationwide religious revival, had passed its peak, but its effect was still being felt in the churches, mindsets, and lifestyles of many of the great number of rural Americans too isolated to be able to attend church regularly.

The New Force in Church Growth

It was only since the Democratic presidential campaign of Jimmy Carter in 1976 that evangelicalism has re-emerged from a relatively dormant phase back into general American consciousness as a dominant religious force in public life. And whereas the Great Awakening revival supported liberal reforms, and especially the political aspirations of Thomas Jefferson, himself not an orthodox Christian, by A.D. 2000 the American evangelical world had swung to the opposite political pole to make possible the election of conservative George W. Bush in 2000 and 2004.

How does the Jesus movement fare in the first decade of the third millennium A.D.? The world total of adherents to Christianity is approximately 2.1 billion; compared with Islam, 1.3 billion; secular-irreligious-atheist, 1.1 billion; Hinduism, 900 million; Chinese traditionalism (Taoism and others), 394 million; Buddhists, 376 million, and many others, all under 25 million (probably of most interest in current events, Judaism has 15 million adherents).

factum

Among the Christian groups, Catholicism is by far the largest, with 1.1 billion adherents, with an estimated 675 million Protestants in the world, ranging from the most traditional (Lutherans, Anglicans, and Calvinists) to some out of the range of the orthodox definition of Christian, like Mormons and Unitarians.

Among the Protestants, the fastest growing group of all is the Pentecostals, who account for an estimated 100 million Protestants worldwide, after having originated little more than a century ago. If Pentecostals are seen as a subset of evangelicals (where, most, but not all Pentecostals fall), it is clear that evangelicalism in general is the fastest-growing segment of Christendom.

Defining Christian groups isn't easy. Some statistical studies want to lump together Catholics and the most Catholic–like groups, by which they mean Anglicans and the Orthodox, though most adherents of Anglican and Orthodox confessions would probably resist this categorizing. Though many Anglicans have taken to resisting being classified as Protestant, English law requires that the monarch be a Protestant, by which it is generally understood to mean "an Anglican," that being the established church of England. So in that sense Anglicanism is definitely Protestant, and its defining thirty-nine articles are definitely part of the Protestant Reformation.

Anglicanism's American branch, the Episcopal Church, was until recent years known officially as the Protestant Episcopal Church. Many Orthodox feel that their differences with Catholicism put them closer to (though by no means in) the Protestant camp, rather than the Catholic one. Orthodoxy's long membership in the World Council of Churches, an agency established and run by Protestants, accords with this opinion.

fallacy

"Speaking in tongues" doesn't appear in church history from the second through nineteenth centuries. In 1901, Agnes Ozman talked in tongues at Bethel Bible College in Topeka. Considered a sign of the Holy Spirit, it spread to the Holiness movement. In 1906, people began speaking in tongues during the Azusa Street Revival in Los Angeles. Many consider that revival the beginning of Pentecostalism.

Likewise, the vast majority of Pentecostals, who are generally defined as believing in a need for "being filled by the Holy Spirit" and in signs of that filling, like gifts of healing and speaking in tongues, are products of American evangelicalism and its exportation to places like Brazil and other far-flung mission areas. But some Pentecostals are not Trinitarian. And some denominations, mostly aligned with theologically liberal mainline Protestantism, most notably the Evangelical Lutheran Church of America, are not in the evangelical column, as that word is popularly used.

Big Names: Graham, Robertson, Dobson

In America, the most visible evangelical denominations are Baptist, especially the Southern Baptists, which is by far the largest Protestant denomination, with nearly 19 million adherents. The only other American religious group to exceed 10 million members is the United Methodists, which is much larger than any other relatively liberal church, with 11 million believers. More or less tied for third place among American religious communities are Jewish people and Evangelical (liberal) Lutherans, with over five million adherents each.

discussion question

What are the post-Reformation Protestant groups?
Baptists and Methodists come from the First Great Awakening, led by John Wesley (the Anglican who founded Methodism), and John Whitfield, the Calvinist whose preaching boosted American Presbyterian, Reformed, and Congregational denominations and ignited the then-fledgling Baptists. Most Pentecostals are offshoots of Methodist Holiness movements.

While English evangelists Wesley and Whitefield, and American Presbyterian intellectual Jonathan Edwards were the spiritual icons of American Revolution-era evangelicalism, the subsequent awakenings as well as the current evangelical movement are seen primarily as revolving around spiritual leaders like Billy Graham, Pat Robertson, Jerry Falwell, James Dobson, and others. All but Dobson are Southern Baptist, and all of them are influential in many other churches and institutions as well.

Billy Graham (b. 1918)

Billy Graham has been the most widely recognized religious leader in the United States since at least 1950, and has been one of the Gallup Poll's "ten most admired men" in the world forty-seven times since 1955, including forty consecutive citations, more than any other world figure, making him the most admired individual by Americans overall for the past four decades.

He was ordained in 1939 in the Southern Baptist Church and received his degree from Wheaton College in Illinois in 1943. He pastored a Baptist church in Illinois for several years before joining the staff of Youth for Christ as an evangelist, later founding the Billy Graham Evangelistic Association in Minneapolis.

factum

Billy Graham's 1949 evangelistic crusade in a tent in downtown Los Angeles was extended because of overflow attendance from the originally planned three weeks to eight weeks, gaining him national media attention. He went on to conduct similarly extended crusades in London and in New York and has been the world evangelist without peer ever since.

Though he began his ministry with messages often characterized as having strong politically conservative implications, criticism of Graham's ministry has come mostly from conservative voices, usually self-identified as fundamentalists to Graham's right, like the late Carl McIntire and, earlier in his ministry, Jerry Falwell. Their main complaint has been regarding the inclusiveness of his crusades, which he has consistently insisted be supported by citywide clergy and church associations, regardless of the orthodoxy of the ministers or their churches.

Graham doesn't respond to such critics, but those who interpret his actions favorably seem satisfied that in the long run his policy has enabled the Gospel to be preached to thousands who wouldn't have been in his audience if he were less inclusive, and that the net effect of his ministry has been strengthening the conservative and evangelical churches, while the liberal ones represented on the dais have consistently experienced membership declines.

A more general criticism has been that most of the commitments to Christ in his crusades don't seem to stick, and, despite his success at reaching probably more people in live appearances than any other preacher in history, no widespread revival comparable to the Great Awakening has taken place during his decades of active ministry (history may eventually dispute this claim).

Through his publishing, radio and television ministries, and his being instrumental in the founding of *Christianity Today* (arguably the only socially significant periodical in the United States with a clearly identifiable religious position), Graham undoubtedly gets major credit for the rise of evangelicalism to its current prominence.

Pat Robertson (b. 1930)

The son of a longtime United States congressman and senator from Virginia, after graduating magna cum laude with his Bachelor of Arts degree from Washington and Lee in 1950, Marion Gordon "Pat" Robertson served as the assistant adjutant of the First Marine Division in combat in Korea. He was promoted to first lieutenant in 1952 upon returning to the United States. Robertson received a J.D. from Yale University Law School in 1955 and a Master of Divinity from New York Theological Seminary in 1959.

Robertson hosts a television program called *The 700 Club*. Approximately half of this program is devoted to reporting and interpreting current events from Robertson's and his other hosts' perspectives.

Though detractors call Robertson a "televangelist," he prefers to be considered a "religious broadcaster, educator, religious leader, businessman, author, and philanthropist" as founder and chairman of CBN Inc., founder of International Family Entertainment, Inc., and because of his involvement with Regent University, Operation Blessing International Relief and Development Corporation, American Center for Law and Justice, The Flying Hospital, Inc., and several other enterprises. He was ordained a Southern Baptist minister in 1961 but surrendered his credential to run for president in 1986. He is also a figure in the charismatic movement by virtue of the word of knowledge healings and other miracles that are a regular feature of *The 700 Club*.

discussion question

How did Pat Robertson become the most visible Christian on television?
In 1960, Robertson raised funds to buy a bankrupt television station in Virginia, launching the Christian Broadcasting Network. Today, CBN produces programs in seventy languages seen in 200 nations. The network's best known program, *The 700 Club*, which Robertson hosts, is one of the longest-running religious television shows, and reaches an average of one million American viewers daily.

The International Family Entertainment company he founded developed the cable Family Channel and branched out into entertainment program production before he sold it to Fox Kids for $1.9 billion. The Family Channel was subsequently acquired by Disney's American Broadcasting Company. Now it is billed as ABC Family Network and is still contractually bound to carry *The 700 Club* as part of the terms of sale.

The American Center for Law and Justice that Robertson launched as an alternative to the American Civil Liberties Union has been in the forefront of legal actions defending Christian expression in the public square, especially public schools. In his 1986 campaign for the Republican nomination for president of the United States, he polled second in the early Iowa caucuses of that campaign, which was eventually won by George H. W. Bush, who was given Robertson's support in the party's national convention and subsequently won the office.

After Robertson's presidential campaign, he founded the Christian Coalition to continue supporting conservative political goals. It was a strong force in George W. H. Bush's second, failing campaign, but Robertson left the Coalition in 2001, turning leadership over to Ralph Reed who, in turn, left it in the hands of Roberta Combs.

Though often criticized in the mainstream press for remarks suggesting that the terrorist attacks on the World Trade Center and the Pentagon were God's retribution for American decadence, and later calling for the assassination of Venezuela's anti-American President Hugo Chavez, his constant exposure to a sizable audience and his generally erudite apologetics for his views tend to keep him one of the most influential American evangelicals.

Jerry Falwell (b. 1933)

A Lynchburg, Virginia, pastor and founder of the now-defunct Moral Majority (1979–1989), Jerry Lamon Falwell was one of the country's first pastors of what is called a megachurch. In Falwell's case, Thomas Road Baptist Church in Lynchburg has grown from a starting core of thirty-five adults in a temporary location in 1956 to a congregation of 24,000 in a city of 65,000. For some decades, the most visible proponent of self-described fundamentalist evangelicalism in the United States, and a member of the Bible Baptist Fellowship International, he changed his membership to the more moderate Southern Baptist Convention.

Voted one of the ten most admired men in America in a *Good Housekeeping* poll, Falwell was named one of the twenty-five most influential people in America in *U.S. News & World Report* in 1983, and has been featured on the covers of both *Time* and *Newsweek*. His Moral Majority claims to have been the first conservative organization labeled as the Christian right by the media, and to have started the campaign to elect Ronald Reagan president in 1980.

James Dobson (b. 1936)

An associate clinical professor of pediatrics at the University of Southern California School of Medicine for fourteen years, James Dobson also spent seventeen years in the division of child development and medical genetics while on the staff of the Children's Hospital of Los Angeles before launching his Christian psychology radio program, *Focus on the Family*.

His book on child discipline, *Dare to Discipline,* got widespread media attention for its approval of moderate spanking of children under age eight. The ministry, begun as a twenty-five-minute weekly discussion radio program in 1977 from Arcadia, California, has been relocated to Colorado Springs, Colorado, and employs some 1,300 staff members. Its public policy arm, the Family Research Council, is considered a major influence on government policies, extending to the White House.

factum

Dobson holds a Ph.D. in child development from the University of Southern California, and his first book, *Dare to Discipline* (1970), sold over three million copies among Christian families. His radio program now airs on 3,000 radio stations in the United States, and thousands more in other countries, and is heard by more than 200 million listeners daily.

Peale and Schuler

In the last half century, the only other members of the American Protestant clergy to become household names to any extent approaching the ones previously mentioned have been the late Norman Vincent Peale of New York City, and Robert Schuler of Garden Grove, California. Both were ordained in the Reformed Church in America, possibly the closest thing to a moderate denomination in the United States, if that is taken to mean midway between theologically liberal and conservative. Though both have described their denomination as similar to Methodism, in theology it is closer to the Presbyterian churches, with a Calvinist background. But socially, or socio-politically, it is very close to the United Methodists, who have many individual conservative evangelicals (like American Family Association founder and head Donald Wildmon) but is controlled by a liberal denominational establishment. Peale and Schuler carefully sidestepped making statements that could be called over the line from orthodoxy, but the emphases of their preaching and books have been more psychological, relational, and inclusive than evangelistic, and are more for believers than aimed at converting non-Christians.

Other Names: D. James Kennedy, Schaeffer, Pearcey

D. James Kennedy (b. 1930)

D. James Kennedy is pastor of the 10,000-member Coral Ridge Presbyterian Church in Fort Lauderdale, Florida, and claims to be "the most listened-to Presbyterian minister in America." His originally forty-five-member congregation was the fastest-growing church in the nation for fifteen years, which was the impetus for his writing *Evangelism Explosion*, which has been used as a cookbook for other congregations wanting to see similar growth results. His weekly televised services, called the *Coral Ridge Hour*, and his daily half-hour radio program, *Truths that Transform*, reach a national audience. His Coral Ridge Ministries includes the Center for Reclaiming America, which provides conferences, literature, and networking opportunities to Christians concerned about the nation's spiritual health.

Francis Schaeffer (1912—1984)

Francis Schaeffer was an evangelical Presbyterian minister who settled with his family in a remote chalet in Switzerland that he named *L'Abri* (French for "shelter") and waited for the world to come to him so he could convert it. Surprisingly, eventually it started to do so, as backpacking young tourists and truth-seekers found L'Abri and soon afterward found their worlds turned upside down this knickers-wearing and goateed American Calvinist transplant. *Time* magazine dubbed Schaeffer "an apostle to the intellectuals," and InterVarsity Christian Fellowship writer Gordon Govier wrote on the observance of the fiftieth anniversary of L'Abri that Schaeffer "may have done more to shape the culture of American evangelicals at the end of the 20th century than any one" other than C. S. Lewis and Billy Graham. This echoed similar sentiments by former University of Notre Dame professor Michael Hamilton in a 1997 piece on Schaeffer in *Christianity Today*.

Though Schaeffer's direct outreach was much smaller than the other evangelical icons discussed thus far—his books like *The God Who Is There*, *Escape from Reason*, *He Is There and He Is Not Silent*, and others had considerably smaller circulations than others cited—his critique of every philosophical trend from the Enlightenment to the current generation; and his knowledge of artists of all eras since the Renaissance and popular culture represented in music and movies reached the intellectuals and future intellectuals who came to visit. Often they ended up staying longer than they expected and coming back for more, and being changed for the rest of their lives. And they, now in places like college and university faculties, the media, politics, entertainment, and the arts are making the kind of impact he said Christians were meant to make in the culture of their times.

factum

James Sire, retired editor of Inter-Varsity Press, which published most of Schaeffer's books, likens him to "Jeremiah, a weeping prophet whose message was that Christians need to be more involved in the public sphere."

Nancy Pearcey

Nancy Pearcey is an example of one of those young seekers who found L'Abri and got converted back to Jesus and new meaning in her life. Raised in a Lutheran family and a devout child, like many she came to wonder if her faith was just there because it was all she'd been taught, and quietly and somewhat sadly, by the time she was in college, she'd left it behind. She says Schaeffer explained and demonstrated what the faith actually was—who Jesus really was—and slowly she started the metaphorical trek back home.

Now she is the author of *Total Truth: Liberating Christianity from Its Cultural Captivity*, a tour-de-force survey of the Christian worldview and its viability in opposition to secularism and post-modernism, which demonstrates that she has been blessed by Francis Schaeffer's influence. Appropriately, she is the Francis A. Schaeffer scholar at the Asheville, N.C.-based World Journalism Institute. Among other topics, her book covers the history of evangelical Christianity in America from colonial times, the chronicle of how American politics became secularized, modern Islam and the New Age movement, and the war between materialism and a Christian worldview.

Campus Crusade for Christ and InterVarsity Christian Fellowship

Probably no other single organization, including any denomination, has impacted the evangelical world more widely and deeply since its founding in 1951 by Bill and Vonette Bright at the University of California at Los Angeles than Campus Crusade for Christ. A veritable army of young evangelists who support themselves by raising pledges of sustaining contributions through friends, family, and churches, it is found at work in most campuses and many other locations, like high schools and military bases, around the world.

Some fellow evangelicals criticize the ministry for superficiality, as its "Four Spiritual Laws" booklet, used to begin most evangelistic conversations on campuses, omits some basic Christian teachings. Defenders maintain any shortcomings in the entrée mechanism are offset by intensive discipleship and fellowship, often spanning years of campus life.

factum

Campus Crusade is the largest evangelical organization in the United States, according to *USA Today* and others. Even governmental offices are targeted for outreach by Crusade staff members, through so-called Christian embassies in Washington and near the United Nations. Its film, *Jesus*, has been shown around the world more widely than any other film ever produced, Crusade spokespersons claim.

Though many see the modern secular university campuses as an unlikely environment for Christians and their faith, ministries like Campus Crusade, InterVarsity Christian Fellowship, Navigators, and other church-based and independent campus ministries help evangelical young adults get through the challenges of college life. These groups usually co-operate and try to be mutually supportive of major programs, though sometimes territorial disputes are claimed.

Part of the International Fellowship of Evangelical Students, InterVarsity, oriented more to serving already-persuaded Christian students than evangelizing, had 810 chapters at 560 campuses throughout the United States in the most recent year for which figures were available. Chapters are often organized around needs of specific student groups, like ethnic minorities (especially Asian Christian students), graduate students, and others. Tracing its roots to Cambridge University in 1877, the American branch has been incorporated since 1941, following InterVarsity's establishment in Canada by British campus missionary Howard Guinness. As of the latest reported figures, there are 1,000 InterVarsity staff members serving 35,000 American student members.

factum

InterVarsity Press supplies academically oriented books (like Schaeffer's, on trends in philosophy, the arts, and culture) to campus groups, adding 100 titles annually, with 800 currently in print. For years, campus chapters sold the books from tables in common areas, but since the 1970s, the books have been widely available through Christian booksellers and, more recently, secular bookstores.

Navigators dates its now-international ministry to 1933, when a southern California Sunday-school teacher, Dawson Trotman, enlisted his high school–aged class to join him in evangelizing sailors serving on nearby U.S. Navy facilities. Out of this work came the Navigators' ministry of spiritual multiplication. Today staff members minister to military installations around the world, on college campuses, and in many other locations. The Navigators have long led the after-decision follow-up ministry to Billy Graham evangelistic crusade converts. Incorporated in California in 1943, its headquarters is currently in Colorado Springs, Colorado.

The Christian College Movement

Though the original universities and other higher educational institutions were begun to serve their understanding of Jesus, many, like Oxford in England, Harvard in New England, and the University of Pennsylvania in Philadelphia (founded with financial support by Great Awakening evangelist John Whitefield) moved away from a Christian worldview once a secular humanist one was being widely accepted in academic circles. American evangelicals have attempted to counter this trend by establishing new Christ-centered (evangelical) colleges and universities.

According to the Council for Christian Colleges and Universities, only 102 American colleges are Christ centered. These member institutions are listed, along with associate members, in Appendix C: Evangelical Christian Institutions.

discussion question

How many American colleges are religious?
According to United States Department of Education figures, there are over 4,000 degree-granting higher educational institutions in the country, 1,600 of which are private nonprofit institutions, and 900 describe themselves as religiously affiliated.

Evangelical Media Initiatives

Pat Robertson's development of the Family Channel and the development of its related businesses were the furthest advances evangelicals ever made into that suspect world. Generations of preachers before Robertson considered the entertainment industry to be too worldly. But Robertson felt creating programming for his network was always a daunting challenge, since he wanted to avoid criticism and yet turn out commercially viable entertainment.

A former student at Wheaton (Illinois) College, who recalled the visit there in 1965 of Francis Schaeffer, told an interviewer that, at that time, some students were pushing school administrators to permit the showing on campus of movies like *Bambi*, a situation reversed over time because of Schaeffer's teaching. His lectures and books say that films and popular culture must be understood in order to better understand how Jesus' teachings apply to current culture.

Since Mel Gibson's phenomenally successful 2004 film, *The Passion of the Christ*, many serious Christians have expressed hope that what they had long perceived as the negative Hollywood attitude toward Christians may be past. *Christianity Today* reports that Christians in the entertainment industry are well entrenched and organized for mutual support and fellowship.

symbolism

For much of movie history, and still true in some evangelical circles, movies and evangelicals have had strained relations, the movies symbolizing the worst of worldliness, according to some preachers. The fact that whole churches went to see Gibson's *The Passion of the Christ* or rented it to show in their halls or sanctuaries is considered a historic turning point.

Many other efforts by Christians to offer viable Christian media, both aimed at the general public and the Christian subculture, have met with mixed reception, most not long sustained. One notable exceptions is *World* magazine, a Christian alternative to the mainstream news magazines, which is in its twentieth year of publication in a full-color format comparable to its much more famous counterparts. An outgrowth of the former *Presbyterian Journal* published by L. Nelson Bell (who also was a co-founder of *Christianity Today*), the founding editor and current CEO of *World* is Joel Belz.

World's editor-in-chief is University of Texas journalism professor Marvin Olasky, the author of *Compassionate Conservatism* and *The American Leadership Tradition*. Olasky has been credited with being the policy wonk behind the Clinton administration's welfare-reform legislation, and critics have blamed him for having had a hand in inspiring the Bush administration's faith-based initiatives programs. Published fifty times a year, *World* magazine claims to follow *Time*, *Newsweek*, and *U.S. News & World Report* as the fourth most widely read weekly newsmagazine in the United States.

Finally in 1965 Billy Graham founded *Christianity Today,* with theologian Carl F. H. Henry serving as its founding editor. Slotted as an evangelical alternative to the liberal and considerably older *Christian Century,* it has since left its competitor far behind, regularly reaching two million readers through its print and online editions.

CHAPTER 18

Jesus and the Culture Wars

During a public debate in 1999 among Republican candidates Steve Forbes, Alan Keyes, and George W. Bush for their party's nomination for president, they were asked which political philosopher or thinker had influenced them. Bush answered, "Christ, because he changed my heart." Some questioned whether the term "political philosopher or thinker" really applies to Jesus, but Bush's answer was well received by the public at large and was quickly taken up by the mainstream media pundits as another volley in the so-called culture wars.

The Apolitical Jesus

In the Sermon on the Mount, Jesus made it plain that he was no revolutionary, and that his was not a political movement (Matthew 5:17–20). In another case, he even advocated that the people of Judea pay their taxes, even though the taxes amounted to tribute the Judeans were forced to pay to their oppressors (see Luke 20:19–26). This "give to Caesar what is Caesar's" passage has been used for centuries to support the doctrine of separation of church and state, which was a founding principle of the American nation. American Protestants, especially, have been partial to this teaching of Jesus because, since the Great Awakening, when the new evangelical converts started to outnumber the old established-church members, it became more popular to be opposed to established churches that had previously been recognized as official state churches.

All of the original American states except Maryland (which was founded by Catholics) had its own established church, but after the Great Awakening, when new denominations came to dominate, the sentiment began to turn against having established churches.

fallacy

Some think that Pat Buchanan—erstwhile White House staff member, syndicated columnist, and conservative TV talking head—wrote the book on the culture wars, but actually he only gave a speech invoking the term at the 1992 Republican National Convention, a reference that ignited significant controversy. Many other books have taken up the culture-war theme.

No Established Church

"No established church" was what the separation of church and state meant for most of American history. The actual words of the First Amendment of the U.S. Constitution prohibit the "establishment of religion," meaning a tax-supported state church. Today most active American Protestants are now much more comfortable and trusting of their Catholic neighbors than they are of secularists, deists, and free-thinkers who claim to be in the tradition of Thomas Paine, Benjamin Franklin, and Thomas Jefferson. This was not the case in the era of the American War for Independence and the century and a half afterward.

Caesar's Due

As mentioned previously, when Jesus was asked if was okay to pay tribute to Caesar, he answered, "Render to Caesar what is Caesar's." Thousands might have been spared martyrdom if they said they were "just rendering to Caesar" and followed Roman law by sacrificing to the imperial deity's likeness. But if any early Christians used that defense, it hasn't been kept in the early church annals, as the memory of those who died is.

Following in the tradition of the martyrs who were burned alive rather than burn incense to Caesar, the fourth-century Christians whom Emperor Constantine consulted about his newfound faith apparently did not tell him he had no political responsibility before God; or that government is politics and faith is religion, and the two shall never mingle. Instead, they introduced him to the many teachings of Jesus, Paul, and the Old Testament concerning the imperative for righteousness and justice in all human pursuits, including law and government, and he immediately began reforming his government.

The discussion in Chapter 8 of Matthew 21:19–21, about the withering of the fig tree and Jesus' promising a faith that would move a mountain, involved interpreting the fig tree as Israel, the nation the church would leave behind; and the mountain as Rome, the empire the church would move from paganism to widespread belief in him. The political implications are apparent: Jesus has the power to change everything, and over time and with faithful obedience and sacrifice, faith moves mountains and can change systems of government from the bottom up.

Red State/Blue State, Left/Right, Sheep/Goats

In Matthew 25:31–33 Jesus foretells the great judgment. "When the Son of Man shall come in his glory, and all the holy angels with him, he shall sit on the throne of his glory and all nations shall be gathered before him. And he shall separate them one from another, as a shepherd divides his sheep from the goats, and he shall set the sheep on his right hand, but the goats on the left." His words no doubt struck a familiar chord with his Jewish audience, familiar with Psalm 33:12, "Blessed is the nation whose God is the Lord; and the people he has chosen for his own inheritance." And a very similar one on the way to win God's favor: "Righteousness exalts a nation, but sin brings reproach to any people" (Psalm 14:34).

Many conservative Christians use these verses from the Psalms to make a case for bringing more godliness to America or even making it, or declaring it, a Christian nation. But liberal critics see a specter of theocracy in such talk, and sociologists suspect that what the conservative Christians are doing is promoting their religion as America's civil religion.

Theocracy

"Theocracy," or a government subject to a religious authority, has become a label in many media treatments of Christian political action, especially when describing the political initiatives of the red-state conservatives. Writing in the *Village Voice* before the second George W. Bush election tallies were complete, James Ridgeway, under the headline, "Bush gets mandate for theocracy," wrote, "The dream of a secular, liberal democracy is lost: Christians are stronger than ever . . . ." It was a note sounded by many magazine feature writers and columnists in the subsequent months.

The president's invocation of Jesus as his favorite thinker and reports from journalists or White House insiders that he has a daily prayer life has been interpreted by some critics to imply that he thinks he has a pipeline to God or that he thinks he is getting his daily assignments through prayer exercises, and this gets him labeled a theocrat.

Though the American liberal political movement also has notable religious leaders among its well-known figures (for example, Jesse Jackson, Al Sharpton, Jim Wallis, Barry W. Lynn, Dr. Bob Edgar), their pronouncements are seldom described as injecting religion into politics, or promoting their own theocratic vision. Looking at the word in its roots, *theocracy* means government (*ocracy*) by God (*theos*) directly. First introduced as a term by Flavius Josephus in *Jewish Antiquities*, it described the way ancient Israel was governed under the Patriarchs (Moses in particular) and the judges (among the best known being Joshua, Gideon, and Samson, plus a dozen others between Moses and the first king, Saul). As Judges 8:23 puts it, "Gideon said to them, 'I will not rule over you, neither shall my son rule over you; the Lord shall rule over you.'"

discussion question

What ended the biblical theocracy?
There is much negotiating in the Old Testament between the people, petitioning God to give them a king so they could look good alongside the other kingdoms of their time, and God, warning that a king will do bad things like raise taxes, draft sons into the military, and lead the nation into idolatry.

Even after the establishment of the new Old Testament government as a monarchy, however, God continued to let his will be known directly to the king and the people through the prophets, whose sermons were God's word to them. For many generations after establishing the monarchy, Israel had good kings and bad kings. Good kings listened to the prophets and acted in accord with God's will revealed through them. Bad kings did "that which was right in their own sight."

Democracy or Anarchy?

As political theorists have observed, the theocracy under the patriarchs and judges was close to a true democracy or anarchy. If the judges told the people what to do and they voluntarily and ungrudgingly did it, it was democratic. If the judges told the people what God wanted and they refused, it was anarchic. Despite there being no physical coercion, rebellion against the judges seldom occurred. The Old Testament simile for this is expressed in 1 Kings 4:25: "every man under his vine and under his fig tree, from Dan to Beersheba." Sitting under his own "vine and fig tree" symbolizes the peace and security in Israel when they were faithful to God. Dan and Beersheba, the southernmost and northernmost cities in the land, is a simile for, "from border to border."

Current use of *theocracy*, as cited above, attempts to apply it to any political theory that supports a role for God or of godliness in any approach to governing. In November 2004, writer Stephen Pizzo said that the Democrats should avoid "values politics" rather than imitate the Republicans, because to do so would even more "Talibanize" the United States. Afghanistan under the Taliban and Iran under the Ayatollahs may be genuine theocracies, but using the democratic process to advocate for one philosophy of what constitutes public morality over another is politically poles away from such totalitarian systems. And though there is much work among Christian scholars to propose the best configuration of democracy in a Christian worldview, no Christian scholar or professor of political theory has been found who advocates turning modern democracies into theocracies.

Christian Theocracy Is an Oxymoron

Though many authoritarian figures in history have claimed to govern as Christians (Spanish dictator Francisco Franco, 1892–1975, to cite one recent example), Christian political theorists say the New Testament precludes theocracy as a viable form of government in pluralistic societies. The way the Gospel should be spread—by voluntary assent of the heart, rather than coercion of either the intellect or the body—favors pluralistic societies for Christians over monolithic or totalitarian ones. Jesus said the tares, weedy plants that grow in grain fields and a symbol of unbelievers, are to be lived with in toleration by the wheat, his metaphor for the believing children of God (Matthew 13:25–30 and 36–40).

Civil Religion

Defined as "the folk religion of a people," civil religion usually appears as a widespread acknowledgement of divine approval, guidance, or help in public life, usually by elected officials like the president, governors, mayors, and professional administrators, and especially in former times, in institutions like public schools and the military. Patriotism and civil religion are intermingled; ceremonies like military funerals, Memorial Day programs, and, formerly, high-school graduations use prayers, and even participation of clergy, but usually without sectarian or denominational distinctions.

factum

All United States presidents have invoked God as the nation's judge and provider, which usually has been perceived as civil religion or "saying what the people think they understand," even if they may be understanding it differently than the speaker does.

Some Christian scholars and authors caution against confusing civil religion or patriotism itself with Christianity, lest the government or its institutions become idols and God be nationalized as America's God, at the expense of any nations opposing America. Scholars also caution against equating the United States with Old Testament Israel or God's chosen people, or failing to understand biblical prophecies for Israel in historical and geographical context. Christian writers on this topic usually advocate looking for the personal and organizational application of biblical teachings, and making them part of a personal or organizational political perspective rather than trying to apply them to the nation. In the Constitution, the nation as a whole considers itself to be "governed by the people," not by God, and biblical revelation does not specify the role God has for the United States, as he had for the Israel of old.

Light and Darkness

A central teaching of Jesus that has been applied to Christian action in political situations is Matthew 5:15–16: "Neither do men light a candle, and put it under a bushel, but on a candlestick; and it giveth light unto all that are in the house. Let your light so shine before men, that they may see your good works, and glorify your Father which is in heaven." The passage was adapted by the Puritan colonists who came to Massachusetts in the early seventeenth century to describe how they perceived their goal and their mission as being "a city on a hill" to enlighten the other nations. Their minister, John Winthrop, used this passage in a sermon given while they were en route to the new world. Christians working on helping the still relatively new nation clarify and pursue its vision have reiterated this passage many times since.

God on All Our Sides

Ronald Reagan characteristically said, "We shouldn't worry so much about whether God is on our side as whether we're on his." Puritan preacher and Massachusetts Governor John Winthrop (of the "city on a hill" allusion made earlier) told his congregation (paraphrased): "if we deal falsely with our God in this undertaking, causing him to withdraw his present help from us, we shall become a story and a byword throughout the world; we shall open the mouths of enemies to speak evil of God's ways and all believers for God's sake; we shall bring shame on many worthy servants of God, and turn their prayers into curses on us, until we are consumed out of the good land that we are going to."

The Old Testament aligns God on the side of victims of unrighteousness, violence, and injustice. He sides with the oppressed, those who mourn, and those who seek him (see Leviticus 25, 1 Kings 21, Isaiah 5:8, Jeremiah 7: 5–7, Isaiah 58: 4–12, Micah 6: 7–8). Jesus affirmed that perpetrators of injustice will be judged harshly (Matthew 24 and Mark 13).

God is on the side of those who take a stand for righteousness, Psalm 14:34 says. He's on the side of justice, Jeremiah says in an Old Testament prophecy about the Messiah, "the day is coming, says the Lord, when I will raise to David a righteous Branch, and a King shall reign and prosper, and shall execute judgment and justice in the earth" (see Jeremiah 23:5).

The church in general says God is on the side of everyone on this planet, because everyone is his child, an object of the redemption Jesus obtained on the cross. God has invested in everyone in his world, and Christian politics is first about justice, a form of God's mercy to all people: "To do justice and judgment is more acceptable to the Lord than sacrifice" (see Proverbs 21:3).

Christian Politics

Lutheran scholar Dr. Gene Edward Veith, Jr., culture editor of *World* magazine and executive director of The Cranach Institute, a research and education arm of Concordia Theological Seminary in Fort Wayne, Indiana, has spoken and written about Martin Luther's seeing the world in terms of two kingdoms, comparable to the realm of darkness and the realm of light in Jesus' teaching. In Luther's view, Veith says, Christ is the Lord of both the secular kingdom and the spiritual kingdom.

In the secular kingdom, Christ reigns whether or not the subjects know they are his. To paraphrase Proverbs 21:1, the hearts of all human kings, all people in authority, are in the Lord's hand. But the main point Veith promotes is that the secular king can be an intentional servant of God just as legitimately as the ministers, missionaries, or evangelists who find their vocations in the spiritual kingdom.

Vocation, God's Calling

A vocation, in Veith's view, is doing one's calling in whatever can be of service to God. And inasmuch as the earth is the Lord's, and Jesus is king of (all) kings and Lord of all, any legitimate life's work is to be seen as a vocation given by the Lord.

This Lutheran foundational worldview is similar to one built on John Calvin's teachings about vocations, similarly legitimizing any work (other than those that are unlawful or immoral) for Christians wanting to serve the Lord through their talents. Since the latter years of the nineteenth century, scholars in the Netherlands and the United States have greatly expanded on Calvin's thoughts.

symbolism

Abraham Kuyper suggested the "kingdoms," which he called "spheres," be enlarged to six instead of two. He added a God or Creator sphere ruling over the temporal, or created, spheres of family, life work, recreation and education.

Abraham Kuyper (1837–1920), a Dutch Reformed pastor, scholar, journalist, educator, and political reformer, made the greatest addition to Calvin's foundation, which he laid out in a series of lectures on Calvinism he delivered at Princeton University in 1899. The main point of Kuyper's Princeton lectures, as McKendree R. Langley of Westminster Theological Seminary said in a centennial essay about these lectures, was "that the Christian faith is both for salvation and for the rest of life." And to show partly what he meant by "the rest of life," Kuyper established a university, The Free University of Amsterdam, which still thrives as a Reformed Christian alternative institution of higher education.

But Kuyper's main contribution was in the field of political theory. He is credited with having introduced democratic representative government to the Netherlands (which was a monarchy but had been won and lost several times as European superpowers ran over it in the eighteenth and nineteenth centuries). He created the country's first political party, and the first in the world to be based on Christian principles for doing politics and statecraft. Originally called the ARP, Anti-Revolutionary Party (a philosophical dig at the French exportation of their Revolution through much of the nineteenth century), it has more recently been merged with several other confessionally Christian parties to become the largest constituency in the Christian Democratic Appeal. From Kuyper's election as prime minister in 1905, the ARP remained in power most of the time, and the CDA, its successor, is at this writing the party in power. The ARP was the model for the other European Christian Democratic political movements, most of which have been based on Catholic teachings and constituencies.

Despite numerous secularist complaints and warnings that theocrats are taking over the United States government, the only Christian movement with a comprehensive approach to political reform for the United States was established on Kuyper's pluralist principles, which include equal treatment of all faiths, not on theocratic principles.

Public Justice

The Washington-based Center for Public Justice (CPJ) has been working for more than twenty-five years to bring principles of public justice to bear on American politics and government. Its most successful effort has been to help define the Charitable Choice provision of the 1996 welfare-reform law (signed by President Clinton), which requires equal treatment of faith-based and all other nongovernment social-service organizations that co-operate with government in delivering services. Stanley Carlson-Thies, the Center's director of social policy studies, also helped organize the White House office of faith-based and community initiatives in the first year of the George W. Bush administration.

The Center established that no helping program, whether conducted by government agencies like FEMA or nongovernmental ones like the Salvation Army, Catholic Charities, and Red Cross, works on a basis of values neutrality. The administrators of government programs can and do impose their own values on their programs and their administration, which competes with more openly defined helping programs.

fallacy

The Center for Public Justice says that although pluralism is widely misunderstood as based on compromise, principled pluralism is a biblically consistent alternative to multicultural politics. Where multiculturalism is based on ethnicity, nationality, and sexual orientation, pluralism is principle-based, with each minority defining itself by its worldview and goals, whether religious or secular.

War in the Flesh and in the Spirit

Besides light and darkness, there is also a clear exposition in the teachings of Jesus and the apostles on the relationship between the flesh and the spirit. However, this is not as simple a division between two kingdoms as it may seem.

Flesh and Spirit as Enemies

On the one hand, some teachings imply that the flesh is the enemy of the spirit, and often this is how the division is taught. Some examples suggest that kind of clear distinction. In Matthew 26:41 (also Mark 14:38), Jesus says, "The spirit indeed is willing, but the flesh is weak." In John 3:6, "that which is born of the flesh is flesh; and that which is born of the Spirit is spirit." John 6:63: "the spirit makes alive, the flesh profits nothing. The words that I speak to you are spirit, and they are life." The Apostle Paul also discusses the dichotomy between flesh and spirit. In Romans 8:1, he states: "There is no condemnation to those who are in Christ Jesus, who walk not after the flesh, but after the Spirit."

Spirit is Able to Cleanse the Flesh

But on the other hand, flesh participates in salvation and receives the spirit in itself. Luke 3:6 illustrates: "All flesh shall see the salvation of God." In Luke 24:39, Jesus says: "See my hands and my feet, that it is I myself. Handle me and see, for a spirit does not have flesh and bones, as you see me have." And in John 1:14 he confirms a positive aspect of the flesh: "the Word was made flesh, and dwelt among us, and we beheld his glory, the glory as of the only begotten of the Father, full of grace and truth."

Finally, the flesh of Jesus is able to purify the spirit of those who receive it. John 6:51–56 states: "'I am the living bread that came down from heaven: if any eats of this bread, he shall live forever, and the bread that I will give is my flesh, which I will give for the life of the world.' The Jews argued among themselves, asking, 'How can this man give us his flesh to eat?' To which Jesus replied, 'Truly I say, except you eat the flesh of the Son of man and drink his blood, you have no life in you. Whoever eats my flesh and drinks my blood has eternal life and I will raise him up at the last day. For my flesh is meat, indeed, and my blood is drink indeed. He who eats my flesh and drinks my blood dwells in me, and I in him.'" This is the institution of Holy Communion, the meal of thanksgiving or Eucharist.

Flesh and Spirit Reconciled

Paul seems to untie the knot in this riddle in Romans 8:3–5. "What the law could not do, in its weakness through the flesh, God, by sending his own Son in the likeness of sinful flesh, and for [the sake of] sin, condemned sin in the flesh in order that the righteousness of the law might be fulfilled in us who walk not after the flesh, but after the Spirit. For those who are born of the flesh are always mindful of the things of the flesh; but those who are born of the Spirit are mindful of the things of the Spirit."

discussion question

Is war inevitable?
There will always be wars between the lusts of the flesh, and those parties in the human community who find their glory in the flesh on one side; and the ineffable freedom of God's spirit renewing our flesh, and those parties that want the glory of the human race to be their risen King.

Verses 8–9 say: "So then, those who are in the flesh cannot please God. But you are not in the flesh but in the Spirit if the Spirit of God dwells in you. Now if any man does not have the Spirit of Christ, he is none of his." And finally, verse 12–13 state: "Therefore, brothers, we are not debtors to the flesh, to live after the flesh, for if you live after the flesh, you shall die: but if you through the Spirit mortify the deeds of the body, ye shall live."

Purification

The Christian mindset is not to be set against "flesh." Christianity is not a dualism like some strands of Gnosticism, which hold that matter is profane, bound, and binding, and the spirit is holy, free, and freeing. Christians believe Christ came to make the flesh holy. In taking his flesh into our own, we begin renewing our bodies into spiritual bodies. In the resurrection, our flesh is raised to new life: "Handle me and see, for a spirit does not have flesh and bones, as you see me have."

The Dividing Line

Spiritual warfare is inevitable for Christians, and one of the ways it makes itself evident is in what is currently called the culture wars. Each side tends to demonize the other and think that the other side epitomizes the evil tendencies in our time and in our socio-political life. But the great pitfall of engaging in such wars is that the focus may shift from the spiritual prize to the flesh-and-blood enemy, and the conflict may shift from fighting in the spirit to fighting in the flesh. "For we wrestle not against flesh and blood, but against principalities, against powers, against the rulers of the darkness of this world, against spiritual wickedness in high places," Paul writes in Ephesians 6:12.

The funny thing about the darkness and the light, the flesh and the spirit, is that all human beings have both of them. To paraphrase Alexander Solzhenitsyn, it would be nice to separate the good people from the bad. But it's not so easy because the line dividing good from evil cuts not through the sides of the culture wars, but through the heart of every human being.

CHAPTER 19

The Jesus of the Future

There is a general sense in human thinking that the end is nigh, our doom is sealed. To some extent every religion in human history has addressed such fears. "Run for the hills" echoes Jesus' words in Matthew 24, "When you see the abomination of desolation spoken of by Daniel the prophet . . . then let those who are in Judea flee into the mountains" (verses 15–16).

The Second Coming of Christ

Jesus' return was promised by two angels who appeared to his disciples at his ascension, as Luke relates in Acts 1:10–11: "While they looked steadily toward heaven as he ascended, two men dressed in white stood by them and said, 'You men of Galilee, why do you stand gazing up to heaven? This same Jesus, who is taken from you into heaven, shall come back in the same manner as you have seen him taken up.'"

Maranatha

Three New Testament texts refer to "Maranatha"; one in the Aramaic, and the other two in translation. In 1 Corinthians 16:22 the Apostle Paul says, "If any man does not love the Lord Jesus Christ, let him be Anathema Maranatha." In other words, "let him be accursed; the Lord comes." Or, more likely, he means the Lord is nearby, as in, "the Lord sees and judges; we do not have to worry about it." Many Bible scholars see Philippians 4:4–5 as having the same point, though the Aramaic form *Maran atha* does not appear there: "Rejoice in the Lord always; I repeat, rejoice. Let your moderation be known to all men. The Lord is at hand."

factum

Maran atha are two Aramaic words that mean "our Lord comes." Evangelicals, and especially Pentecostals, have anglicized it, and use the word as an indication of their expectation of and orientation toward the Second Coming or Second Advent of Jesus.

Jesus Returns

All Christians believe in the Second Coming (among those who hold the Nicene Creed, Apostles Creed, or both as definitive, which all but some liberal and post-Christians do). In the Apostles Creed that belief is expressed: "He ascended into heaven and sits at the right hand of God the Father Almighty, whence he shall come to judge the living and the dead."

In the Nicene Creed, the same belief is stated as follows: "he suffered and was buried; and the third day he rose again, according to the Scriptures; and ascended into heaven, and sits on the right hand of the Father; and he shall come again, with glory, to judge the living and the dead; whose kingdom shall have no end."

The epistle of James the Lord's brother has a similar teaching in chapter 5:8–9: "Be patient; establish your hearts, for the coming of the Lord draws nigh. Don't hold grudges against one another, brethren, lest you be condemned. Behold, the judge stands at the door." James' take on the Lord's nearness incorporates both the idea that the Lord is always present, watching, and also that his "coming back is drawing near," ambiguously connecting his omnipresence with his Second Advent.

Ambiguity Is Key

Most references to the Second Advent are widely believed to include this ambiguity. In fact, in Paul's epistles, this ambiguous sense of his presence and his return is thought of as the essence of the Christian's hope, which is a major theme in Paul's writing. The most pointed instance of this in Paul's writings is Titus 2:13–14: "Looking for the blessed hope and the glorious appearing of the great God and our Savior Jesus Christ, that being justified by his grace, we should be made heirs according to the hope of eternal life." Here, Paul specifically refers to our hope as the Second Coming, but also ties every other kind of hope we have arising from our faith in him to that event.

Patience Required

One of the most provocative passages about the Second Coming is Hebrews 10:36–39: "You must have patience so that, after you have done the will of God, you might receive what has been promised. For a little while yet, then he who shall come will come, and will not tarry. The just shall live by faith, but if any man draws back, my soul shall have no pleasure in him. But we are not the type who draw back to perdition; but the type who believe to the saving of the soul."

symbolism

Another way of referring to the Second Coming is as a metaphor for death or faith in the Lord. Evangelicals' use of the phrase "if the Lord tarries," has as its first meaning "if the Second Coming doesn't happen first," but people often mean by it "if the Lord doesn't take me first" or "if I live that long."

In other words, it won't be long until the Lord comes, so wait patiently. In fact, as seen in the previous passage, he's already at the door. The writer of Hebrews seems to think Jesus' coming is going to happen at any time in this first generation of the church, but as it did not occur, many Christians think the point that God wants to convey is that we should always live as though Jesus is at the door, but not be anxious about it. Death is, after all, a type of Second Coming also, as God sends his angels to escort home those of his faithful who have believed to the end.

Are These the Last Times?

Some believe that when Jesus refers to "the last times," he is referring only to the last times for the covenant of God with Israel, which these believers think ended with the First Jewish-Roman war and the destruction of Herod's Temple in Jerusalem in A.D. 70. Though this has some truth, others say the references to "last times" refer to the era of the church, and see that as extending from the time of the Book of Acts to the present, as suggested earlier in the point made about the intentional ambiguity of the meaning of the Second Coming.

When Will it Happen?

William Miller, a nineteenth-century Baptist farmer in New York state, studied the Bible according to prophetic tools he had developed, and with the help of Bishop James Ussher's dating of the biblical time periods, concluded that the Second Coming of Christ would take place in 1843. Upward of 100,000 people anticipated the fulfillment of the prophecy that year, many of them divesting themselves of their assets to prepare, but they were disappointed (or relieved).

In 1970, Hal Lindsey, one of the most widely read prophecy experts in American evangelical circles, wrote in *The Late Great Planet Earth* that, based on biblical prophecies about the restoration of the nation of Israel, within a generation of modern Israel's founding in 1948, all things prophesied in Matthew 24 should come to pass.

Critics say that, biblically, a generation is about forty years, so by 1988 all the prophesies Jesus made about the end times should have come to pass, according to Lindsey's timetable. But there is no evidence that the scenario presented in Matthew 24 was being played out between 1948 and 1988.

discussion question

What is eschatology?
Eschatology is the technical term in theology for the study of "last things" or the age to come, which in Greek is *eschaton*. Speaking of a church's or a teacher's eschatology refers to the view held concerning the end times or the culmination of the age, based on the interpretation of the biblical teachings on these questions.

Harold Camping, founder of the Family Radio network and its major on-air personality, predicted in 1994 that the apocalypse would occur in September that year, but that he could not predict the exact date because Matthew 24:36 says, "no man knows the day and hour, no, not the angels of heaven, but my Father only." Many in his radio audiences were disappointed, and some, it has been reported, were relieved when the apocalypse didn't occur.

Prophecy-based Cults

There have been many secular and cult groups built around prophecies. Some of these groups are infamous, like David Koresh's Branch Dividians,

Jim Jones' People's Temple, and the "Heaven's Gaters" with their Hale-Bopp Comet prophesies. The prophecy experts cited previously profess to be traditional Christians, and are generally accepted as such within Christian circles.

Considering the way Old Testament prophecies about the Messiah are used by the writers of the New Testament (emphasizing the failure to discern the prophecies), it's not surprising that Christians in later times would look for signs that the Second Coming might happen soon. Many believe, even, that it would be an error to fail to look for such signs.

Christian Disagreements about "Ultimate Things"

In *The Church and the Last Things*, Dr. Martyn Lloyd-Jones, a South Wales native who became what some believe to be "possibly the greatest British preacher of the twentieth century," describes the difference between the preterist and the futurist views of biblical prophecies. Preterists believe the prophecies have now been fulfilled; futurists believe they are still to unfold in the future.

factum

Isaac Newton allegedly said, "About the time of the end . . . men will . . . turn their attention to prophecies, and insist upon their literal interpretation." And Blaise Pascal is quoted as saying, "Prophecies are to be unintelligible to the ungodly but intelligible to those who are properly instructed."

Controversy over the Millennium

One of the major points contested within theological schools is what the Bible teaches about the millennium, meaning "the thousand-year reign of Christ" that many find in Revelation 20. In the church at large, there are three major divisions of thinking regarding how prophecy about the millennium is to be interpreted.

AMILLENNIALISM

Also known as nunc millennialism, or no millennium, amillennialism holds that the thousand-year reign of Christ is figurative, not to be taken as referring to a literal thousand-year period. The reign of the church as the body of Christ is seen as the symbolical or spiritual millennium, which has already exceeded two literal millennia; this opinion also includes that the church is the earthly, spiritual expression of the Kingdom of God. Though some people believe in the relative inactivity of satanic forces in areas of the world where the church is influential, as opposed to those areas where paganism still prevails, amillennialists believe the church and the forces of evil will coexist throughout the reign of Christ as head of the church. With some variations, amillennialism is the traditional eschatology of the Catholic, Orthodox, Lutheran, Calvinist (Presbyterian, Reformed), Anglican, and Methodist Churches.

discussion question

What is the Great Tribulation?
It is a seven-year period of persecution under the reign of the antichrist. Pretribulationists believe that the rapture of the believing church occurs before the antichrist begins his reign of destruction, mid-tribulationists pinpoint it at three and a half years in, and post-tribulationists believe the rapture will come after the tribulation.

PREMILLENNIALISM

Premillennialism teaches that the Second Coming of Christ will occur before the millennium, which will be a literal thousand-year reign on earth of the conquering Prince of Peace. In the United States and in the parts of the world where missionaries are primarily American evangelicals, premillennialism is by far the most widely held view among Baptists, Pentecostals, and most other evangelicals. Though advocates see a belief in premillennialism reaching back to early church history, it has had its greatest growth since the dispensational system introduced by John Nelson Darby (1800–1882).

POSTMILLENNIALISM

Postmillennialism teaches that the Second Coming will occur after the millennium, and therefore, like the amillennialists, they believe that the thousand-year reign of Christ is figurative, in and through the church, not literal, as from an earthly throne. The postmillennial emphasis is on purifying the church and, through the church, defeating and binding Satan in the world, and bringing about the peace of the Prince of Peace. In this way the postmillennialists hope to purify the world in order to make it ready to meet Christ as his bride. Postmillenialism is often characterized as triumphalism, pushing for the victory of the church in the present age. No major denominations are identified as postmillennial, but individuals like the late R. J. Rushdoony, Gary North, and Greg Bahnsen, and their movements (theonomy, reconstructionism) advocate it.

Dispensationalism

Dispensationalism, which is traced to a pietistic movement in England in the 1820s called Plymouth Brethren, interprets the whole Bible in terms of particular ways God interacts with his people under different covenants and time periods. So something true of one group of believers in one dispensation, meaning believers of a specific time period and under a specific set of covenants, may not apply to or be required of other believers in another dispensation. And there can be more than one dispensation at the same time, according to some dispensationalists. Followers of this approach think that God interacts simultaneously with the Jewish people under one dispensation, and with Christians under another.

Taken to its logical conclusion, the system ends up asserting that the teachings of Jesus in the Gospels are entirely for the Jewish people, and that only the teachings of Paul and part of the book of Acts are for the church. The *Scofield Study Bible* (1909) formalized dispensationalist teaching in some detail, and this system's major academic defense has come from Dallas Theological Seminary. For all Christians, at its simplest, the Old Covenant and the New Covenant (synonymous with the Old Testament and the New

Testament) have at least two dispensations, but adding other modes of inter-action between God and his people (beside the two basic ones—Old and New Testaments) becomes dispensationalism.

factum

Many churches believe these opinions about the millennium are not required for salvation and so they are willing to tolerate any of these among their clergy. Positions that were described previously as being held by certain denominations and communions are indicative of the great majority in those communions, but are not necessarily the only view permitted.

Chiliasm

Strongly committed amillennialists equate premillennialism with chiliasm (from the Greek, *chiliasmos*, meaning "a thousand years"), which the church condemned as a heresy at the second Ecumenical Council in 381. Critics of premillennialism say that the words in the Nicene Creed, "he shall come again, with glory, to judge the living and the dead; whose kingdom shall have no end" were specifically intended to oppose the teaching that Christ's reign would be for a specific thousand-year period, as chiliasm taught and contemporary premillennialists also teach.

discussion question

Why do some believe the millennium will be a time of decadence?
Early chiliasts believed that the thousand-year kingdom of Christ would be a time of gluttonous feasting and sexual excess, which others say contradicts Paul's declaration in Romans 14:17, "the kingdom of God is not food and drink."

Anabaptists in 1533 established the German city of Munster as the New Jerusalem, in fulfillment of the chiliast belief in the establishment of a physical kingdom of God on earth. According to Owen Chadwick in *The Reformation*, the "radical reformers" (mostly Anabaptists) banned all who refused to be baptized, and they proclaimed John of Leyden the king of New Zion. They interpreted Old Testament teachings as permitting polygamy, and some of their men took multiple wives.

The "kingdom" declared war on the rest of the world, calling for the annihilation of all the ungodly. Only after two years, when some saner minds in the city conspired against their leaders and opened the gates to outside troops, who had been sent to quell their revolution, was the insurrection put down.

The Kingdom of Munster revolution has remained infamous in church history as the saddest instance of Reformation fever gone wild. Luther was apparently chagrined that his declarations of independence from the Pope had been taken to such extremes. This disaster encouraged Luther and Calvin to speak and write against chiliasm and any efforts to establish a literal Kingdom of God in the temporal world. The Lutheran Augsburg Confession and the Reformed Second Helvetic (Swiss) Confession specifically condemn chiliasm.

The Prophecy Trap

Dr. Martyn Lloyd-Jones in *The Church and the Last Things* cautions his readers against becoming "exclusivists," meaning they shouldn't be unwilling to consider views of the millennium and "ultimate things" other than the one they find most accord with. Dr. Lloyd-Jones feels exclusivism sometimes leads to an obsession about what will happen before the Second Coming.

Dedicated followers of Hal Lindsey and other dispensationalists generally have strong opinions about the modern State of Israel, based on their view of its role in the End Times. Some of them think the Jewish Temple must be restored in fulfillment of prophecy in order that the antichrist can rule the world from a throne there during the Great Tribulation. Lindsey has told audiences that he has been invited to present his eschatological views at the Pentagon and other governmental agencies, which he implies has helped mold United States policy toward Israel and her enemies.

factum

When interest in prophesy turns into obsession, it often leads to foolish moves like those made by the followers of William Miller, who sold homes and other assets to be unencumbered when the Lord returned, only to find themselves in embarrassing straits, if not dire ones, when he failed to appear at the prophesied time.

Christian financial planner Jim Parris has warned his audiences that "not investing because the Lord may be coming back soon" is a prophecy-based financial trap that may lead to years of regret, and investing or liquidating assets based on one's own interpretation of end-times events, or those of a favorite prophet, can be disastrous for yourself and those putting trust in you. Jesus himself, in his most prophetic sermon, warns, "There shall arise false Christs, and false prophets, who shall demonstrate great signs and wonders; so much so that, if it were possible, they shall deceive the very elect" (Matthew 24:24). Even some of God's chosen leaders have been deceived, as shown in the biblical record. Usually it was their own conceits that led them into error, relying on their own judgment rather than depending on God's guidance.

Jesus' Teaching on the End Times

Most of Jesus' teaching on the end of the age takes place on the Mount of Olives, and therefore scholars refer to it as the Olivet Discourse. Matthew's Gospel, chapter 24, begins with Jesus' describing the destruction of the Temple in A.D. 70, followed by his disciples asking for more input about the things that must come to pass before the end of the age.

Jesus' speech seems ambiguous, as though in the same sentence his focus may be on the disciples and the generation they still have to live out, but a few words later seems to be focusing a millennium or two into the future. It is not hard to see why Christians of every age since the first generation want to find in these words, which seem to scan down the centuries, ways to apply parts of them to themselves. At the very least, these words are intentionally, ambiguously, speaking to both the end of the age of Israel under the Old Covenant in A.D. 70 and the culmination of the age of the church some undefined time in the future.

symbolism

> Prophetic passages in the Old Testament symbolize things taking place when the prophet speaks and preaches, but at the same time other phrases are dropped in that foreshadow the coming of the Messiah and the ultimate salvation of Israel.

Tribulations

At least some Catholics, Orthodox, and amillennialist Protestants take this discourse as speaking of both the end of the age of Israel and the culmination of the age of the church. Jesus is talking about the persecution of the church under Emperor Vespasian and Military Commander Titus in the first Jewish-Roman war, and of the persecutions of the Christians that would be just beginning when the abomination of desolation takes place in the Temple and it is destroyed.

Jesus' description of how Christians will die and will want to run for the hills closely captures the waves of persecutions that began when the Temple fell in the church's first generation, and continued for the next three centuries. He mentions repeatedly that those who withstand the tribulation, the great persecutions, meaning those who do not turn back on their baptisms to be spared, will be saved. The Orthodox churches have always said he does not give the people hope that they will escape the tribulation by being raptured.

Signs of the End

Yet amillennialists, too, find prophecies here pertaining to the Second Coming, still in the future. An anonymous Orthodox writer finds "signs of the second coming" in the Olivet Discourse, beginning with "The Gospel of the Kingdom shall be preached in all the world as a witness unto all nations; and then the end shall come" (Matthew 24:14). There are signs that this is being fulfilled in the twenty-first century as never before.

Another sign appears in Luke's Gospel, where Jesus asks, "when the Son of Man comes, will he find faith on the earth?" (Luke 18:8). Though the Gospel is being spread far and wide, its faith, especially in the churches established for many years in the West, seems to have waned, its depth eroded. Another sign of the end is the proliferation of false messiahs and false prophets trying to lure away the faithful, as Jesus says will precede the Second Coming: "many shall come in my name, saying, I am Christ; and shall deceive many" (Matthew 24:5), "for false Christs and false prophets shall arise and show great signs and wonders so much so that, if it were possible, they shall deceive the very elect" (Matthew 24:24).

Fulfillment of Prophecy

The Jewish people figure in this anonymous Orthodox writer's interpretation of what signs will precede the Second Coming, based on Paul's prediction in Romans 11:25–33:

For I would not have you be ignorant, brethren, of this mystery, lest you be wise in your own conceits; that blindness in part has befallen Israel, until the fullness of the Gentiles be complete. And so all Israel shall be saved, as it is written, 'There shall come out of Zion the Deliverer, who shall turn away ungodliness from Jacob. For this is my covenant to them, when I shall take away their sins. As concerning the gospel, they are enemies for your sakes, but as touching the election, they are beloved for the fathers' sakes. For the gifts and calling of God are without repentance. For as you in times past have not believed God, yet have now obtained mercy through their unbelief, even so these have also now not believed, that through your mercy they also may obtain mercy. For God has concluded them all in unbelief, that he might have mercy on all. O the depth of the riches of the wisdom and knowledge of God! How unsearchable are his judgments, and his ways past finding out!

Dispensational premillennialists see the church as a small part of the larger plan of God for Israel. Under the amillennialism that sees the church as the inheritor of all the covenant promises of God to Israel, it is the church that becomes the fulfillment of what God promised to Abraham, that through his seed all the nations shall be blessed and his descendants would be uncountable.

The Apocalypse

The only book in the New Testament that is, as a whole, prophetic is The Book of Revelation, also known as the Apocalypse, which is Greek for revelation or disclosure. John wrote the Book of Revelation on the island of Patmos in Greece when, the biblical scholars of the Orthodox and Catholic churches generally say, he was nearly one hundred years of age and was living in exile after being spared in the latest round of persecutions. In *The Church and the Last Things*, Dr. Martyn Lloyd-Jones says that in the preterist view, all the prophecies in Revelation have now been fulfilled, while the futurists see most of them as still awaiting fulfillment.

Lloyd-Jones says that most Protestant Reformers looked at Revelation as a laying out (in advance) the stages of the church's history. His own view of it is what he called a "spiritual historicist" view, which sees Revelation as a spiritual map of where the church should be in its journey, and what it should do to avoid the pitfalls described in John's visions of various local churches. The early church interpretation of John's Apocalypse has been that the churches in his visions are actual congregations that the apostle had ministered to, and that he was writing to guide and comfort the people through the persecution they were enduring, and which he could foresee would not be ending soon (not for at least another two centuries, as it turned out).

factum

> The important point of the Jesus of the future, for Christians who profess the Nicene or Apostles' Creed, is that, regardless of whether they are amillennial, premillennial, postmillennial, or dispensationalist, he is coming again, and his return is nearer every day.

Lloyd-Jones gives his readers premillennial, postmillennial, and spiritual readings of Revelation 20, a chapter very much under debate, as it presents the "chaining" of Satan for a thousand years, which has been interpreted as being the thousand years in which Jesus will reign on earth by the premillennialists, as an indeterminate period for the church to grow in the amillennial view, and for the church to gain dominion over the world in the postmillennial one. Catholic writer Mark A. McNeil writes about Revelation 20 as well. He reports that the church traditionally has interpreted the chaining by Jesus of Satan as occurring as part of the crucifixion and resurrection, at which time Jesus defeats Satan and binds him sufficiently so that the church can take up its work of being light and salt in the world and spreading the good news of the kingdom.

CHAPTER 20

Jesus as Lord and Savior

One of the favorite slogans of the "Jesus People" Revival of the 1960s and '70s was "if you won't have Jesus as your Lord, you don't have Jesus as your Savior." The Jesus freaks, as they affectionately called themselves, meant it is not enough to assent to an invitation to confess Jesus as Savior if you aren't willing to live for him. It was a restating of Jesus' own words, "If you love me, keep my commandments" (John 14:15).

In All Things the Pre-eminence

If you've become a believer in Jesus as your Savior, been baptized, and joined a church, you might be thinking: so now what? You attend church every week and gradually get involved in some chores around the church. Perhaps you hear an almost-identical sermon every week. It may be along the lines of, "are you sure you're really saved, and if there's any doubt, don't you think you should come up and get saved or recommitted to Jesus?" Or, "How much have you done for the church? What's your ministry? Couldn't you do more, like singing in the choir, leading a class or a clean-up crew, making the coffee, or bringing snacks for the fellowship hour? Have you talked to your friends and neighbors about the church? Are you doing enough for Jesus?"

Is that all there is? Admittedly, the homilies (or sermons, for the down-to-earth) are not the *sine qua non* of being a Christian, but they are the first line of initiation into what may seem like insider stuff. Isn't being a Christian supposed to bring some excitement, or at least some purpose into life? Is the only cost of discipleship what you put in the offering plate?

Some critics have said that people often experience church as either so seeker friendly and geared to making everyone feel at home that it's barely different than being in meetings at work or at the school parents' night. Or that the church takes the safe middle road of not rocking anyone's boat, making church seem like little more than a series of cerebral exercises in looking at safe, noncontroversial texts.

Christian Life Beyond Chores at Church

The Apostle Paul offers some radical propositions about what Christ should mean to believers, and what the Christian life is meant to be:

[Jesus] is the image of the invisible God, the firstborn of every creature. For by him all things were created, that are in heaven, and that are on earth, things visible and invisible, whether they be thrones, or dominions, principalities, or powers; all things were created by him, and for him. And he is before all things, and by him all things consist. He is the head of the body, the church; the beginning, the firstborn from the dead, so that in all things he might have the pre-eminence. For it pleased the Father that in him

all fullness should dwell, and, having made peace through the blood of his cross, by him to reconcile all things to himself, by him, I say, whether they be things in earth, or things in heaven (Colossians 1:15–20).

Advocates of the Christian worldview like the late Francis Schaeffer, contemporary authors Nancy Pearcey and Gene Edward Veith, Jr., and minister D. James Kennedy have taken Paul's text as a homily worth taking to work on Monday morning. If "by him all things were created," and if the goal is that "in all things he might have the pre-eminence," they say your work is cut out for you. That work is figuring out, and applying, what it means for Jesus to have the pre-eminence in your particular vocation, and how the work you start again every Monday morning brings glory to him and points the people served by your work to his kingdom.

Everything Belongs to God

The separatist Puritans, better known as Pilgrims, who are given a nod of remembrance every American Thanksgiving Day, also took this sense of everything being Christ's seriously. Leland Ryken, author of *Worldly Saints: The Puritans As They Really Were*, says Puritans believed that "everything was God's." Nothing was experienced outside their commitment to God and their faith. For support they might cite "The earth is the Lord's, and the fullness thereof; the world, and they who dwell therein," as David the Psalmist wrote (Psalm 24:1), or "For the earth is the Lord's, and the fullness thereof," echoed by Paul the Apostle (1 Corinthians 20:26).

The influential Christian novel *In His Steps* is Charles M. Sheldon's story of a single congregation in a small American city taking a single sermon seriously. The takeaway thought for that homily was "What would Jesus do?" The 1886 novel doesn't present a full-fledged Christian worldview, but its message of making every decision in light of Jesus' teaching is powerful enough to change lives. And as Sheldon himself demonstrated though his example in civic projects, like pioneering kindergartens and being among the first to work for racial justice in his own city, it can change institutions and societies. Today the question "What would Jesus do?" (often abbreviated as WWJD) graces thousands of items, such as

T-shirts, hats, bumper stickers, pens, magnets, and all kinds of jewelry, from silver necklaces to silicone bracelets.

The Christian Mind

In 1963, Oxford scholar (and former student and friend of C. S. Lewis) Harry Blamires wrote *The Christian Mind* in an attempt to encourage "integrated thinking" by Christians committed to taking a stand against the secularization of Western culture. It became an instant classic—a little book to treasure, reread often, and disseminate—among Christian thinkers moved by the profundity of its simple apologetic. Blamires has gone on to write *Recovering the Christian Mind* and *The Post-Christian Mind*, which challenge popular myths like private morality, calling the term an oxymoron, as any morality based on less than the universality of its principles is no morality.

factum

A keystone of Abraham Kuyper's writings and sermons was the advocacy of the creation of a Christian mind or the redemption of the intellect as the first line of defense against the eroding effects of the higher critical thinking of the eighteenth century Enlightenment.

Russian Orthodox educator and philosopher Paul Evdokimov (1900–1969) expressed the same understanding of New Testament declarations: "the educational concern of Christifying rational life, the saturation of every domain by the light of Christ, a saturation that is inherent to the Christian faith, derives organically from Christian anthropology." Christian anthropology, the Christian understanding of what being human means, was described by Evdokimov's former colleague at St. Sergius Orthodox Institute in Paris, Alexander Schmemann, as "the first, the basic definition of man [as] priest." Schmemann is not referring to priesthood here as the clergy of the church but is referring to a mandate from God to all human beings to mediate the blessings of God to every aspect of the world. "You are a chosen generation, a royal priesthood, a holy nation, a peculiar people; that you should show forth the praises of him who has called you out of darkness into his marvelous light," as the Apostle Peter says (1 Peter 2:9).

Academic Lordship

Christian philosophy is a growing discipline that is beginning to influence the academic world. In *Total Truth*, Nancy Pearcey says that, almost single-handedly, Notre Dame University philosopher Alvin Plantinga has launched something of a revolution in academic philosophy. Pearcey cites naturalist philosopher Quentin Smith as "blaming" Plantinga for making Christian philosophy creditable and a major movement in American secular university philosophy departments, saying these new faculty members are having the effect of desecularizing the discipline of philosophy. Smith noted that, in other disciplines, Christian faculty members departmentalize their discipline and their private, religious, lives (being careful not to come out as Christians, in other words), but in philosophy the trend is in the other direction, with scholars openly discussing Christian foundations for their work and ably defending them.

Trickle-Down Philosophy

If one of Francis Schaeffer's recurring themes holds true—the claim of Quentin Smith that the Christian faculty members in other departments of most secular universities are reticent to come out—it may not remain true much longer. Schaeffer believes that whatever happens in the field of philosophy trickles down over a few years to become the trend into the arts next, and into other academic disciplines a few years later, and a generation or two after that becomes the trend in popular thinking. Today's post-modernism could actually give way to a new-Christian movement, academically, artistically, and socially.

The Dominion

Paul Evdokimov's call, quoted earlier, for "Christifying rational life, the saturation of every domain by the light of Christ" echoes the many Old Testament prophesies and New Testament declarations that "He shall reign forever and ever." Handel had passages like Psalms 97:1 and Revelation 19:6,

11:15, and 19:16 in mind when he wrote his Messiah oratorio. The dominion of Christ on earth is what every Christian prays for every time she recites the Lord's prayer, "thy kingdom come," or utters the simplest and most basic Christian creedal declaration, "Jesus is Lord."

Dominionism (the belief that Christians are mandated to bring the entire world under the rule of God) is sometimes confused with Christian obsession with politics and wanting to wrest control over society or government through nefarious means, but for many Christians, it entails learning to think consistently as disciples of Christ as Lord. One of the church's favorite texts regarding Jesus' dominion is Hebrews 1:2–3: "[God] has in these last days spoken to us by his Son, whom he has appointed the heir of all things and by whom also he made the worlds, being the brightness of his glory, and the express image of his person, and upholding all things by the word of his power, when he had by himself purged our sins, sat down on the right hand of the Majesty on high."

Every Knee Shall Bow

Paul in his epistle to the Philippian church writes, "at the name of Jesus every knee shall bow, of things in heaven, and things in earth, and things under the earth," (Philippians 2:10) echoing Isaiah's prophecy (45:21–23), "there is no other God beside me, a just God and a Savior, there is none beside me. Look unto me and be saved, all the ends of the earth, for I am God and there is none else. I have sworn by myself, the word is gone out of my mouth in righteousness, and shall not return, that to me every knee shall bow, every tongue shall swear." It seems that, if Jesus is what he claims to be, either he could force every knee to bow by simply saying the word, or he wants the bowing to be unforced and motivated by love in the hearts of those bowing.

The Temptation of Triumphalism

Triumphalism, as the word implies, means being sure you're right and that your truth shall prevail. But as the term is generally used in a negative and pejorative sense, it carries with it a connotation of conceit, pride, or cocksureness. Triumphalism is seen as woefully lacking in humility, and triumphalists fail to realize the universality of Jesus' principle that it is the meek who shall inherit the world. Such pride precedes a fall, and as pride is the mother of all other sins, it is to be avoided even in confessing the Lordship, dominion, and sovereignty of Jesus the Lord.

symbolism

"Confessing" faith is the most symbolic expression for expressing faith because to confess implies meekness of heart and attitude. Confessing acknowledges that even if the right shall eventually prevail, its defenders have often failed and been defeated by the wrong because of poor timing, poor planning, poor weapons, and most typically, poor attitudes.

A major factor requiring caution against triumphalism is the not-yet aspect of Jesus' redemptive work. The kingdom is "already here" in its formative stage; the church is its best but imperfect evidence. That imperfection is the rub; when the kingdom comes in its fullness, but not before, the triumph will be *fait accompli*. "The kingdom of God has not arrived, nor have we Christians arrived," Isaac C. Rottenberg says in a *Christian Century* article cautioning against triumphalism. If the kingdom had already fully arrived, we would be in error to pray "thy kingdom come."

The Last Enemy

Triumphalism forgets the last line of the Lord's Prayer: "yours is the kingdom, and the power, and the glory forever. Amen." The kingdom is Jesus'; the power is his, and his is the glory. The triumph is his, and for those he has saved to get triumphal means they have forgotten who is the servant and who is the Master; who is the sinner and who the Savior: "The disciple is not above his master, nor the servant above his lord" (Matthew 10:24). The Apostle Paul describes the greatest triumph in human history, part of which is still to come, in 1 Corinthians 15:21–28: "Then cometh the end, when he shall have delivered up the kingdom to God, even the Father; when he shall have put down all rule and all authority and power. For he must reign, till he hath put all enemies under his feet."

The Holy City

Revelation Chapters 21 and 22 relate the vision John the Beloved Apostle received on the Isle of Patmos, of Jesus enthroned in the New Jerusalem.

discussion question

How are we to understand "the new creation"?
The new creation in the New Jerusalem far exceeds the new creation that is the mandate all of his disciples are given to work at in this, their meaningful, integrated physical and spiritual lives in their priesthood callings. But rather than brush away the best efforts of his people, he transforms them into the new creation.

"And he that sat upon the throne said, Behold, I make all things new" (Revelation 21:5). From the lowliness of a stable in Bethlehem, Jesus is finally seen in Scripture enthroned over the New Jerusalem. And here we see Him finally, through John's masterful depiction. See Revelation 21:10–27; 22:1–4, the theme of which is, "I saw no temple therein: for the Lord God Almighty and the Lamb are the temple of it. And the city had no need of the sun, neither of the moon to shine in it: for the glory of God did lighten it, and the Lamb is the light thereof."

APPENDIX A

Web Resources

Online Bible, King James Version. Downloadable text of both Old and New Testaments; also various other languages are available. Though there are several online sources like this, this is one of the most varied in terms of languages and file types available.
bible.ccim.org/dcb.html

History of the celebration of Christmas
www.christmas-time.com/cp-hist.html

Astronomer Susan S. Carroll's star of Bethlehem Web site
sciastro.net/portia/articles/thestar.htm

John Charles Webb Jr.'s star of Bethlehem, astronomy, and astrology Web site
www.aloha.net/~johnboy/sitemap.htg/sitemap.htm

Christmas in public schools
www.catholicleague.org/research/religious_expression_christmas.htm

Chronology of dates in Jesus' lifetime
http://en.wikipedia.org/wiki/Chronology_of_Jesus'_birth_and_death

Traditional icon of the Virgin Mary
www.iconsexplained.com/iec/00011.htm

The synoptic problem
www.mindspring.com/~scarlson/synopt/index.html

The synoptic problem by Daniel B. Wallace, Th.M., Ph.D.
www.bible.org/page.asp?page_id=669

Wikipedia concise summary of the Synoptic Problem
http://en.wikipedia.org/wiki/Synoptic_problem

Calvin College Ethereal Library, Fox's *Book of Martyrs*
www.ccel.org/f/foxe/martyrs/fox101.htm

The presentation in the Temple and the flight into Egypt discussed
christianwritings.net/chapt-2.htm

The Infancy Gospel of Thomas (an apocryphal Gnostic text)
www.gnosis.org/library/inftoml.htm

PBS page on Jewish life in first century Israel.
www.pbs.org/wgbh/pages/frontline/shows/religion/portrait/judaism.html

Source for Gnostic texts
www.gnosis.org

Hidden Gospels article by Phillip Jenkins, Penn State University
www.bibleinterp.com/articles/hiddengospel.htm

Divine liturgy of St. John Chrysostomos (main Eastern Orthodox liturgy)
www.ocf.org/OrthodoxPage/liturgy/liturgy.html

The Koran, one of many online sources
etext.virginia.edu/koran.html

Complete words of Flavius Josephus
www.ccel.org/j/josephus/JOSEPHUS.HTM

St. John of Kronstadt
www.fatheralexander.org/booklets/english/johnkr_e.htm

Information about St. Photini (Samaritan woman at the well)
home.it.net.au/~jgrapsas/pages/photini.htm

Joseph of Arimathea in England
asis.com/~stag/glastonb.html

Bible maps
biblia.com/jesusm/maps.htm

Catholic Encyclopedia of 1911 (public domain)
www.newadvent.org/cathen/

Encyclopedia of Christianity
www.ccel.org/php/wwec.php

The Gospel of Nicodemus (aka The Acts of Pilate)
www.ccel.org/fathers2/ANF-08/anf08-76.htm#P6567_1985111

Eusebius, church history
www.ccel.org/fathers2/NPNF2-01/TOC.htm

St. Ignatius, Bishop of Antioch
www.ccel.org/fathers2/ANF-01/anf01-22.htm

All about Jewish Passover
www.jewfaq.org/holidaya.htm

The Internet Medieval Sourcebook Web site at Fordham University
www.fordham.edu/halsall/basis/goldenlegend/

Statistics—Christian communions and denominations
en.wikipedia.org/wiki/List_of_Christian_denominations_by_number_of_members

World religions
en.wikipedia.org/wiki/Major_world_religions

Billy Graham and the Billy Graham Evangelistic Association
www.wheaton.edu/bgc/archives/bio.html

Pat Robertson and The 700 Club
www.cbn.com/

Christianity Today Online
www.christianitytoday.com/

Eastern Orthodox philosophical statements
www.hkbu.edu.hk/~ppp/HKPC/Orthodox_Wisdom_intro.htm

www.incommunion.org/articles/previous-issues/issue-36/becoming-the-jesus-prayer

Harper's article on the National Religious Broadcasters Association
www.harpers.org/FeelingTheHate.html

Christian Century article, "Christian Fulfillment and Jewish-Christian Dialogue"
www.religion-online.org/showarticle.asp?title=842

Lloyd-Jones' book on eschatology reviewed
www.bible.org/page.asp?page_id=1652

Catholic view of the millennium, rapture
www.diogh.org/youngacm/left_behind.htm

Schweitzer and the quest for the historical Jesus
www.mcmaster.ca/mjtm/2-51.htm

*www.westarinstitute
.org/Jesus_Seminar/jesus_seminar.html*

Billy Sunday's baseball statistics
*www.baseball-reference.com/s/sundabi01
.shtml*

Billy Sunday's sermons, stories
*articles.christiansunite
.com/preacher5-1.shtml*

The Book of Revelation of St. John the Divine in
both English and Greek
*www.ellopos.net/elpenor/greek-texts/
new-testament/revelation/1.asp*

Icons and iconography
www.orthodoxinfo.com/general

The Roman emperors
www.roman-emperors.org/

APPENDIX B

Bibliography

Biblical Texts

The Scripture texts quoted in this book are drawn from:

THE HOLY BIBLE: OLD AND NEW TESTAMENTS
> Self-pronouncing edition, conforming to the 1611 edition, commonly
> known as the Authorized or King James Version. (Cleveland and
> New York: The World Publishing Company).

Other Texts

Additional, supporting sources are as follows:

Boice, James Montgomery. *Foundations of the Faith: A Comprehensive and Readable Theology.* (Downers Grove, IL: InterVarsity Press, 1986).

Bultmann, Rudolf. *Jesus and the Word.* (New York: Charles Scribner's Sons, 1934).

Bultmann, Rudolf. *Jesus Christ and Mythology.* (New York: Charles Scribner's Sons, 1958).

Bultmann, Rudolf. *Kerygma and Myth.* (London: S.P.C.K., 1953).

Bultmann, Rudolf. *Theology of the New Testment.* 2 volumes. (London: SCM Press, Ltd., 1967).

Cairns, Earle E. *Christianity Through the Centuries: A History of the Christian Church.* (Grand Rapids, MI: Zondervan, 1981 [1954]).

Chilton, Bruce. *Mary Magdalene: A Biography.* (New York: Doubleday, 2005).

Dobson, James. *Dare to Discipline.* (Wheaton, IL: Tyndale House, 1970).

Dobson, James. *New Dare to Discipline.* (Wheaton, IL: Tyndale House, 1992).

George, Margaret. *Mary, Called Magdalene.* (New York: Penguin, 2002).

Gillquist, Peter. *Becoming Orthodox.* (Ben Lomond, CA: Conciliar Press, 2002).

Hanegraaff, Hank, and Maier, Paul L. *The Da Vinci Code: Fact or Fiction?* (Wheaton, IL: Tyndale House, 2004).

Harrison, R.K. "Higher Criticism," in *Evangelical Dictionary of Theology*. Walter A. Elwell, 511–512 (Grand Rapids, MI: Baker Book House, 1984).

Kennedy, D. James. *Evangelism Explosion*. (Wheaton, IL: Tyndale House, 1977).

Kraeling, Emil G. *The Old Testament Since the Reformation*. (New York: Harper and Brothers, 1955).

Lester, Meera. *Everything Mary Magdalene*. (Avon: Adams, 2006).

Lester, Meera. *Mary Magdalene: The Modern Guide to the Bible's Most Mysterious and Misunderstood Woman*. (Avon: Adams, 2005).

Lewis, C.S. *Mere Christianity*. (New York: Macmillan, 1943).

Malet, A. *The Thought of Rudolf Bultmann*. (New York: Doubleday, 1969).

Pearcey, Nancy. *Total Truth: Liberating Christianity from Its Cultural Captivity*. (Wheaton, IL: Crossway, 2004).

Pokrovsky, Gleb. *The Way of a Pilgrim*. (Woodstock, VT: Skylight Paths Publishing, 2001).

Rice, Anne. *Christ the Lord: Out of Egypt*. (New York: Knopf, 2005).

Roberts, Robert C. "Bultmann, Rudolf," in *Evangelical Dictionary of Theology*. Edited by Walter A. Elwell, 180 (Grand Rapids, MI: Baker Book House, 1984).

Roberts, Robert C. *Rudolf Bultmann's Theology: A Critical Interpretation*. (Grand Rapids: Eerdmans, 1976).

Schaeffer, Francis, and Koop, C. Everett. *Whatever Happened to the Human Race?* (Wheaton, IL: Crossway, 1983).

Schaeffer, Francis. *Escape from Reason*. (Downers Corners, IL: InterVarsity Press, 1968).

Schaeffer, Francis. *He Is There and He Is Not Silent*. (Wheaton, IL: Tyndale House, 1980).

Schaeffer, Francis. *How Should We Then Live?* (Wheaton, IL: Crossway, 1983).

Schaeffer, Francis. *The Church Before the Watching World*. (Wheaton, IL: Crossway, 1994).

Schaeffer, Francis. *The God Who Is There*. (Downers Corners, IL: InterVarsity Press, 1998).

Schaeffer, Francis. *The Great Evangelical Disaster*. (Wheaton, IL: Crossway, 1984).

Schaeffer, Francis. *The Mark of a Christian*. (Downers Corners, IL: InterVarsity Press, 1976).

Schmithals, W. *An Introduction to the Theology of Rudolf Bultmann*. (London: SCM Press, 1968).

Thiselton, A.C. *The Two Horizons: New Testament Hermeneutics and Philosophical Description*. (Grand Rapids: Eerdmans, and Paternoster, 1980).

Ware, Kallistos, Palmer, G.E.H., and Sherrard, Philip. *The Philokalia*. (London: Faber and Faber, 2005).

CCCU Member Colleges

Abilene Christian University, Abilene, Texas

Anderson University, Anderson, Indiana

Asbury College, Wilmore, Kentucky

Azusa Pacific University, Azusa, California

Belhaven College, Jackson, Mississippi

Bethel College—Indiana, Mishawaka, Indiana

Bethel University, St. Paul, Minnesota

Biola University, La Mirada, California

Bluffton University, Bluffton, Ohio

Bryan College, Dayton, Tennessee

California Baptist University, Riverside, California

Calvin College, Grand Rapids, Michigan

Campbellsville University, Campbellsville, Kentucky

Carson-Newman College, Jefferson City, Tennessee

Cedarville University, Cedarville, Ohio

College of the Ozarks, Point Lookout, Missouri

Colorado Christian University, Lakewood, Colorado

Corban College, Salem, Oregon

Cornerstone University, Grand Rapids, Michigan

Covenant College, Lookout Mountain, Georgia

Crichton College, Memphis, Tennessee

Crown College, St. Bonifacius, Minnesota

Dallas Baptist University, Dallas, Texas

Dordt College, Sioux Center, Iowa

East Texas Baptist University, Marshall, Texas

Eastern Mennonite University, Harrisonburg, Virginia
Eastern Nazarene College, Quincy, Massachusetts
Eastern University, St. Davids, Pennsylvania
Erskine College, Due West, South Carolina
Evangel University, Springfield, Missouri
Fresno Pacific University, Fresno, California
Geneva College, Beaver Falls, Pennsylvania
George Fox University, Newberg, Oregon
Gordon College, Wenham, Massachusetts
Goshen College, Goshen, Indiana
Grace College & Seminary, Winona Lake, Indiana
Greenville College, Greenville, Illinois
Hardin-Simmons University, Abilene, Texas
Hope International University, Fullerton, California
Houghton College, Houghton, New York
Houston Baptist University, Houston, Texas
Howard Payne University, Brownwood, Texas
Huntington University, Huntington, Indiana
Indiana Wesleyan University, Marion, Indiana
John Brown University, Siloam Springs, Arkansas
Judson College—AL, Marion, Alabama
Judson College—IL, Elgin, Illinois
Kentucky Christian University, Grayson, Kentucky
King College, Bristol, Tennessee
King's University College, The, Edmonton, Alberta, Canada
Lee University, Cleveland, Tennessee
LeTourneau University, Longview, Texas
Lipscomb University, Nashville, Tennessee
Louisiana College, Pineville, Louisiana
Malone College, Canton, Ohio
Master's College & Seminary, The, Santa Clarita, California
Messiah College, Grantham, Pennsylvania
MidAmerica Nazarene University, Olathe, Kansas
Milligan College, Milligan College, Tennessee
Mississippi College, Clinton, Mississippi
Missouri Baptist University, St. Louis, Missouri

Montreat College, Montreat, North Carolina
Mount Vernon Nazarene University, Mount Vernon, Ohio
North Greenville College, Tigerville, South Carolina
North Park University, Chicago, Illinois
Northwest Christian College, Eugene, Oregon
Northwest Nazarene University, Nampa, Idaho
Northwest University, Kirkland, Washington
Northwestern College—IA, Orange City, Iowa
Northwestern College—MN, St. Paul, Minnesota
Nyack College, New York, New York
Nyack College, Nyack, New York
Oklahoma Baptist University, Shawnee, Oklahoma
Oklahoma Christian University, Oklahoma City, Oklahoma
Oklahoma Wesleyan University, Bartlesville, Oklahoma
Olivet Nazarene University, Bourbonnais, Illinois
Oral Roberts University, Tulsa, Oklahoma
Palm Beach Atlantic University, West Palm Beach, Florida
Point Loma Nazarene University, San Diego, California
Redeemer University College, Ancaster, Ontario, Canada
Roberts Wesleyan College, Rochester, New York
Seattle Pacific University, Seattle, Washington
Simpson University, Redding, California
Southeastern University, Lakeland, Florida
Southern Nazarene University, Bethany, Oklahoma
Southern Wesleyan University, Central, South Carolina
Southwest Baptist University, Bolivar, Missouri
Spring Arbor University, Spring Arbor, Michigan
Sterling College, Sterling, Kansas
Tabor College, Hillsboro, Kansas
Taylor University, Upland, Indiana
Trevecca Nazarene University, Nashville, Tennessee
Trinity Christian College, Palos Heights, Illinois
Trinity International University, Deerfield, Illinois
Trinity Western University, Langley, British Columbia, Canada
Union University, Jackson, Tennessee
University of Sioux Falls, Sioux Falls, South Dakota

Vanguard University of Southern California, Costa Mesa, California
Warner Pacific College, Portland, Oregon
Warner Southern College, Lake Wales, Florida
Wayland Baptist University, Plainview, Texas
Waynesburg College, Waynesburg, Pennsylvania
Westmont College, Santa Barbara, California
Wheaton College, Wheaton, Illinois
Whitworth College, Spokane, Washington
Williams Baptist College, Walnut Ridge, Arkansas

Member status in the CCCU requires that colleges be four-year under-graduate institutions that hire only professing Christian faculty members. Affiliate status is provided to institutions that want to promote Christian education but do not meet the criteria for member status. Affiliates in North America, many of which are post-graduate schools such as theological seminaries, Toronto's Institute for Christian Studies, and Regent University in Virginia, include (arranged alphabetically by province and state):

Canada

Alliance University College, Calgary, Alberta
Canadian Nazarene University College, Calgary, Alberta
Prairie Bible Institute, Three Hills, Alberta
Taylor University College & Seminary, Edmonton, Alberta
Providence College & Seminary, Otterburne, Manitoba
Atlantic Baptist University, Moncton, New Brunswick
Institute for Christian Studies, Toronto, Ontario
Tyndale University College & Seminary, North York, Ontario
Tyndale University College & Seminary, Toronto, Ontario
Briercrest College, Caronport, Saskatchewan

United States

Grand Canyon University, Phoenix, Arizona
Crestmont College, Rancho Palos Verdes, California
Fuller Theological Seminary, Pasadena, California
San Diego Christian College, El Cajon, California

William Jessup University, Rocklin, California
North Haiti Christian University, Sarasota, Florida
Emmanuel College, Franklin Springs, Georgia
Toccoa Falls College, Toccoa Falls, Georgia
Moody Bible Institute, Chicago, Illinois
Central Christian College, McPherson, Kansas
Asbury Theological Seminary, Wilmore, Kentucky
Andrews University, Berrien Springs, Michigan
Reformed Bible College, Grand Rapids, Michigan
North Central University, Minneapolis, Minnesota
Campbell University, Buies Creek, North Carolina
Franciscan University of Steubenville, Steubenville, Ohio
Mid-America Christian University, Oklahoma City, Oklahoma
Lancaster Bible College, Lancaster, Pennsylvania
Philadelphia Biblical University, Langhorne, Pennsylvania
Valley Forge Christian College, Phoenixville, Pennsylvania
Charleston Southern University, Charleston, South Carolina
Columbia International University, Columbia, South Carolina
Baylor University, Waco, Texas
Criswell College, The, Dallas, Texas
Dallas Theological Seminary, Dallas, Texas
Bluefield College, Bluefield, Virginia
Regent University, Virginia Beach, Virginia
Walla Walla College, College Place, Washington
Ohio Valley University, Vienna, West Virginia

Member Denominations of the National Association of Evangelicals

Member denominations and their year of joining the NAE are listed below.

Advent Christian General Conference (1986)
Assemblies of God (1943)
Baptist General Conference (1966)
The Brethren Church (1968)
Brethren in Christ Church (1949)
Christian Catholic Church (Evangelical Protestant) (1975)
The Christian and Missionary Alliance (1966)
Christian Church of North America (1953)
Christian Reformed Church in North America (1943–51; 1988)
Christian Union (1954)
Church of God (Cleveland) (1944)
Church of God Mountain Assembly, Inc. (1981)
Church of the Nazarene (1984)
Church of the United Brethren in Christ (1953)
Churches of Christ in Christian Union (1945)
Congregational Holiness Church (1990–92; 1994)
Conservative Baptist Association of America (1990)
Conservative Congregational Christian Conference (1951)
Conservative Lutheran Association (1984)
Elim Fellowship (1947)
Evangelical Church of North America (1969)
Evangelical Congregational Church (1962)
Evangelical Free Church of America (1943)
Evangelical Friends International of North America (1971)
Evangelical Mennonite Church (1944)
Evangelical Methodist Church (1952)
Evangelical Presbyterian Church (1982)
Evangelistic Missionary Fellowship (1982)
Fellowship of Evangelical Bible Churches (1948)
Fire Baptized Holiness Church of God of the Americas (1978)
Free Methodist Church of North America (1944)

General Association of General Baptists (1988)
International Church of the Foursquare Gospel (1952)
International Pentecostal Church of Christ (1946)
International Pentecostal Holiness Church (1943)
Mennonite Brethren Churches, USA (1946)
Midwest Congregational Christian Fellowship (1964)
Missionary Church, Inc. (1944)
Open Bible Standard Churches (1943)
Pentecostal Church of God (1954)
Pentecostal Free Will Baptist Church, Inc. (1988)
Presbyterian Church in America (1986)
Primitive Methodist Church USA (1946)
Reformed Episcopal Church (1990)
Reformed Presbyterian Church of North America (1946)
Regional Synod of Mid-America (Reformed Church in America) (1989)
The Salvation Army, National Headquarters (1990)
The Wesleyan Church (1948)
Worldwide Church of God (1997)

Mary

Top Ten Facts About Mary

1. Dante said that Mary's face is the one that most closely resembles the face of Christ.

2. Apparitions of Mary have been reported in every era in history and every country in the world.

3. The early church fathers compared Eve to Mary. As Eve was the mother of humanity who fell into sin, Mary was the mother of a new humanity.

4. The Christian representation of Mary helped early converts from paganism connect with the Church.

5. Mary is regarded as a helper for those who grieve and to those who are in need of comfort. Grieving parents have taken comfort in her because she lost her own child in a tragic way.

6. Despite the widely secular nature of the twenty-first century, pilgrimages to Marian sites seem to be increasing in frequency.

7. Many of the earliest churches devoted to Mary were built on old pagan holy sites.

8. Despite Mary's significant place in the lives of the Christian faithful for centuries, she is mentioned less in the Bible than in the Koran.

9. Many scholars think that Mary may have only been thirteen or fourteen years old when she gave birth to Christ.

10. Mary has garnered the praise of writers such as Dante, Jack Kerouac, Flannery O'Conner, and Sue Monk Kidd.

Introduction

YOU'VE PROBABLY SEEN EVIDENCE of devotion to Mary in our society—you may have seen the shrines that adorn backyards across America, an image of Our Lady of Guadalupe dangling from the rear-view mirror in a taxicab, or statues or icons of the Virgin Mary in people's homes. Perhaps you've wondered what is at the heart of this love for the Virgin Mary.

The phenomenon of devotion to the Virgin Mary is wider and deeper than you may imagine. Apparitions of her are reported to have occurred in every country in the world, spanning the centuries, and crossing cultural barriers. She has inspired more artistic renderings than any other woman in the history of the world and has nudged the pens of poets, the hearts of kings, and the history of nations.

Her influence even extends to our gardens. Did you know that in a very simplistic way the flowers and plants in your backyard witness to the history of Marian devotion, with its many peaks and valleys? Originally, flowers and plants were named for ancient pagan gods and goddesses. In the medieval era, hundreds of them were renamed with Marian names, which helped the faithful to draw close to her even in the fields. Think about the names of marigolds, lady's slippers, and Madonna lilies. After the Reformation, when devotion to the Virgin Mary was curtailed, these flowers were again renamed—or in some cases, their connection to Mary just became more subtle, so that only a serious devotee would be able recognize the connection. For example, the Milk Thistle was known before the Reformation as "Our Lady's Milk Drops," and forget-me-not was known as "Our Lady's Eyes."

Think of this book as a quilt of the Virgin Mary with many squares stitched together to tell the story of the history, legends, art, culture, and controversies that have been connected to Mary. Most of us know only our own square; by stepping back from that one square and glimpsing the whole quilt, we have an opportunity to glimpse the whole—to see patterns, shapes, and possibilities that may not have been apparent before.

It is an exciting process of discovery to learn how people have related to the Virgin Mary throughout the ages, how her presence has inspired and transformed lives, how her very being has helped Christianity to connect with the patterns and seasons of Earth, and how we can be strengthened as we face the great mysteries of life—birth and death.

As we remember the way that Mary walked through these thresholds, we find courage as we face our own thresholds. We see that there is more to life than meets the eye, that only by stepping back to see the whole can we begin to see patterns in the ways in which devotion to Mary crosses cultures, spans seasons, and transforms lives around the globe, both historically and in the present day.

If we come to Mary with humility, with an open and seeking heart, we are sure to learn something, no matter who we are and where we come from. This book discusses so many cultures and peoples. For some of us, it may help us to better understand our spouses, our in-laws, our neighbor's devotion and it may help us make sense of the bewildering variety and intensity of devotion to this lady whose life, in so many ways, still remains a mystery.

Foreword

THERE IS SIMPLY NO doubt about it. The woman who has had the most impact on the history, art, culture, and literature of the human race from the dawn of time till now is clearly Mary, the mother of Jesus. The ironic thing about this, however, is that good information about Mary is not always easy to come by. Usually what you can find is either incomplete, dry, or sectarian.

This book is none of the above. It represents something that has been desperately needed for a long time—a fascinating, comprehensive, provocative, and eminently readable introduction to every aspect of Mary and her 2,000-year relationship with the sons of Adam and the daughters of Eve.

This book does not stop with the various and sundry Christian perspectives on Mary. It also reviews the very important role she plays in the Islamic faith confessed by over a billion of the earth's inhabitants. In fact, the book makes a rather startling claim—that the Virgin Mary, far from being a bone of contention, is actually a bridge-builder of monumental proportions. This book explores Mary's ability to cross boundaries and build connection between Jewish and Christian Scriptures, Christians and Muslims, poor and rich, and men and women.

In fact, in a feminist age fascinated by the "divine feminine," Mary holds greater importance than ever. What she represents is the key to unlocking the secret of true feminine dignity and power, and how best to understand and access the feminine dimension of the Divine.

But make no mistake about it—this is no academic tome of mere theoretical interest. Its focus throughout is how Mary has impacted the faith and lives of *real* people. Here we learn about devotions as well as doctrines, art as well as literature, and folk customs along with their surprisingly profound meanings. Weeping icons, statues crowned with May flowers, apparitions, healing Marian springs, rosaries, and scapulars are covered along with what church councils, Protestant reformers, New Testament Scriptures and even the Koran have had to say about the most modest, yet most pivotal, woman in human history.

This book will not only provide you with information *about* Mary, it will also introduce you *to* her. As you read about the ways she has influenced the lives of millions across the centuries from every religious tradition imaginable, you may just find her story striking a chord in you. Your knowledge of culture and religion will certainly be enriched, as will the quality of your own life and spirituality.

This book demonstrates that Mary is more than a plaster statue on a pedestal or an icon on a wall. She is a very real person who is strangely approachable, given her lofty role, because she is not very much different than we are. She experienced many of the same doubts, fears, and limitations that beset us every day. Perhaps that's why she's been such a sought-after prayer partner and an inspiring model. For Mary achieved what many of us, at least secretly, desire to achieve—loyalty to the truth, courage in the face of fear, and surrender to the One whose love and power surpasses everything we can possibly imagine.

Marcellino D'Ambrosio, Ph.D.
Adjunct Professor of Theology
Ave Maria University
Naples Florida

CHAPTER 1

Our Lady of Paradox

Many people are surprised to discover how little the New Testament says about Mary, especially in light of her profound influence throughout the ages. Although few, if any, would claim to know exactly what Mary looked like, artistic renderings of her appear in almost every culture in the world. Likewise, millions continue to be inspired or baffled by news of her "appearances." To express the inexpressible, the ancient church often used paradoxes to speak about Mary. This chapter will use paradoxes to introduce a teenage virgin from Galilee who changed the world.

Who Is Mary?

In C. S. Lewis's *Prince Caspian*, Lucy notices that Aslan seems to have grown since the last time she saw him. When she asks him about this he tells her that he only seems bigger because *she* has grown. It is like that with Mary. She seems simple at first glance and becomes more complex and significant the more you learn about her.

Throughout the centuries, Christians have debated about what to call Mary, how to view her life, and how to integrate her witness into their own spiritual journeys. The Roman Catholic and Eastern Orthodox Churches have retained a deep love for her. Although the two churches have not always expressed their devotion in the same ways, they have generally shared the guiding premise that every statement and image of Mary is ultimately intended to bring people closer to her son.

Icons depicting Mary holding her infant son express the reason that Mary is most revered. Her witness is not only one of profound courage and obedience, but is ultimately one of maternal love. Her love for her own son has often been seen as a role model for mothers as they seek to care for their own children.

symbolism

In some icons of the Virgin Mary, she holds the infant Christ with her left arm. Her right hand gestures toward the face of her son, guiding our eyes back to him. He leans into her, with the eager devotion of a child, expressing his quiet, steady love for her, and ultimately, for all of us.

Friends in High Places

Anne Rice's novel *Christ the Lord* offers a unique glimpse into the clannish culture in which Jesus was born. According to Rice's depiction, the nuclear family as we know it now was rarely seen in ancient times. Instead, a family would have multiple generations and relations (including first and second cousins) living under the same roof. When a family would travel, they would often journey as a tribe.

This image fits well with the lengthy genealogies offered at the beginnings of the Gospels of Luke and Matthew. These meandering lists of barely pronounceable names are read in many churches in the days and weeks leading up to Christmas. Some might wish to skip them and get on to the gist of the story—the no-room-at-the-inn scene starring the very pregnant Mary and Joseph. But these lists are important because they help place the newborn Jesus in the context of generations of faith, a community stretching through time and space.

Even today, every Christian life is rooted in a heritage of faith and has a sense of continuity with all of those who have come before, who have carried the Gospel with their lives through the centuries. In many churches, this "Great Cloud of Witnesses" (Hebrews 12:1) is understood to be full of holy people who, though deceased, nevertheless continue to pray and support those struggling to live for God. Throughout Christian tradition, this intangible, invisible community of saints has been made tangible and visible through icons and statues and other religious objects.

Those within the churches that believe in the living example of the "Great Cloud of Witnesses" have also continued the ancient practice of asking for the prayers of those who have gone before them, believing that those who now live with God know far better than the earthbound how to pray. Within this community, there is no prayer partner more beloved than the Virgin Mary.

So Few Words—So Much Influence

Despite Mary's significance for many Christians around the world, the Gospel accounts only provide the barebones of Mary's life. Many details from the Gospels about Mary's life have leaked into Christmas hymns and Nativity scenes and have been repeated year after year. Sometimes, the story seems so familiar that it can be hard to grasp the full impact of the event. Mary lived with her parents in Nazareth. During her engagement to a man named Joseph, an angel came to her and told her that she would conceive a child through the Holy Spirit. The angel told Mary that the child's name would be Jesus, because he would save people from their sins (Luke 1:31–32).

discussion question

What is the significance of the name Jesus?
The Hebrew name for Jesus, Y'shua, is a shortened form of the name Joshua (Y'hoshua). The name Joshua literally means "the Lord saves."

When Mary shared her frightening, awe-inspiring news with her fiancé, he did not rejoice. In fact, according to the Gospel of Matthew, he did not actually believe her, and secretly resolved to quietly end the relationship to prevent a scandal (Matthew 1:19). But Joseph's sense of betrayal and disbelief changed as a result of a dream in which an angel came to him, assuring him about the more-difficult-to-explain parts of the pregnancy (specifically, how Mary came to be pregnant when she and Joseph had not yet been married). The angel also told Joseph not to be afraid to take Mary as his wife.

Joseph's initial apprehension about Mary's news is reflected in early Christian icons of Jesus' birth. In these icons, Joseph is often portrayed with his back to Mary and the newborn Jesus, looking away from the infant Jesus toward a small demon. Because icons often include images of events that may have occurred at different times, the image of Joseph here jumps back in time to show his earlier temptation to disbelieve Mary. He seems lost in his own private world of doubts and fears. This image expresses the ancient belief that temptations tend to be most fierce when we are alone, and that sin increases isolation.

In one of the great giddy moments of the Gospels, Mary hears the news that her relative Elizabeth (who had been barren) is also pregnant. She journeys to Elizabeth's home, and as she steps through the front door, Elizabeth makes the first public proclamation about the miracle inside of Mary. Elizabeth calls Mary "the mother of my Lord" and the babe in Elizabeth's womb leaps with joy (Luke 1:39–45).

During her pregnancy, Mary traveled with Joseph to Bethlehem for the census (Luke 2:1–7). When they realized that the birth of the baby was near, Mary and Joseph attempted to find a room at an inn, but there were no openings, so Mary gave birth in a stable where animals were kept, and Jesus was laid in a manger (which is something like a cattle trough).

The accounts from Matthew and Luke differ in many elements, including the structure in which Jesus was born. Many Christmas hymns make it seem as if Jesus was born in a wooden barn, but according to ancient church tradition Jesus was actually born in a cave. This tradition is based on Luke's account (Luke 2:7), because shepherds would have likely kept animals in a cave. Matthew, however, refers to a house (Matthew 2:11).

factum

The oldest continually operating church in the Holy Land, the Church of the Nativity in Bethlehem, is located on the spot where many believe Jesus was born. Each year, thousands of pilgrims journey to Bethlehem to light a candle and pray beside the gold star that marks this holy spot.

After Mary gave birth, Jesus was circumcised and the family visited the temple in Jerusalem. Shortly after this, the family fled to Egypt to avoid Herod's wrath, and then returned after Herod's death (Matthew 2:13–23). They lived in Nazareth for thirty years until the beginning of Jesus' public ministry (Luke 2:39–40). Scholars believe that Mary was eventually widowed, because Joseph was never mentioned again.

From the cross, Jesus asked his beloved disciple John to care for Mary until her dying day (John 19:26–27). In Ephesus, there is a small stone house that Christian and Muslim pilgrims visit to this day, where many believe John and Mary lived for several years. You'll learn more about the house of Mary in Chapter 18. According to Scripture, Mary was also present with the apostles at Pentecost (Acts 1:14, 2:1).

These bare-bones accounts demonstrate how very little we know about Mary from the Gospels. They don't seem to explain the widespread influence of Mary. Because the Biblical accounts are so sparse, many Protestants are reluctant to say too much about Mary. Unlike the Reformers (discussed in more detail in Chapter 10) who generally expressed devotion toward

Mary, modern Protestants often avoid saying anything about her that doesn't directly come from Scripture. Within the Roman Catholic and Eastern Orthodox Churches, however, devotion to Mary is so strong that hyperbole is often used in speaking about her—not unlike the way that some people rave about their own mothers.

The next sections will explore some of the ways in which the ancient church used to speak about this woman of so few words and so much influence.

Unwedded Bride

One of the paradoxes that has been used to describe Mary, especially in Byzantine hymnography, is the phrase "unwedded bride." This expresses something profound about Mary's relationship with God. Throughout the centuries, many have believed that by choosing Mary to be the mother of Christ, God entered into a unique, almost spousal relationship with Mary. Mary has been considered the Bride of the Holy Spirit in a relationship that echoes the Scriptural reference to the marriage between Christ and the Church (Ephesians 5:23–32). For Saint Paul, there was no imagery more potent than that of a wedding to express this joyful union between Christ and the Church.

symbolism

In the Gospels, the kingdom of heaven is compared to a wedding banquet, and the relationship between Christ and the Church is compared to a marriage between a husband and a wife. The use of nuptial imagery remains a common way for Christians to express the mystical depths of the relationship between God and his beloved creatures.

Mary was, of course, married to Joseph in the official sense of the word, but church tradition has held that, in a more transcendent sense, Mary was actually the spouse of the Holy Spirit. Because of the particular nature of

Mary's role as the mother of Christ and her unique place in salvation history, both the Roman Catholic and the Eastern Orthodox Churches believe that Mary and Joseph's marriage was never consummated.

Currently there is much debate between Protestants, Catholics, and Eastern Orthodox over whether the Virgin Mary remained a virgin all of her life. Although most of the Reformers did believe that Mary remained a virgin (including Protestant reformers John Calvin, Ulrich Zwingli, Martin Luther, and John Wesley), Protestantism has generally moved away from this earlier belief, while Orthodoxy and Catholicism continue to teach that Mary was "ever-virgin."

Virgin Mother

The idea of a Virgin Mother is extremely difficult to grasp, because children are the fruit of a sexual union. But Christ's unusual entry into the world set him apart as the unconventional sort who would no doubt turn the world upside down.

factum

In the Bible, the term "to know" is often used to imply sexual relations. When Mary asks, "How shall this be, since I know not a man?" (Luke 1:34 KJV) she is saying, quite simply, that she is still a virgin. This term "know" implies that a rich intimacy is found in sexuality—an intimacy that creates physical, emotional, and spiritual union.

Most Christians have been able to agree that Mary was a virgin when Christ was born, but the idea of her being ever-virgin has been hotly contested by many. Those who do not believe that Mary was ever-virgin have pointed out that the Gospel accounts mention that Jesus had siblings. Some also express concern about the passage in the Gospels that says that Joseph did not *know* Mary until after Christ was born (Matthew 1:25). Part of the problem here may be the particular connotations of the word *until* in English—in Greek, it simply means "up to the time of" and does not imply anything about what came afterward. The word *until* simply emphasizes the idea that Mary was a virgin when Christ was born.

Although the Roman Catholic and Eastern Orthodox Churches share the conviction that the Virgin Mary was ever-virgin, each church has found ways to explain the fact that the Gospels speak of the "siblings of Christ." Their different explanations are based on the different sources they have generally relied on for the traditions surrounding Jesus' family.

The East follows the story in the Protoevangelium of James (an apocryphal book), which says that Joseph was a widower, and that they were Joseph's children from a previous marriage. It would not have been unusual for a young virgin to be betrothed to an older man. Christians in the West, following St. Jerome (A.D. 331–420), have usually regarded the siblings of Jesus as merely cousins.

Over time, more and more discussion has been generated about these basic questions. Some scholars have said that if Jesus did have siblings in the modern sense of the word, then it would be rather odd for Jesus to ask his relative John to care for his mother after his death (John 9:27).

Whichever account is accepted, it is clear that the Greek and Aramaic terms for brother are more expansive than the English term, which could account for some of the confusion surrounding these passages. In Aramaic and Greek, this term is more generic, sometimes meaning "relative" or someone who is part of one's extended family as opposed to a blood sibling. There are other scriptural examples of Biblical brothers such as Lot and Abraham, who were not brothers in the English sense of the word.

The cultural context of the Scriptures certainly offers a picture of family relations that is much more expansive than the American version of the nuclear family. Because of this, modern readers might be skeptical of the theory that the word *siblings* could actually refer to cousins.

Frail, but Powerful

In his 1898 painting of the Virgin Mary, Henry Ossawa Tanner depicts Mary as a young girl, seated on the rumpled sheets of her bed, looking vulnerable and afraid. She is looking toward a light-filled being in the corner of the room. The radiance of the angel seems to pull her face upward, toward some hope and purpose, as she is being told that she will bear the Christ child in her womb, risking alienation from her fiancé and community.

Mary must have understood the real risks of what was about to happen to her. As a betrothed woman, she could have been stoned to death for adultery. This is part of why Joseph, evidently a gentle man, planned to quietly end the relationship, to protect Mary (Matthew 1:19).

This painting also says something about the progression of the way Mary has been viewed throughout time. This image expresses an important truth about Mary. She is not a simple, one-dimensional character, aloof and separate from our struggles and experiences. She experienced the full complexity of human emotions and struggled for courage. Fear and wonder must have mingled on her face as the angel spoke, which is why she was told, "Be not afraid."

symbolism

In the early centuries, Christians often emphasized the ways in which Mary was set apart and holy. In more recent times, however, Mary has been better known for commiserating with the poor and oppressed and the ways she lived with empathy, compassion, and vulnerability.

But there is another side to Mary that is rarely emphasized in modern times. As much as she can be seen as vulnerable and frail, she can also be viewed as a woman of incredible strength and power because of her closeness with God. Her strength was seen as so great that entire armies—from Byzantium, through the Crusades, and up through the time of Imperial Russia—would ask for her protection before heading into battle. Mary was also seen as a protector for those heading out to sea, because she was viewed as able to quell the waves and storms as her son had.

When Christopher Columbus set sail for the Americas he named his ship the *Santa Maria,* for Mary. By naming ships after Mary, mariners often felt that they were evoking her special blessing upon them as they journeyed. It was widely believed that her prayers could hold back storms and protect those at sea in the midst of them, as her son did in the Scriptures.

The image of Mary as "Star of the Sea" or *Stella Maris* may be based on an error a scribe made when he was copying the works of Jerome. Although Jerome is often viewed as the first author to use this title, the title he actually used was *Stilla Maris*, which can be translated as "Drop of the Sea."

Revered and Shunned

Despite the widespread devotion to her through the ages, Mary has remained something of an enigma. Check your local bookstore and you may be surprised by how few titles there are related to the Virgin Mary. While most bookstores have large selections of books on Christianity, books on Mary are often difficult to find.

But perhaps this lack of literature speaks to the historical dilemma. People just don't know how to feel about the Virgin Mary. While Eastern Orthodox and Roman Catholics revere her, Protestants often feel uneasy about Marian Devotion, sensing that it could distract people from Christ. And while no woman has been a model to more women, some strains of feminism have expressed disdain for Mary, saying that her submissive attitude only fosters a culture of male oppression. Yet the paradox only grows, because to so many of the people who love her most, Mary is the ultimate female representation of strength and power—transcending time and transforming lives.

factum

During the Reformation, bandits knocked off the heads and limbs from statues as a way of expressing their rage at some of the practices of the Roman Catholic Church. In our day, random vandals topple and shatter statues of Mary as a way of defacing all that she represents.

The final way in which our culture seems to have a paradoxical relationship with Mary is demonstrated through some of its popular images. While many images of Mary are created with great love and reverence, others seem to mock her. The "artistic" depiction of the Virgin Mary covered in dung and pornography, which went on display at the Brooklyn Museum of Art is one example of this. (You can read more about this in Chapter 15.)

Another way that Mary is both loved and shunned is through statues. After Hurricanes Katrina and Wilma devastated Louisiana and Florida, many people cared gingerly for pieces of the statues of Mary that had been shattered by the storm. They felt that their loving care for these broken images translated into loving care for Mary and her son. But as much as people have respected these images, over the course of history people have also defaced and intentionally destroyed them.

As much as Mary is shunned, mocked, and feared, she is also adored and cherished. The wide variety of reactions to Mary is suggestive of the wide scope of realities that she represents. So much of who and what she was seems simple at first glance, and then becomes increasingly complex as she is explored. For this reason, paradoxes have offered an invaluable tool for glimpsing this woman who continually stretches beyond the grasp of our language and comprehension.

CHAPTER 2

Gospel Glimpses

The Gospels do not give much attention to Mary, because they are far more focused on detailing the works of Christ and the establishment of his ministry. References to her may be sparse, but each one has grown richer and deeper through time, as generations of Christian theologians have engaged and reflected upon the texts. This chapter will explore the different Gospel representations of Mary, as well as the unique approach taken by each of the Gospel writers.

Prophecies

The New Testament builds upon and expands the Old Testament. The writers of the New Testament were steeped in the Scriptural world of Judaism. One way many of the New Testament writers emphasize this connection to the writings of Judaism is by pointing to prophecies or other verses from the Old Testament that, according to the writers of the New Testament, were fulfilled in events the New Testament writers were recording.

Isaiah's Prophecy

One of the prophecies woven into Matthew's Gospel was taken from the Old Testament book of Isaiah (7:14). Matthew embedded this prophecy into his account of the birth of Christ (Matthew 1:18–24), which differs significantly from the account offered by Luke (Luke 1–2). Matthew's account offers the bare-bones of the birth, skipping the central story of the angel's visitation to Mary and emphasizing the way that the angel appeared to Joseph in a dream just as he was considering leaving Mary.

According to Matthew's account, the angel's words echoed the Old Testament prophecy from Isaiah when the angel said, "Now all this took place to fulfill the words of the prophet when he said, 'The Virgin will conceive and give birth to a son, and they will call his name Emmanuel, which means "God is with us,"' (Matthew 1:18–24).

This connection with the Old Testament prophecy helped to demonstrate that both Christ and the Virgin Mary were part of a divinely orchestrated plan, which was intimately connected to the Old Testament.

Jesus in the Temple

Another prophetic event in the Gospels is related to something that happened shortly after Jesus' birth. In this case, it is not an Old Testament prophecy but a prophecy that was first mentioned in Luke's Gospel that had implications for Mary's life and for later generations to come.

This prophetic event occurred when Joseph and Mary took Jesus to the temple as an infant. Simeon was there and he said to Mary, "You see this child. He is destined for the fall and for the rising of many in Israel, destined to be a sign that is rejected—and a sword will pierce your own soul, too—so the secret thoughts of many will be laid bare" (Luke 2:33–35).

symbolism

In later Roman Catholic piety, images of Mary with her heart exposed became popular. These images offered a way of understanding the love she experienced for Christ and the suffering she endured for his sake. Many of these images show her heart pierced by a sword, based on the image from Luke's Gospel.

This passage from Luke's Gospel has many theological implications, which will be felt personally by Mary. Mary will suffer because of her love for her son. Just as Jesus experienced rejection and death, Mary will feel this pain acutely, as only a mother could.

Mary's Family Tree

One of the first ironic things that one might notice about the lengthy lists of names that trace Joseph's lineage back to King David is that these genealogies are specifically related to Joseph, who was not, according to Christian teaching, biologically related to Christ. At first glance, it seems strange that these writers would go to such great lengths to establish a royal line if this royal line were only connected to Joseph. However, in Jesus' time, the father's lineage would be of utmost importance for establishing legal parentage. Matthew emphasizes Jesus' adoption into this line. There is a church tradition that Mary was also a descendant of King David, but the Bible is ambiguous about this. In any case, all four of the Gospels—Matthew, Mark, Luke, and John—speak of Jesus as the son of David.

There is an interesting divergence between the way the Koran and the Gospels present these genealogies. In the Gospels, the genealogies seem to be chiefly intended to show that Jesus came from the royal house of David. In the Koran, however, Christ's genealogy offers a different set of Old Testament figures than any of the Gospels. These figures are not from the kingly line but from the line of prophets. This variation between the two texts parallels the different teachings about Christ. Within Christianity, Christ is the Son of God and a descendant from the royal line of David. In the Koran, however, Christ is a great prophet, but is not considered divine.

factum

Some theologians have pointed out parallels between the Virgin Mary and the Old Testament prophet Abraham. Both struggled with the question of how they would bear children, and both heard, "Fear not!" in response. Just as Abraham pleaded with God to save the people of Sodom and Gomorrah, Mary was seen as one who interceded for people seeking God's mercy.

Matthew's genealogy mentions four women: Tamar, Ruth, Rahab, and "the Wife of Uriah," or Bathsheba. Although all of these women's lives were significant, each of their names was at least slightly tainted by scandal.

Tamar, who was a widow without children, dressed up as a prostitute so that she could trick her father-in-law into sleeping with her in order to claim her legal right to continue the family line of her deceased husband. Ruth was not Jewish by birth, but her Jewish mother-in-law Naomi helped her into a marriage with Naomi's wealthy relative, Boaz, so that Ruth could also perpetuate her family line. Rahab was herself a prostitute, but she put her efforts toward helping the Jews to enter the promised land.

Finally, there is Bathsheba. King David spied her bathing naked one day as he was walking on his roof. David lusted after her to such an extent that he gave orders that she be brought to his palace, and he committed adultery with her. When she became pregnant, he commanded that her husband, Uriah, be put on the front lines of battle so that he would be killed and David could marry Bathsheba. (2 Samuel 11) The child born of her was Solomon, who later became king and was renown for his wisdom. It was Solomon who built the temple for God that David dreamed of, and through whom the royal line continued. All of these women used unconventional methods to accomplish extraordinary things that profoundly affected the history of the Jewish lineage.

In these women, many theologians have seen a suggestion of what was to come—another woman who would enter into an equally unconventional marriage for the greater good of her people.

The Brave Yes

Because stories of the Annunciation (the revelation to Mary by Gabriel that she will conceive and give birth to the Son of God) have become so familiar, many of us miss the unusual aspect of the conversation between the angel and Mary that is recorded in Luke. Mary's agreement with God's plan was not automatic. She had to struggle through the implications first (Luke 1:26–38).

The account in Luke begins with the story of Zachariah serving in the temple and having an angel appear to him to tell him that his prayers will finally be answered and that his barren wife (Mary's cousin, Elizabeth) will give birth. Zachariah is struck silent by the vision and is unable to report to anyone in the temple what he saw or heard. Only when he names the child, John, by writing the name on a tablet, does he regain his speech.

This story of miraculous conception sets the stage for Jesus' birth. According to Luke's account, when Elizabeth was six months pregnant, the angel Gabriel appeared to Elizabeth's relative Mary, telling her to not be afraid because she will bear a son, and her son will be great and will rule over the house of Jacob forever.

symbolism

Many Christian interpreters see parallels between the Holy Spirit overshadowing Mary in the Gospel account (Luke 1:35), the Spirit descending like a dove at Jesus' baptism (Matthew 3:16, Mark 1:10), and the passage in Genesis about the Spirit of God hovering over the waters at the creation of the world (Genesis 1:2). Jesus' birth heralds the beginning of new creation.

After Mary questions the angel, asking how this can be possible because she has not known man, the angel explains that the Holy Spirit will come upon her and the holy one in her womb will be called the Son of God.

After the angel explains how Mary's conception will occur, the angel goes on to report another miracle to Mary that may likely help her to see that she was at the center of concentric circles of miracles—that the child she had conceived came at a time of other extraordinary events.

The angel explained to Mary that her relative Elizabeth, who had been barren, had also conceived and was six months pregnant. The angel then said, "For with God, nothing will be impossible" (Luke 1:37).

Mary is amazed by this news and travels to the hill country of Judea to be with her relative. As soon as she greets Elizabeth, the babe leaps in Elizabeth's womb, and Elizabeth immediately recognizes the holiness of the moment, as she loudly proclaims the words that would later become the foundation of the Hail Mary prayer: "Blessed are you among women, and blessed is the fruit of your womb." Then she goes on to say, "But why is this granted to me that the mother of my Lord should come to visit me?" (Luke 1:43).

factum

The Annunciation has been the source of much creative interpretation. The beauty of this encounter between Mary and Elizabeth caused the great contemporary poet Rainer Maria Rilke to write, "She had to lay her hand upon the other woman's body, still more ripe than hers . . . each one a sanctuary, sought refuge with her closest woman kin."

Both of these statements must have confirmed for Mary and Elizabeth that they were part of a Divine plan. After Elizabeth's greeting, Mary replies with the words that are now known as the Magnificat. In Eastern Christian usage, the Magnificat is the ninth chapter of the *Biblical Odes*, a book that was used liturgically and included in many Bibles right after the Psalms.

Here is this famous "Song of Mary":

My soul proclaims the greatness of the Lord; my spirit rejoices in God my savior.

For he has looked with mercy on the lowliness of His handmaiden; for behold, from now on all generations will call me blessed.

For the Mighty One has done great things for me, and holy is His name.

His mercy is on those who fear him from generation to generation.

He has shown strength with his arm;

He has scattered the proud in the imagination of their hearts.

He has thrown down the mighty from their thrones, but lifted up the lowly.

He has filled the hungry with good things, but the rich he has sent away empty.

He has helped Israel his servant, in remembrance of His mercy;

As He spoke to our fathers, to Abraham and to his seed forever.

(Luke 1:46–55)

With these words, Mary expresses her sense of wonder and joy at the news of her role in God's plan for the salvation of the world. Because of the way it proclaims God's salvation, these verses have sometimes been called "The Gospel of Mary."

Christ's Birth

Luke's and Matthew's accounts of Jesus' birth do not offer all the same details. For centuries, Christians have been piecing together different elements from each Gospel in an effort to create one cohesive account, but in reality, the Gospel accounts sometimes contradict each other. Likewise, only Matthew and Luke offer details from Christ's birth and only Luke mentions Jesus' childhood.

discussion question

Has there been an attempt to blend the Gospel stories together?
In the latter half of the second century, a man named Tatian attempted to create a synthesis of all the four Gospels called the *Diatessaron*. This was used by many Christians but was ultimately dismissed by the fifth-century Bishop of Cyrrhus, Theodoret. He believed that the Church needed to preserve the original Gospels in their full integrity.

Luke's Gospel is the only one in which a census forced the holy family to journey to Bethlehem, where Mary gave birth to her firstborn son, wrapped him in swaddling clothes, and laid him in a manger (Luke 2:7).

The next striking aspect of Luke's account occurred when the shepherds were minding their flocks at night and an angel appeared to them, announcing that a child named Christ had been born in Bethlehem. The shepherds, like Mary before them, were extremely frightened by the glory of the Lord that shone upon them as the angel spoke. But also like Mary's Annunciation, the angel offered reassuring words—he was again bearing good news that would bring joy to all the people.

The shepherds were then told to go to Bethlehem to find the babe wrapped in swaddling clothes and lying in a manger. Then, a whole host of angels surrounded the shepherds and began to sing, "Glory to God in the highest and on earth peace, good will toward men" (Luke 2:14).

When the shepherds arrived at Bethlehem, they found the babe just as the angel had prophesied. They were amazed at all the things they had experienced and shared their story with Mary and Joseph. Everyone marveled, and Mary "kept all of these things and pondered them in her heart" (Luke 2:19).

In the Gospel of Luke especially, Mary often seems to be storing up bits of information in her heart as she ponders the changes that are happening to her son as he grows toward his vocation. After Mary and Joseph lose Jesus in Jerusalem and then search for their twelve-year-old son for three days, they finally find Jesus in the temple. Mary says, "Son, why have you done this to us? Your father and I have been looking for you with great anxiety" (Luke 2:48).

Jesus responds with a statement that some contemporary scholars believe was one of rebuke when he says, "Did you not know that I must be in my father's house?" (Luke 2:49). According to Sally Cunneen in the book *In Search of Mary*, the response Mary gives to Jesus is interesting, because Mary does not scold Jesus for a remark that might have sounded arrogant coming from the lips of a twelve-year-old. Instead, she keeps silent, and according to Luke's Gospel she kept all these things in her heart (Luke 2:51).

In the Gospel stories, Mary, like her son Jesus, seems to be growing toward understanding. She holds experiences in her heart because she needs time to understand them. Mary seems amazingly flexible in this way—she is able to adjust to her son's evolving ministry even when it causes him to say or do things that might have appeared rude coming from any other child. She recognizes that there is a larger purpose at work in her son, even if she does not claim to fully understand the implications of it or the shape that it will take over the next several years.

The Wedding at Cana

In this story, found only in the Gospel of John, Jesus and Mary are at a wedding. It seems that Mary is one of the wedding coordinators, and when the wine begins to run out, she becomes alarmed. She tells Jesus that they are out of wine. Jesus responds to his mother's prompting with some very blunt words. He says, "Woman, what have I to do with you? My hour has not yet come" (John 2:4).

Mary, however, does not seem to be offended. Her son eventually responds to her concern, though. The wine that he creates from the water is so good that one of the guests comments that usually one puts out the best wine first, and when it has been consumed puts out the lower-quality wine, but at this wedding, the best was saved for last. This miracle is significant, because it is one of Jesus' first acts at the very beginning of his public ministry. Because this was a significant turning point for Jesus, his reluctance may have been warranted—when he said "My hour has not yet come," he might have had in mind everything that was to happen to him in the future.

This story has also been quoted as an antecedent to the later mystery of the Eucharist in both the Roman Catholic and Eastern Orthodox Churches, in which bread and wine become body and blood. Another echo of this story is seen when Jesus is stretched out upon the cross and a soldier pierces his side with a sword and both blood and water stream from the wound.

Perhaps the most popular bit of folk piety, however, that rose from this passage is the idea that Mary is a great intercessor because in this story at least, she was able to get Jesus to do the thing she most wanted him to do, even though it went against his initial wishes. People reading this story in the Bible see a different side of Mary, who is a strong and determined woman who has the power to get things accomplished.

Mary at the Cross

According to the book of John, Jesus' mother was said to be at the cross during Jesus' Crucifixion, along with Mary Magdalene, and another Mary. According to John's account, Jesus speaks from the cross and commits his mother to the care of his beloved disciple. He says to John, "Behold your mother," gesturing at Mary, and then he says to Mary, "Behold your son" (John 2:4).

According to John's account, from that time forward John took Mary to live with him in his own home. According to Church tradition, John moved to Ephesus after the Crucifixion.

At the wedding at Cana, in which Mary asked Jesus to turn water into wine, he states, "Woman, what have I to do with you? My hour has not yet come" (John 2:4). Jesus addresses his mother as "woman." While many people have viewed this statement as profoundly disrespectful, some recent scholars have suggested that when Jesus called Mary "woman," he was addressing her as one of his disciples, as opposed to his mother. It would have been an honor to be considered one of Christ's disciples.

This statement seems to connect well with the verses in Acts which mentions that after the Crucifixion, Mary went to the upper room with the disciples to pray. She was present as if she was a disciple—she bore a responsibility to Christ that went beyond her biological connection to him and related directly to the spiritual responsibility she felt to continue to bring his message into the world.

discussion question

If the Virgin Mary had children other than Jesus, why were none of them present at the cross with her? Although this issue is sometimes debated among Protestants, Roman Catholics, and Eastern Orthodox, Christians have pointed to the Crucifixion passage as evidence that Jesus had no blood siblings, because siblings would have been a more logical choice as guardians of Mary than his disciples.

Mary and the Apocalypse

The book of Revelation, also known as the Apocalypse of John, describes a "woman clothed with the sun" who labors with child (Revelation 12:1–6). She stands upon the sun and has twelve stars upon her head. She cries out in anguish as she gives birth to the child.

The child she brings into the world is a male child who will rule all the nations with an iron scepter. This woman is never explicitly identified as Mary in the Biblical text, but many Christians have drawn out the parallels. Many of the Marian apparitions seem to confirm this interpretation, especially because of the solar miracles associated with her visitations at Fatima and Medjugorje. This image also parallels the prophecies given to Mary at the Annunciation when she was told that Jesus will rule over Judea forever and his kingdom will have no end.

Although the passages in the New Testament related to Mary are sometimes sparse and occasionally contradictory, these passages became the basis for much of the piety that would surround Mary for generations to come. Each passage offers fresh insights into her heart, her person, and her unique role in her son's ministry.

CHAPTER 3

Mary in the Apocrypha

Besides the books that eventually became collated into the New Testament, many other books were written around and after the time of the apostles. While these books never achieved the full status as canonical (or universally accepted) books of the Bible, some of them came to have a wide influence and were much loved by Christians, while others were considered dangerous and shunned. This chapter will explore the stories of Mary found primarily in one apocryphal book, the Protoevangelium of James.

What Is the Apocrypha?

The term *Apocrypha* can refer to two very distinct bodies of texts. First, the Old Testament Apocrypha connotes a group of texts that are part of many Greek versions of the Old Testament around the time of Christ, but are not considered authoritative in Judaism or the Protestant churches today. These texts, however, remain part of the officially accepted Roman Catholic and Eastern Orthodox versions of the Old Testament. Because the Reformers used the Hebrew text instead of the Greek as the basis for their translations, these apocryphal books are not generally accepted by the Protestants, although the Anglicans tend to use the books to some extent.

The Old Testament Apocrypha

The Old Testament, as we know it now in most English-language Protestant texts, reflects the decision of a council of non-Christian Jewish rabbis around A.D. 90. Because these were non-Christian rabbis who met after the Church had already begun to be established, their decisions did not have weight for the early Christians. To make matters more complex, there has been some debate between the Roman Catholic and Eastern Orthodox theologians about which of these texts are authoritative. The Roman Catholic scholar Jerome did not believe that some of these books should be used at all.

The New Testament Apocrypha

The focus of this chapter, however, is on those texts that are sometimes called the New Testament Apocrypha. These have a much different origin and status than the Old Testament Apocrypha, and vary greatly in character and content. Some of them, particularly the Protoevangelium of James, were accepted as useful even if not fully canonical, while other texts, such as the Gospel of Thomas, which showed many Gnostic tendencies, are full of ideas that were contrary to the Christian gospel and were shunned as heretical.

The Gnostics were an offshoot of early Christianity—early enough that some parts of the New Testament are crafted as an argument against them, particularly 1 John. Gnosticism is a diverse phenomenon, but it can be broadly characterized by a few traits held in common by these disparate (and quarreling) groups. Gnostics:

- Understood themselves to possess a secret knowledge ("gnosis") that others did not have
- Believed that the God spoken of in the New Testament was different from, and superior to, the God of the Old Testament
- Viewed the body, and the material world in general, as insignificant or evil, fundamentally opposed to that which is spiritual

Because of the belief that the body and the material world are evil, many Gnostics sought liberation from the flesh through extreme ascetic practices. Although these sometimes resembled orthodox practices—trying to become liberated from the tyranny of the flesh through fasting and abstinence from sexual intercourse—Gnostics practiced asceticism for different reasons. While Christians believed the world was fundamentally good, but fallen, Gnostics viewed the world as something to be escaped entirely.

factum

Some Gnostics took their beliefs and practices in an opposite direction from the majority of Gnostics, believing that if what happened with the flesh was meaningless, there was no reason to avoid indulging the lusts of the flesh.

As noted above, Gnostics also generally taught that there was a deep division between the Old and New Testaments—that the God of the Old Testament was inferior to the God of the New, and that this inferior God had created the material world, and that childbirth merely prolonged people's enslavement to this lesser world. These teachings were considered heretical by the early church because Gnosticism viewed the body as evil, and viewed death as the ultimate separation of the body and soul, while more mainstream Christians taught that although the body and soul were separated at death, they would be reunited at the Resurrection. Although the lusts of the flesh were to be overcome, the body itself was to be sanctified, not despised. Marriage and procreation were defended as good things—as gifts from God.

The Making of Scripture

The first canon of Scripture, or list of official books, was drawn up by a Gnostic teacher named Marcion in the second century A.D. His list of books included only parts of the Gospel of Luke and some of Paul's letters, and specifically excluded the Old Testament. It was only in the fourth century that a final and authoritative list of the books of the New Testament was agreed upon. This wasn't arbitrary, though.

The books that were finally accepted had to meet certain criteria. They had to:

- Be written by one of the apostles or their close associates
- Conform to the understanding of the Gospel message passed down by the apostles or to those they appointed as successors in the churches and those who came after them (thus giving birth to the doctrine of Apostolic Succession)
- Be more or less universally known and accepted in all of the churches

Thus it could be said that the current New Testament was not invented in the fourth century, but rather was formally recognized and sealed by the church leaders at that time. One amazing thing about this process was how much agreement there actually was with regard to which books were to be included.

Mary's Conception

The story of Mary's conception is not recorded in the any of the New Testament canonical books. Authors of noncanonical books such as the Protoevangelium of James attempted to provide the details that were lacking in the Gospels by writing their own narratives, which would have likely included elements from the oral tradition. This is especially likely with the Protoevangelium of James, because this book was written around A.D. 150, only eighty years after the destruction of the Temple of Jerusalem.

The memories of the events that occurred in the Gospel, as well as the stories that were not recorded in the Gospels but reflect the lives of those most intimately connected with Christ, would have still been fresh in the memory of the society as well as in the mind of the author of the Protoevangelium.

The Question of Authorship

Most scholars believe that the Protoevangelium was compiled by a single author, who attached the name of the apostle James to it to give it an air of authority. The Protoevangelium offers more details about the life of Mary and birth of Christ than any other text, although the bulk of these details are not viewed as straight historical facts.

Some scholars have suggested that the genre of the Protoevangelium of James is closest to a Midrash, which is literature from the Jewish rabbinical tradition based on the original sacred texts. According to scholar Addison Wright, the authors of Midrash sought to make the Biblical stories "understandable, useful and relevant" to later generations by means of creative, extended reflections upon the Biblical texts.

The Protoevangelium is valuable because it offers useful insights into the life and theological significance of the Virgin Mary. It is also very moving and even humorous and tragic in turns, as the characters are shown in their full human complexities.

The Holy of Holies

In the Protoevangelium, Mary is brought to the temple when she is only three years old, and she remains in the temple until adolescence. Upon her arrival, she is brought by Zachariah, the high priest, into the Holy of Holies, the innermost part of the temple where the Ark of the Covenant was once housed. This place was considered so holy that even the high priest would only enter once a year, on Yom Kippur, the Day of Atonement. According to tradition, the Holy of Holies was not illuminated by the sun or by artificial light, but shone with the Glory of God. This text helped form an association in the minds of early Christians between Mary and the temple. Like the physical temple, God dwelt within Mary. Unlike the temple building, God took on her own flesh and was, in a sense, even physically present within her womb.

factum

> The depiction of Mary's parents, Joachim and Anna, in the Protoevangelium seems to echo that of another Old Testament apocryphal couple named Joachim and Susanna. This couple is described in a book called *Susanna*. They were also wealthy and unable to bear children.

Joachim and Anna

According to the Protoevangelium, Mary's parents, Joachim and Anna, were a wealthy and generous couple who had struggled with infertility for many years. The Protoevangelium is also very intentional about stating that Joachim was from the Royal line of David, which would mean that Mary, and ultimately her son, Jesus, would also be descendants of David.

When Mary's father Joachim goes to the temple to make an offering, his offering is rejected by the priest Rubin because Joachim and his wife had not yet been able to produce a child. Joachim was aggrieved by this, but when he studied the Old Testament Scriptures he discovered that it was true that all of the great people in the Scriptures had, in fact, produced offspring. Instead of returning home to his wife, Joachim decided to go out into the wilderness and fast and pray for forty days.

It is significant that Joachim was away for forty days because of the significance of the number forty in the Bible. The number forty in the Old and New Testaments is intended to signify many years, but it is not necessarily related to the literal numerical value. Noah was in the ark for forty days and nights (Genesis 7), the Israelites wandered for forty years in the wilderness (Exodus 16:35), Moses was on the mount for forty days and nights (Exodus 24:18), and Jesus fasted for forty days (Matthew 4:2).

When Joachim disappeared for forty days, Anna did not immediately guess that her husband had gone to the wilderness to pray. Instead, she feared the worst, imagining that she was both infertile and a widow.

Anna prayed and moped at home, while one of her servants made matters worse by pointing out to her that her infertility was a curse. Anna went into her garden and looked up at a tree and saw that there were newly hatched baby birds in the nest. She felt that everyone in the world was able to have babies except her.

She made this plea to God, "O God of our fathers, bless me and hear my prayer as thou did bless the womb of Sarah . . ." This prayer connects her own plight to the ancient story of Abraham and Sarah's struggle with infertility. Like Abraham and Sarah, Joachim and Anna were ultimately blessed with a miracle, but they had to struggle for it first.

An Angel Appears

While Joachim was in the desert and Anna was praying at home, angels appeared to both of them to tell them that they would have a child. According to the angels, this child would be "a gift of the Lord." Anna responded to this message with great joy, and made a promise that she would dedicate her child to the Lord's service for the rest of her life. Joachim immediately made an offering of lambs, kids, and calves. He then rushed to the gates of Jerusalem to embrace his wife. Anna does conceive and bear a child, who is born exactly nine months, minus one day, after her parent's embrace.

symbolism

The embrace shared by Anna and Joachim has become the subject of many icons. In these icons, one can often see the wedding bed just behind the embracing couple, as if to report that Mary was indeed conceived in the traditional way.

According to a medieval text that is partially based on the Protoevangelium of James and called *The Golden Legend* (see Chapter 9), just after Anna gave birth she asked her midwife about the sex of her child. When the midwife replied that Anna had given birth to a little girl, Anna said, "On this day is my spirit exalted."

This passage is especially interesting because a similar tale is also told in the Koran, although in the account in the Koran, Anna is initially distressed and disappointed to discover that she has given birth to a girl, because she had hoped for a boy.

Child Mary in the Temple

According to the Protoevangelium, Anna watched her daughter closely. Just after the infant Mary took her first seven steps, Anna scooped her up and said, "As the Lord my God lives, you shall walk no more upon this ground until I take you to the temple of the Lord."

From that day forward, Anna kept Mary in her room, which she set apart as a sanctuary and allowed only "undefiled" people to enter. When Mary was a year old, her father had a great feast in celebration of her birthday, and the priests and high priests came and blessed Mary.

When Mary was two years old, Joachim and Anna debated over whether or not they should send her to the temple in fulfillment of Anna's promise to God. They decided to wait because they felt it would make the two-year-old Mary sad if they left her at the temple.

At age three, Mary was taken to the temple to live as a virgin. Joachim and Anna wanted to offer her to the temple as a dedicated virgin, but they were afraid that she might not be able to stay there. To their amazed wonder, however, the priest received Mary, kissed her and said, "The Lord has made your name great among all generations. At the end of days, the Lord will reveal in you his redemption for the sons of Israel."

The priest then placed Mary on the third step leading to the altar, and the spirit of God filled her and she danced with Joy. According to the Protoevangelium, "The whole of Israel loved her." Mary then lived in the temple for many more years, and according to tradition, was fed by an angel.

The account of Mary being miraculously fed is quite similar to the account offered by the Sufi Muslim mystic, Jalal-ud-Din Rumi. According to this account, the priest Zachariah continually brings food to Mary, but each time he does so, he finds an exact replica of the food he is bringing to her. Finally the priest asks where the other food is coming from and Mary responds, "Whenever I feel hungry, I ask God, and whatever I ask for, God sends. His generosity and compassion are infinite; whoever relies wholly on God finds that his help never fails."

Rumi's account of Mary being miraculously fed is very similar to the account offered by the Koran, which you will learn more about in Chapter 18. There are many parallels between the Christian extra-Biblical texts and the Koran.

According to the Protoevangelium, Mary lived in the temple for many years, but had to leave when she was twelve years old, because as soon as she began to menstruate, her blood could defile the temple. This concern was based on ancient views of purity which held that blood (and other bodily fluids) must be kept out of the temple because of the risk of pollution.

Mary's Engagement

After Mary had to leave the temple, priest Zachariah then went into the Holy of Holies and prayed to God about what to do. The response to his prayer came through an angel, who told him that he should assemble all the widowers from Judea. They would all bring their rods and drop them and then Zachariah would take all the rods into the temple and pray over them. Whoever received that last rod back would take Mary as his wife.

This process of selection was a little bit like the "casting of lots" which occurred in both the Old and New Testaments (see, for example, 1 Samuel 14:36–42 and Acts 1:24–26). Occasionally, lots (coins, polished sticks, dice, or cards) were tossed in an effort to make difficult, significant decisions. When lots were cast, nobody could complain of favoritism. According to Proverbs 16:33, "The lot is cast into the lap, but its every decision is from the Lord."

factum

The dove has symbolic value in Scripture. After the flood, Noah sent a dove to check for land. When Christ was baptized, a dove hovered over him. In Christian tradition, the dove represents the Holy Spirit. The dove was also present in the apparitions of Mary in Zeitun, Egypt, in which doves flew from a form resembling the Virgin Mary.

When the selection process commenced, a trumpet sounded and all the widowers came running. Joseph's rod was the last to be returned, so he was selected to be Mary's husband and guardian. As he received the rod, a dove flew from it and landed on his head.

Joseph, however, initially refuses to take Mary as his wife, because he feels that if he takes such a young bride, he will be seen as a laughing stock among his people. The priest, however, offers Joseph reassurance, and Joseph finally agrees to take Mary. The priest then performs the betrothal service, which is something like an engagement, only more binding.

Mary's Work

According to the Protoevangelium, Mary was part of a group of twelve virgins who were asked to return to the temple to help weave the holy veil for the tabernacle. Mary was pleased with this work and considered it a great honor to be entrusted with the very valuable scarlet and purple threads for her weaving.

During this time, Mary went out to a well to draw water and was startled by the appearance of an angel who said to her, "Hail, thou art highly favored, the Lord is with thee, blessed art thou among women." When Mary returned home, the angel appeared to her again, and spoke words that echo the account of the Annunciation in Luke.

One of the differences between the Gospel account of the Annunciation and the accounts of the Annunciation in the Protoevangelium of James is that in the Protoevangelium, Joseph responds more harshly to the news that Mary is pregnant, accusing her of being deceitful like Eve.

Joseph mentions that Mary, of all people, should never have done what she did, because she was raised in the Holy of Holies. This statement is important because it forms the basis for one of the central teachings about the Virgin Mary as a temple of the Holy Spirit, and yet, ironically, it seems to be thrown in as an afterthought—it is only in the course of Joseph's rant that Mary being raised in the Holy of Holies is ever stated explicitly.

Mary and Joseph then went before the priest Zachariah, who also accused them of immorality. They were required to do the ancient "bitter water test," which is described in the Old Testament book of Numbers (5:11–31). This test was meant to show whether a wife had been unfaithful or not (since Mary was betrothed, any infidelity would have been considered adultery). According to the results of this test, Mary was found innocent.

Mary's Vision

Mary and Joseph then had to travel to Bethlehem, where Mary would give birth to Jesus. While they were traveling, Mary had a vision in which she saw two infants, one weeping and one rejoicing. This vision seemed to echo the vision Rachel experienced soon before she gave birth to Esau and Jacob. In Rachel's vision, she sensed that there would be great struggle between her twins.

discussion question

How can Mary's vision be interpreted?
The struggle between the two infants from Mary's vision has been viewed as a metaphor for the tensions between Judaism and Christianity. It is also viewed as a representation of the fact that although Christians rejoiced at the birth of Christ, Jews soberly continued to await the Messiah.

Soon after the couple finally arrived in Bethlehem, Mary gave birth to Jesus while Joseph was away. Shortly afterward, Joseph saw a cloud surrounding the manger and realized that Mary had given birth. The Protoevangelium ends with the Slaughter of the Innocents, which was also recorded in the Gospels (Matthew 2:16). In the Slaughter of the Innocents, Herod hears that the Messiah had been born and becomes furious, so he decrees that every firstborn child shall be killed. According to the Protoevangelium, Mary hides Jesus in the manger until Herod's soldiers pass by.

Mary's relative Elizabeth fled to the mountains with her baby John, and he was also spared, although her husband, the high priest, Zachariah, who served in the temple, was often questioned about his son's whereabouts. When Zachariah refused to give any clues about his son, he was killed, causing great grief in the Jewish community. Eventually, Simeon was appointed as Zachariah's replacement, and Simeon believed in the promise that he would not die until he had seen the Savior with his own eyes.

Jesus' Siblings

There are two traditional ways of understanding who the Scriptural "brothers" of Jesus were. According to one tradition, rooted in the Protoevangelium of James, these "siblings" are from Joseph's prior marriage (because Joseph was a widower). This perspective is the standard explanation found in Eastern Orthodox Churches.

Roman Catholic theologians, on the other hand, have been more inclined to say that that these siblings were cousins. This statement is based in the teaching of Saint Jerome, a Biblical scholar who didn't like the way the Protoevangelium of James described the siblings of Jesus as stepbrothers.

factum

Saint Jerome preferred the argument that the siblings of Jesus were cousins because he felt that it was most appropriate for both Mary and Joseph to have been virgins. Saint Jerome felt that it would have been improper for Joseph to have fathered other children even if he did remain chaste with Mary.

Ever since Jerome's statement, Roman Catholic theologians have been more inclined to emphasize the Pseudo-Gospel of Matthew, a later text that shares many elements with the Protoevangelium. According to the Pseudo-Gospel of Matthew, the siblings of Jesus were actually his cousins. The pseudo-Gospel of Matthew is also distinct in that it offers more information about Mary's education in the temple. Stories from the Protoevangelium became popular in the West many years later, when they were incorporated into *The Golden Legend* (see Chapter 9 for more information).

Mary's Death

Likewise, there are two main traditions related to Mary's death. One of the great unsettled debates within Christianity surrounds the question of where Mary lived out her final years. According to many people, most notably the second-century writer Saint Irenaeus of Lyon, Mary died in Ephesus. Irenaeus based his belief on the immediate disciples of the apostle John. Because this traditional teaching is based on the passage from John in which Jesus commits Mary to John's care from the cross, and because it is widely believed that John moved to Ephesus to preach after the Crucifixion, a strong case can be made for this position.

Another tradition holds that Mary died in Jerusalem. This tradition is reported in the medieval text the *Legenda Aurea* (or *the Golden Legend*). This text was compiled in the thirteenth century, by the Dominican Archbishop of Genoa, Jacobus de Voragine. According to this account, Mary lived in a house on Mount Zion for many years after the death of her son.

According to this account, one day, as the Virgin Mary was again pondering her son's death, an angel appeared to her and announced her death. But Mary protested, because she wanted to see the apostles one more time. In response to Mary's request, Saint John was brought on a white cloud from Ephesus, and all of the other apostles came as well. Just as Mary was believed to have given birth to Jesus without suffering, according to the *Golden Legend*, Mary also died without suffering, as her soul flew directly into the arms of her son.

An account called the Transistus, or Passing, offers an additional detail about Mary's death. In this account, Saint Thomas also arrived just after Mary's death on a cloud from India. Because the apostles knew that Thomas was a doubter and needed to be reassured with evidence, they took him to Mary's empty tomb. But Thomas explained that he didn't need to see the empty tomb, because he had already spotted Mary ascending when he was passing by on his cloud.

These accounts of Mary's death are all attempts to fill the gaps about an event that we know very little about. Some of the traditions are more reliable than others, and much of the mystery remains. No relics of Mary's body have ever been found. While some have suggested that they could have been lost, this is unlikely, considering how much care and attention have been given to relics throughout Christian history.

The search for Mary's relics began more than 1,500 years ago when Constantine's mother Helen began her excavations in Palestine in the fourth century to try to find relics from the life of Christ. Drawing from the collective memory of local Christians, Helen was able to successfully locate the cross on which Christ died, but she never found the Virgin Mary's body.

symbolism

Several icons show a large Jesus holding his mother wrapped in her burial shroud as if she is a tiny baby. This image is an exact reversal of the Nativity icon, which shows a tiny Jesus wrapped in swaddling clothes. Most icons of the Virgin Mary and child show a small Jesus held in his mother's arms.

In 1950, the Roman Catholic Church officially proclaimed that the Virgin Mary was taken up into heaven after she completed the course of her earthly life. Although the Eastern Orthodox believe that Mary was assumed into heaven, they teach that she "fell asleep" first (and thus celebrate the feast of the Dormition instead of the Assumption). Roman Catholics are divided on whether Mary died or not before being assumed. The Eastern Orthodox celebrate Mary's Dormition, or falling asleep, on August 15.

Although it was widely believed among the early Christians that Mary was taken directly up to heaven without suffering the separation of body and soul that is customary at death, there is little certainty surrounding Mary's death. The earliest written mention of her ascension is found in a text that dates from the fourth or fifth century. It is difficult to know for sure how strongly this teaching was affirmed in the oral traditions before that time.

According to the fourth-century writer Ephiphanius, no one knows exactly what happened to Mary at the end of her life. As we can see, this debate continued well into the Middle Ages and continues even now, particularly between Protestants and Catholics. In 1950, Pope Pius XII declared the Assumption to be a formal dogma of the Catholic Church. The lingering questions that surround the Virgin Mary's death remain part of the larger body of mysteries that continue to surround her life.

CHAPTER 4

Spotting Mary in the Old Testament

In novels, many writers employ a literary device called foreshadowing in which they offer a hint of what is to come later in the book. The early Church Fathers viewed the Old Testament in a similar way. According to their thinking, there were both Christ types and Mary types in the Old Testament that foreshadowed the appearance of Christ and Mary in the New Testament. This chapter will explore ways in which the early Church Fathers saw Mary in the Old Testament.

Multiple Meanings

In contemporary times, people often debate about literal interpretations of different Biblical stories. For example, whether the world was created in a literal seven days or whether the term "day" in Genesis 1 might not correspond perfectly to the twenty-four-hourdays experienced on Earth.

The earliest Christians, however, did not hold to a strictly literal interpretation of the Scriptures. Because they believed that the Scriptures were wholly true and inspired by God, they believed that many stories of the Old Testament implicitly spoke about the truths that were revealed more fully in the events surrounding Jesus' life.

discussion question

What is typology?
In a Christian context, typology is way of reading the Bible in which Old Testament figures, events, or prophecies are interpreted through the lens of Jesus Christ. Practically speaking, typology allowed Christian interpreters to fully integrate some of the more difficult parts of the Old Testament in a Christian context.

The Church Fathers saw multiple meanings in every passage, especially in the lives of the great ancestors of the faith, such as Abraham, Isaac, Jacob, and Moses. They interpreted everything through the lens of Christ, and saw references to Jesus and Mary throughout the text.

In allegorical interpretations of the Scriptures, passages contain additional meanings apart from the plain sense of the text. These meanings would have been readily understood within the whole context of faith. One of the most famous and universally accepted uses of allegorical interpretation was used in the Song of Songs, the great love poem of the Old Testament. This book was seen as not just a love poem between two individuals, but more profoundly, a love poem between God and Israel, God and humanity, or in later understanding, humanity and Jesus Christ or the Virgin Mary.

Typological interpretations allowed later thinkers to look back on earlier texts and to understand them as precursors of things that were yet to come. Typology was also used more broadly by many Christian thinkers to refer not only to the Old Testament, but also to elements of other religions, showing how they were all fulfilled in Christ.

One example of this kind of typological interpretation is Jonah, who was often viewed as a type of Christ because he spent three days in a dark, deathlike place (the belly of the fish) and then was brought back into the light of day. Similarly, the sacrifice of Isaac (Genesis 12) is understood to foreshadow Jesus' on the cross. Just as Abraham was called to offer his only son as a sacrifice, so too, according to Christian belief, God gave up his only son for the life of the world.

These typological and allegorical interpretations extended beyond Christ to his mother Mary, who came to be seen by the Church Fathers in many of the most significant events of the Old Testament. Typological interpretation allowed for a clear sense of Mary's significance as well as the way in which her actions helped to bring many of the Old Testament stories together into a more complete picture of creation, fall, and redemption.

The Burning Bush

In his work *On the Birth of Christ*, the fourth-century Church Father Saint Gregory of Nyssa wrote eloquently about the Virgin Mary and her connection to the burning bush from the Old Testament. He said, "What was prefigured at that time in the flame of the bush was openly manifested in the mystery of the Virgin . . . As on the mountain the bush burned but was not consumed, so the Virgin gave birth to the light and was not corrupted."

These images captured the imaginations of many of the early and medieval Christians, who felt that the Virgin Mary's body was something like the bush, which burned with the flames of the presence of God, yet miraculously survived. According to the Old Testament account, through that flaming bush, the angel spoke to Moses, who discovered that he was standing on holy ground.

Saint Gregory of Nyssa believed that not only did Moses experience this miracle as an encounter with God, but that he may have even been able to see into the future in that moment in which the presence of God burned within the bush. For Saint Gregory, even Moses was looking toward what was to come. The image of Mary as the burning bush has been depicted both in Eastern Orthodox iconography and in Western medieval art.

symbolism

In Nicholas Froment's 1476 painting, *Moses and the Burning Bush*, Mary holds the infant Christ and is seated on a flaming rose bush. Moses is also in this image, tending his flock of sheep as an angel appears to him. Froment depicts the connection between Mary and the burning bush that had been made by many early Christians.

This image of Mary in the burning bush is part of a larger collection of images that connects Mary to the natural world. In the Middle Ages, hundreds of plants and flowers were named for Mary's different attributes. The natural world was seen as a school through which the Church could educate people about the life of Mary and of Christ. You'll learn more about the connections between the Virgin Mary and the natural world in Chapters 16 and 19.

Jacob's Ladder

The story of Jacob's Ladder from the book of Genesis is read in the Eastern Orthodox Church on the Feast of the Nativity. In the minds of the early Church Fathers, this image pointed to the Virgin Mary. Just as in Jacob's dream, where a ladder ascends to heaven and angels climb down the ladder, so, in Christian tradition, God climbs down the ladder toward Earth through Mary, who becomes the ladder—the bridge between heaven and Earth.

When Jacob awoke from sleeping on his stone pillow, he declared, "How awesome is this place! This is the gate of heaven!" (Genesis 28:17). This proclamation is read by Christian interpreters to connect Jacob's vision to Mary because in other writings, Mary's womb is "the gate of heaven." She is also viewed by many early Christian writers as the house or the temple of

God, because God dwelt in her and made her holy. The images used by the fathers and in the Scriptures are all related, complementing each other and each offering a fuller picture of the Virgin Mary.

The Ark of the Covenant

The Virgin Mary is also viewed as the Ark of the Covenant because God dwelt within her. She also carried within her womb the creator of all things, and she herself became "the holy of holies." This image is closely connected to the apocryphal story from the Protoevangelium of James, in which Joseph accuses Mary of adultery. Her close association with the temple was directly linked to the fact that in the Christian tradition Mary is viewed as the temple. While all Christians are in some sense the temple of the Holy Spirit when they bear the Word of God, Mary's role as a temple of the Holy Spirit was unique, because only she nourished Christ in her womb.

The fourth-century bishop of Alexandria, Athanasius, also wrote eloquently about the Virgin Mary, making strong connections between her and the Ark of the Covenant. He was an extremely influential writer, expressing many of the mysteries of the Incarnation in powerful, lucid terms. He wrote, "O [Ark of the New] Covenant, clothed with purity instead of gold! You are the Ark in which is found the golden vessel containing the true manna, that is, the flesh in which divinity resides. You surpass them, for it is written: 'The earth is my footstool' (Is 66:1). But you carry within you the feet, the head, and the entire body of the perfect God."

The East Gate of the Temple

Another image often used for the Virgin Mary was the East Gate of the temple. Like the other Old Testament types, this image highlights the way in which Mary's role in salvation history is intrinsically linked to Christ. Mary is the portal through which the Lord entered his creation. Because of this, exploring the Old Testament typology becomes a means of contemplating the Incarnation.

According to Jewish tradition, the Messiah would enter through the East Gate (see, for example, Ezekiel 43:1–5). Christians also celebrate Jesus' entry through the East Gate into Jerusalem on Palm Sunday (Luke 19:35–38).

The Golden Gate

In the Book of Acts, the East Gate is called the Beautiful Gate (Acts 3:2–10). Because of the way Jerome translated the book into Latin, it is also known as the Golden Gate. This is appropriate, not only because of the way this gate was once decorated, but also because, according to the Bible, it was the place where the glory of God (the Shekinah) entered the temple.

This gate is also said to be the place where the Last Judgment will take place. This is based on passages from both the Old and New Testaments, as well as other traditions. Jews, Christians, and Muslims have traditionally buried their dead outside of this gate so that they could be close to the Lord when he returns to judge the living and the dead (see Zechariah 14:4–5 and Matthew 24:27). This is why there are many cemeteries to this day on the Mount of Olives, just east of the Temple Mount. The Mount of Olives is located on the east side of Jerusalem and is a popular holy site for Jews, Muslims, and Christians. Among Jews, the Mount of Olives has been a popular burial site since the time of the first Temple. According to Jewish tradition the Messiah is to enter Jerusalem through the nearby Golden Gate and those who are buried on the Mount of Olives will be the first to be resurrected. Today many important churches are located on this mountain, and according to Christian tradition, this was the last place where Jesus prayed before he was taken captive by the Romans.

The imagery of the East Gate was also connected to the teaching of Mary's ever-virginity. Ezekiel writes, "And the Lord said to me, 'This gate shall be shut; it shall not be opened; and no man shall enter by it because the Lord God of Israel has entered by it; therefore, it shall be shut'" (Ezekiel 44:2).

There is a further significance connected to this temple door facing east. Christians have traditionally prayed facing east, and it is from the east that the sun rises—an image that the Church has often connected to rising of the "son."

A Garden Enclosed

The image of a gate that remains closed is closely connected to the images of Mary as a "garden enclosed" (Song of Solomon 4:12). This image would also have been connected to her ever-virginity. She became, in the minds of Christians, a sealed-in garden that no man could enter after God did. This image was also featured in medieval tapestries and paintings, in which Mary is shown surrounded by animals and flowers that had a particular connection to her (such as roses and lilies) and surrounded by a walled-in gate. She would be shown near her infant child Christ, if not holding him.

The image connecting Mary to the East Gate of the temple is similar to the image of the door, which is featured in the writings of Saint Romanos. In his hymn for the Nativity of Christ, he writes that Mary "opens the door and receives the company of the magi. She opens the door—she the unopened and yet in no way robbed of the treasure of her purity. She opened the door, she from whom was born the door." This passage symbolically connects Mary, who was herself a door, since it was through her that God came into the world, with Christ, who is himself "the way," or the door, to eternal life (John 14:6).

The Root of Jesse

The rod (or root) of Jesse was interpreted by early Christians as a Christ-like figure. This imagery was connected to David's royal line, from which both Joseph and, according to Church tradition, Mary were descendants. The lineage grew through the ages and blossomed in the persons of Mary and Christ. Isaiah 11:1–10 says, "There Shall come forth a Rod from the stem of Jesse, and a Branch shall grow out of his roots . . . and in that day there shall be a Root of Jesse, who shall stand as a banner to the people; for the Gentiles shall seek him and his resting place shall be glorious."

According to the Church Fathers, the Virgin Mary (not just her husband Joseph as is shown clearly from the Gospel lineages) was a descendant from the house of David. This lineage was important to the Church Fathers because it connected Mary's son, Jesus, with the royal line. In Romans 15:12, Saint Paul explicitly makes the connection between Christ and the root of Jesse.

The root-of-Jesse imagery is similar to the vine imagery from the Gospel. The Gospel that states, "I am the true vine, and my father is the vine grower. He removes every branch in me that bears no fruit. Every branch that bears fruit he prunes to make it bear more fruit . . . Just as the branch cannot bear fruit by itself unless it abides in the vine, neither can you unless you abide in me" (John 15:1–4). In this passage, Jesus is the vine and his followers are the branches. Mary, as the mother of Jesus, would have been the first to receive this seed from God and to nurture the vine as it grew. According to the book of Isaiah, "a staff shall spring forth from the root of Jesse, and a flower shall come up from his root; and the Spirit of God will rest upon him" (Isaiah 11:1).

The image of Mary as springing from the root of Jesse was also another reference to the miracle of her ability to bring life into the world although she was a virgin. Many times, in both the writings of the fathers and the Koran, much is written about Mary's ability to bring forth life without any seed from man. This gift is a sign of divine favor as well as miraculous intervention. Saint Jerome brought out the paradox of this event by marveling at the miracle that she, who never had the seed of man, was able to bear fruit—she herself was the fruit of the earth but she bore the Lord in her womb.

factum

Within Islamic thought, there is also a connection between Mary and fruitfulness. In the Koran's account of the birth of Jesus, Mary went to an isolated place to give birth. When the pain of childbirth became intense, she reached up and grabbed a fig tree, which immediately bore sweet figs to nourish and refresh Mary.

The Buttery Mountain

The Church Fathers also made a connection between Mary and a mountain. She is like a mountain in the sense that she stretched toward the heavens with her life. Her life is viewed as higher than any of the other saints, because she was chosen for the ultimate calling of bearing God in her womb.

These interpretations are sometimes connected to Psalm 67, in which God dwelt inside of a mountain in the same way that Jesus dwelt inside of the Virgin Mary's womb. Psalm 67:17 describes this mountain as "God's mountain, a rich mountain, the mountain in which God has been pleased to dwell."

Some translations of this verse have used the word *fertile* instead of *rich*— a translation that strengthens the Marian association. This image of the "buttery mountain" has also been translated in a way that may sound strange (and not very appetizing) to modern ears. The other image was "a Curdled Mountain." In the Eastern Orthodox Church these mountain images are used in a Vespers hymn for September 6, "O immaculate one, Daniel describes you as a great mountain, while Habbakuk calls you a mountain shaded by virtues, and David regards you as a curdled mountain, from which God has become incarnate and redeemed the world."

This was another reference to the Virgin Mary's fertility, which was connected to the ancient understanding of how babies were made. In the ancient world, it was believed that babies were made when the seed of the man mingled with the blood of the woman, causing that blood to "curdle" into a kind of cheese. This image was also stated in Job 10:10, "Did you not pour me out like milk and curdle me like cheese?"

Saint Romanos, who wrote beautiful chanted sermons in the sixth century, picked up on this image and puts the words in Christ's mouth as he speaks to his mother on his way to the cross saying, "Do not make the day of my passion bitter, because for it I, the sweet one, came down from heaven, like the manna, not onto Mount Sinai, but into your womb. For within it, as David prophesied, I was curdled like cheese." Christ goes on to make the reference even more direct in Saint Romanos's hymn, saying, "Understand, honored Lady, the curdled mountain, I now exist because being word I became flesh in you."

The Rose of Sharon

The Rose of Sharon image was used by Saint Jerome and is taken from the Song of Solomon (also known as the Song of Songs), "I am the Rose of Sharon and the Lily of the Valleys" (2:1). These images suggested the Virgin Mary's purity and beauty. The image of a rose with petals not fully opened was connected to her virginity and youth. Just as young flower does not open completely until it has reached maturity, the Virgin Mary was chosen to become the Mother of God when she was still a pure, young girl.

There is some ambiguity surrounding this particular passage in the Song of Songs. The Song of Songs is a passionate love poem from the Old Testament. Traditional rabbinic Jewish interpretation understood it to symbolize the special relationship between God and Israel, while Christians have generally taken it to refer to the love between Jesus and the Church (as spoken of in Ephesians 5), or more recently, between Christ and the individual Christian soul. Many have also seen it as speaking of Mary's relationship to God.

Some of the confusion that has come about related to this poem is the fact that it can be difficult to parse out *who* is speaking. In some cases it seems that the bride is speaking, while in other cases it seems as if the bridegroom is speaking. The confusion surrounding this passage has extended into later commentaries on the passage, because while some people took the reference to the Rose of Sharon and the Lily of Valley to be a reference to Mary, still others thought it was a reference to Christ.

symbolism

The Rose of Sharon imagery is also a symbol for the bride. In this case, these references would have called Mary to mind as the spouse of the Holy Spirit, chosen by God for a very unique and significant purpose, set apart from the rest of creation, united to God through her perfect obedience.

Several centuries later, Saint Thérèse of Lisieux picked up on this imagery when she wrote, "Thou art the flower with petals still unclosed; I gaze upon Thy beauty undefiled. Thou art the Rose of Sharon long foretold, Still in Thy glorious bud, Thou heavenly Child!" This reference can be confusing, because it sounds as if it is referring to Mary. But clearly, in this passage, it is only the final verses that refer to Mary. "Thy dearest Mother's arms, so pure and white, form for Thee now a royal cradle-throne; The morning sun is Mary's bosom bright, thy sunlit dew her virginal milk, my own!"

In the minds of the Church Fathers, Mary pulled together the disparate aspects of creation and wove them into a single seamless garment, bringing harmony to a world broken by sin. These images come together beautifully in the seventeenth century when Johannes Scheffler, under the penname Angelus Silesius, wrote, "Ark, fortress, tower, house, garden, mirror, fountain; The sea, a star, the moon, the rose of dawn, a mountain; She is another world so can be all things freely."

These images provide just a sampling of the many visual images that were used both by early Christians and during the medieval period to point to the multiple connections between the Old and New Testaments, and the ways in which these images come together in representations of Mary. All of these images serve to create a rich tapestry of belief that provides a helpful backdrop for understanding the multiple facets of devotion to Mary.

CHAPTER 5

Mary and the Councils

During the first few centuries after the death of Christ, there were sometimes fierce debates over what constituted legitimate Christian teaching. In order to bring unity and clarity to the churches, the famed Roman emperor, Constantine the Great, called the first church council, which met in Nicea in 325. This chapter will offer a basic framework of some the earliest church councils and the ways these councils helped to form an early understanding of Mary's place within Christianity.

No Easy Answers

People often assume that more unity existed in the early Church than actually did. In truth, the earliest Christians had to struggle to define their faith. Throughout history, Christians have struggled to distinguish between true and false teaching. Even some books in what is now known as the New Testament were the subject of heated debate among early Christians. Together, these believers had to struggle and prayerfully discern which books would be included in the final canon, and which would be kept within the tradition of the Church, but not given authoritative status.

Likewise, many of the central teachings of Christianity became more defined through time. For example, although the doctrine of the Trinity—the belief that there are three divine persons, Father, Son, and Holy Spirit, who exist and work together in unity—is rooted in Scripture, it would not necessarily be plainly apparent from a reading of the Bible.

In this context of division, church councils were often called by the Roman (Byzantine) emperor as a way to unify the churches. This was in the interest of the civil authorities since, as Christianity became more widespread, doctrinal disputes had a marked effect on civic peace. These councils provided a forum for Christians to meet and struggle through the different issues, seeking a prayerful consensus on matters that were critical to the life of faith.

discussion question

Why were councils called ecumenical?
These councils were called ecumenical because they brought together representatives from all over the Christian world. The word *ecumenical* comes from the Greek word *oikos*, or house, so what is ecumenical pertains to the whole ecumene, meaning the household of the Empire, or the inhabited world.

Sometimes the battles about theology were quite fierce. People believed things with all their hearts and fought for them, only to have their views rejected by the Church as a whole. There is an old saying attributed to Tertullian that "the blood of the martyrs is the seed of the Church," meaning that the teachings of the Church come from the blood, sweat, and tears of the earliest Christians. Long before official councils were called, bishops had been assembling to dispute and define theology for their flocks. One of best-known and earliest examples of this is the Council of Jerusalem, which is spoken about in Chapter 15 of the book of Acts.

Constantine

The earliest Christians struggled under the continual threat of persecution. This situation changed dramatically, however, when Constantine issued the Edict of Milan, also known as The Edict of Toleration, in A.D. 313. Under this edict, freedom of religion was proclaimed, and Christianity was even specially favored. Some years later, under Theodosius the Great (379–395), Christianity would become the official religion of the Empire.

factum

Like many secular rulers before and after him, politics and religion were intermixed for Constantine. He was concerned with unifying both Church and Empire. Constantine was baptized on his deathbed in A.D. 337, having legalized Christianity while still a catechumen (a student preparing for Baptism).

About six years after the Edict of Milan was issued, a *presbyter* (a Greek term meaning "elder," usually translated as "priest") named Arius of Alexandria began to teach concerning the Word of God (John 1:1) that "God begat him, and before he was begotten, he did not exist." Athanasius was at that time a newly ordained deacon, secretary to Bishop Alexander of Alexandria, and a member of his household. His reply to Arius was that the Father begat the Son from all eternity—this was not an event in time. Arius was condemned by the bishops of Egypt (with the exceptions of Secundus of

Ptolemais and Theonas of Marmorica), and went to Nicomedia, from which he wrote letters to bishops throughout the world, stating his position.

Calling a Council

Constantine sought to resolve the dispute by calling a council of bishops from all over the Christian world. This council met in Nicea, just across the straits from what is now Istanbul, in A.D. 325, and consisted of 317 bishops. Athanasius accompanied his bishop to the council, and became recognized as a chief representative for the view that the Son was fully God, co-equal and co-eternal with the Father.

The party of Athanasius was overwhelmingly in the majority. (The western, Latin-speaking, half of the Empire was very sparsely represented, but it was solidly Athanasian, so that if its bishops had attended in force, the vote would have been still more lopsided.)

symbolism

The term *catholic* comes from a Greek word that can mean both "whole" and "universal." The Church of the councils used this word both to refer to "those things which were held by Christians everywhere" and to the idea of the fullness or holistic character of the faith.

Those at the council first attempted to find a formula from Holy Scripture that would express the full deity of the Son, as well as his equality with the Father. However, the Arians cheerfully agreed to all such formulations, having interpreted them already to fit their own views. Finally, the Greek word *homoousios* (meaning "of the same substance, or nature, or essence") was introduced, chiefly because it was one word that could not be understood to mean what the Arians meant, which was that the Son was somehow less divine than the Father. On the contrary, it made absolutely clear that the Son's divinity was exactly the same as the Father's (the only difference being that the Son was begotten of the Father, that his divinity derived from the Father, the "source" of the Godhead).

Ultimately, this council sought to formulate a creedal statement that would express the consensus belief, which was that Jesus Christ was eternal with the Father, and not "made" or "begotten." This creed was called the Nicene Creed.

Here is one version of the Nicene Creed as it is often said in churches today:

We believe in one God, the Father Almighty, Maker of heaven and earth, and of all things visible and invisible;

And in one Lord, Jesus Christ, the Son of God, the Only-begotten, Begotten of the Father before all ages, Light of Light, True God of True God, Begotten, not made, of one essence with the Father, by Whom all things were made:

Who for us men and for our salvation came down from heaven, and was incarnate of the Holy Spirit and the Virgin Mary, and was made man;

And was crucified also for us under Pontius Pilate, and suffered and was buried;

And the third day He rose again, according to the Scriptures;

And ascended into heaven, and sits at the right hand of the Father;

And He shall come again with glory to judge the living and the dead, Whose kingdom shall have no end.

And we believe in the Holy Spirit, the Lord, and Giver of Life, Who proceeds from the Father, Who with the Father and the Son together is worshipped and glorified, Who spoke by the Prophets;

And we believe in One, Holy, Catholic and Apostolic Church.

We acknowledge one Baptism for the remission of sins.

We look for the Resurrection of the dead,

And the Life of the world to come. Amen.

You may recognize the basic wording, which has been translated in a variety of ways. This statement of faith is often said in conjunction with baptism, as it offers a helpful summary of Christian belief. Many Christians have memorized and said it every day of their lives in an effort to remain faithful to the teachings of the Gospel.

The Filioque Clause

A long-standing dispute between the Eastern Orthodox Church and the Protestant and Catholic Churches is related to an addition to the creed. This is called the Filioque clause. The word *filioque* means "and the Son" in Latin and refers to the part of the creed that says, "the Holy Spirit, the Lord, the Giver of Life, Who proceeds from the Father and the Son" (in the West). The phrase, "and the Son" was first added at the Synod of Toledo in Spain in A.D. 447. It was adopted by Charlemagne in the ninth century, and finally by Rome in 1014 (at the request of the German emperor Henry II). The East never accepted this addition, both questioning its theology, and citing concerns about the way it was adopted (without the approval of an Ecumenical Council).

Ephesus, A.D. 431

Even as the Councils sought to define the creeds, the nature of the Trinity, and the person of Christ—both divine and human—discussions arose about titles for his mother, the Virgin Mary. The most important council in relation to the Virgin Mary was the council at which her name, Theotokos, was officially declared. The word Theotokos is rooted in the two Greek roots *theos* (God) and *tokos* (bearer). This term can be translated as "The one who gave birth to God," although a more simple (and widely used) translation is "Mother of God." ("Mother of God," however, is a more direct translation of the phrase *meter theou* which is also used in Greek, so some prefer to keep this distinct in their translations.)

Within the Eastern Orthodox context, the single most important title associated with the Virgin Mary was the title Theotokos. By the fourth century, this title was so widely used among Christians that the famed anti-Christian emperor Julian (whose short reign lasted from A.D. 361 to 363), referred to by Christians with the unflattering title of "the Apostate," complained about it.

Although the term *Theotokos* was used as early as A.D. 230 by Origen of Alexandria, and was widely used in the fourth century (there are references from Athanasius, Gregory the Theologian, Cyril of Jerusalem, John Chrysostom, Augustine, Gregory of Nyssa, and many others), it had never been universally sanctioned, and some Christians vehemently opposed it. This title for the Virgin Mary also appears in the most ancient prayer to Mary that exists, dating back to at least A.D. 300. This prayer was originally written in Greek and is preserved on a scrap of parchment. This short prayer, commonly known in the West by its Latin name, *Sub Tuum Praesidium*, reads, "We flee to your protection, O Holy Mother of God; Do not despise our petitions in our necessities, but deliver us always from all dangers, O glorious and blessed Virgin."

As significant as the title Theotokos was for many of the early Christians, those who opposed this title felt that they must object to it because it seemed crazy to them. They asked a question many might ask today, which was "How could God have a mother?"

Some feared that this title made it seem as if the Virgin Mary existed from the beginning of time, whereas those who used this title and were devoted to it always understood that it was to be used in a very specific way—Mary gave birth to God only in the sense that she gave birth to Christ. She did not conceive and give birth to God the Father.

Some who believed in the divinity of Christ didn't particularly like this title because they felt that it might be confusing to some, making it sound as if Mary came before God the Father, while others felt that it was very important as a way of expressing the teaching that Jesus united the human and divine natures in this one person. So much controversy surrounded this title that a council was held in which some of the questions surrounding it were formally addressed. The two central figures on opposite sides of the debate were Cyril and Nestorius.

Nestorius and Cyril

Nestorius, who had been appointed patriarch of Constantinople in A.D. 428, was deeply concerned that the title Theotokos could lead to exaggerated beliefs about the Virgin Mary. When he was in Constantinople, a famous speaker named Proclus preached an exuberant sermon about the Virgin Mary. When Proclus exclaimed that the Virgin Mary was the Theotokos he struck a sour note with Nestorius, who stormed up to the pulpit and accused him of mingling Christianity and pagan mythology.

Nestorius always felt squeamish about this term. He felt that it was more theologically acceptable to call Mary *Christokos*, Christ-bearer, or simply *anthropotokos*, "human-bearer." Nestorius felt that it was essential to view the Incarnation in terms of two natures that remained separate. He did not like the idea of two natures mingling, and he was put off by the idea that God was born in a manger. He also struggled to believe in a God who died and rose again.

factum

The sparring between Nestorius and Cyril was not just rooted in theology. There was also long-standing competition between the two places they represented, Alexandria and Constantinople. These geographical tensions very likely contributed to the bitter fight between the two men.

The most powerful opponent of Nestorius was Cyril, bishop of Alexandria. After Nestorius publicly criticized Proclus, Cyril not only came to the defense of Proclus, but he also sent several letters to important people, accusing Nestorius of separating the Christ into two separate people. Nestorius refused to take back his words. Both in writing and verbally he would not call the Virgin Mary Theotokos. He felt bitter, even, that others would press him this way.

Cyril taught that it was absolutely essential to retain the unity of the human and divine persons in Christ. The symbol of this perfect unity was the Virgin Mary as the "Theotokos," or God-bearer. Nestorius countered that he did not like the idea of the divine nature of Christ seeming to overwhelm his humanity, while Cyril hoped to hold the two natures in perfect balance, seeing them as two natures functioning, unified, in one person. The battle between Nestorius and Cyril was so fierce that it could only be settled by calling together the leaders of the Church to talk through the issues at hand.

The Third Ecumenical Council was held at Ephesus in June of A.D. 431. Nestorius had hoped that through this council he could convince others that he was right, but from his perspective, the council did not go well at all. Although the council had been called by Pope Celestine at Cyril's urging, Pope Celestine actually died before the council began. Cyril had been given permission to open the council, and Nestorius's views were condemned.

Nestorius was both excommunicated and deposed, meaning that he was kicked out of the Church and he lost his job as patriarch of Constantinople. To further his shame, the very man he had so sharply criticized for his flowery sermon, Proclus, was appointed to replace Nestorius as patriarch of Constantinple.

Results of the Council

The Third Ecumenical Council had a variety of results. Following the decree from the council that it was acceptable to call the Virgin Mary, Theotokos, people from the town marched through the streets, cheering. That night, after the council, those who led Cyril to his lodgings shouted, "Praised be the Theotokos, Long live Cyril!"

The official pronouncement of Mary as Theotokos at Ephesus was worded quite strongly. Cyril said, "If anyone does not confess that Emmanuel is God in truth, and therefore that the Holy Virgin is the Mother of God (Theotokos), let him be anathema."

discussion question

In what sort of place was the Third Ecumenical Council held?
This council was held in a large church that was dedicated to the Virgin Mary. About 200 bishops attended. The ruins of this church can still be seen in Ephesus.

Ever-virgin

The term *ever-virgin* was used officially at the Fifth Ecumenical Council in Constantinople in A.D. 553. This term is connected to the belief that the Virgin Mary was a virgin both before she gave birth to Christ and afterward. References to Mary's ever-virginity can be found, for example, in the writings of Peter of Alexandria, Epiphanius, Athanasius, Didymus the Blind, Jerome, Cyril of Alexandria, Leo, Sophronius of Jerusalem, John of Damascus, John Cassian, Ephrem of Syria, and the Second Council of Constantinople in A.D. 553, which said, "If anyone shall not confess that the Word of God has two nativities, the one from the Father, from all eternity, without time and without body; the other in these last days, coming down from heaven and being made flesh of the holy and glorious Mary, Mother of God and ever-virgin, and born of her: let him be anathema."

The word *anathema* means "cut off from the community." It is used by Saint Paul in 1 Corinthians 16:22, "If anyone does not love the Lord Jesus Christ, let him be anathema." It becomes a kind of technical term used as a way to denounce a person's immoral behavior or false teachings.

These terms—*theotokos, panagia,* and *aeiparthenos* (ever-virgin)—were continually used in traditional Christian liturgies, especially after these disputes, as a way to seal the declarations in people's hearts and to bring clarity to their prayers. There is an ancient saying that "the rule of prayer is the rule of belief" (*lex orandi, lex credendi*)—in other words, theology and prayer reinforce each other, so they shouldn't be separated.

Mary as All-holy

Another term used for the Virgin Mary is "all-holy" (*panagia* in Greek). This title was not officially decreed at a council, but was invoked at the Seventh Ecumenical Council, which occurred at Nicaea in A.D. 787. At this Council, the Virgin Mary was called a title that is very close to Panagia in meaning, which was "most pure."

The use of the word Panagia also has very ancient roots. It may be have been used to describe Mary by Origen in the middle of the third century. By the early fourth century, this name was clearly linked to the Virgin Mary by Eusebius.

The term *panagia* provides a helpful perspective on the unity of teaching between East and West. Even though the Orthodox Church does not hold to the doctrine of the Immaculate Conception (see Chapter 14), this term articulates views that the Virgin Mary did not sin during her earthly life, but rather, she lived a pure and holy life. It does not, however, imply that something unique occurred at her conception that released her entirely from the consequences of sin that occurred in the Garden of Eden. Just as all Christians must struggle to live lives of purity and grace, Eastern Orthodox theologians emphasize that the Virgin Mary was Panagia not so much because of the miracle of her birth, but because of her consistent desire to choose a holy and pure life.

factum

The idea of Mary as the Mother of the Church is related to her role as the first to accept Christ. Mary's motherhood is also related to the idea that spiritual ties could be as strong (or stronger) than biological ones. This is illustrated at the cross, when Christ said to Mary, "Behold your son" while gesturing to Saint John.

In A.D. 787, the Seventh Ecumenical Council, held at Nicea, once again restated that the Virgin Mary is *Theotokos* and *panagia*.

All of these councils sought to bring clarity to the confusions surrounding Jesus Christ, to define essential theological positions, and to help bring unity to the Church. The Virgin did play a prominent role in these councils, as the titles ascribed to her had tremendous implications for how Christians understood Jesus and the way in which he brought about the salvation of the world.

CHAPTER 6

Images of Mary

No woman in history has inspired more artists than the Virgin Mary. Within Eastern Orthodoxy, she has been captured by a very particular form of stylized art called iconography. Icons are two-dimensional images of holy people or events, which nevertheless are meant to capture or present some kind of spiritual reality to the faithful. They find their context in the midst of church life—in the cycles of feasts and fasts and days of remembrance, as well as in relation to the whole scope of Christian theology. This chapter will explore the meaning of icons within Eastern Orthodoxy, especially when they are used to depict the Virgin Mary and the infant Christ.

Heaven on Earth

The use of icons within the Eastern Orthodox Church cannot be understood apart from the whole context of worship. Eastern Orthodox services strive to reflect heavenly realities in their services with candles, incense, icons, and *a cappella* singing. In this way, Eastern Orthodox worship engages not just the mind or heart, but all of the senses. Images of saints and Biblical events cover the church walls. These icons are an integral part of the services because they help make present the holy people and saving events from the history of Christianity.

The Eastern Orthodox Church is the second largest Christian group in the world (after the Roman Catholic Church). It is made up of more than twenty national churches that are in communion with each other. The Eastern Orthodox Church has many ethnic manifestations around the world but shares a common theology.

factum

One can visit any branch of the Orthodox Church—Greek, Romanian, Georgian, and so on—for a Sunday service, and while the worship may have some ethnic and cultural variations from one church to the next, it will be essentially the same service, a liturgy that is more than 1,500 years old.

Other than Christ, there is no single figure within Eastern Orthodox iconography who is depicted more than the Virgin Mary. Her face is beloved because it was her face that most resembled Christ's face—she was his closest biological kin, and it was she who experienced the quickening of Christ in her womb.

Orthodox Christians also find theological support for creating and honoring icons through the event of the Incarnation. According to Orthodox theology, if Christ could take on human form, then he could be depicted in earthly ways. Within the East, however, statues have never been embraced.

Eastern Christians have been historically wary toward statues because of their lifelike qualities.

According to official Eastern Orthodox teaching, it is unacceptable as well to create images of God the Father because no living human has seen God the Father. An exception is made for depicting, for example, the "Ancient of Days" figure of the prophet Daniel's vision in Daniel 7:9 because this refers to what he *saw* rather than being a depiction of God himself. Similarly, the Holy Spirit may be depicted as a dove in the icon of Theophany (the Baptism of Christ, from Matthew 3:16 and Mark 1:10), or as tongues of fire in the icon of Pentecost (Acts 2:3) but otherwise is not to be depicted.

Encountering Icons

When Eastern Orthodox Christians enter their churches, they will often greet the many icons around the church, kissing them, bowing before them, and taking a moment of silent prayer before them as they light candles. While some might view the practice of kissing icons or bowing before them as idolatrous, the Eastern Orthodox do not view it this way. The Eastern Orthodox believe that the icon makes present the holy person or event in the same way a photograph might. They believe that the honor that is paid to the image passes through the image to the holy person the image represents. In this way, they can continue to show honor and love for those who have departed this world but continue to live with Christ.

Images Not to Be Worshipped

Icons are not worshipped, because worship is reserved for God alone. This position was emphasized at the Seventh Ecumenical Council, which took place in Nicea, Asia Minor, in A.D. 787, and was held in response to this controversy about the use of icons. According to the iconoclasts (those who opposed the use of icons, literally the "destroyers of icons"), icons were idolatrous and should be destroyed. Many others, especially the monks, believed strongly that the icons were valuable for the faithful because they helped teach and make present the lived theology of the Church. The Council made a sharp distinction between *proskynesis* (a relative respect or veneration that could be shown to images, saints, and other human beings, literally, a bowing before), and *latreia*, which is the worship due to God alone.

One of the great ironies of history is that new battles are not always being fought but often the same battles are waged from age to age. In our age, the Eastern Orthodox, Roman Catholic, and Anglican Churches generally hold to an anti-iconoclastic perspective, believing that images can help glorify God. Certain other churches, however, still hold to a strict iconoclastic perspective, teaching that images are idolatrous. Some contemporary Protestant churches have an iconoclastic perspective that loosely resembles the thinking of the historical iconoclasts.

Because Eastern Orthodox Christians believe that icons are an invaluable link to these heavenly realities, they refuse to destroy or abandon their images. To this day in Eastern Orthodox Churches, icons are treated with great respect and love because they help connect the Eastern Orthodox faithful to "The Great Cloud of Witnesses" from Hebrews 12:1.

symbolism

Within Orthodoxy, symbols are intimately connected to the realities they represent, in the same way that in American culture, coins and bills are directly linked to an actual amount of gold, which is why it is illegal to deface or destroy American dollars or coins.

Icons also serve as a tangible reminder of intangible realities. Icons accompany the Eastern Orthodox believer through every phase of life. They are often presented to an infant at baptism, hung on the wall of one's home, and kissed and used for daily prayer. At the end of life, when the person dies and is placed in the casket, the much-loved icon is tucked into their hands as a sign of God's continual presence.

Icons are powerful images in the life of the Eastern Orthodox Church because they make the communion of saints—the fellowship of all the Christian faithful who have departed this life, and even now participate in the Resurrection—present to the faithful, expressing heavenly realities in a language that is rich, visual, and transcendent. Because icons are so precious, the faithful generally treat them with great care, and do not set them on the ground or use them in ways that might be viewed as careless. If an icon accidentally falls to the ground, the person who caused it to fall will usually quickly snatch it up and kiss it before placing it back on the stand or wall.

Because icons are intended to show eternal realities, the figures on the icons usually have sober expressions that go beyond the realm of human passion. Their faces are often full of love, but they do not laugh or smile. The gaze of holy people through icons is steady and unchanging, much like the changeless realities they intend to represent.

Icons are also called "windows to heaven" because they offer a glimpse into heavenly realities. For this reason, the Eastern Orthodox Christians create prayer corners in their homes with icons of Christ, the Virgin Mary, and the particular saints that are significant for each family member.

Creating an Icon Corner

Icon corners offer a way to make heavenly realities present. They also serve as a reminder that all Christians are called to keep watch for the return of Christ. Many families also keep a "lampada" or small, oil-filled lamp, burning at all times before the icons.

factum

In Orthodox Churches, the priest censes the icons. The smoke that rises at Vespers, an evening prayer service, echoes the words of the Psalm 140: "Let my prayer arise in thy sight as incense." Because the Orthodox Church teaches that humans are "living icons" the priest also censes the people, who bow in response, acknowledging the image of God in the priest.

Icons also express profound realities related to each person's unique vocation. Just as in Genesis Adam and Eve were created in the image of God, all human beings reflect this image. According to Eastern Orthodox theology, the ultimate call is to make this image shine forth more and more clearly in our own lives (and to see it more clearly in others) as one grows closer to God. The saints depicted in icons are shown in their glorified or resurrected state—fully complete in the divine life. In this way, the images of the saints reveal our own calling to be saints.

Icons often depict saints—people who fully embraced the reality of Christ in their own lives and now live with God in heaven. In the Eastern Churches, icons of the Virgin Mary and infant Christ are of primary importance because they reflect the Incarnation, the way in which God took human form and dwelt on this earth, placing himself in a profoundly vulnerable position.

The Craft of Iconography

Icons are quite unlike most art, because they are not only subject to artistic discipline but the creator of icons (or iconographer) must follow guidelines while working. Iconographers usually learn their craft under the guidance of an experienced iconographer. These apprenticeships help guarantee that new generations of iconographers follow the ancient form. Iconographers are expected to fast and pray when working, so that their icons become the fruit of prayer as much as the end result of their artistic endeavors.

Creating Icons

The process of creating icons is laborious. Most iconographers prepare their own boards for painting, and also mix their own egg-tempura paint. Icons also depart from Western art in the perspective they employ. In most Western art since the time of the Renaissance, a "vanishing point" perspective is used. This makes objects at a distance seem smaller than those that are closer. Vanishing-point perspective is something like the illusion created when one stares at train tracks and the tracks at the farthest distance seem to come together.

Inverse Perspective

In iconography, the opposite perspective, inverse perspective, is used, so that the vanishing point is in the viewer. The person who gazes at the icon becomes the central focus of the icon. This perspective engages the viewer and helps him to see that he is not on the outside of theological realities but at the very heart of the Biblical stories. The inverse perspective suggests that each Christian stands at the center of narrative—that our lives are directly connected to the history of Christianity.

symbolism

The iconographer's work is sometimes referred to as "writing icons." Some people prefer this terminology because it captures the idea that icons constitute a specific symbolic language, and contain a lot of theology. Similarly, the act of deciphering the symbolic language of icons can be called "reading," just like a person might search a holy book for spiritual insights.

Another interesting distinction between Western art and iconography is an iconographer begins his work with a layer of dark earth tones (called "the chaos"), slowly adding lighter colors as the icon develops, so that when the icon is complete the holy person seems to radiate light. (In Western art, it is more typical to begin with light colors, and slowly add the darker ones.) This process is symbolic of the dynamic movement of the Christian life—always toward the light and away from the darkness.

The craft of iconography follows strict guidelines of form and style so that from generation to generation, holy people and events remain recognizable. Saint Paul, for example, is almost always shown with an elongated and hairless forehead because, according to tradition, he was mostly bald. Likewise, children are often portrayed as little balding adults to demonstrate their wisdom. The Virgin Mary is most often shown with a red robe and a blue mantle, which is the inverse of what Christ wears. The blue is associated with Christ's divinity, and the red with his humanity.

Icons of the Virgin Mary

It is rare to see an icon of the Virgin in which she is shown by herself, without Christ present. This also illustrates an important theological point about human nature: we fully become ourselves through relationships. Our relationships are integral to our identity, which is why traditional Christianity has recognized only two "stable" states for the human person—marriage or monasticism. In both situations, the challenges of interacting with others are a catalyst for spiritual growth and increased maturity.

There are a variety of types of icons of the Virgin Mary. There are three types that are the most famous, known in Greek as:

- The *Hodegetria*, translated as "the One who points the way"
- The *Orans*, or "the Virgin of the Sign"
- The *Eleousa*, or "the Virgin of Loving Kindness"

All of these images show Christ as an infant with Mary, but each one has particular theological significance. Rowan Williams, Archbishop of Canterbury, authored a book called *Ponder These Things* which offers some beautiful, thought-provoking insights into these three main Marian icon types.

factum

Though Islam prohibits the use of images in worship, when the prophet Muhammad destroyed the images he found in the Kaaba in Mecca, he left one image untouched—the image of the Virgin Mary, which he could not bear to deface. Similarly, when the Turks invaded Greece, they defaced many icons in the churches, but often left the ones of Mary intact.

Eleousa Icons

In the *Eleousa*, the infant Christ appears as almost any child—eagerly, desperately, even, seeking the loving attention of his mother. The infant Christ pushes his cheek against his mother, and she leans into him with a look of tenderness on her face. Her eyes are often shown with bags beneath them, perhaps to express the weariness of loving this child who was born to die. Whatever the bags beneath her eyes express in terms of theology, the image certainly resonates with the parents of any young children. The task of parenting is awesome and, at times, overwhelming.

In this icon, the infant Christ clutches his mother's veil in his fist in the same way any infant might grab onto his mother's clothing or hair, his face pressed to her cheek with the eagerness of a child seeking his mother's love. One leg seems to be digging into her, as if he is trying to climb up her side as small children love to do. The Virgin Mary holds the child close, gathering him up in her embrace.

According to Rowan Williams, this icon is not only an image of the tender love between Mary and Christ, but is also an image of God's seeking, eager, love for humanity. One can also view this icon as a reminder of Christ's searching, intense, personal love for every person in the world.

Orans Icons

In the *Orans* or "Virgin of the Sign" icon, Mary stands in prayer with her arms raised up and Christ is shown in her womb. Often, there are one or more seraphim surrounding Mary, expressing the presence of the angels in prayer and the mystery of redemption. This image has been considered for centuries to be an image of the Church, in which each person is called to "give birth" to Christ in their own way by faithfully responding to his call.

As Mary prays in the ancient tradition of the church with arms raised, we are reminded that through prayer God becomes present in our lives and in our world.

Sometimes in this image, the Virgin Mary will hold a shawl over her hands, which is symbolic of her protective veil over the Church. You will learn more about the Virgin Mary's veil in Chapter 12, because it is associated with one of the ancient apparitions of the Virgin.

Hodegetria Icons

The *Hodegetria* or "She Who Points the Way" style of icon originated in Byzantine times. This icon offers an effective balance to the concern some hold that churches that honor the Virgin Mary occasionally fall into idolatry. In this icon, the Virgin Mary holds Christ with one arm, but with her other arm she gestures toward him, as if to say, "Look to him." In most icons of this type, Christ gazes at his mother and his hand is raised in blessing.

Icons for Parents

One of the moving things about this icon is how fully Christ and his mother engage each other. The icon seems to suggest that Mary is best known by the way that she points to or guides people to her son, while at the same time, one is better able to understand Christ in light of his love for his mother. In this icon, neither Christ nor his mother seem to call attention to themselves. Both draw the viewer in with their eyes, and each directs the eyes of the viewer to the other person, so that one's eyes move from child to mother and then back again to child.

symbolism

One of the beautiful themes in icons of Christ and Mary is universal among parents and children. When children are small, they depend upon their parents, but as they age and grow increasingly independent, their parents tend to depend on them.

One of the most striking depictions of this role reversal can be seen in the icons from Mary's death, in which she is a small form wrapped in linen, held in the arms of her much larger son Christ. The burial shroud she wears closely resembles the swaddling cloths worn by the infant Christ. In a sense, she has become the infant and he has become the parent.

Images from Christ's infancy show him as a small child, leaning into his mother's arms. As much as Mary was the first person to embrace Christ in her own life, she is ultimately the one who shows us what it is to be embraced by Christ. These images demonstrate the cycle of life, which moves from dependency to interdependency and then back again to dependency.

When Icons Weep

Accounts of the phenomenon of weeping icons are widespread, and several icons have been reported to have begun weeping in North America within the past decade. When an icon weeps, moisture tends to form on the surface of the icon, then begins to gather as tears in the eyes. The oil-like tears then drip down the face of the icon. This "holy oil" is then used to anoint the faithful. Often, so much oil streams down the icon that it soaks through the icon and leaves a stain on the back.

One such weeping icon is located in Chicago. Weeping icons have also been reported in New York and Texas. In most cases these icons are of the Virgin Mary, but sometimes icons of Christ or the saints have also been reported to weep. In 1996 in the Church of the Nativity in Bethlehem an icon of Christ began to weep red tears. The tears were first seen by a Muslim woman who was startled by them and could not imagine why she, a Muslim, would be the first to witness the weeping icon. She immediately brought the local monks to see the icon and they felt that they were witnessing a miracle. The weeping icon was viewed by thousands of pilgrims over the course of the next several days.

factum

In the early seventies in Akita, Japan, a statue of the Virgin Mary wept 101 times. This statue produced tears, sweat, and blood that were tested in a local laboratory. Scientists discovered that the blood, sweat, and tears were from a human source—the tears were type AB while the blood was type B.

Witnesses often describe the tears shed by icons as having an oily consistency and sometimes exuding a sweet smell that some describe as a heavenly aroma. This aroma is similar to the sweet aroma that is said to rise up from the bodies of saints, most notably Saint Demetrius in Thessalonica, Greece. The Eastern Orthodox Church has historically connected these oil-like tears with myrrh, which is the aromatic spice associated with the beginning and end of Christ's life—the three wise men brought gold, frank-incense, and myrrh when Christ was a newborn, and after he died, three women went to his tomb to anoint his body with myrrh.

Chapter 13 describes the miracle that occurred at Damascus, Syria, in which a young woman experienced olive oil coming from her fingers as she prayed, as well as myrrh-like tears coming from her icon. It was also reported that over 100 copies of this icon also began to weep.

The Gift of Tears

Many people wonder why icons or statues seem to weep, especially those of the Virgin Mary. There have been no conclusive responses to this question from the Eastern or Western Churches, although many theories have been suggested.

Within the Eastern Orthodox tradition, the gift of tears has been viewed as a rich manifestation of the Holy Spirit. The gift of tears is an experience of weeping that arises out of prayer. This gift is not associated with emo-tional upheaval, but is said to be spiritual, and associated with the weeping of repentance and the compassion of God.

The prevalence of this gift within the Eastern Church is something like the widespread manifestation of the "gift of tongues" in some contemporary Pentecostal and Charismatic Churches.

symbolism

The gift of tears is associated with drawing near to God. In particular, in the ninth century Saint Symeon the New Theologian made a connection between weeping and the dwelling of God in our hearts. The weeping icons seem to mirror those who have experienced this gift.

Many in the East believe that the phenomenon of the weeping icons of Mary is associated with her role as an intercessor (someone who prays to

God on behalf of other people). Because she prays so fervently for those in the Church and in the world, some believe that it makes sense that she would also weep through her icons.

Others have suggested that the tears are related to the state of the world today, which is full of brokenness and pain. Another theory about the weeping icons is that they are signs of God's continued love, which pours out through the icons and the prayers of the Virgin Mary to the faithful. The myrrh-scented tears are also sometimes viewed as a sign of the mingled sorrow and joy that is often associated with the Virgin Mary because at Christ's birth, one of the three Magi brought myrrh to present to him. Because of its bitter, balsamic smell, myrrh is also traditionally associated with mourning. Many interpreters see the myrrh as a foreshadowing of Christ's death. The myrrh-stained icons speak both of sorrow and joy— sorrow at the suffering of the world and its separation from God, but joy at the grace of God that brings salvation, and at the divine love that abides eternally.

Those who have witnessed weeping icons report that they are incredibly beautiful, and many also report having experienced healing from the myrrh-scented oil that drips from them. The icons of the Virgin Mary express profound realities about her person, her role in the church, her relationship with her son, and her protective role. These icons demonstrate the tremendous variety of theology that comes from the pivotal events in the Virgin Mary's life, and also all of the theology that she made possible through her willingness to say "yes" to God.

CHAPTER 7

Seasons of Salvation

Within the liturgical calendar, shared to some to degree by Anglicans, Roman Catholics, and Eastern Orthodox, there are several major cycles that span the year. One of the most significant is related to the Virgin Mary. This chapter will explore this cycle as well as her place within the liturgies of all three churches. The Church, just like Earth, marks time through the passing of seasons, returning year after year to the same patterns, which grow deeper and more meaning-ful with time.

Cycles of Faith

The books of the Bible are filled with references to the natural cycles of the earth. While the Christian faith offers a taste of the transcendent, it also takes its form in an earthly way. Early on, Christians saw a confirmation of their faith in the cycles of nature. The Bible is full of references to the natural world, such as "unless a grain of wheat falls into the earth and dies, it remains alone; but if it dies, it bears much fruit" (John 12:24, *ESV*). Christians saw a reflection of divine truth in the natural patterns of the earth. Furthermore, the church drew out these patterns in the arrangement of an ordering of feast days. Christmas Day, for example, was set on the winter solstice, just before the days would get longer and brighter after the bleak month of December. Easter has been traditionally celebrated at sunrise, in an effort to connect with the rising sun, which has been viewed as a powerful natural image of the Son of God who rose from the darkness of death.

Natural Associations

The piety surrounding the Virgin Mary was also rooted in the natural world. She has been associated with the sea, stars, soil, flowers, and snow. Her body, which went through nine months of pregnancy following the Annunciation, experienced one of the great seasons of the female life. She is intimately connected with the beginning and end of life, and the feasts that are devoted to her are largely connected with these critical thresholds. These thresholds are connected to the seasons of our bodies, the seasons of the earth, and the seasons of the Church.

Liturgical Calendars

In particular, liturgical churches such as the Roman Catholic, Eastern Orthodox, and Anglican are anchored by events that repeat themselves year after year. Life in these churches is cyclical, meaning that the same Scriptures are read on the same Sundays year after year, the same feasts are celebrated on the same days, and the same colors are used during particular seasons to visually mark the event that is being celebrated.

These churches move through time and through seasons. Historically, there have been special seasons in these churches connected to the Virgin Mary. These seasons encapsulate her conception, her birth, the Annunciation, Christ's birth, and her death. The seasons are intimately connected with the fundamental realities of life—conception, birth, and death. These feasts have been celebrated in a way that at least partially corresponds to the realities they represent. In particular, in the Eastern Orthodox Church the Virgin Mary's birth is celebrated exactly nine months minus one day after her conception. This placement of the feasts is intended to show that she was human, although quite extraordinary, coming a day early—fulfilling the dreams of her parents and ushering in a new era of faith. (In contrast to this, the time from Jesus' conception—Annunciation on March 25—and his birth on Christmas is exactly nine months.)

fallacy

Those who worship in liturgical churches do not feel that the repetitive nature of the church seasons are dull. Just as the first snow of winter inspires awe as do the first buds of spring, liturgical seasons repeat themselves but remain fresh for those who are open to them.

Mary in Anglicanism

Of all Protestant churches, the Anglican Church (known in America as the Episcopal Church) has historically had the deepest relationship with the Virgin Mary. This is because the Anglican Church was not founded primarily for theological reasons but because of practical concerns related to the English king of the sixteenth century, King Henry VIII, who reigned from 1509 to 1547. In his quest for a male heir to take over the throne after his death, Henry VIII sought the permission of the Roman Church to divorce his wife so that he could marry again.

When the Pope would not grant King Henry the divorce he requested, Thomas Cranmer, the king's ally, was appointed as Archbishop of Canterbury (the seat of highest authority in the Anglican Church), and immediately allowed the divorce. Because Pope Clement VII did not approve of the divorce or of King Henry's flagrant disobedience, he excommunicated him. King Henry's response to the Pope's act of excommunication was to remove England from the control of the Roman Catholic Church and to start the Church of England (called the Anglican Church).

Although the new Anglican Church embraced some aspects of the newly forming Protestant theology, the Church of England retained many of the forms and devotions of the Roman Catholic Church. King Henry never really intended to have a clean break from Rome; he had the short-term goal of attaining the freedom to do as he chose in regards to divorce.

In one of the most wrenching ironies of history, Henry VIII was never successful in producing a male heir who could be king. Despite his efforts with six wives, Henry only had one son, Edward VI, who was sickly and died when he was just fifteen years old. Still, the difficulties surrounding Henry's quest for a male heir had a profound impact on the history of England and the history of Christianity.

The Act of Supremacy

In 1534, King Henry VIII established The Act of Supremacy. Under this act, the Church in England was placed squarely under the authority of the king. Under King Henry VIII, who was quite conservative, the Church retained many of the liturgical practices and piety of the Roman Catholic Church, while mixing in some Protestant sentiment for good measure. During this time, Thomas Cranmer wrote *The Book of Common Prayer,* which contained specific articles of faith. During the early era of Anglicanism, the Church demonstrated varying degrees of warmth toward the Virgin Mary.

On August 15, the day on which the Roman Catholics celebrate the Assumption and the Eastern Orthodox Celebrate the Dormition (or falling asleep of Mary), the Anglicans also remember this event by praying, "O God, who hast taken to thyself the blessed Virgin Mary, mother of thy incarnate Son: Grant that we, who have been redeemed of his blood, may share with her the glory of thine eternal Kingdom; through the same thy Son Jesus Christ our Lord, who liveth and reigneth with thee, in the unity of the Holy Spirit, one God, now and forever. Amen."

discussion question

How many wives did King Henry VIII go through in his effort to produce a male heir?
King Henry had six wives: Catherine of Aragon, Anne Boleyn, Jane Seymour, Anne of Cleaves, Catherine Howard, and Catherine Parr. Henry divorced Catherine of Aragon and Anne of Cleaves, beheaded Anne Boleyn and Catherine Howard, and outlived Jane Seymour. Catherine Parr, lived to tell her tale.

One of the chief distinctions between the Anglican Church and the Roman Catholic and Eastern Orthodox Churches, however, is that although the Anglican Church heartily embraced the idea that the saints in heaven continue to pray for those on earth, from very early on, the Anglican Church expressed reservations about asking for the prayers of the saints. Although the Anglican Church retained much of the forms, calendar, and piety of the Roman Catholic Church, it had a strong desire to separate itself from some of the perceived "excesses" of the Roman Catholic Church.

Contemporary Anglicanism

In contemporary times, there are pockets of devotion to the Virgin Mary within the Anglican Church. Historically, the more robust Marian devotion that remained under Henry VIII gradually gave way to a more subtle Mariology, but Mary still has a position of esteem within the Anglican Church. Many Anglican chapels have been devoted to her, and she still occupies a place within their calendar.

In 1931, a Society of Mary was formed within the Anglican Church. This group describes itself as "Episcopalians dedicated to the Glory of God and the Holy Incarnation of Christ, under the invocation of Our Lady, Help of Christians." This group exists with the desire to promote devotion to the Virgin Mary within the Episcopalian context, although its membership is not limited to Episcopalians.

Within the Anglican Church, there are six major feasts of the Virgin Mary. Many of these feasts are not celebrated in all parishes, but they exist in the richness of the liturgical calendar. Depending on the spiritual emphasis of each individual parish, these services may or may not be celebrated.

▼ **THE MAJOR FEASTS OF THE VIRGIN MARY IN THE ANGLICAN CHURCH**

The Purification of Saint Mary	February 2
The Annunciation	March 25
The Visitation	May 31
The Day of Saint Mary (known in the West as Assumption and in the East as the Dormition)	August 15
The Nativity of Mary	September 8
Our Lady of Walsingham	October 15
Mary's Conception	December 8

The Seattle Statement

Historically, there has been enough common belief surrounding the Virgin Mary between the Roman Catholics and the Anglicans that in 2005, a statement called Mary, Grace and Hope in Christ (often referred to as the Seattle Statement) was formally presented. This statement was the fruit of many years of dialogue between a small group of Anglicans and Roman Catholics who sought to find common ground between the two churches in relation to the Virgin Mary.

The Seattle Statement offers an interesting glimpse into the fruits of ecumenical discussions surrounding the Virgin Mary, although this statement is not generally viewed as authoritative because it has not yet garnered universal approval within these churches. Instead, it is seen as a starting place for discussion on an issue that has at times been divisive.

This statement affirms the positions that the two churches hold in common in relation to Mary. In particular, it says that it is theologically acceptable for both Anglicans and Roman Catholics to pray to the Virgin Mary. It also states that the Roman Catholic dogmas of the Immaculate Conception and the Assumption can be viewed as consistent with Anglican methods of Biblical interpretation. On the Roman Catholic side, admissions are made that there have been some "past excesses" related to the Virgin Mary. Although they may not be explicitly opposed to the dogmas of the Immaculate Conception and the Assumption, Anglicans were primarily concerned with the way these dogmas came about—through Papal pronouncements instead of through a more organic kind of consensus. This issue was a major sticking point between the two churches. In another statement that was released in 1981, the Anglicans expressed deep concerns about a dogma that is binding to all believers and is proclaimed on the basis of papal authority.

In 2002 the current Archbishop of Canterbury, Rowan Williams, published a beautiful book about praying with icons of the Virgin Mary and infant Christ titled *Ponder These Things*. In this book, he expresses a classic Christian position on the relationship between Christ and Mary. "It is not only that we cannot understand Mary without seeing her as pointing to Christ: we cannot understand Christ without seeing his attention to Mary," he writes, continuing, "Jesus does not appear to us as a solitary monarch, enthroned afar off, but as someone whose being and loving is always engaged, already directed toward humanity."

The Roman Catholic Cycles

Roman Catholicism has historically had an extremely robust love for the Virgin Mary. Of all the churches, the Roman Catholic Church has the most days set apart for her commemoration. In fact, the entire month of May is set aside as Mary's month, and traditionally during this month, statues of Mary are crowned with flowers. October is also set apart as a month of the Rosary. The first Saturday of each month is also dedicated to Marian Devotions, a practice which began in the Middle Ages.

▼ **THE FOUR PRINCIPLE MARIAN FEASTS OF THE ROMAN CATHOLIC CHURCH**

The Immaculate Conception	December 8
The Assumption	August 15
The Divine Motherhood of Mary	March 25
The Annunciation	March 25

Almost fifty days are marked on the calendar with special Marian emphasis, although these Marian feasts are not equally important.

Apparitions and Calendars

Many days of remembrance are related to the phenomenon of Marian Apparitions—times in which Mary appeared to Christians offering healing, warnings, or messages. Apparitions that have received formal approval from the Church have sometimes found places of designation on the Roman Catholic Calendar. Days are set apart for remembering Mary by her many titles—such as Our Lady of Lourdes (February 11), Our Lady of Fatima (May 13), Our Lady of the Snow (August 5), and Our Lady of Knock (August 21). These dates create a formal way for the church to remember these apparitions.

Titles to Be Remembered

On the Roman Catholic calendar there have also been days set aside for the purpose of remembering specific titles of the Virgin Mary that have had implications for those within the Church such as Our Lady Help of Christians (May 24), Our Lady, Mediatrix of All Graces (May 31), and Our Lady of the Most Blessed Sacrament (May 13). All of these feasts help refresh the memory of the faithful as they move through the Church year, offering fresh insights into Marian possibilities.

symbolism

It is interesting to note the unity of major Marian feasts between the Roman Catholic, Eastern Orthodox, and Anglican Churches that symbolize events in Mary's life. Although these feasts do not always share the same name (and each name may have meanings specific to the context of a particular tradition) the commonalities demonstrate a significant amount of unity.

On top of these many Marian Feasts, the Roman Catholic Church also has several major Marian feasts on the same days which are set apart in the Eastern Orthodox and Anglican Churches. In particular, Mary's Assumption is celebrated on August 15, the Annunciation is celebrated on March 25, and the Immaculate Conception is celebrated on December 8 (the same day on which the Eastern Church celebrates her conception, without using the word "immaculate").

After Vatican II (a major council of the Roman Catholic Church that took place from 1962 to 1965), there were several adjustments made to the Roman Catholic calendar. Important distinctions were made between the different feasts to help distinguish which feasts were most important, making some of the less significant feasts optional, although all of the feasts do help to complete the picture of the Virgin Mary's role in the Roman Catholic Church.

The Orthodox Cycle

The Eastern Orthodox Church may not have all the same feast days of Mary found in the Roman Catholic Church, but the Virgin Mary certainly plays a powerful role in the seasons of the Orthodox year. Her feasts are always linked to the Christian message, each one demonstrating something about what it is to be a Christian, what it is to be open to the Gospel message, what it is to become a temple of the Holy Spirit, and what it is to experience conversion and salvation.

Within the Eastern Orthodox context, there are four feasts that are most important in relation to the Virgin Mary, although there are other minor feasts connected with the Virgin Mary's life and some of the miraculous icons associated with her.

▼ **THE FOUR PRINCIPLE MARIAN FEASTS OF THE EASTERN ORTHO-DOX CHURCH**

The Nativity of the Virgin	September 8
The Presentation of the Theotokos in the Temple	November 21
The Annunciation	March 25
The Dormition	August 15

The feast of the Nativity of the Virgin commemorates the day that Mary's parents, Joachim and Anna, conceived her. This feast does not have a Scriptural basis, but the tradition surrounding this feast is deep and beautiful. It is the celebration of the beginning of the reversal of the curse that occurred in Eden. Joachim and Anna, who were barren, conceive the Virgin Mary after prayerfully pleading with God that they could become parents. Just as Mary's life will begin to reverse the curse of Eden because of her willingness to give birth to the Redeemer, the curse of Joachim and Anna's life, their infertility, was reversed at the moment of conception.

The feast of Presentation of the Theotokos in the Temple is the celebration of the day the Virgin Mary was brought into the temple by her parents, who had promised to devote her to God. According to Church tradition, the Virgin Mary was raised in "the Holy of Holies," she herself preparing to eventually become, in a very unique way, the temple of God by giving birth to Christ.

The feast of the Annunciation is the most universally celebrated feast. This one commemorates the day the angel came to the Virgin Mary and told her that she was to bear a child who would be God Incarnate.

The feast of the Dormition celebrates the memory of the Virgin Mary's death, or in the Eastern Orthodox Church, "her falling asleep." This belief is rooted in the idea that Christians do not die but only sleep in anticipation of ultimately waking with God. In the case of Mary, both the Eastern Orthodox and Roman Catholics believe that the Virgin Mary ascended into heaven.

Liturgical Traditions

Within the Eastern Orthodox tradition, prayers devoted to Mary are very common. She is remembered at the end of the various cycles of intercessions, hymns, and dismissal prayers. For example, most litanies end with the priest remembering the three great titles associated with the Virgin Mary as well as her place among the saints. He prays: "Calling to remembrance our all-holy, most-pure, most blessed and glorious Lady, the Mother of God and ever-virgin Mary, with all the saints, let us commend ourselves and one another and our whole lives unto Christ our God."

According to the late Eastern Orthodox theologian, Father Alexander Schmemann, a mention of the Virgin Mary offers the final note of Eastern Orthodox prayers. "This pattern applies to all liturgical units: the daily, weekly, and yearly cycles . . . Whatever the theme of any particular celebration, its last word, its seal, will always be the Theotokos."

factum

The belief that Mary ascended directly to heaven has been enforced by the fact that no relics have ever been found from the Virgin Mary's body. The relics associated with her are linked to her clothing and breast milk. Unlike other saints who have left behind their bones and bodies, there is no physical evidence of the Virgin Mary's body.

Akathists and Novenas

Akathists and Novenas are special prayer services in the Eastern Orthodox and Roman Catholic Churches. These services are often devoted to a particular saint, and in many cases this saint is Mary. One of the most beloved Akathists in the Eastern Orthodox Church is in honor of Mary, and is usually referred to simply as "The Akathist Hymn." This hymn dates back to about the middle of the sixth century, and is usually attributed to Saint Romanos the Melodist.

The word *Akathist* literally means "not sitting." Akathist hymns give honor to a particular holy person, and for this reason, people stand while praying them. The Akathists alternate between repetitive verses and unique stanzas. "The Akathist Hymn" uses poetic language to demonstrate the cohesiveness of the Scriptural message. Many Old Testament images that are often linked to Mary are mentioned in the Akathist. Mary is called the "Heavenly Ladder by which God came down," a reference to Jacob's Ladder, as well as the "Tabernacle of God the World." The Akathist also features language that demonstrates the way in which the Virgin Mary is symbolic of all of creation. She is seen as the earth, while Christ is the life-giving wheat that comes from it. Likewise, just as Christ will ultimately become "The Bread of Life" through his sacrifice on the cross, the Virgin Mary is seen in this hymn as the table upon which the feast is spread. These images express the multiple ways through which creator and creature were unified in the person of Christ, all of this made possible by the Virgin Mary's willingness to bear the seed of God in her womb.

The Akathist also describes Mary as the star causing the sun to shine. Star imagery surrounding the Virgin Mary comes up quite frequently. Just as a star led the shepherds to the manger where the Virgin had given birth, and the Virgin Mary is often adorned with stars in her icons, the term *Stella Maris* or "Star of the Sea" is frequently used as an image of Mary's guiding presence through the storms of life.

Stations of the Cross

The Stations of the Cross is a primarily Roman Catholic devotional practice that is sometimes performed by Anglican and other churches. This devotional practice, which goes all the way back to the Middle Ages, is also referred to as "The Way of the Cross" or "Via Dolorosa."

discussion question

How did the Stations of the Cross develop?
The devotional practice of Stations of the Cross developed during the Middle Ages when wars made it impossible for Christians to visit the Holy Land. Pilgrimages were a central part of the life of faith, so the Stations of the Cross was developed as a way of having a "mini-pilgrimage" right in one's local church.

You may have seen a Catholic Church decorated with fourteen images related to these central events in the life of Christ. The events are best commemorated on foot, as a person walks through the stations, pausing to pray and contemplate each step that Christ took. The Stations of the Cross can also be done in an outside space. A wooded area or garden is especially well-suited to this meditative and prayerful devotional practice.

For Roman Catholics, the Stations of the Cross are often associated with Lent and Good Friday, but they can be performed at any time of the year, both at church and at home. Nowadays, you can even walk with Christ in a virtual way through an online Stations of the Cross (*www.catholic.org/clife/ prayers/station.php*).

The Stations offer an opportunity to literally follow in the footsteps of Christ during the most critical hours of his life. This devotional practice requires one to stop and prayerfully consider each step of Christ's journey to Calvary.

The liturgical and devotional practices surrounding the Virgin Mary offer a rich way to draw close to Christ as one considers the experience of the woman who was clearly closest to him—his mother.

A survey of these feasts and cycles offers a glimpse into the unity and diversity of liturgical traditions surrounding the Virgin Mary. These traditions have developed over time, as Christianity has spread around the globe. The feasts of Mary have served as a way to contemplate the Incarnation, the mystery of God becoming human. They bring an element of humanity to the Church, a glimpse of the feminine through Mary, and help keep worship rooted in the seasons and the earth.

CHAPTER 8

Mary among the Saints

Because the Virgin Mary had such a profound role in the history of Christianity, and because she was chosen to do the thing that no other person has ever been chosen to do before or since—to bear God Incarnate in her womb, you might think of Mary as a woman apart from the other saints. While Mary is special in her own right, she is better understood within the context of the Church. This chapter will explore Mary's unique role in this regard.

Mary, Mother of the Church

The title of Mary as Mother of the Church is an ancient description that has had many controversies surrounding it. This idea was based on the premise that had Mary not said "yes" to God, there would have been no Christian Church. Her very willingness to become the mother of God also made her, in effect, the very first Christian and the mother of the Church. This term also implied that Mary was the very first to do the work that all Christians are called to do, which is to birth Christ into the world by living in a way that faithfully expresses his love for humanity. Mary has also been called the Mother of the Faithful.

Motherly Icons

The theme of Mary as the Mother of the Church is also present in icons. In one icon, she is shown with Christ still in her womb giving a blessing. This icon has been interpreted by some as symbolic of her role as Mother of the Church because it offers a glimpse of how Mary gave birth to Christianity.

Many of the reported apparitions also testify to Mary's ongoing concern for the Church. Not only has one of the themes of the apparitions been that Mary often asks for churches to be built in specific locations, such as Lourdes, Guadalupe, and Rome, but she also shows an ongoing concern for people within the Church.

Sibling Rivalry

Another theme that has surfaced through the apparitions is that of the Virgin Mary's concerns about divisions in the Church. If Mary is the Mother of the Church, then it is only fitting that the painful separation between the Eastern and Western Churches would not go unnoticed by her.

Whether one ascribes authority to these apparitions or not, it is notable that at least one of the themes seems to be entirely consistent with the Virgin Mary's role as Mother of the Church. Just as a mother does not wish her children to fight with each other, the Virgin Mary (along with her son, Jesus) surely longs for the Church to one day become one again, to struggle toward this end in prayer and in dialogue.

symbolism

In the apparitions that occurred in Damascus, Syria, the Virgin Mary said that anyone who divides the Church is in sin. She also promised to bring special blessings to both the Eastern and Western Churches when Easter is finally celebrated on the same day in all churches.

Controversy about the title "Mother of the Church"

The title Mother of the Church has certainly not been without controversy, even during this century. At Vatican II, there was a good deal of discussion about whether this title should be used in the official documents or not. In his homily in December 2005, Pope Benedict recounted the moment when the final proclamation was made by Pope John XXIII. He said, "There is a moment fixed indelibly in my mind, when on hearing his words, 'Mariam Sactissimam declaramus Matrem Ecclesiae' ('Let us declare Mary the Most Holy Mother of the Church'), the [Council] Fathers leapt out of their chairs and stood applauding, paying homage to the Mother of God, our Mother, the Mother of the Church. In fact, it is with this title that the pope summed up the Marian doctrine of the Council and gave the key for its understanding."

Mary, Bride of Christ and Sign of the Faithful

The Virgin Mary has often been referred to as the Bride of Christ, especially in medieval Western devotion. This term may seem strange, in particular because the Virgin Mary is most obviously the mother of Christ. But when you consider the first title, that Mary is considered the mother of the Church, coupled with the scriptural idea that the Church is the Bride of Christ, you can see how the images of Mary and the Church are sometimes used interchangeably.

The other idea that is closely linked to this one is that the Virgin Mary acts in perfect harmony with her son. Clearly Mary is Christ's mother, but she is never above him, and she never dominates him. Instead, she cooperates with him. The two of them function in perfect unity in the way that a healthy married couple might. This may be part of the reason why when couples are married in the Eastern Orthodox Church the wedding icons given to them are often of Christ and the Virgin Mary. The perfect harmony of their relationship provides an image of how all of our relationships should be.

The Virgin Mary is also seen as a sign for the faithful because her life was a perfect witness. She pointed the way for all believers by living in dynamic obedience to the will of God. Her desire to open herself to God's will for her entire life is an image of the life that all Christians are called to—a life of surrender, brave faith, and obedience to the will of God. The Virgin Mary is also seen as a sign to the faithful because her example offers guidance to all those who seek it—especially those who are living in difficult circumstances.

Mary's life was a sign that things are never quite as they seem—an unmarried, pregnant teenager from Nazareth was able to show how the coming of Christ represented shifting realities in both the temporal and ultimate sense. The Virgin Mary was also seen as a sign because her story made the spiritual world a visible and real part of the mundane realities of secular life.

Champion Leader

The Virgin Mary is not seen only as the epitome of motherhood and femininity—she is also represented within the Church as a woman of great strength. So common is the image of Mary as powerful protector that her strength is often evoked by young men going into battle. People have felt that if they dedicated battles to her, she would help them to be victorious. One of the classic battle images associated with the Virgin Mary has to do with her battle with snakes or the dragon (which can symbolize the devil and temptation).

In Revelation 12, a woman groans in childbirth and a dragon waits for the child to be born, threatening to consume the child when he emerges from the womb. The woman seems to represent Mary, based on the description of the woman being clothed by the sun and with the moon at her feet. When the woman gives birth to a boy, the child is taken away to God and the woman flees into the wilderness, where she "has a place prepared by

God"(Revelation 12:6). The child seems to represent Christ, because he is described as "a male child, who is to rule all the nations with a rod of iron" (Revelation 12:5). The image of this woman not being conquered by the dragon is similar to one that shows up frequently in Western art, in which the Virgin Mary conquers the serpent from Genesis 3, reversing the curse that resulted from Adam and Eve eating the forbidden fruit. In this art, instead of being seduced by the snake, Mary steps on it and conquers it. This image also serves as an example of the life of victory to which all Christians are called.

The Protection of the Mother of God

The other side of this emphasis on the Virgin Mary as the Champion Leader or Woman of Valor is that she has also, historically, been evoked as a protector for those who are struggling in times of political unrest. Many countries, such as Poland and Russia, believe that the Virgin Mary was responsible for protecting them during times of invasion, driving away foreign enemies and preserving peace.

In some cases, countries were invaded by large armies and were able to stand up to overwhelming forces and prevail over them. Often the successful defense was directly attributed to the Virgin Mary. There has been a long-standing belief connecting the Virgin Mary's love for people with her willingness (and ability) to protect them. Medjugorje, Bosnia, although torn apart by wars, seems to have been miraculously protected through some of the bloodiest battles during World War II. The village has remained intact and virtually unharmed. Medjugorje continues to be the location of some of the most famous apparitions.

Constantinople

The Great Eastern Christian city of Constantinople was also miraculously protected multiple times by the intercessions of the Virgin Mary. Throughout history, when rumors of war reached the emperor, processions around the city would be held. The emporer or Patriarch might carry an icon of Mary or her clothing-related relics. The crowds would pray and sing and wait to see what happened.

In 860, for example, Russians attempted to invade the city with a fleet of 200 ships. They were forced to withdraw after the Virgin's Robe was processed around the city and a great storm rose up and scattered their fleets.

An icon of Mary was again brought out in 1453 just as Constantinople was about to fall to the Ottoman Turks. Emperor Constantine XI commanded that this icon be carried through the city as a way of offering prayers and comfort to the Christians there. During this procession, however, the sky filled with ominous clouds and the icon slipped and fell. Immediately, the streets were deluged with hail and rain and the procession halted. The city fell to the invading armies and is now known as "Istanbul."

discussion question

Who is thought to have been assumed into heaven?
According to 2 Kings 2:9, Elijah was whisked to heaven by a whirlwind, accompanied by chariots and horses of fire. His disciple, Elisha, was also blessed enough to receive Elijah's gift of prophecy after Elijah departed.

The Blachernae Palace Church possessed this very valuable relic associated with the Virgin Mary, and in that church, an apparition directly linked to this particular relic was reported. On October 1, A.D. 911, this church was having an extremely long prayer service called an All-night Vigil.

It is said that during the service, Saint Andrew looked up and saw the Virgin Mary kneeling in prayer in the church, weeping and praying for all Christians. Saint Mary was not alone but was in the company of Saint John the Baptist and Saint John the Theologian. She was radiantly beautiful.

As the Virgin Mary prayed and wept, she eventually came close to the bishop's throne and continued to weep and pray. Saint Andrew could hardly believe his eyes as he watched the Virgin Mary complete her prayer and then spread her veil over all the people who were praying in the church. The veil was luminescent.

Saint Andrew watched in astonishment and then he nudged his companion, Epiphanius, to ask him if he also saw the Virgin. Epiphanius replied, "I do see, holy father, and I am in awe."

symbolism

Within the Eastern Orthodox Church, the Virgin Mary's veil is a much-loved symbol that represents the Virgin Mary's tender care and her ability to protect the faithful through her intercessions on their behalf.

The feast of the Pokrov (Protective Veil of the Mother of God) is celebrated on the day that the apparition is reported to have occurred, October 1. Although the event occurred in Constatinople, the feast is also zealously celebrated in Russia, where many churches are named for this feast, and an entire city, Pokrov, was named in memory of this event.

Mary and Weather

Historically, the Virgin Mary has also been connected with weather in the minds of the faithful. Many sailors, in particular, have believed that the Virgin Mary saved their lives when they prayed to her during stormy weather.

factum

The connection between Mary and stars may also relate to the appearance of the star of Bethlehem, which guided the Magi to the baby Jesus.

In Russia, where long, harsh winters are one of the undeniable realities of life, the connection between the need for the protective care of the Mother of Christ and the feast of Pokrov has been strong. A variety of folk traditions that have had particular significance for agricultural families surround this day.

In Russia it is widely believed that the first cold blast of winter wind blows on the day of this feast, which coincides with the time in which the weather begins to change from autumn to winter. The feast of Pokrov also marks a significant deadline—before this day, all harvesting and fieldwork must be completed, so people can settle in safely for the coming winter. One Russian folk saying captures the sentiment of Pokrov well. According to this saying, "On Pokrov, before dinner is autumn, after dinner is winter."

Traditionally, Russian families waited until this day to burn their first wood for warmth, believing that if they did not kindle their hearths until Pokrov they would be able to stay warm all winter long. The first fires of winter were often lit with a sort of prayerful devotion as the family committed itself to the tender loving care of the Virgin Mary in the face of the long, bleak winter that was to come.

Mary as Intercessor

Some of the most ancient images of the Virgin Mary come from the catacombs in Rome (catacombs are underground burial places found in many parts of the world) where Christians would hold their services during times of persecution. Most of the images from the catacombs do not directly show Christian themes because the Christians needed to keep their identities hidden.

One of the images of Mary recovered from the catacombs dates back to the fourth century. She is shown with her arms raised in the "orans" position. The image of raised arms symbolized prayer, and there were many depictions in the catacombs of figures in the orans position from the period during the persecution of Christians in the first few centuries after Christ. But in this fourth-century fresco image, a child is shown in the woman's belly. In contrast with the less defined images of earlier times, this would have been a more explicit reference to the Virgin Mary bearing Christ in her womb. This image demonstrates the classical relationship between the Virgin Mary and the Church.

Mary's arms are raised in prayer as a demonstration of her ministry of ongoing intercession, as she is praying for the good of the faithful. In this position, Mary demonstrates not only who she is, but what all Christians are called to become—intercessors for the sake of the world.

Another, more contemporary Western image of Mary that demonstrates her role as intercessor was first manifest through an apparition experienced by Catherine Laboure in France in 1830. This image was later engraved on the Miraculous Medal, which has been distributed all over the world (you'll learn more about the Miraculous Medal in Chapter 14). In this apparition, the Virgin Mary lifted up a golden globe topped by a cross, as if she was praying for mercy for the world. Then, the globe disappeared and she spread out her arms. Her fingers shone with luminous rings from which streaks of light poured down about the earth, illustrating the blessings that she pours upon those who seek them.

There are so many images of Mary as intercessor that it is impossible to detail them all here. But it is helpful to understand that all images of Mary are connected. Her role as intercessor is also connected to her role as Mother of the Church, demonstrating to all what it means to live a life of prayer, love, and action.

Star of the Sea

Another classic title for the Virgin Mary is *Stella Maris*, or Star of the Sea. This title is most often attributed to a manuscript written by Saint Jerome, from the fifth century. Saint Jerome, however, actually used the term *Stilla Maris* instead of *Stella Maris*, which would have been translated as "a drop of the sea" instead of "star of the sea." Many historians believe that this linguistic confusion could have been caused by a copyist's error. The term *Stella Maris* was nonetheless used by many other later Christians, including Isidore of Seville.

There are also some ancient Christian hymns from the eighth to the eleventh centuries that used this title to describe Mary, such as "Ave Maria Stella" and "Alma Redemptoris Mater."

One of the Scriptural verses that is sometimes used to explain this term comes from a story in 1 Kings 18:41–45. In this passage, a small cloud appears above the sea. The cloud is interpreted as a hopeful sign to people suffering through a drought. Seeing the cloud, they know the rains will come and the drought will end. This Biblical image is almost a perfect reversal of other events connected to the title Stella Maris, specifically the image of Mary helping those who are trapped at sea during a storm—here, she gives hope of rain instead of stopping the storm. Mary is often viewed as a person who gives hope to the hopeless and help to those who are in despair.

The star imagery that is associated with the Virgin Mary has multiple dimensions. A six-pointed star is a reminder that Mary is from the line of David (as the Star of David has six points). Mary is also associated with the qualities assigned to stars—most specifically the use of stars for navigation. Stars lead you to your destination, and allow you to always know in what direction you are heading, guiding followers to the truth.

The association between Mary and stars gave birth to much imagery of the Virgin Mary as a protector of sailors. Many sailors have prayed to the Virgin Mary and felt that she miraculously protected them. In one legendary tale (which reflects some anti-Muslim bias, unfortunately), three men were on a boat, and a storm rose up. Two of the sailors cried out to Mary to protect them—these men were Christians. The other man, who was a Muslim, cried out to Allah for safety and then began to chastise the other sailors of crying out to Mary instead of Allah. As he scolded them, a great wave rose up and tossed him into the sea while the other two survived.

The image of Mary as "Star of the Sea" is also closely connected to some pagan-goddess imagery, particularly that of Isis, who came from the sea and was able to preserve seafarers. The parallels between the Virgin Mary and Isis have been especially significant because Isis had a sacrificial child (see Chapter 19 for more information about Mary and the goddess Isis).

The image of storm-tossed sailors calling out to the Virgin Mary for assistance can be understood metaphorically as well—the world itself is a stormy sea that is difficult to navigate and dangerous. As Saint Bernard said:

"Take not your eyes from the light of this star if you would not be overwhelmed by the waves; if the storms of temptations arise, if you are thrown upon the rocks of affliction, look to the star, invoke Mary . . . In dangers, in distress, in doubt, call on Mary. She will not be far from your mouth, or your heart; and that you may obtain her intercession, omit not to imitate her conduct. When you follow her, you will not go astray; when you invoke her, you will no longer be in doubt; when she supports you, you will not fall; when she leads

you, you will surely come to eternal life, and will find by your own experience that she is justly called Maria—that is, Star of the Sea."

The Heart of Mary

The significance of the Virgin Mary's heart is deeply connected to the heart of her son, which is called "The Sacred Heart." The Sacred Heart imagery is often connected to four apparitions from the 1670s, which were experienced by Saint Margaret Mary Alacoque.

The Sacred Heart

The name for Jesus' heart connects the heart of Christ to his ongoing love for humanity. It is often shown with thorns as an expression of Christ's suffering for the sake of the world, as well as the suffering he experiences when his love and message of salvation is rejected. The Sacred Heart of Christ has been widely connected to Roman Catholic devotional practices; to meditate on his heart is to contemplate his love and to draw closer to him in love.

Especially within Catholicism, there has been much discussion of the Virgin Mary's heart. In Paris, one of the most beautiful churches, set high on a hilltop overlooking the city, is named Sacre Coeur, which can be translated as "Sacred Heart." Many Western Christian monastic orders and parochial schools have been dedicated to the heart of the Virgin Mary. This piety may at least partially be connected to the idea that through the Virgin Mary's heart, one is able to glimpse her suffering, love, compassion, and unceasing prayer.

The Virgin Mary's heart is also a frequent theme of Western art and apparitions. This image came through strikingly in the vision that reportedly took place at Rue de Bac in Paris when a young postulant named Catherine had a vision of the Virgin Mary, which was ultimately made into the Miraculous Medal (you will learn more about the Miraculous Medal in Chapter 14). One of the significant elements of this apparition is that Catherine saw two hearts beside each other. One was encircled in thorns while the other was pieced by a sword. These two hearts were intended to represent the heart of Christ (as he suffered the pain of persecution), and the other heart was intended to symbolize the heart of Mary, which was prophesied in the New Testament. When Mary and Joseph took the infant Christ to the temple for his dedication, Saint Simeon greeted the Holy Family and prophesied to Mary that a "sword would pierce her soul" (Luke 2:33–35). This prophesy has been most often connected with the suffering the Virgin Mary would experience as she watched as her son was rejected and crucified. In popular piety, it is sometimes said that, besides Christ, no one suffered more than Mary at the Crucifixion.

Two Holy Hearts

These two hearts, shown so closely together, both pierced, also express the way in which the hearts of Jesus and his mother were linked. Within Catholicism, there has been much piety surrounding the Immaculate Heart of Mary. This piety finds inspiration from a number of passages in the Gospels, especially Luke 2:19, which says, "But Mary treasured up all these things [that had happened to her], pondering them in her heart," and Luke 2:35, where Simeon prophesies to Mary, "a sword will pierce through your own soul also." This second passage seems to be fulfilled in John 19, where Mary stands at the foot of the cross, and in which Jesus' side is pierced.

Within the Roman Catholic tradition, there is even a feast day on August 22 to celebrate the Sacred Heart of Mary. A special prayer is said on this day, which shows the significance of the Virgin Mary's heart within the Roman Catholic Church: "ALMIGHTY, everlasting God, Who didst prepare in the Heart of the Virgin Mary a worthy dwelling-place for the Holy Ghost; mercifully grant that we, devoutly contemplating the festivity of the same Immaculate Heart, may be enabled to live according to Thy Heart."

The Virgin Mary's heart has a significant place in the faith of many Roman Catholics because a glimpse of what she felt in her heart offers an understanding of who she is. The symbolic representations of Mary prevalent in the Church help to flesh out a picture of a woman who was fully human but fully transformed by her complete willingness to live for God.

CHAPTER 9

Medieval Mary

Many of the devotional practices surrounding Mary that grew up in the East eventually found their way to the West and blossomed in fresh ways during the medieval period. This chapter explores the artistic and poetic forms and devotional practices that developed during this era, which is known for its courtly romances, the Crusades, and flowering of mysticism.

The Cult of Courtly Love

Many of our modern ideas about romance are rooted in the medieval cult of courtly love, which developed from a mingling of many sources. These sources include older traditions of Arab love poetry, which first found their way to Spain and then became popular in Europe by the eleventh century. During the Middle Ages, these passionate expressions of love blossomed.

Courtly love was a school of thought in which courtiers could learn how to be charming and graceful. Famed poets, or troubadours, were attached to specific wealthy courts. They created poetry and songs to entertain and educate those in the court.

According to the model of courtly love, love was important as a catalyst for growth and transformation. When the notion of the transformative power of love migrated to Europe, it was easy for medieval Christians to apply this practice to Christianity. The Virgin Mary came to be seen as a lady worthy of devotion, and as people drew closer to her, they felt that their love for her made them bolder, braver, and more faithful.

Troubadour Poetry

Troubadour poetry became popular in Europe during the twelfth century. The Troubadours were a class of musicians and poets based in France, Italy, and Spain who wrote poems and music about chivalry and love. They were most prominent between 1100 and 1350. Many of their writings focused on sexual love.

By the thirteenth century, both the Arab love poetry and the troubadour poetry found a new subject—the Virgin Mary. The Virgin Mary served as an ideal subject of love poetry because she was viewed as paradoxically accessible and unattainable.

Courtly love was full of grace, longing, and devotion. According to the mores of the time, love made people better than they would otherwise be; and to love another person would be to raise that other person above oneself. Love was always restless, always seeking, and never fully satisfied. The desire to acquire the beloved only intensified with time. Mary could be sought, but never captured; passionately loved, but never possessed.

May Day Celebrations

One of the ancient romantic traditions rooted in the cult of courtly love is still celebrated today. May Day celebrations offered a way to integrate the pre-Christian practice of crowning a "lady" into the Christian tradition of devotion to the Virgin.

The ancient May Day celebrations included various courting rituals and were a celebration of the springtime and the pagan deities associated with fertility and the land. Increasingly, as the Church sought ways to translate these folk festivals into events that would be compatible with Christianity, they adapted to the rituals of the culture.

symbolism

Today, the ancient tradition of crowning a lady is still practiced during the month of May—but the lady crowned has become the Virgin Mary. Many American Catholics who attended parochial schools during this past century have fond memories of crowning the Virgin Mary with a wreath of flowers during the month of May (which is designated Mary's Month).

Many of the references to the Virgin Mary as "Our Lady" reflect the medieval obsession with courtly love. *Our Lady* serves as the counter-term to Our Lord. This title is suggestive of the pious notion that Mary was a royal lady who must be wooed and honored.

The Face That Resembled the Face of Christ

Mary was also the subject of more love poems during this time period than any other woman, and imagery surrounding her figured mightily into Dante's *Divine Comedy*. It was through the *Divine Comedy* that Dante first coined a famous description for Mary's face, stating that it was "the face that most resembled Christ."

This idea that by peering into the face of Mary one might able to glimpse her son powerfully influenced both the art and theology of the day. Increasingly, artistic images (such as the Black Madonna images, which you will learn more about in Chapter 19) demonstrated the startling resemblance between the mother and her child. In these images, both mother and son were carved from a single block of wood and their resemblance was undeniable.

During the Middle Ages, Mary often seemed more accessible than Christ. For peasants, her femininity would have provided some continuity with the ancient goddesses they worshipped and prayed to as they tilled their fields. For the ranks of celibate monks, the presence of Mary as a "safe" woman in their lives might have fulfilled some need for female companionship—the famed Saint Francis of Assisi, for example, adored the Virgin Mary. Just as his monastic life called him to take vows of poverty and chastity, Saint Francis found a positive way to interpret these restrictions. Instead of viewing his life in terms of deprivation, he saw himself as united to these values in the way that a married person might be united to their spouse. Specifically, he felt a particular closeness with Mary, whom he thought of as his Lady, "Holy Poverty."

The Flowering of Western Art

For the teachers of theology, images of the Virgin Mary helped them convey her role in the history of salvation. Mary's role in art and piety was profound during this time, perhaps prone to excess, but certainly worth exploring if we are to understand the presence of Marian devotion in our world today.

During the Middle Ages, most people were not able to read or write the Latin that was used for theological documents, prayer books, and the Mass. Because they did not have access to the printed word, art and architecture served as the theological textbooks of the day.

According to Sally Cunneen in her book *In Search of Mary: The Woman and the Symbol*, the people of the Middle Ages would have readily understood the bulk of the images from the Old Testament that had been viewed by the Church Fathers as "types" of Mary. They would have been able to grasp Mary as the burning bush who had the presence of God within her but was not consumed; Mary as Jacob's Ladder, the link between heaven and earth; Mary as the Ark of the Covenant; and Mary as the flowering of the root of Jesse.

These images were powerfully woven together in churches, manuscripts, and sermons. The visual continuity of these images allowed medieval communities to grasp some of the earliest theology in a fresh way. The medieval period also brought about one of the most significant transformations related to the Virgin Mary. If piety helped create the art that made the Virgin Mary appear more elevated during the Middle Ages, the art also informed the increasing piety that helped Mary be more accessible and available.

The *Pieta*

One piece of art that powerfully influenced the devotion of the Middle Ages was Michelangelo Buonarroti's *Pieta*, the famed marble image created in 1499 in which Mary holds the body of her limp, crucified son. Unlike the stylized and richly symbolic icons of the East, this image was intentionally realistic. Although any mother would agonize during a moment like this, Mary's youthful face remains dignified and full of grace. Her incredible expression of calm speaks to the courage and serenity that is so often associated with her.

discussion question

Where is the *Pieta* now?
Housed in the Chapel of the Pieta in Saint Peter's Basilica in Rome, the *Pieta* is one of Michelangelo's most famous works (and the only one he signed). It is also one of the most recognizable pieces of religious sculpture. Michelangelo carved the *Pieta* when he was only twenty-four years old.

Like the images of Mary that link her role in the New Testament to some of the famed events from the Old Testament, the *Pieta* is a visual depiction of the early sentiments that come from the poetry of the East that would have expressed the sorrow of the mother at the death of her son. In his book *Mary Through the Ages,* Jaroslav Pelikan connects the image of the *Pieta* to the poetry of Romanos the Melodist, in which Mary and Jesus discuss his death. She begs him to let her be present at the cross because she wants to remain close to him through his darkest hour. Christ encourages her to lay aside her grief because she is "in the bridal chamber."

The Hope of a New World

The *Pieta* is not merely a grief-filled image. It is also a profoundly hopeful one. Christ's death must occur so he can fulfill prophecies of his resurrection, so that he can return like a bridegroom seeking his bride, the Church. He expresses his desire to return to his mother, Mary, who was often viewed as an image of the Church.

Mary grieved the death of her son, and shared in his sufferings as only a mother could. It was she who would have been most able to grasp that even in his death there were the fresh seeds of a promise. Even as she held her deceased son in her arms, she must have sensed that his death was the beginning of new life for the world.

The image of the *Pieta*, which showed Mary with Christ in her arms after his death, is also connected with Saint Teresa of Avila, who had a vision of Christ in her own arms after his death. Through this vision, Saint Teresa experienced what it would have been like to be Mary, holding her dead son in her arms.

Our Lady of Legends

During the Middle Ages, legends of Mary were widespread and influential, and were treasured for their spiritual significance and teaching value. These ancient legends also helped inform the piety of the day, shaping people's liturgical and private devotional practices.

The Legend of Theophilus

One of the most popular legends from the Middle Ages involved a sixth-century archbishop named Theophilus who lived in what is now Turkey. He was a humble man who served as archdeacon for the Archbishop of Celia. When he was unanimously elected to serve as bishop, he turned down the post because of his humility.

Later, however, when Theophilus was forced to step down as archdeacon for no clear reason, he was so filled with rage that he turned to the devil. The devil encouraged him to sign a pact in which he would renounce God and the Virgin Mary in exchange for the position as bishop. Theophilus signed the pact with his own blood.

He became bishop, but his conscience troubled him. After he fasted for forty days, the Virgin Mary appeared to him and chastised him for what he had done. After he repented, she agreed to intercede before God on his behalf. Later, she appeared to him in a dream and tore up the pact. He awoke surrounded by scraps of parchment. He made a confession to his bishop and died in peace.

This legend offers a glimpse into the medieval perspective of the Virgin Mary. During the Middle Ages, she was increasingly viewed as the woman who had the power to cancel the works of the devil, to make right even lives that had gone horribly awry.

factum

> The medieval notion of Mary's ability to restore lives was expressed well by the eleventh-century writer Peter Damian, who offered this prayer to Mary: "Pay what we owe, avert what we fear, obtain what we wish, and accomplish what we hope."

Increasingly, Mary was viewed as this type of mediating (some might even say meddling) mother who makes things right for her children. Despite her exceptional example of piety and purity, she was not generally viewed as a figure of judgment but of mercy and reconciliation. Christ, on the other hand, was most often portrayed as a stern judge. According to Sally Cunneen, in her book *In Search of Mary,* many of the surviving medieval images of Christ show him as the stern Shepherd who separates the sheep from the goats. It was during the middle ages especially that Mary came to be associated with mercy while Christ came to be associated with judgment.

Images of Mary generally shifted during the Middle Ages as well. The early art from this period often emphasized Mary's greatness, while the art produced later emphasized her tenderness. As she came to be seen as increasingly tender and accessible, prayers to her for intercessions increased as well. Some people even prayed to Mary instead of Jesus.

The influential writer Bernard of Clairvaux expressed this progression away from the son and toward the mother this way, "If you fear the Father, go to the Son; if you fear the Son, go to the Mother."

The Golden Legend

Another influential text that developed during the Middle Ages was called *The Golden Legend.* This collection of stories of the lives of the saints was most likely compiled around 1290 by Jacobus de Voragine.

The Golden Legend was much loved for the way it both humanized and spiritualized the lives of holy people. For example, it drew from a variety of ancient and apocryphal texts to fill in many biographical details about Jesus and Mary which had not been supplied by Scripture.

The Golden Legend was something like a medieval encyclopedia of the saints, containing stories of varying pedigree. These stories were valued for the way they offered spiritual lessons to the faithful, but were not always accepted uncritically. Some of the details supplied in these accounts were more fanciful than historical, more symbolic than miraculous.

Mary and Medieval Mysticism

The monastic communities of the day did a great deal to encourage and increase Marian devotion, in part by establishing additional feast days for Mary. In particular, Saturday came to be set apart as a day for commemorating Mary. This decision was based on multiple traditions related to Mary. According to one, because the world was completed on the seventh day and Mary was an essential part of the ultimate plan of redemption, it was appropriate to commemorate Mary on that day.

One of the reasons that the seventh day seemed fitting as a day to commemorate Mary was related to the Genesis account. According to Genesis, after God created the world, he rested on the seventh day. Likewise, it was sometimes said that, when the infant Christ came into the world, he was able to find rest in the arms of his mother.

symbolism

Saint Alcuin was a Benedictine monk who was the Minister of Education. He was attached to the court of Charlemagne, and under his direction, each day of the week came to commemorate and symbolize a different event in Scripture. A Mass was to be celebrated on each day, and two were to be celebrated for Mary on Saturday.

The Venerable Bede, an eighth-century English monk who was a famed historian and theologian, wrote some of the earliest Western sermons devoted to Mary. A twelfth-century devotee of Mary, Saint Bernard of Clairvaux, who served as Abbot of Cistercian Monastery for thirty-eight years, also wrote beautiful and influential sermons about the Virgin Mary.

Saint Bernard

Saint Bernard was titled the "mellifluous doctor" because of his poetic writing, especially about the Virgin Mary. His first few writings about the Virgin Mary were composed when he was only twenty-five years old. He had loved her since he was a small child because, according to one legend, once while he was praying to the Virgin in a church, he received three drops of her milk as a sign of her love for him.

factum

Sometimes Bernard used particularly romantic terms to describe the Virgin. In one sermon he wrote, "Our Queen has gone before us, and so glorious has been her entry into paradise that we, her slaves, confidently follow our mistress, crying: 'Draw us after you, and we shall run in the fragrance of your perfumes.'"

Bernard had a tender relationship with Mary for all of his life. He called her the "aqueduct" of God's grace. Through his sermons, Bernard made connections between the Virgin Mary and the bride in the Song of Songs.

Saint Bernard's devotion to Mary was so great that he often attributed things to her that some might only be comfortable attributing to Christ. He encouraged people in every kind of distress to call on Mary, and he firmly believed that she would assist people in their time of need. Some of his reasoning seemed to follow the medieval notion of Mary as interceding mother.

Saint Bernard is also credited with helping to perpetuate the image of Mary as the Star of the Sea. Many contemporary scholars see this particular title for Mary as one that is based upon a scribal error that occurred during one of Saint Jerome's translations. Yet, the image of Mary as the Star of the Sea was valuable because it provided some continuity for the local people between the ancient pagan deities who were associated with the sea and the figures of Christianity.

One of the ancient goddesses associated with the sea was Isis. Many throughout history have drawn parallels between the Virgin Mary and Isis (a connection you will learn more about in Chapter 19). Because of Saint Bernard's great and sometimes effusive devotion to the Virgin Mary, he was sometimes criticized as carelessly reviving the ancient goddesses for the local people. Some people felt that he was not careful enough to make a clear distinction between the Virgin Mary and the ancient goddesses.

Female Mysticism

The medieval period was also a time in which many women entered the monasteries. By the twelfth century, the monastic life was an increasingly popular choice for women. Monasticism not only offered an opportunity to devote one's life completely to the service of God, but it also offered women the opportunity to join tight-knit communities of women, to make valuable contributions to their society, and to escape the rigors and dangers of childbearing.

Some of the female nuns of this age authored some of the most beautiful writings about the Virgin Mary. One of the most famous medieval mystics was Hildegard of Bingen, who experienced multiple visions of the Virgin Mary during the twelfth century.

symbolism

Hildegard of Bingen emphasized the ways in which the Virgin Mary restored to women the dignity that had been compromised through Eve's sin. Just as Eve was viewed as the mother of all, Mary became the mother of the new creation.

Hildegard was sickly as a child, suffering from migraine headaches. She had her first taste of the monastic life at just eight years old when she was sent to live at a hermitage where she could receive her education. Eventually, she became an influential leader, or abbess, within her community. She composed songs for her monastic sisters, many of which she wrote, like the visions she experienced all of her life, were specifically centered on the Virgin Mary.

Hildegard's songs echoed some of the central themes of Marian devotion. Mary's virginity served as the link between heaven and earth, and the Virgin birth was as significant as the cross because of the way that it connected humanity to divinity.

In one of her writings on Mary, Hildegard addressed Mary this way: "You are the luminous matrix through which the Word breathed forth all virtues, as in the primal matrix it breathed into being all that is."

The Crusades

One of the most tragic chapters in the history of Christianity is related to the Crusades, which occurred during the Middle Ages. The Crusades were a series of eight military expeditions launched by Western Christians in an effort to reclaim the Holy Land from Muslims, whom the Christians deemed infidels. The Crusaders waged war against others too. During the Fourth Crusade in 1204, for example, the Crusaders sacked the city of Constantinople and zealously killed many of the Eastern Christians there. Just as the bitter memory of the Crusades continues to fuel hostility between the Islamic and Christian worlds, so too the memory of Western Christians attacking Eastern Christians remains a stumbling block in attempts to reunite the Eastern Orthodox and Roman Catholic Churches (which some believe is one of Mary's goals).

Writers such as Sally Cunneen have suggested that perhaps one of the most profound ironies of the Crusades is that Mary was sometimes invoked by English armies for her strength and cited by these armies and their leaders as a reason to engage in holy war. The First Crusade was initiated in 1095 by Pope Urban II. At a famed Marian shrine, in Claremont-Ferrand, France, Pope Urban encouraged his soldiers to pray to Mary for victory and promised that those who participated in Saturday Marian devotions would be forgiven for their sins. The Second Crusade was announced by Pope Eugenius III in 1145 and popularized by the famed scholar Bernard of Clairvaux.

factum

During the Crusades, monks brought chess to Europe from Syria. They made changes to the game to reflect their devotion to Mary. In Syria, the figure who followed the King was the Minister. In the Crusaders' version of the game, this figure could move in any direction—becoming the most powerful piece of the game—and was renamed the Queen or the Virgin.

As the soldiers marched into battle, they may have prayed the Salve Regina: "Hail Holy Queen, Mother of Mercy, our life, our sweetness, and our hope. To you do we cry, poor banished children of Eve, to you do we send up our sighs, mourning and weeping in this valley of tears. Turn then, most gracious advocate, your eyes of mercy toward us; and after this our exile, show us the blessed fruit of your womb, Jesus. O clement, O loving, O sweet Virgin Mary."

During the medieval period, the Virgin Mary was not only present in the minds and hearts of the Crusaders. Her influence permeated the hearts of the majority of medieval Christians, and their love for her was intimate, earthly, and sometimes romanticized.

It was during the medieval period that ancient Eastern practices of devotion to Mary were expressed through artwork, architecture, and writings, leaving us with a rich tapestry of insights into Marian devotion, and into her role as intercessor, guide, and mother.

CHAPTER 10

Toppling Mary: The Reformation

Some modern Protestants believe that the original reformers, especially Martin Luther, rejected all of the more ancient teachings associated with the Virgin Mary, especially the invocation of her prayers and the belief that she was ever-virgin. But most of the reformers had a fairly complicated relationship with Mary. This chapter explores the ways that different reformers viewed the Virgin Mary and also considers the gradual decline of Marian devotion within Protestantism, as well as the faint glimmers of a contemporary Marian revival.

The Rise of Protestantism

In our day, modern Protestants often define themselves in terms of doctrines that have a specifically anti-Catholic slant. The very term "Protestant" speaks to the reality that this movement was sparked by a protest that was originally related to some medieval Catholic abuses such as the widespread practice of selling indulgences. Indulgences were passes that, for a fee, guaranteed the buyer the right to be spared time in purgatory.

The sale of indulgences was not only viewed as spiritually beneficial to the purchaser, but was also a great fundraiser for the Roman Catholic Church. Reformer Martin Luther was especially appalled by the sale of the Peter Indulgence, the profits of which funded the Roman Catholic Church's completion of the construction of Saint Peter's Basilica in Rome.

discussion question

What does *sola fida, sola gratia, et sola scriptura* **mean?** One of Luther's most famous Latin sayings related to his convictions about salvation and theology is *sola fida, sola gratia, et sola scriptura*. This saying can be translated as "by faith alone, by grace alone, and by Scripture alone." This conviction is one of the central creeds of many Protestant Churches.

Protestants have also pointed to the concern that was foremost on Martin Luther's mind—anxiety related to his own salvation. As Luther studied the Bible, he became increasingly convinced that salvation came through "grace alone and faith alone," and not from purchasing indulgences from the Church. This newfound conviction brought him profound inner peace and courage, as well as the desire to share this good news with others.

Luther was a professor at a university in the German town of Wittenberg. Many students responded enthusiastically to his teachings about the sufficiency of faith, grace, and Scripture for salvation. Much of what he taught, however, grew out of a personal reaction to a particular context and time in the history of the Roman Catholic Church.

Tumultuous Times

It is nearly impossible to understand Martin Luther's drive to challenge the Roman Catholic Church without considering the historical times in which he lived. Luther lived in Germany in the sixteenth century. As the son of a father who had worked his way out of the peasant stock and owned a mine, Luther's parents expected much of him and encouraged him to study hard. He completed his bachelor's degree in one year, went on to receive his master's degree, and then proceeded to study law. In 1505, he found himself in the midst of a raging storm. After lightning nearly struck him, he prayed to Saint Anna (the mother of Mary) to save him. He promised her that if he survived the storm he would become a monk.

factum

During Luther's years in the monastery, he became so obsessed with the idea of trying to be perfect that the Vicar General of the German Augustinians, John Staupitz, encouraged him to focus on the love of Christ, and to study the Scriptures.

A Nagging Question

Martin Luther survived the storm and kept his promise to Saint Anna by becoming an Augustinian monk. Although he devoted himself to the prayerful monastic life, he found that all of his work brought him no peace. A question that had plagued him before he joined the monastery continued to haunt him within the walls of the cloister. How was he to know that he was going to be saved? How much work did he have to do to be accepted by God, who in Luther's eyes (and perhaps the eyes of many of his contemporaries) was a righteous judge who looked upon all of his efforts with a disapproving frown? The harder Luther worked, the more aware he became of his own sins. As he grappled with his many sins, God's love seemed increasingly far away.

The Vicar General of the German Augustinians, John Staupitz, instructed Luther to commit himself to academic work as a way to busy his mind and to keep from falling into the trap of endless ponderings. Luther was ordained a priest, began teaching theology at the University of Wittenberg, and went on to receive a second bachelor's degree in Biblical Studies. Eventually, he received a doctorate of theology from the University of Wittenberg.

A Way Out?

As Luther immersed himself in the Scriptures, he discovered that according to Paul from the book of Romans, salvation was not dependant on works but on the grace of God, which was accomplished through Christ's death on the cross. This insight brought much-needed clarity to Luther's life. Just as he found liberation through his study of the Scriptures, he sought to liberate others. Luther's formula appealed to many, and his influence was widely felt both by his fans and by his enemies.

Christendom Cracked

On October 31, 1517, Luther nailed his *95 Theses* to the door of a Catholic church in Wittenberg. This document made multiple accusations against the Church, but Luther's central objections were related to the sale of indulgences and a teaching that is often referred to as "works based salvation."

Luther's *95 Theses* are not only significant from a theological perspective, but also from a historical perspective, because the *95 Theses* were subsequently published and distributed all over Europe (tens of thousands of copies were generated). This was made possible by the advent of the printing press in the 1450s.

The Roman Catholic Church did not take Luther's views as constructive criticism, which is what Luther might have hoped would be the reaction to his work. In 1520, a papal bull (official statement) of excommunication was issued against Luther, which Luther publicly burned along with a stack of church books.

fallacy

It is a fallacy that the Roman Catholic and Eastern Orthodox Churches teach that salvation is through works alone. Neither church endorses faith alone, but both believe that while faith is the central component of salvation, faith without works is dead (James 2:14). Both churches emphasize that while we are ultimately saved through faith, authentic faith is always connected to works.

The Diet of Worms

Ultimately, Luther was brought before the Diet of Worms, a council in which he was to deny or affirm his previous writings. His books were laid out on a table and he was asked if he had written them all. He said yes and was then asked if he still believed all the things that had been written. He asked for time to think and pray about it, and this request was granted.

Eventually, Luther apologized for the harsh tone of some of his writing (especially the writing that criticized specific individuals), but he refused to repudiate his work. He felt that to deny those statements would be tantamount to encouraging abuses to continue. "Here I stand," Luther is reported to have said. "I can do no other. God help me, amen." Many contemporary scholars question whether these words were actually said or are merely part of the tradition. No official documents from the Diet of Worms actually contain this quotation.

Outlawing Luther

In 1521, the "Edict of Worms" was issued by Holy Roman Emperor Charles V, officially banning Luther's writings and claiming that Luther was an outlaw. According to the "Edict of Worms," anyone was welcome to kill Luther without legal ramifications.

Although Luther was promised safe passage to and from the Diet of Worms, many believed that he would be arrested and possibly taken prisoner on his way home from the council. Because of this, Luther's ally,

Prince Frederick, arranged to have him secretly snatched by his envoys and taken to the Wartburg palace. There, Luther began work on his famous German translation of the Bible.

Luther's writings (although officially banned) continued to attract widespread popular support. By the time he died in 1546, he was still calling for reform within the Church, yet the seeds of Lutheranism had already been planted in the hearts of some of his followers. While he was still alive, some Christians who believed in his famous formula *sola gratia, sola fida et sola scriptura* began calling themselves Lutherans.

Martin Luther and Mary

The earliest Protestant Churches retained many of the beliefs and practices of the Roman Catholic Church. As the years progressed, however, these churches resembled Roman Catholicism less and less. Few people recognize how significant Marian devotion was to many of the reformers, although the reformers were generally cautious in their Mariology.

Luther was outspoken in his concerns about some of the excessive forms of Marian devotion, and was especially appalled by some practices that he saw as being on the level of folk piety—he did not like to see the Virgin Mary equated with God. Sometimes, Luther made the common mistake of lumping together practices that were accepted on the level of popular practice with actual dogma of the Roman Catholic Church.

factum

Luther did not intend to start a new church, but rather to bring about reform within the Roman Catholic Church. Although passionate about taking a stance against the abuses he experienced, he was deeply conflicted over the possibility of schism. His excommunication indeed did bring about an era of schism in which Protestant churches broke apart from each other.

Praying to Mary

Although early in his ministry he sometimes seemed to invoke the prayers of the Virgin Mary in a public way, over time Luther became increasingly wary of the practice of invoking the prayers of the saints. He was especially uncomfortable (as many Protestants are to this day) with the idea of Mary as a mediator or intercessor. As Luther's ministry evolved, he came to distrust the practice of invoking the prayers of the saints. His caution, however, did not suppress his belief that the departed saints do continually pray for those on earth and that Mary, especially, prays for the Church.

Luther also offered some cautions related to the saying of the Hail Mary. While he believed that this prayer could be useful for believers who wanted to meditate on Mary's faith, he was concerned that those who didn't believe in God might say the "Hail Mary" in a way that was spiritually dangerous. He was troubled that some people would pray to Mary instead of Christ.

Luther's Catholic Convictions

Luther did, however, believe in most official Roman Catholic teachings related to the Virgin Mary, especially her ever-virginity and her Immaculate Conception, although the latter was not officially proclaimed as dogma by the Roman Catholic Church until 1854. Although Luther called this doctrine a "sweet and pious belief" and embraced it on a personal level, he did not believe that the Immaculate Conception should be forced upon believers because he did not see sufficient Biblical evidence to support it.

fallacy

It is fallacy to believe that the Immaculate Conception refers to Jesus' birth from a virgin. The Immaculate Conception is a view held by the Roman Catholic Church that Mary was conceived without the original stain of sin which had been passed on to every person since the fall in the Garden of Eden.

Luther also believed in the ancient Christian idea that Mary was the spiritual mother of the Church. And he believed that Mary was a wonderful person to meditate on and emulate, especially because of her extreme humility and obedience to the will of God.

According to Martin Luther, not only was devotion to Mary a spiritually helpful practice, but it was an almost intrinsic aspect of healthy spirituality. According to a sermon he gave on September 1, 1522, "the veneration of Mary is inscribed in the very depths of the human heart."

Ulrich Zwingli

Although he came before Luther, the Swiss reformer, Ulrich Zwingli (1484–1531) often takes a back seat in discussions about the Reformation, perhaps because he did not have the same commanding personality as Luther. But while Luther was studying the Scriptures in Germany and coming to the conclusions that would ultimately cause him to be excommunicated, Ulrich Zwingli, a Catholic pastor in Switzerland, was also troubled by abuses within the Roman Catholic Church and was personally engaging the Scriptures. Both men began to call for reform within the Catholic Church.

Devotion to Mary

Some theologians say that Zwingli was the most devoted to Mary of all the reformers. It is certainly the case that the first wave of reformers, including Zwingli and Martin Luther, were far more Marian in their personal devotions and sermons than the second wave of Reformers, including John Calvin.

Zwingli had a very particular devotion to the Virgin Mary, and he was concerned that people knew about it, especially because his calls for reform may have caused some to think that he held positions that he did not. On September 17, 1518, he sent a sermon he'd written to his brothers with a note attached that said, "If you are told that I despise God or his Mother, or that I falsify God's teaching, do not believe it."

Like Luther, Zwingli felt that a measure of reverence for Mary was intrinsic to Christian piety. Many people may be surprised to discover that Zwingli held the conviction that good Christians would be in the habit of reciting the

Hail Mary, although he, like Luther, he would have only been familiar with the first, Biblical portion of this prayer, "Hail Mary, full of grace, blessed art thou among women and blessed is the fruit of thy womb, Jesus." He would not have been familiar with the later addition, "Holy Mary, Mother of God, pray for us now and at the hour of our deaths. Amen."

discussion question

Did Zwingli ask for Mary's intercessions?
Zwingli was not comfortable with the idea of asking for Mary's intercessions. Because of this, he said that the Hail Mary was merely a greeting and a praise, but not a prayer—as prayers generally contained petitions. Still, from Zwingli's perspective, the Hail Mary offered a valuable means of contemplation.

Zwingli often spoke of Mary when he commented on the Bible. This was especially the case between 1516 and 1518 when he served as a chaplain at the monastery. During these years, one of his primary responsibilities was to offer sermons to flocks of pilgrims who came to venerate a statue of the Virgin Mary. Mary would have naturally been on the minds of these pilgrims and she was certainly part of the equation in Zwingli's thinking.

Like Luther, Zwingli held to the the ever-virginity of Mary. He was also comfortable with the title Theotokos, as a term for describing the Virgin Mary's unique role in the history of salvation.

Zwingli also often referred to Mary as Immaculate. He believed that she occupied a special place among the saints because the weakness toward sin was not passed on to her through her parents, Joachim and Anna, as it had been passed down to every single human being since the Fall. Zwingli was, however, concerned about the widespread practice of asking the saints, and particularly Mary, for prayers. He did not feel that this was an appropriate way to pray.

Contemplating Mary

Zwingli did encourage contemplation of Mary, especially contemplation of her heart. He believed that the practice of meditating on her heart was rooted in Luke 2:51. According to this passage, when Mary was pregnant with Jesus she pondered all things in her heart and kept them. Because of this, Zwingli felt that it was a fruitful project to contemplate Mary's heart, which was so full of God's intention for the world. Like Luther, Zwingli felt that Mary's witness was also to be contemplated. But Zwingli was always careful to make clear that Mary never intended to draw attention to herself. Her value was directly related to her relationship with her son and her obedience to God. According to Zwingli, Mary was not just a great example in her faithfulness, but also in the struggles she faced. He stated, "therefore may you, with your poverty and your weariness, find an example in her: this misery that is so well known to humans must be borne, since the holy Mother of God was not sheltered from it."

John Calvin

French-born Swiss reformer John Calvin (1509–1564) participated in the second phase of the Reformation, moving toward a Christianity that was increasingly less Catholic. Of all the reformers, Calvin was perhaps the least effusive about the Virgin Mary, and the most critical toward the Roman Catholic Church.

Protestant Commonalities

There are a few areas, however, in which Calvin shared the convictions of Luther and Zwingli. Calvin firmly believed, for example, in the ever-virginity of Mary. He was familiar with a theory circulating during his time that Mary had other children with Joseph after Jesus was born, but he dismissed this theory as an ancient, recycled heresy, based on the teachings of Helvidius, who lived in the fourth century and provoked the ire of Jerome over the issue of Mary's ever-virginity. Calvin went so far as to say that this ancient heresy had been brought back into fashion by those who speculated upon Scripture in a way that was dangerously imaginative.

factum

Calvin is most well known today for Calvinism, a theory based upon Luther's model related to salvation through faith alone. Calvinists emphasize the grace of God in pre-destining souls to heaven or hell, teaching that chosen people experience "irresistible grace," which means that they are powerless to turn away from the grace of God once selected to receive it.

For Calvin, whose father suffered for many years under a ban of excommunication from the Roman Catholic Church, it was very important to approach Christian theology with a healthy dose of intellectual sobriety. He derided those who took a more speculative approach to Scripture, reading things into the text that weren't there. According to Calvin, one of the key ways to combat the "terrible confusion" of the Roman Catholic Church of his day was to remain intellectually sober. Calvin also expressed concerns about some of the reformers who seemed to love speculating and coming up with new theories that were not firmly grounded in Scripture.

In light of Calvin's concern for sobriety, it is no surprise that he railed against some of the common practices of his day related to Mary. Like Zwingli, he was firmly opposed to images of Mary. He felt that the excessive Roman Catholic pomp surrounding the Virgin Mary bordered on blasphemy.

He was also opposed to the saying of the Rosary, as well as to the practice of naming churches and chapels after Mary. He was appalled by what he perceived as the increasingly superstitious quality of the Hail Mary, which had mysteriously changed from a mere greeting to a prayer, and was increasingly viewed on the popular level as one of the only ways to attain the grace of God. Calvin was disturbed when he saw people praying the Hail Mary instead of approaching God directly.

The Mirror of Faith

Ironically, as much as Calvin deplored physical images of the Virgin, his chief way of speaking about her involved mental images. Mary was an invaluable example to believers because of the ways in which she represented the epitome of an obedient life of service to God. According to Calvin, Mary had no merits in her own right, but because of her obedience to God, her witness can help the faithful live in a way that is more consistent with Scripture. According to Calvin, "She was a mirror of the faith that we must bring to God."

Calvin expressed the ancient connection between Mary and the Church in a profound way:

"Let us learn from the sole title of mother how useful, indeed necessary, is the knowledge of her, inasmuch as there is no entrance to permanent life unless we are received in the womb of this mother, and she begets us, and feeds us at her breasts and finally she preserves us and keeps us under her guidance and government . . . it is also to be noted that outside of the womb of this Church one cannot expect forgiveness of sins or any salvation."

Calvin suggests that, like Mary, all believers should be open to receiving the Word of God in their own hearts. Mary is a model, not only of a faithful life that embraces Christ, but also of the Church.

A Marian Revival?

In December 2003, the prominent Evangelical magazine *Christianity Today* featured an article called "The Blessed Evangelical Virgin Mary." This article begins with a striking anecdote from John Knox's book *History of the Reformation in Scotland.* In this story, a young man who had left the Roman Catholic Church was forced to row in a galley ship for nineteen months. Soon after the boat arrived in Nantes, France, an image of the Virgin Mary was brought to those in the ship to kiss. This young man took the image and threw it into the water, saying, "Let our Lady now save herself: she is light enough; let her learn to swim!"

According to the author of the article, Timothy George, this attitude toward Mary often resurfaces in the Evangelical response to Mary. Evangelicals generally have an extreme wariness and instinctive distrust of Marian piety. But George asks the question voiced by many of his contemporaries: "Does Protestantism have a place for the Virgin Mary or, like Knox of the galleys, must we throw her overboard once and for all?"

This question is currently being answered in a variety of ways. On a personal level, many Protestants are slowly warming to the idea of asking for Mary's intercessions, or at least very intentionally contemplating her example.

Princeton theologian Robert Jensen, a Lutheran, and coeditor of the book *Mary, Mother of God* now encourages the practice of praying to Mary in stark contrast to his father, who was a strict Lutheran pastor. According to Jensen, asking for Mary's intercessions does not decrease our focus on God or take away from prayers to God. Instead, this practice is more like asking for the prayers of a deceased friend or family member—these prayers allow for participation in the Communion of Saints and are not a negation of God.

fallacy

It is a fallacy that all Protestant churches reject Mary. The worldwide Anglican Communion (to which the Episcopal Church in the United States belongs) has, in certain quarters, retained some measure of veneration of Mary.

A recent joint commission of Anglicans and Roman Catholics issued a statement that it is officially theologically acceptable within both contexts to ask for the prayers of the Virgin Mary. The statement also clarified that according to Anglican principles of Biblical interpretation, the Immaculate Conception and the Assumption of Mary are not necessarily contrary to Scripture, although concerns were raised about the fact that the Scripture does not explicitly recount these events. Anglicans also expressed some concerns about the ways that these doctrines were proclaimed by popes without a church council.

Increasingly, Protestants are expressing desires to find ways to integrate Mary's witness into their own spirituality. Although many have historically felt that Mary "belonged to the Catholics," more and more churches are now seeking ways to make Mary their own. In a recent article in *U.S. News & World Report* Senior Pastor Mark Roberts stated that the increasingly warm feelings toward Mary within Protestant churches suggests "that the dividing wall between Catholics and Protestants has come down a bit." As this wall comes down, questions about Mary begin to surface, and some Protestants are finding ways to integrate Marian devotions into their own lives.

CHAPTER 11

Messages from Mary

During the course of the last century, apparitions of the Virgin Mary seem to be increasing in frequency. Apparitions, however, are not a new phenomenon. Reports of apparitions have circulated since at least the first century. Although these apparitions have varied according to the time in which they occurred, certain themes have emerged. This chapter will explore some of the questions surrounding apparitions, as well as some of the universal themes that come through them.

A Global Phenomenon

Often, when we think of apparitions of the Virgin Mary, well-known locations come to mind, such as Fatima or Lourdes. But apparitions of the Virgin Mary are a wider phenomenon than most people realize. The full scope of these apparitions is detailed in Roy Abraham Varghese's book *God-Sent: A History of the Accredited Apparitions of Mary*. Almost every culture in the world has a story to tell of an encounter with the Virgin Mary. Some of these stories seem more credible than others, but each account helps create a more cohesive picture of the phenomenon that is reported to occur around the world.

Vatican Investigations

Before the Enlightenment, apparitions were not subject to scientific investigation. These apparitions were valued, however, because the communities that experienced them firsthand testified to their authenticity and because apparitions cohered with the larger witness of church life and teaching. In the last several hundred years, apparitions have been subject to scientific investigations, and when the scope of the apparitions has warranted it, the Vatican has commissioned investigations.

fallacy

It is a fallacy that the Roman Catholic and Eastern Orthodox Churches embrace apparitions without careful investigation. Apparitions are not necessarily considered valuable publicity for the churches. The most significant apparitions—those that draw the largest crowds and create the greatest followings—tend to be investigated by theologians, civil authorities, and secular medical and scientific professionals.

The Vatican has a policy of investigating only apparitions that have far-reaching effects, such as those at Fatima and Medjugorje (discussed in greater detail in Chapter 13). When the apparitions are smaller in scope, Vatican officials allow local bishops to carry out their own investigations.

The investigations vary from case to case, but they generally employ theologians, scientists, medical professionals, and forensic specialists—particularly when the apparitions involve blood or other bodily fluids.

Scientific Investigations?

To date, scientific evaluation has had only limited use in terms of being able to prove or disprove an apparition, as the actual phenomena transcend the understanding of science. Because the actual apparitions cannot be tested by empirical means, investigations have generally focused on those things which can be studied—in particular the mental health and responsiveness to external stimuli of the people (known as visionaries) who experience the apparitions. During an apparition, visionaries are thought to enter into an ecstatic state and do not respond to pain, heat, or bright lights being flashed in their faces.

When statues have emitted bodily fluids, such as blood, sweat, or tears, scientists have taken samples of these fluids so that they can be identified in the laboratory setting.

A Case Study

The apparitions that occurred in Akita, Japan, began in 1973 and ended in 1981. They were primarily experienced by Sister Agnes Sasagawa, a nun in the convent at the Institute of the Handmaids of the Eucharist. Sister Agnes experienced many unusual phenomena, including the stigmata (meaning that she developed the painful, bleeding wounds of Jesus), as well as the restoration of her hearing, which had been lost shortly before the apparitions began. She also witnessed the statue bleeding, weeping, sweating, and speaking to her on multiple occasions.

This apparition had some unusual elements—for one, the entire nation of Japan was able to view the statue weeping on national Japanese television. In 1975, the blood, sweat, and tears were sent to professor Eiji Okuhara, a Catholic physician at Akita University's department of biochemistry. When he tested the samples, he determined that the tears and sweat were type AB and the blood was type B. These samples were then sent to a non-Christian forensics specialist named Dr. Kaoru Sagiska, who confirmed professor Okuhara's findings. A later test contradicted the results from the first two examinations, and it was finally concluded that the blood was type O, while the other bodily fluids were types A and AB. (It seems that the earliest tests were flawed because the blood sample had accidentally been contaminated by some of the handlers.)

factum

The Vatican eventually said that the apparition in Akita, Japan, was authentic. In a statement from the Vatican dated June 1988, Joseph Cardinal Ratzinger, now Pope Benedict XVI, stated that the "Akita events and messages were reliable and worthy of belief."

After the samples had been tested and confirmed, the Church brought in a Mariologist from Toyko named Fr. Garcia Evangelista, who was a well-known critic of the apparitions. He developed a highly unconventional theory. He said that the blood, sweat, and tears that flowed from the statue were actually being transferred to the statue through Sister Agnes's ectoplasmic powers (meaning that this holy person could actually weep, bleed, and sweat *through* the statue). Many individuals, including Roy Varghese, felt that there were some significant flaws in Fr. Garcia Evangelista's theory, most notably the fact that Sister Agnes's blood type was B, while the blood, sweat, and tears from the statue were type O, AB, and O, respectively. Fr. Evangelista ultimately admitted that he could not account for the differences in blood type. When he tried to claim that another nun was using her ectoplasmic powers, all the nuns were tested and none were shown to have the same blood type as the samples from the statue.

In 1984, after seven years of investigation, this apparition was deemed to be authentic. The local bishop, Most Reverend John Shojiro Ito, confirmed that the apparition was "of supernatural origin" and officially allowed the diocese to venerate the "Holy Mother of Akita." More than 500 Christians and non-Christians, as well as the Buddhist mayor of the town, also testified to witnessing the weeping statue. These events were also deemed authentic by Vatican authorities.

Evaluating Claims—Psychological Reflections

Often, people are tempted to write off apparitions as "hallucinations." This term, however, is rarely applicable to the accredited apparitions. The apparitions that are deemed authentic tend to have many common elements.

discussion question

What is the difference between an apparition and a hallucination?
In most cases, hallucinations are connected to ideas that would already have been in the mind of the person who experienced the hallucination. But with the authentic apparitions, the visionaries often found that they were unable to understand what they had seen, and in many cases, they could not easily convey what they had experienced.

According to Roy Abraham Varghese in his book *God-Sent: A History of the Accredited Apparitions of Mary*, the first element that has been significant from a psychological perspective is that those who experience authentic apparitions are consistently of sound mental health. They demonstrate no more suggestibility than their peers. A person who experiences an apparition is often called a visionary. On the other side of the spectrum are those who experience hallucinations. Hallucinations tend to be experienced by those who have specific mental conditions related to neurosis or psychosis, which predispose them to experience altered states of reality. Hallucinations may also be drug-induced. Visions are also frequently (but not always) experienced by at least a few people, while hallucinations are generally experienced by an individual.

The Making of a Visionary

Certain people are more likely to see the Virgin Mary than others. Poor children, for example, are far more likely to see Mary than adults. Children make for more trustworthy witnesses because they are less successful at deception. Some skeptics, however, claim that children are also more likely to fabricate encounters with the Virgin Mary because of their overactive imaginations.

This theory, however, seems less plausible when one considers the scrutiny that these children often face after experiencing an apparition—in Fatima, a nine-year-old shepherd girl named Lucia Dos Santos was beaten by her mother after describing her encounter with the Virgin Mary. Her mother repeatedly tried to force her to take her story back, but Lucia held to her original account. Later, all three children seers were kidnapped by a local civil administrator. He separated the children and threatened them with death in a red hot frying pan if they did not retract their stories or share their "secrets." All three children endured three days of interrogation and did not alter their stories or surrender their secrets.

During a Vision

During a vision, those who see the Virgin Mary are thought to enter into an ecstatic state where they are unresponsive to external pain or stimuli. Often, their faces radiate peace and joy as they gaze toward a specific location. Witnesses to the apparition who aren't visionaries will not actually see the Virgin Mary, but may be able to observe the progress of the vision through the face of the visionary. They may also experience companion phenomena that are distinct from what the visionaries are seeing, such as the miracle of the sun at Fatima and the lunar miracles at Medjugorje.

Scientists and medical professionals have tested the authenticity of apparitions in ways that may seem barbaric. During the course of an apparition, they have sometimes stabbed the visionaries with needles or knives or attempted to burn them with flame. When the ecstatic state is authentic, the visionaries do not flinch from the pain and their bodies are unable to receive injuries.

Visionaries report lifelong transformation after encounters with the Virgin Mary. Some apparitions recur multiple times and are followed by extreme periods of persecution from local authorities. In some cases, visionaries have suffered martyrdom after experiencing an apparition. Such was the case with the apostle James, who according to Christian tradition, was both the first Christian ever to experience an apparition of the Virgin Mary, and the first apostle to be martyred for the faith.

Evaluating Claims—Theological Reflections

After the cycle of sightings has come to an end (in some cases over 1,000 visitations will occur over the course of several years), the apparitions are investigated. Apparitions are not considered accredited until church authorities have had an opportunity to evaluate them. Some Christians believe that apparitions are demonic. To this concern, writers such as Roy Varghese respond that authentic apparitions cause conversions, something that Satan could not (or would not) do.

A Call to Prayer

In almost every apparition, the faithful are urged to pray more. This call to prayer is often accompanied by warnings about events that might occur if people do not change. In many cases, predictions have come through the apparitions, including predictions of World War II, and of the rise, spread, and eventual collapse of Communism.

symbolism

Many of the contemporary apparitions echo the catastrophes referred to in the Book of Revelation. Although these messages come from a great variety of cultural contexts, apparitions that are deemed authentic generally are theologically consistent, both with one another and with the broader church tradition.

Apparitions in Context

Apparitions have occurred in such locations as India, China, Vietnam, South Korea, Croatia, Russia, and Japan. After these apparitions have occurred, statues and paintings have sometimes been created to commemorate them. These works of art testify to Mary's ability to transcend cultures. She tends to be universally recognizable as the Virgin Mary but is also depicted as a person native to the country and culture in which the apparition occurred. In the statue of Our Lady of LaVang, Vietnam, created in 1798,

Mary appears as a Vietnamese woman, holding an Asian infant Christ—both appear in gowns that would be appropriate to Vietnam's culture. In the statue Our Lady of Good Health from India, she and the Christ child wear shimmering gold saris and have distinctly Indian faces. In Our Lady of Akita, in Japan, Mary appears as an elegant Japanese woman.

One of the fascinating aspects of apparition accounts is that Mary most often seems to come in a form and context that will be recognizable to the locals. The messages she gives (as well as the ways in which she communicates them) tend to be ideally suited to the culture in which she appears. This was certainly the case with the recent apparitions in Damascus, Syria, in which a woman began to experience olive oil dripping from her own fingertips (and then her icon of the Virgin Mary began to weep myrrh-scented tears). Olive oil is an ideal conduit for a miracle in the context of the Middle East because in the Christian Middle East, olive oil is associated with sacred rituals, health, and healing.

Each accredited apparition has left a profound mark not only on the individuals who report having witnessed the event but also on the heritage of each nation that includes apparitions in their national history. Mary's ability to be present in a variety of cultures is celebrated in the great variety of international depictions of her.

Comfort and Consolation

The Virgin Mary often seems to come to offer comfort or consolation particularly to the poor and vulnerable. While many of the apparitions include requests or warnings, at least a few of them seem to be connected to the Virgin Mary's desire to bring comfort to those who are in need.

This was particularly the case in apparitions that were reported to occur in Vietnam. Christianity was introduced to what is now Vietnam in 1533. Since then, Christians have suffered much persecution. In the past three centuries, thousands have been martyred for the faith. In 1798, an apparition of the Virgin Mary occurred in LaVang, Vietnam, to a group of Christians who had escaped to the jungles in the mountains. One day, this group was praying the Rosary when a radiant woman appeared to them, flanked by angels and holding the infant Christ in her arms. She assured them of her protection and care.

factum

In the apparition in LaVang, the Virgin Mary is said to have done something quite intriguing. She pointed to several plants and flowers and explained how they could be used medicinally.

There have been numerous "silent apparitions" in which the Virgin Mary has appeared to people, offering healing and hope without saying a word. Her presence in places like Zeitun, Egypt, has been taken as a sign of God's continual love for the people of the world.

Health and Healing Springs

Many who experience apparitions also experience healing. This has been particularly the case in places like Lourdes, France, and in India, where the shrine of Our Lady of Good Health exists to this day. Many apparition sites contain healing springs (this is true of both Lourdes and India) where people can wash themselves and drink of the water as they seek healing.

It is remarkable to consider the vast number of healing springs or ponds associated with the Virgin Mary all over the world, in places such as Vailankanni, India; Lourdes and LaSalette, France; Banneux, Belgium; and many other locations, including the one at the House of Mary in Ephesus, Turkey.

The Virgin Mary is often referred to as Our Lady of Good Health in India because of the continual healing she has brought to people of many faiths beginning with the healing of a boy, who was lame, to whom she appeared personally during the sixteenth century.

Although many seek physical healing when they visit apparition sites, often the healing that they experience is instead emotional or spiritual. Some also report finding strength to endure suffering in their lives as a result of visiting apparition sites.

Pope John Paul II lost his mother at a very early age, and many people have connected his deep devotion to the Virgin Mary to his experience of early loss as a child. This is also the case with the much-loved Saint Thérèse of Lisieux, who became devoted to the Virgin Mary at a young age after her own mother died.

Saint Thérèse of Lisieux came from a very pious Catholic family in which all of the girls were named for the Virgin Mary. Because Thérèse lost her mother at a young age, she experienced intense anxiety, insomnia, and headaches. She suffered from these afflictions for most of her childhood. When she was ten years old, she was praying before a statue of the Virgin Mary and she saw the statue smile at her (this statue had also spoken to her mother twice). From that moment forward, Thérèse reported experiencing a mental wholeness and healing that she had not experienced since her mother's death. This sense of mental wholeness continued for the rest of her short life until her death from tuberculosis at age twenty-four. Although Thérèse did experience feelings of intense darkness and despair near the end of her life, she always said that just beneath that darkness there was great joy.

discussion question

How does one know when healing will occur?
In some cases, healings come as a result of multiple prayers and requests, and in some cases, people pray earnestly for healing and do not receive it. There is no uniform rule for how, when, or if healings will occur.

Warnings

Many of the more recent accounts of apparitions—especially those at Fatima and Medjugorje—have contained dire warnings about things that will come if people do not change their lives and begin to pray. In some apparitions, the Virgin Mary describes the threat of a third world war that could employ germ and biological warfare. She also sometimes describes natural disasters, widespread destruction, and loss of life. Some people have made a connection between the content of her messages and the ways in which she comes to people—often through weeping statues and icons.

factum

In apparitions, the Virgin Mary sometimes expresses motherly frustration and anguish over people's unwillingness to change. She also constantly encourages people to pray, not only for themselves but for all of the people who have no one to pray for them.

During many of these apparitions, the Virgin Mary has said that the end of the world is near and that a period of intense suffering will be followed by a period of relative peace before the return of Christ.

Although some of the messages of the apparitions can be frightening, in most cases, visionaries experience a sense of confidence despite the dire predictions, because they believe that despite difficulties ahead, God will be present with them.

Fatima Predictions

At Fatima, Portugal, the Virgin Mary told three shepherd children that there would be a world catastrophe during the time of Pope Puis XI if people did not repent. During the last year of the reign of Pope Pius XI, World War II began. It was also at Fatima that the Virgin Mary predicted both the rise and fall of Communism in Russia, as well as the spread of Communism to many other parts of the world.

The apparitions that occurred at Hrushiv, Ukraine, in 1914 and 1987 also contained predictions. In these apparitions, the Virgin Mary told a group of villagers that Russia would turn away from God and endure two wars. She also predicted that although the Ukraine would endure hardship for eighty years, it would eventually become an independent state.

An apparition that reportedly occurred in 1830 in Paris, France, also contained a warning of an event that is now well recorded in history books. A postulant of the Sisters of Charity named Catherine Laboure went to bed the night before the feast of Saint Vincent de Paul after swallowing a small fragment of the deceased saint's surplice. Nobody is quite sure why she did this. Perhaps Catherine felt that by swallowing this small fragment, she would be able to draw closer to the saint.

Like many other holy people, Catherine had a lifelong devotion to the Virgin Mary that was most likely connected to her own loss of her mother as child. When she was nine years old and grieving the death of her mother, Catherine held a statue of the Virgin Mary and said, "Now Blessed Mother, you will be my mother."

The night of the Eve of the feast of Saint Vincent De Paul, Catherine woke in the middle of the night to a small child standing near her bed who told her to go to the church because the Virgin Mary was there waiting for her.

discussion question

Do visionaries experience special protection?
In many cases, visionaries do experience protection, such as Catherine Laboure whose convent remained safe despite all of the violence in Paris during the French Revolution.

Catherine dressed quickly, rushing quietly to the church, which was fully illuminated—every candle in the church had been lit as if for midnight mass, but the church was empty. Suddenly, Catherine heard the sound of silk rustling. She looked up and there was the Virgin Mary seated in the chair that belonged to the father director of the monastery.

Coming Sorrows

The Virgin Mary told Catherine that France's throne would come toppling down and that misfortunes were on the way. "Sorrows will befall France," the Virgin Mary said. "The throne will be overturned. The whole world will be plunged into every kind of misery." The Virgin Mary went on to predict that bishops and priests would be killed, and that many monasteries would be attacked, although Catherine's monastery would be protected.

The French Revolution

Just a few days later, the throne of King Charles X was overturned and mass rioting broke out. Churches were desecrated and bishops' palaces were attacked. Although many monasteries and convents were destroyed, Catherine's monastery remained unharmed just as the Virgin Mary had predicted.

Marian Secrets

Some apparitions have also contained "secrets," such as those reported in Fatima. These secrets were statements made by the Virgin Mary during apparitions that are not supposed to be revealed immediately. Although some people are fascinated by the secrets, the phenomenon of secrets is not unusual from a Biblical perspective.

In the Scriptures, Christ often asks people not to speak of his miracles because they are not to be revealed until the appointed time. In essence, he asks direct witnesses to keep secrets on his behalf, just as many of the visionaries (particularly in Fatima and Medjugorje, discussed in detail in Chapter 13) have been asked to guard secrets that Mary has shared with them.

Many of the secrets are actually prophecies that are not supposed to be known until the appointed time. The secrets are often deeply Biblical. When Sister Lucia, one of the visionaries from Fatima, was pressured to reveal a secret from Fatima, she said, "Just read the Gospels and the Book of Revelation. It's all in there."

Sister Lucia's words highlight one of the larger themes of the apparitions: for these spiritual experiences to be deemed authentic, they must be consistent with Scripture. As Pope Benedict XVI said in an interview with Roy Varghese in 1991, "Apparitions are never required for salvation. The Old and New Testament revelations have all that is necessary for salvation." Although the Roman Catholic and Eastern Orthodox Churches have both affirmed that authentic apparitions can aid the faithful, these subjective experiences are never supposed to overshadow the Scriptures or the witness of the Church.

CHAPTER 12

Ancient Appearances

Apparitions of the Virgin Mary date back to the first century. In the earliest apparitions, Mary often came to offer comfort and consolation. In some cases, she requested that churches be built to commemorate the spot where she appeared. Remarkably, from some of these earliest apparitions, tangible reminders still remain. This chapter will explore a selection of the earliest apparitions.

The First Apparition

After the death of Jesus, his apostles sought to spread the message of the good news all over the world. According to church tradition, the apostle Thomas made it all the way to India, and Saint James (the brother of John) is said to have traveled to Saragossa, Spain.

Around A.D. 40 James had become deeply discouraged. He felt that his mission was not progressing in the way that he'd hoped. One day he was preaching beside the Ebro River when the Virgin Mary, flanked by angels, appeared to him and gave him a statue of herself and a six-foot-tall pillar made of jasper wood. Her gift came with directions as to how the statue and pillar were to be used.

factum

The word *apostle* means "one who is sent." It is particularly used for Jesus' twelve disciples as well as for the seventy who formed the larger circle of coworkers for the Gospels, the good news about Jesus. More generally, it can refer to anyone who has been commissioned to preach the Gospel.

According to James, the Virgin Mary told him, "This place is to be my house, and this image and column shall be the title and altar of the temple you shall build." Shortly after the visitation, James began work on a small chapel in honor of the Virgin Mary.

Like many ancient holy sites, this chapel has been destroyed and rebuilt multiple times throughout the centuries. After almost 2,000 years, the pillar and the statue are still venerated at the Basilica-Cathedral of Our Lady of the Pillar in Zaragoza, Aragon, Spain. Throughout the centuries, this statue and pillar have had multiple healings attributed to them, and they can be visited to this day, although they are not always kept on display.

symbolism

The miracle of James's vision of Mary occupies a special place in the national memory of Spain, and is linked to the discovery of the Americas. The Spanish Feast of El Pilar is commemorated on October 12. It was on this day in 1492 that Christopher Columbus arrived in the New World, after traversing the ocean on his ship, the *Santa Maria*.

While this visitation must have brought James joy and comfort, it probably also brought him dread, as it was through this apparition that the Virgin Mary informed him that God had requested that he return to Jerusalem so that he could become the first martyr for Christ.

Four years later, James was martyred in Jerusalem. His own death is part of a larger trend that continues in our own day—visionaries sometimes suffer terribly for sharing what they've experienced. Some child visionaries have been beaten by their parents, others have been interrogated by church and civil authorities, and still others, like James, discovered through a vision that they would die unjustly.

As you will see as you explore the other apparitions, the Virgin Mary is often reported to leave behind tangible reminders of her visits. Although skeptics might say that these "reminders" could have easily come from other sources, all that we have now (especially in the case of the most ancient apparitions) are the stories that communities tell about how these objects—pillars, statues, and churches—came to them. These stories are valuable, both for what they convey about the communities that guard these reminders as well as for what they convey about beliefs surrounding the Virgin Mary.

Patmos, Greece, A.D. 81

According to tradition, the Book of Revelation was written by Saint John after a series of revelations that occurred on the Island of Patmos in Greece.

In one of the visions, Saint John saw a "woman clothed with the son" (Revelation 12) who stood upon the moon and was crowned with twelve stars. The woman was in the process of giving birth to a son who was to rule the nations. As she cried out from the pains of childbirth, a dragon waited nearby to consume the child. After the child was born, however, he was protected by God and enthroned. The woman escaped to the wilderness.

Although this woman is never directly identified as the Virgin Mary, the parallels between this vision and later apparitions are quite strong. Over time, Mary came to be associated with the moon and stars, and this theme has often been incorporated into many artistic representations of her. In icons, her veil is adorned with stars, and in many of the statues and paintings of the Virgin Mary, she stands upon the moon.

Neocaesarea, Asia Minor, A.D. 238

When Saint Gregory the Wonderworker was preaching in Asia Minor, he became confused about the doctrine of the Trinity. One night, Gregory couldn't sleep because he was so anxious about his inability to articulate the theology of the Trinity. At some point during the course of this long, restless night, two beings are reported to have appeared to him. He might not have known who they were, had they not addressed each other by name.

discussion question

How could Gregory be confused about the Trinity?
At the time of Gregory's vision, the full doctrine of the Trinity had not yet been formulated. Many of the definitions and creeds developed slowly over time. Especially tricky were doctrines like the Trinity, which were implicit in Scripture, but could not be properly understood without a good deal of interpretation.

The radiantly beautiful female figure turned to the aged male figure and addressed him as "Saint John the Evangelist." She and he discussed Gregory's dilemma and then she asked Saint John to explain the doctrine of the Trinity to Gregory. Saint John replied that he would certainly comply with the wishes of "The Mother of the Lord."

After Saint John offered a basic explanation, he concluded with these words, "There is therefore nothing created, nothing greater or less in the Trinity . . . The Father has never been without the Son, nor the Son without the Spirit; and the same Trinity is immutable and forever unalterable." The content of this message has been continually affirmed by the Church ever since.

Rome, A.D. 352

Children and peasants are generally more likely to report apparitions than wealthy people. In a few cases, however, wealthy people have encountered the Virgin Mary, particularly those who were generous and seeking guidance as to how to better use their resources for God.

This type of apparition occurred during the fourth century when a wealthy, childless couple in Rome was struggling over how to best use their fortune. They had often prayed to the Virgin Mary for guidance, and on August 4, A.D. 352, she finally appeared to them in response to their multiple requests.

On that day, she instructed them to begin construction on a church located on one of Rome's hills. Just to be clear about exactly which hill and exactly how large she intended the church to be, she promised to send snow to cover the earth on the exact spot where the church was to be built.

August is the hottest time of the year in Rome, so the idea of snow was baffling to this couple. But just as they were receiving the message about the church they were to build, Pope Liberius received a parallel message.

The next morning, Pope Liberius and the wealthy couple were astonished to discover that a portion of Esquiline Hill was blanketed in snow. They had just enough time to measure the space where the church was to be built before the snow melted. Within eight years, the world's largest church devoted to the Virgin Mary, Saint Mary Major, was constructed. This church still stands to this day.

One of the themes of this apparition—that the Virgin Mary is able to cause a reversal of weather patterns, such as snow in the middle of August—

is often repeated in the apparitions. Sometimes the miracle is poetically reversed and instead of summer snows, roses bloom in the dead of winter.

Walsingham, England, 1061

Like the apparition in Rome, in Walsingham, England, the Virgin Mary appeared to a wealthy person—in this case, it was a widow named Lady Richeldis de Faverches, who had been praying about how to best use her resources. One night that year, the Virgin Mary came to her with a request: build a mini-replica of the house from Nazareth, where the Annunciation occurred. The Virgin Mary wanted the replica to serve as a reminder to the people that she was available to help them.

According to accounts of these apparitions, the Virgin Mary is often quite detailed in her requests, not leaving much to the imagination of the visionary. In Walsingham, she not only asked Lady Richeldis de Faverches to create the replica, but she also transported the Lady through space and time to her original house in Nazareth so that she could get the measurements exactly correct.

A year after the visitation, the house was completed. A chapel called the Slipper Chapel was also built about a mile away from the house so that pilgrims could leave their shoes behind and travel the last mile without them.

Walsingham became an extremely popular pilgrimage spot during the Middle Ages but was destroyed during the Reformation. Only the Slipper Chapel survived the pillaging.

symbolism

Walsingham, which was once one of the most popular pilgrimage sites in Europe, has attracted the attentions of prominent people. During construction, Edward the Confessor offered the entire country of England to the Virgin Mary as a dowry. After the replica was completed, all of the English kings up to Henry VIII made pilgrimages there.

Many centuries later, when English Catholics were once again permitted to practice their faith in England, the shrine was rededicated to Mary. Presently, a remnant of the original Slipper Chapel shares space with an Anglican shrine for Our Lady of Walsingham. Walsingham is now considered one of Europe's great ecumenical sites.

Czestochawa, Poland, 1382

In Poland there is an icon that is often referred to as the Black Madonna. This icon, which is one of the most famous in the world, is part of a larger school of dark-skinned images of the Virgin Mary and the infant Christ. There are several Black Madonna icons as well as statues that were especially popular during the medieval period in Europe.

The Black Madonna icon in Poland, Our Lady of Czestochawa, is one of the most famous icons in the world. Some even believe that this icon changed the course of history in Poland. According to one church tradition, this image was painted by the apostle Luke. Reportedly, while he was painting it, the Virgin Mary told him many things about the life of Christ, which he ultimately included in his Gospel.

Although one tradition holds that the icon was created by Luke in the first century, the icon seems to have disappeared from the popular eye for a few hundred years, resurfacing in A.D. 326, when it was discovered by Saint Helen in Jerusalem. Saint Helen passed the icon to her son, the Emperor Constantine who was reportedly able to scare off an invading army by placing the icon on the walls of the city. According to accounts of this event, the soldiers took one look at the icon and fled.

After this event, the icon passed through many hands and finally found its way to Poland. In 1382, the Virgin Mary appeared to the man who possessed the icon at the time, Prince Ladislaus of Opolo. During the course of this apparition, the Virgin Mary asked that the icon be placed at a mountain-top monastery, Jasna Gora, located in Czestochowa.

After the icon was moved, many miracles were reported and recorded in a book at the monastery. One of the most remarkable events occurred in 1430, when the Tartars took over the monastery. When one of them attempted to steal the icon, he found that it became heavier and heavier the farther he walked. Finally, in a fit of desperation he took out a knife and slashed the cheeks of the Virgin Mary and threw the icon into a river. Although it was eventually recovered and the slashes were repaired multiple times, the wounds mysteriously continue to be visible.

symbolism

In Sue Monk Kidd's bestseller *The Secret Life of Bees,* a small paper replica of a Black Madonna icon linked a child to the mysteries surrounding her deceased mother. The girl carried the icon to a house inhabited by African American beekeepers who possessed such deep love for this image that they affixed it to all of their honey jars.

Many believe that Our Lady of Czestochowa helped protect Poland during invasions and wars. In 1655, the entire country was taken over by Charles X of Sweden. Only a few Polish soldiers and monks from Jasna Gora were able to fight for resistance. Although they were sorely outnumbered, they successfully resisted the Swedes for forty days, and the Swedish soldiers fled.

On September 14, 1920, the Russian army was preparing to attack Warsaw, but their plans changed when they saw a vision of a woman in the skies over Warsaw. After that frightening experience, they felt they could not invade Warsaw.

During World War II, when Poland was occupied by the Nazis, Hitler demanded an end to all pilgrimages. In a brave show of defiance, nearly half a million Polish people ignored Hitler's orders and visited their precious icon. When Poland was liberated in 1945, one-and-a-half million Polish people visited the shrine to offer their gratitude to Our Lady of Czestochowa for her deliverance and protection. Three years later, when Russia captured Warsaw, 800,000 Polish people again risked their lives, passing the Communist soldiers who patrolled the roads as they made their way to visit the sanctuary at Czestochowa for the Feast of the Assumption.

Kazan, Russia, 1579

Russia treasures a number of ancient icons that may date back to the age of the apostles. Perhaps the most famous of these is called Our Lady of Kazan. According to Church tradition, this icon was brought to Russia from Byzantium around the thirteenth century. Its name comes from city where it was housed, Kazan.

In the thirteenth century, when the city of Kazan was destroyed, the icon disappeared beneath the rubble of a monastery and was lost for almost three hundred years.

In 1579, a nine-year-old girl named Matrona had a vision of the Virgin Mary. In this vision, Mary told Matrona to seek and find the icon. The Virgin Mary told Matrona exactly where to look.

After Matrona witnessed three apparitions, a bishop and several others began digging in the location described to them by Matrona, but they failed in all of their attempts to find the icon.

On July 8, 1579, the authorities finally allowed Matrona to dig. Almost immediately, she found the icon, wrapped in a red cloth. After this discovery, many miracles and healings came to be attributed to the icon. Just as Our Lady of Czestochowa was viewed by the Polish people as a protective icon, Our Lady of Kazan eventually came to be seen as the protector of Russia.

During the Communist revolution on October 13, 1917, the church that housed the icon that Matrona unearthed was destroyed, and the icon disappeared. Perhaps not coincidentally, the reverberations of this day in Russia were felt throughout the world.

factum

In Fatima, Portugal, on October 13, 1917, the miracle of the sun occurred. Through an apparition, the Virgin Mary reported that Russia would spread its errors throughout the world. Many believe that through these apparitions Mary predicted the rise and fall of Communism in Russia.

There are conflicting reports about what happened to the icon of Kazan after the church was destroyed. Some believe that the icon was destroyed, and others say that it was whisked away to safety.

Through a mysterious sequence of events, a valuable copy of Our Lady of Kazan eventually made it to the United States, where the Roman Catholic Church raised more than one million dollars to purchase the icon from a private collector.

The icon was displayed at the New World Exposition in New York in 1964, where thousands kissed and prayed before it. Afterward, it traveled to Fatima and was held by the Blue Army, a Catholic organization that seeks to raise awareness of the Fatima apparitions.

discussion question

How did the Roman Catholic and Eastern Orthodox Churches grow apart?
For the first thousand years of Christianity, the two churches were united. The great schism between them was the result of a growing sense of alienation on both sides. The biggest disagreements between the churches were over the role of the pope and the Western addition of the phrase "and the Son" (*fillioque*) into the Nicene Creed.

In 1993, the icon was presented to Pope John Paul II. For many years, he housed it in his private apartments in the Vatican, although he never wavered in his commitment to return the icon to Russia, hoping that this gesture could be the beginning of healing the rift between the Roman Catholic and Eastern Orthodox Churches.

Tensions in Russia between the Eastern Orthodox and Roman Catholic churches made it difficult for Pope John Paul II to personally return the icon to Patriarch Alexei II. Finally, on August, 30, 2004, Pope John Paul II sent a commission to Russia with the icon, which traveled there in a special jet. The pope sent a statement with the icon that said he had often prayed before that icon for the day that the two churches would again be one.

Patriarch Alexei II thanked the pope for this act of unity, although he also expressed his concern that unification would only be possible if the Roman Catholic Church would make concessions to Eastern Orthodox theological positions. Roman Catholic newspapers have reported that relations between the two churches have warmed slightly since the historic return of the icon.

Guadalupe, Mexico, 1531

During the sixteenth century in Mexico, tensions between the Spanish invaders and local Aztecs were fierce. By 1531, the Aztecs were so outraged by the abuses they experienced that they threatened to kill every Spaniard in the country. Although Spanish missionaries were simultaneously working to bring Catholicism to the native Aztecs, the political tensions between the two groups created an impossible climate for missionary work.

This tense situation set the stage for the most dramatic apparition-related mass conversion in the history of the world. Juan Diego was a fifty-seven-year-old Aztec peasant and a convert to Catholicism. One day while he was walking to Mass, he heard birds singing. The song sounded like it was coming from a nearby hill.

As he drew closer to the hill, the song stopped and he heard a female voice calling to him. "Juan, Juan Diego, Juanito," she said. Juan Diego climbed the hill and saw a stunning fourteen-year-old Aztec girl. Speaking in his own language, she told him that she was the Virgin Mary. She wanted a church to be built on that hill where she stood. She asked Juan Diego to go to Mexico City and inform the bishop of her request.

A Request Denied

Juan Diego went immediately to the bishop to make his request, but the request was denied. Although the Bishop believed that Juan Diego was sincere, he struggled to believe Juan Diego's extraordinary account. Defeated, Juan Diego returned to the Virgin Mary and told her that if she wanted to get her message across, she should have chosen somebody more important to deliver it.

To this, the Virgin Mary replied that she knew what she was doing; she reassured Juan Diego that she wanted him to deliver the message. She urged him to go back and try again with the bishop.

When Juan Diego returned to the bishop, the bishop requested a sign. Juan Diego returned to the Virgin Mary again, who told him to come back at daybreak. When Juan Diego arrived home that day, he discovered that his uncle was fatally ill with a fever. Juan Diego nursed him all night long and through the following day, and he was unable to meet with the Virgin Mary at sunrise.

As Juan Diego rushed into town seeking a priest, he attempted to sneak around the East side of the hill, hoping that he wouldn't be interrupted by the Virgin Mary. Although on other occasions she had appeared on the West side of the hill, she came down the East side of the hill just as he tried to rush by.

When Juan Diego told the Virgin Mary about his uncle, the Virgin Mary said, "Am I not your mother?" Then she told him that his uncle was being healed even as they spoke.

The Virgin Mary spoke many consoling words to Juan Diego. She said, "Hear me, my littlest son: Let nothing discourage you, nothing depress you. Let nothing alter your heart or your countenance. Do not fear any illness, anxiety, or pain. Am I not your mother? Are you not under the protection of my mantle? Am I not your fountain of life? Is there anything else that you need?"

She then asked Juan Diego to climb the hill and pick flowers, and these flowers would be her sign. Juan Diego obediently climbed the hill, although he could not imagine flowers growing during the coldest month of the year. To his astonishment, he found that the hill was covered with Castilian roses.

The Tilma of Guadalupe

Juan Diego picked several roses and carried them back to the Virgin Mary. She took the roses from him and arranged them in his tilma (a cloak made of cactus fibers that was worn by the Aztecs of the time). She handed Juan Diego the roses bundled in the tilma and instructed him to not let anyone other than the bishop see them.

When Juan Diego arrived at the bishop's residence, servants tried to take the tilma from him, but he refused. When he finally met with the bishop, he unrolled the tilma and the roses fell to the floor. Juan Diego was confused and amazed as the bishop and those who surrounded him dropped to their knees before his tilma.

On his tilma, there was a luminescent image of the Virgin Mary appearing as an Aztec, just as she had in the apparitions. Her image also bore a striking resemblance to the woman from Revelation 12. The image on the tilma convinced the bishop that the apparition was authentic.

symbolism

The Tilma of Guadalupe is one of a few images that many Christians believe was actually created by Mary. This image almost perfectly mirrors imagery from Revelation. On the tilma, Mary stands on the moon, and rays of light emanate from her body. Her outer cloak is blue, covered with gold stars—a constant theme in images of Mary.

The bishop immediately traveled with Juan Diego to see the hill where the chapel was to be built, and then the bishop's assistants traveled with Juan to visit his uncle. They found his uncle in perfect health. He explained that the Virgin Mary had also come to him and told him that the image on the tilma was to be called Santa Maria de Guadalupe.

This event transformed the practices of the over 8 million Aztecs who converted to Christianity in the wake of the apparition. According to Roy Abraham Varghese in his book *God-Sent: A History of the Accredited Apparitions of Mary,* one of the descriptions that Mary used for herself in Guadalupe can be translated as "Entirely perfect, holy Mary, who will crush, stamp out, and abolish the stone serpent." This title is sometimes linked to the end of the Aztec practice of sacrificing humans because the Aztecs worshiped a god called Quetzalcoatl, whose name can be translated as "the stone serpent." After the apparitions at Guadalupe, human sacrifices to the stone serpent abruptly (and permanently) halted.

The spiritual dimensions of the apparition, however, are just one aspect of the larger phenomenon. The events that occurred at Guadalupe also have political and social implications: the conversion of the Aztecs saved the lives of thousands of Spaniards, who would have likely been killed had not the Virgin Mary appeared to Juan Diego.

Likewise, some contemporary writers have focused on the way that this apparition marked a Biblical reversal of order—a peasant member of an oppressed people was chosen to bear a message that would change the history of his country, and by extension, the lives and beliefs of millions of Latin Americans. As Megan McKenna wrote in her book *Mary, Shadow of Grace* of Our Lady of Guadalupe, "She is the sister to the poor and the mother of compassion and healing for all those who live on the edges of life . . . She is the symbol of the small of the earth, inconsequential except to God, found with all those who live faithfully in situations of darkness, despair, lack, and need, yet powerful in their very weakness and numbers."

Although historically it has been believed that the tilma was made of cactus fibers, a recent scientific inquiry has cast some doubt on this theory. In 1999, when two fibers of the tilma were tested by Professor John J. Chiment from the Department of Earth and Atmospheric Sciences at Cornell University in Ithaca, New York, he determined that the fibers are not from native cactus plants, nor are they made of wool or cotton. Instead, he believes that they are actually made of hemp, an extremely durable fiber that could account for the long lifespan of the cloak.

To this day, the tilma and image remain intact. Scientists have been unable to identify the source of the pigments in the image. One of the most mysterious aspects of this image is the Virgin Mary's eyes, which reflect the images of three people, as if she is looking at them still—Juan Diego, the bishop and his interpreter. The tilma remains on display at the Basilica of Guadalupe and is visited by five to ten million people annually.

CHAPTER 13

Modern Sightings

Over the past several hundred years, apparitions of the Virgin Mary have continued to occur, and, according to the late scholar Jaroslav Pelikan, this phenomenon seems to be increasing. The following chapter will explore a wide variety of modern sightings that have spanned the globe and addressed a variety of contemporary concerns: Communism, the rift between the Eastern and Western Churches, and conflicts between believers and secular governments. This chapter will explore some of the most famous and unusual apparitions to date.

Vailankanni, India, Sixteenth Through Seventeenth Centuries

During the sixteenth through seventeenth centuries, the Virgin Mary came to the small Indian town of Vailankanni, and healed a lame boy and a young shepherd boy. When the Virgin Mary appeared with the infant Jesus to the lame boy, the boy was selling buttermilk in the shade of a large banyan tree. The Virgin Mary requested some buttermilk for her baby. When the boy gave her buttermilk, she asked her son to heal him, which he did immediately, although the young boy did not realize what had happened.

She then asked the lame boy to seek out a wealthy Catholic Vailankanni to ask him to build a chapel in the Virgin Mary's honor. The boy said that there was no way he could do this, because he couldn't walk. The Virgin Mary smiled at him and encouraged him to stand up and try. Upon trying, the boy realized that he was able to walk.

At this, the boy leapt for joy and rushed to the village to find the man at the Virgin Mary's request. When he found him, he had no trouble convincing him because the older man had also had a vision of the Virgin Mary the night before in his sleep. In his vision, the Virgin Mary bore exactly the same message that she had given to the little boy who could not walk.

The two returned together to Vailankanni and the older man began construction on a small, thatched church with the assistance of the locals, who were moved by the sight of the lame boy walking. The older man placed a statue of Our Lady of Good Health on the altar.

Matha Kulam

Another young boy also had an encounter with the Virgin Mary. This young boy was a shepherd who was carrying milk to his master's house. On a hot day he took refuge in the shade of a banyan tree beside a pond. While he was resting there a beautiful woman appeared with a child in her arms. She asked him for milk for her baby, and the young shepherd gave it to her immediately. As he did this, a smile spread across the infant's face.

The shepherd then rushed to his master's house with the remaining milk. When he arrived, he tried to explain why his milk pot wasn't full. When the lid was removed, however, he discovered that the pot was full and overflowing. His master was astonished and rushed with him back to the site, falling down on his knees and putting his head to the ground on the spot where the shepherd reported having seen the Virgin and child. This pond is now known as *Matha Kulam*, meaning "Our Lady's Pond." Pilgrims continue to flock there, believing that the waters have miraculous, healing powers.

Our Lady of Good Health

Later in that same century, a Portuguese ship encountered a fierce storm in the Indian Sea. The sailors fell to their knees and prayed that Mary would calm the storm, promising to build a church in her honor if they made it safely ashore. The storm halted immediately, and the tattered ship washed ashore at Vailakanni.

As soon as the sailors set foot on the land, they knelt on the ground and thanked God and the Virgin Mary for their safe journey. When locals saw them kneeling they realized the sailors must be Christians and directed them to the chapel of our Our Lady of Good Health.

The Portuguese began work shortly afterward, constructing a larger brick and mortar church to honor Mary. They placed the statue of Our Lady of Good Health on the altar in the newly built chapel, and they dedicated the church to the Nativity of Our Lady, in honor of the day they washed ashore, September 8—the day of the Nativity of the Virgin Mary.

After Vatican II, Pope John XXIII officially recognized this pilgrimage site as the Lourdes of the East. India is now graced with many shrines to Our Lady of Good Health. Many have reported miraculous healings associated with the shrine and pond. Adjacent to the church is a "museum of offerings" where hundreds of pilgrims have left offerings behind. Presently, thousands of Catholic, Protestants, Hindu, Parsee, and Muslim people visit this basilica daily.

Lourdes, France, 1858

Lourdes is a small town located at the foothills of the Great Pyrenees Mountains in France. A young girl named Bernadette, the oldest of four children, lived with her family in a single room that had once been the town jail.

One day, she, her sister, and a friend went searching for dry wood for her mother. Bernadette's sister and friend crossed a small stream, but Bernadette hesitated at the bank. Suddenly, she heard a loud crashing noise and looked toward a stone grotto where a single bush was waving as if it was a windy day. Then, a golden glow came from the center of the grotto, and a beautiful woman appeared. Although Bernadette was initially terrified, when the woman smiled, her fear vanished.

A Healing Well

Bernadette then experienced multiple visions of Mary. In one of these encounters the Virgin Mary told Bernadette, "Go and drink from the spring and wash yourself there." Bernadette saw no spring, so she got down on her hands and knees and began to dig. Soon, the small hole was filled with water, from which she drank and washed her face. This small pool became a river, and very quickly, people came to believe that this river had healing properties because a man who was going blind regained his vision after submerging his face in the water. Another woman with a paralyzed hand was able to use it completely after immersing it in the water.

Bernadette experienced eighteen apparitions of the Virgin Mary. Word of the apparitions spread, causing concern among local and church authorities. A local doctor subjected Bernadette to a battery of tests. She was repeatedly shown to be of normal mental health. In one of the more humorous incidents related to this apparition, Bernadette's local priest Abbe Peyramale refused to believe in the apparitions and requested a sign. But the Virgin Mary was unwilling to perform this sign for the skeptical priest. When Bernadette reported back to her priest she told him, "She smiled when I told her that you were asking her to work a miracle. I told her to make the rose bush, which she was standing near, bloom; she smiled once more. But she wants a chapel."

When Bernadatte visited the grotto, others would flock there in the hopes of witnessing the visitation. During one apparition, 20,000 people were present. In August 1858, the Emperor of France, Napoleon III, ordered that water be brought from the well to be sprinkled on his two-year-old son who had contracted dangerous sunstroke with the threat of meningitis. When his son was cured, Napoleon III ordered that the barricades be removed from the grotto.

fallacy

It is a fallacy that intellectuals did not recognize the significance of apparitions. In Sigmund Freud's book *The New Introductory Lectures on Psycho-Analysis*, he wrote, "I do not think our cures can compete with those of Lourdes. There are so many more people who believe in the miracle of the Blessed Virgin than the existence of the subconscious."

Lourdes Today

Today, five million pilgrims annually flock to Lourdes, which is called the Capitol of Prayer, seeking healing and spiritual refreshment. The small well that Bernadette uncovered now produces 15,000 gallons of water daily. Many drink from the wells, and over 400,000 visitors annually immerse themselves in the water in a nearby bathhouse.

A recent medical study demonstrated that over 2,500 healings have occurred in Lourdes, although church authorities to date have only officially recognized a small number of cures (about 65). Many more potential healings are currently under investigation, and more than 5,000 people claim to have experienced miracles at Lourdes.

Bernadette eventually joined a convent, although she was sickly for most of her life and died at thirty-five. To this day, her body remains incorrupt. She was canonized a saint on December 8, 1933.

Fatima, Portugal, 1917

The apparitions that occurred in Fatima are the most famous and influential of all known apparitions. Four million pilgrims visit Fatima annually. Like many of the apparitions, these came during a time of local Christian persecution, shortly after the monarchy in Portugal had been overthrown, causing anti-Christian groups to seize power and kill more than 1,700 Roman Catholic priests and monastics. In the wake of this violence, three shepherd children, named Jacinta Marto, Lucia dos Santos, and Francisco Marto experienced some of the most dramatic reported apparitions in history.

These apparitions of Mary were preceded by the appearance of an angel to the three young children telling them to pray this way, "My God, I believe, I adore, I hope and I love you. I ask pardon of you for those who do not believe and do not adore, do not hope, and do not love you." The angel also offered them Holy Communion.

After the angel's visit, the Virgin Mary appeared to the children six times, on the thirteenth day of each month.

Visions

The first apparition occurred when the children were out with their sheep in an area called the Cova da Iria. They saw a bolt of lightning come from the clear blue sky. They ran toward their sheep, and as they did this they saw another flash of light and then a globe of light that landed in a nearby oak tree.

Before their eyes, the Virgin Mary emerged from this globe. She asked the children if they wanted to offer themselves to God and to suffer for Him. They said yes, and she told them that they would suffer much but would be strengthened by the grace of God. She also told them that two of them would be in heaven shortly. The shepherd girl who would be left behind, Lucia, would be responsible for spreading the word about the apparition and spreading devotion to the Lady's Immaculate Heart.

In the next vision, the Virgin Mary offered the children a terrifying glimpse of hell. She told the children that the Lord wanted them to help establish devotion to her Immaculate Heart to bring more souls to salvation. All of this took place during World War I. Mary then told the children that this war would end, but a worse war would later begin. She told them that Russia would spread its errors all over the world and entire nations might be obliterated if it was not consecrated to her Immaculate Heart. Its consecration, however, would lead to "the conversion of Russia."

The next apparition did not occur as planned because the children were kidnapped and held prisoner for three days. They survived and the prison administrator was forced to release them. On August 13, eighteen thousand people witnessed what they interpreted as a sign of God's anger for the kidnapping of the children. They saw lightning and thunder, the sky turned pale, and a yellowish haze hung about. A white cloud hung in an oak tree and transformed into all the colors of the rainbow.

On August 19, the Virgin Mary appeared to the children again and asked them to pray for all those who did not pray, saying that many souls are damned because there is no one to pray for them.

The End of the World?

On October 13, 70,000 people arrived at the Cova. A storm had just swept through Europe the night before. The Virgin Mary told the children that she was "the Lady of the Rosary" and that people must change their lives and not offend the Lord anymore because He was already greatly offended. She stretched her hands toward the sun and rays of light streamed from her fingers and the sun began to spin—the event that is now known as the famous Miracle of the Sun.

discussion question

How do many people interpret the "conversion" Mary spoke of?
Although some people have interpreted the "conversion" Mary reportedly spoke of to mean that Russia would become a Catholic country, others have linked this to the fall of atheist Communism and the reemergence of the local churches.

Rays of color streamed from the sun and then the sun seemed to fall from the sky and rush toward the earth. All the onlookers dropped to their knees praying for forgiveness because they thought the world was ending. Just when it seemed the sun was about to collide with the earth, it returned to its place in the sky. While onlookers as far as thirty miles away were witnessing this solar phenomenon, the visionary children were watching scenes from the heavens. They saw Jesus in a red robe blessing the crowds, the infant Jesus with Joseph and Mary, and then Mary in brown robes. This was the final public vision at Fatima.

Sister Lucia

Both Francisco and Jacinta died of influenza. Lucia was later sent to a girls' school run by the sisters of Saint Dorothy. In 1934 she became a nun, after having one more vision of the Virgin Mary and Jesus in 1925. In 1929 the Virgin told Sister Lucia that it was time for the pope to consecrate Russia to his heart.

In 1989, Sister Lucia sent a message to the world to let everyone know that the pope's consecration of Russia had been accepted and that the results of his action would become clear later that year. In late 1989, the Berlin Wall fell. By 1991, Communism had collapsed in Russia. On August 19, 1991, in a Communist coup, Mikhail Gorbachev was captured and held for three days, just as the three visionary children at Fatima had been held for three days. This all occurred on the same day as the delayed fourth apparition at Fatima. The coup ultimately failed and Gorbachev was set free on August 22, which is also the Roman Catholic feast of the Queenship of Mary.

Zeitun, Egypt, 1968

Zeitun is a district of Cairo, Egypt. St. Mary's Church is said to be located right along the path traveled by Joseph, Mary, and Jesus when they journeyed into Egypt to avoid King Herod's wrath. In 1918, at a time when the shrine marking this spot (which had been torn down and rebuilt many times through history) had completely vanished, a wealthy Coptic Christian family owned the property. A member of the family had a vision of the Virgin Mary in which she told them that this location was important to her, and if they would built a church there, many special blessings would come fifty years after the church was built. The family donated the property to the Coptic Orthodox Church, and church authorities constructed a church according to the lady's request.

The Lady on the Dome

Exactly fifty years later on April 2, 1968, Muslim workers noticed a luminescent woman walking back and forth on a dome of the church. These men thought she was a nun who was about to jump off the roof. One of them pointed a finger at her to try to get her to stop. His finger had been riddled with gangrene and was going to be amputated. According to accounts of this unusual event, his finger was healed within the day.

Many gathered to watch the woman walking on the roof of the church, observing her until she vanished. She was seen again over the church seven days later. From that time forward, she reappeared multiple times until May 2, 1971. Many who witnessed these visions reported miraculous healings. Crowds occasionally swelled to as many as 250,000 people from many backgrounds, including Muslims, Jews, Catholics, Orthodox Christians, and Protestants. Occasionally she would bow to the crowd or bless them.

symbolism

A few times, in Zeitun, Egypt, the apparition of Mary was reported to have appeared holding an olive branch. This is appropriate because the name of the town, Zeitun, means "olive" in Arabic.

Other unusual phenomena accompanied her appearances; sometimes incense would come from the church domes into the crowd and occasionally dovelike creatures would take flight around her.

The Official Statement

The Coptic Pope, Kyrillos VI, appointed a committee of high-ranking priests and bishops to investigate these phenomena, and on May 4 issued a statement recognizing the legitimacy of the apparitions. In it, he wrote:

"Thousands of people from different denominations and religions, Egyptians and foreign visitors, clergy and scientists, from different classes and professions, all observed the apparitions. The description of each apparition as of the time, location, and configuration was identically witnessed by all people, which makes this apparition unique and sublime.

Two important aspects accompanied these apparitions: The first is an incredible revival of the faith in God, the other world, and the saints, leading to repentance and conversion of many who strayed away from the faith. The second are the numerous miracles of healing which were verified by many physicians to be miraculous in nature."

The apparitions were also confirmed by Fr. Henry Ayrout, a Jesuit priest, Rev. Dr. Ibrahim Said of the Protestant Evangelical Ministries, and authorities from the General Information and Complaints department of Zetiun. They were also witnessed by a group of Catholic nuns, who sent a report to the Vatican. Pope Paul VI then sent an envoy, whose members also witnessed the apparitions.

Damascus, Syria, 1982–1990

Many of the places where apparitions occur have historical and spiritual significance. This is certainly the case with Damascus, Syria. When Saint Paul was approaching Damascus, he was blinded for three days after seeing a heavenly light (Acts 9:3).

It was also in Damascus that a young, nominally religious couple named Myrna (a variation of Mary) and Nicholas were married in 1982. In that same year, Nicholas's sister Layla became very sick. While Myrna was praying for her, Myrna's fingers started to drip with olive oil. Another woman who was praying with Myrna suggested that Myrna anoint her sister-in-law with the oil. As soon as Myrna did this, her sister-in-law was healed.

A Weeping Icon

On November 27, 1982, Myrna's icon of the Virgin Mary, called Our Lady of Soufanieh, began to exude large quantities of olive oil. This oil was subsequently tested and found to be chemically pure. While praying for discernment with family members, Myrna suddenly could not hear anyone around her. She heard a voice calling, telling her to not be afraid, but to open the doors so that all could see.

On December 15, 1982, Myrna was led to her rooftop garden by an invisible being. There, she saw the Virgin Mary shining as if she were covered with diamonds. Myrna ran away in terror, but was helped by a priest who had experience with supernatural events. Three days later she was again led up to her rooftop garden, this time accompanied by her husband and several friends. She saw a globe of light on the highest point in a nearby tree. A woman emerged from the globe and approached Myrna by climbing over a "bridge of light" to her. The Virgin Mary encouraged her to spread the good news about Mary's son—a particularly challenging task in the largely Muslim Middle East. Mary also said, "Love one another. I am not asking for money to give to churches, nor for money to distribute to the poor. I am asking for love."

discussion question

What is the significance of olive oil?
Within Middle Eastern cultures olive oil is considered to be useful for many purposes beyond cooking. Not only is it used in religious services for anointing, but it is also used in the blessing of homes, and for family folk cures. Within theses cultures, olive oil signifies healing, peace, wholeness, and life.

The Virgin appeared many more times and continued to convey messages. Over 100,000 people came to see the oil flowing from the icon and from Myrna, and many reported healings. Again, both Eastern Orthodox and Roman Catholic church officials conducted investigations and agreed that these sightings were authentic.

In 1984, two years after the first apparition, Myrna experienced three days of painful blindness (just as Saint Paul had experienced almost two thousand years before in that same city). Her eyes exuded oil for all three days. On Holy Friday of that year, Myrna experienced the stigmata (the painful, bleeding wounds of Christ), including wounds from Christ's thorny crown. After four hours the wounds began to close and heal on their own.

Healing the Rift

On August 4, 1984, Myrna heard the words of Jesus at the end of Mass, as she went into ecstasy. She was reportedly told by Jesus that anyone who divides the church or rejoices in the divisions is guilty of sin. To this day, Myrna, is devoted to struggling to heal the historic divisions between the Eastern Orthodox and Roman Catholic Churches. She is no stranger to this painful separation, because she is a Melkite Catholic and her husband is Eastern Orthodox.

factum

> Many copies of the icon of Our Lady of Soufanieh have been anointed by the olive oil tears from Myrna's icon. Of these, more than one hundred have been reported to weep.

Medjugorje, Bosnia, 1981 to the Present, and Rwanda

Like the warnings reported in France in which the Virgin Mary predicted the French Revolution, warnings have more recently occurred in Rwanda and in Medjugorje, Bosnia-Herzegovenia. In the early eighties in Rwanda, visionaries were warned that rivers would fill with blood, and that the visionaries should flee to safety. During the devastating civil war in Rwanda, more than a million people were killed, and the rivers became clogged with dead bodies just as the Virgin Mary had predicted.

In Medjugorje, the Virgin Mary focused on the theme of peace. In one of the Virgin Mary's messages at Medjugorje, she said, "Peace. Peace. Peace. Be reconciled with one another."

Parallels Between Fatima and Medjugorje

Some theologians have seen parallels between the apparitions at Fatima and the apparitions at Medjugorje. Both series of apparitions contained warnings and secrets. Some have even said that the apparitions at Medjugorje are a continuation and fulfillment of the apparitions that began in Fatima.

Like Fatima, in Medjugorje there have been multiple reports of "miracles of the sun" in which the sun has become a spinning disk during the visions. Many people have reported miraculous healings, and hundreds of thousands (some estimate millions) of people have converted to Christianity as a result of these apparitions. Upon returning home from Medjugorje, some pilgrims have reported that metal beads on their rosaries turned to gold.

Some have also made a connection between the apparitions at Medjugorje and Fatima because of issues related to Communism. In Fatima, many believe that the rise, spread, and fall of Communism was predicted. In Medjugorje, some have suggested the widespread effects of the apparitions in Bosnia-Herzegovenia, a Communist country, seemed to indicate the continual demise of Communism around the world.

discussion question

How common are reports of sightings of the Virgin Mary?
During the past twenty years, there have been more than 2,000 claims of Mary sightings. Of these, only 65 have won the status of "accredited apparitions" by the Roman Catholic Church.

Some believe that Medjugorje was supernaturally protected during the war in Yugoslavia. Medjugorje was located in the center of the Republic of Bosnia-Herzegovinia, where some of the most intense battles raged. Though great bloodshed broke out in the surrounding area, the village of Medjugorje remained virtually unharmed. Strangely, only one air raid was attempted on Medjugorje, and the few bombs that were dropped did little damage.

On November 9, 1992, *The Wall Street Journal* reported, "The war has enhanced Medjugorje's fame as an oasis of peace and mystery." The same article quoted Dragan Kozina, the town's mayor, as saying, "You have to believe that either we are very lucky, or that someone is protecting us."

CHAPTER 14

Mary in Catholic Thought

When many people think of the Virgin Mary, they associate her with the doctrines and devotions of the Roman Catholic Church. Marian theology has evolved slowly, taking on different meanings and emphasis through the centuries. This chapter will explore the history and practical applications of Roman Catholic doctrines associated with the Virgin Mary, including that of the Immaculate Conception.

The Immaculate Conception

One of the most significant Roman Catholic dogmas associated with the Virgin Mary is the belief that at her conception, the stain of original sin that had been passed down to every living person since the fall of Adam and Eve was not passed on to her.

Although the dogma of the Immaculate Conception was not officially proclaimed until December 8, 1854, there were many precursors to this historic event. The Immaculate Conception is rooted in a particular understanding of the fall of man in Genesis and its consequences, articulated by influential theologians such as Saint Augustine and Ambrose of Milan.

Ambrose, for example, was particularly interested in the passage from Psalm 51:5: "Behold I was brought forth in iniquity and in sin did my mother conceive me," and sought to articulate the way Mary was set apart from this cycle of sin. Augustine, on the other hand, emphasized a passage in the book of Romans 5, which emphasizes the radical difference between those "in Adam" and those "in Christ." Augustine wrote about how deeply sin has infected and corrupted those who have not been reborn to a new humanity "in Christ."

factum

Christian theologians have likened Mary to the Ark of the Covenant in the Old Testament. For them, Mary's purity was vitally important. She had to be a pure vessel, because otherwise she might be destroyed as was Uzzah, who accidentally touched the Ark of the Covenant in which God dwelled (1 Samuel 6:6–7).

Because of the belief that Mary needed to be a completely pure vessel to bear God in her womb, it has been long understood in the West that Mary was the singular exception to the rule of sin being passed down through the human generations since Adam.

On December 18, 1439, an official statement was made about the Immaculate Conception at the Council of Basel. According to this statement, the doctrine of the Immaculate Conception was consistent with the teachings of the worship of the Church, the Holy Scriptures, and reason, and should be proclaimed universally. This council also condemned anyone who spoke against the Immaculate Conception.

This council was never viewed as universally authoritative, however, because other council statements related to the authority of the pope were condemned by the Church. Although there were questions surrounding these statements and this council, by the end of the fifteenth century, the Immaculate Conception had gained widespread popular acceptance. Some even used the statements from this council to condemn those who spoke against the Immaculate Conception, saying that although there was once a time when the issue could be debated, those debates ceased with the Council of Basel.

Apparitions Related to the Immaculate Conception

During the next three centuries, belief in the Immaculate Conception was widespread, if not completely universal in the West. A few decades before the dogma was officially proclaimed in 1854, an apparition was reported in France that some have interpreted as foreshadowing this official pronouncement.

The Miraculous Medal

In 1830, a postulant at a Paris convent for Our Sisters of Charity named Catherine Laboure had a vision of the Virgin Mary. In this vision, the Virgin Mary wore a long white silk gown and stood upon a globe. Near her chest, she held a golden ball, and each of her fingers had three jeweled, luminescent rings upon them. The Virgin Mary explained that that light was a demonstration of the graces that would come to all who asked for them. Some of the jewels on Mary's fingers were darkened, and Mary explained that these were symbolic of the graces that people forgot to ask for. On the ground near her feet was a green and yellow snake.

As Catherine watched, Mary seemed to turn around. Catherine then saw a large *M* surmounted by a cross. Two hearts were beneath the cross, one wrapped in thorns, the other pierced by a sword. A large oval surrounded

Mary and she was encircled by these words, which were written in gold: "O Mary, conceived without sin, pray for us who have recourse to thee."

The Virgin Mary instructed Catherine to have this image printed as a medal, and the image of the "Miraculous Medal" was born. These medals were extremely popular in Catherine's day—more than fifty thousand were given out in 1832 and 1833 and millions more each year after that. The medals were taken by missionaries to other countries, and the apparition gained global recognition. Over one billion miraculous medals have now been distributed. These medals are commonly associated with miraculous healings and cures. During the apparition, the Virgin Mary said of the Miraculous Medal that, "Those who wear it will receive great graces; abundant graces will be given to those who have confidence."

Pope Pius IX

The widespread popularity of this image may have helped pave the way for the dogma that was proclaimed by Pope Pius IX twenty-four years after the apparition. Pope Pius, who believed that the Virgin had healed him from epilepsy when he was a child, had a lifelong personal devotion to her. His papacy was set against the backdrop of the Enlightenment. During this period, the church was in an increasingly vulnerable position, because more and more people were buying into the ideas of the Enlightenment, which championed science and reason over religion. Pope Pius felt that he might be able to counteract some of this mentality by demonstrating the power of the Virgin within the Roman Catholic Church.

When Pope Pius began to consider proclaiming the Immaculate Conception as dogma, he met with a team of theologians who offered overwhelming (although not universal) support for endorsing the dogma. Pius then contacted several bishops, nine-tenths of whom agreed that he should proclaim the Immaculate Conception as dogma. His actual proclamation took place against a distressing backdrop—Italian nationalists threatened the Church: Massini and Garibaldi were preparing to attack Rome.

factum

During the French Revolution, numerous ancient statues of the Virgin Mary were destroyed, and revolutionaries put up a statue called the "Goddess of Reason" in Notre Dame. The revolutionaries also sang a mock Ave Maria to the allegorical figure Marianne, "Hail Marianne, full of strength, the people are with thee, blessed is the fruit of thy womb, the Republic."

On the day of the Feast of the Immaculate Conception, December 8, 1854, Pope Pius IX read *Ineffabilis Deus*, through tears:

"The Doctrine holds that the blessed Virgin Mary, at the first instant of her conception, by singular privilege and grace of the omnipotent God, in consideration of the merits of Jesus Christ, the savior of mankind, was preserved free from the stain of original sin from the moment of her conception, has been revealed by God and is to be firmly and constantly believed by all the faithful."

Differences of Opinion

Although the Immaculate Conception had been a popular belief among many Western Christians many centuries before the dogma was officially proclaimed, there had always been those in the West who opposed the doctrine, such as Thomas Aquinas, Anselm of Canterbury, and Saint Bernard of Clairvaux.

Bernard of Clairvaux was concerned that the doctrine of the Immaculate Conception made it seem as though Mary had no need of a savior herself. His reasoning went something like this: if she was born without the stain of sin and if she never sinned during her earthy life, why would she be in need of a redeemer?

Those who were uncomfortable with the idea of the Immaculate Conception had two major objections. Some objected to the Augustinian idea that all conception was evil, based on Psalm 51, which reads "In sin did my mother conceive me." Some simply objected to this seemingly negative view of sexual intercourse. Still others felt uncomfortable with the way this dogma seemed to separate Mary from the rest of humanity.

When the dogma of the Immaculate Conception was proclaimed, many of these old objections resurfaced, along with some new ones. In particular, Anglicans and Eastern Orthodox expressed concerns about how the dogma was proclaimed. These churches felt that the pope seemed to be acting too much in isolation. Perhaps they sensed what was to come: later that same century at the First Vatican Council in 1869–70, the doctrine of Papal Infallibility was officially proclaimed. This doctrine is quite foreign to the understanding of papal primacy and church authority that developed in the Christian East.

In her book *In Search of Mary*, Sally Cunneen highlights a fascinating aspect of the proclamation of this dogma: the proclamation was both preceded and followed by apparitions that seemed to echo the underlying themes of this teaching.

Four years after Pope Pius IX proclaimed the dogma of the Immaculate Conception, a young girl named Bernadette Soubirous experienced several apparitions of the Virgin Mary. When Bernadette asked the woman who she was, the woman spread her arms in a way that would have been recognizable to Bernadette as her pose upon the Miraculous Medal. The Virgin Mary responded, "I am the Immaculate Conception."

Vatican II

Vatican II was a council that began on October 11, 1962. At this council, religious officials attempted to remain faithful to the ancient heritage of the Roman Catholic Church while also bringing a renewal of church life. Vatican II was infused with a desire to return to some of the original Scriptural and patristic understandings of the faith, while helping the Church to remain relevant to the modern world.

Changes Resulting from Vatican II

Most people who lived through Vatican II are most familiar with the ways in which the Catholic worship experience was transformed as a result of the council. The services were no longer in Latin, but instead used the language of the locals (the vernacular). The priest no longer served facing the altar, but instead faced the people. In many cases, statues were removed from churches or placed in less conspicuous locations in an effort to appease Protestants.

symbolism

The day Vatican II opened, October 11, 1962, was the day dedicated to the motherhood of the Virgin Mary (before the introduction of a revised liturgical calendar). The council closed on December 8, the Feast of the Immaculate Conception.

Vatican II also represented a shift from the more rigid scholastic thought that had dominated official church theology since the Council of Trent to a more Biblical and patristic form of exegesis, meaning that the Church's revised interpretation of the Bible would be based more on the writings and beliefs of the fathers of the Christian Church. Vatican II encouraged lay ministry, the self-organization of convents, and an increasingly strong desire to reach out to "the separated brethren"— Protestant and Eastern Orthodox Christians.

One of the most significant debates related to Mary from this Council revolved around the question of how teachings about Mary would be incorporated into the documents from the council. Some of the more "progressive" theologians argued that the statements about Mary should be included as one chapter in the larger context of all of the writings from the Council, while some of the more traditional Catholics had hoped that the writings related to Mary would be preserved as a separate document.

These more traditional Catholics feared that if the teachings about Mary were not kept separate, they might be reduced or minimized. Those who felt that Mary should occupy a chapter of the larger collection of statements instead of an entire document felt that it was more appropriate to place Mary in the context of the larger church. The vote between these two groups was extremely close: 1,114 people were in favor of including the documents related to Mary in the larger body of work, while 1,074 wished to keep documents related to Mary separate. So the decision was made to include the writings about Mary as the final chapter of the council's constitution.

factum

Each side of the Vatican II discussion posed the argument in terms of "what Our Lady would want." Those desiring a separate document insisted, "Our Lady would like a separate document" while those who pushed for including Mary as one chapter in the set of documents stated, "Our Lady would prefer to be treated within the entire context of the Church."

The decisions that resulted from Vatican II about Mary were extremely deliberate in their wording. There was a conscious effort to minimize "past excesses" while also avoiding the error of being too narrow-minded in statements surrounding Mary.

Statements were made about Mary's role in the Church and her role in the history of salvation. Mary was called a "helper." Controversial titles such as Advocate and Mediator were carefully qualified; Mary could be called by those titles only when they were being used in a minimalist sense, which would imply that Mary shares in these ministries of Christ because of her relationship with him.

The Wake of Vatican II

Many theologians feel that Vatican II produced significant documents related to Mary, which brought helpful clarity and nuance to discussion about Mary in the Catholic Church. At the same time, in the wake of Vatican II, the role of the Virgin Mary has often been downplayed. Charlene Spretnak, in her book *Missing Mary*, describes the aftermath of the council, in which statues disappeared, rosary use in the parishes became more infrequent, and certain novenas for the Virgin Mary were no longer said. In Spretnak's opinion, one result of Vatican II is that there is now an entire generation of American Catholics who have not experienced the full scope of Marian devotion that would have been a staple of their parents' and grandparents' spirituality.

John Paul II

Although in the years since Vatican II many liturgical practices associated with the Virgin Mary have become less popular, there are still many Catholics who have a deep love for her and devotion to her. During this past century, Marian shrines have become extremely popular. Some people believe that there is something of a Marian revival going on, both within and outside the Catholic Church.

One of most prominent figures from modern times who held a deep and unwavering devotion to the Virgin Mary was Pope John Paul II. His lifelong devotion to her may have been fueled by the loss of his own mother when he was only eight years old. His mother, whom he had once described as "the soul of the house," adored him and had always felt that he would one day be a priest and a great man.

Pope John Paul II (whose birth name was Karol Wojtyla) always carried the memory of his mother with him, and even as an adult, when he traveled to faraway pilgrimage sites, he carried with him a photo of his mother holding him as a young child. After his mother died, his father took him to one of Poland's famous Marian shrines, Kalwaria, near Wadowice, Poland. It was most likely on this pilgrimage that he was able to transform some of his grief into a deep love for the Virgin Mary.

A Tragic Childhood

Although Karol Wojtyla's father devoted himself to caring for his young son, their lives were marked with tragedy. When Karol Wojtyla was twelve years old, his only brother died of scarlet fever. When he was twenty, his father died. Karol was deeply grieved that he had not been able to be present with his mother or father when they died. After his father died, he knelt by his body and prayed for twelve hours.

symbolism

The phrase *Totus Tuus* originated with Saint Louis-Marie Grignion de Montfort in the eighteenth century. Saint Louis-Marie Grignion de Montfort advocated utter devotion (almost slavery) to Mary, which was intended to symbolize complete surrender to the will of God through Marian devotion.

All of these factors may have contributed to Karol's devotion to Mary. By the time he was fifteen years old, he was leading a large society in his hometown which was dedicated to the Virgin. Later, when he was a young priest, he made a special place for Mary in his soul. When he became an archbishop he included a large *M* in his coat of arms, a symbol of Mary. When Pope John Paul II was newly elected as pope, he made an unusual request for his papal coat of arms. He asked for a gold cross with a blue Marian background as well as a large *M* for Mary. Although he was told that this request was quite unusual he was ultimately allowed to wear this coat of arms.

The papal slogan he selected for his papacy, *Totus Tuus* or "My whole self is Yours," also reflected his deep love for the Virgin Mary.

An Assassination Attempt

In 1981, when Pope John Paul II was riding in his Jeep through Saint Peter's Square to greet people, a Turkish man named Mehmet Ali Agca shot him. As he was rushed to the hospital, he cried out to the Virgin Mary to save his life. After his condition was stable, the pope made a television broadcast in which he thanked everyone for their prayers. He also attributed his survival directly to the intercessions of the Virgin Mary, taking note of the fact that the assassination attempt occurred on the anniversary of the apparitions at Fatima. During his convalescence, he read through all of the documents associated with the apparitions at Fatima. After recovering from the assassination attempt, the pope went to the prison cell of Mehmet Ali Agca and offered him forgiveness.

A year later, John Paul II made a pilgrimage to Fatima to deposit the fragments of the bullet that nearly took his life into the crown of a statue of

Our Lady of Fatima. While there, a priest lunged at him with a knife, but the priest was stopped before any harm was done.

The Pope of Many Pilgrimages

Pope John Paul II wrote beautifully about the Virgin Mary; his *Book of Mary* is a compilation of his many writings on Mary. One of the most beautiful quotes from the book comes from a section near the beginning. On October 6, 1976, he wrote:

"This woman of faith, Mary of Nazareth, the Mother of God, has been given to us as a model of our pilgrimage of faith. From Mary, we learn to surrender to God's will in all things. From Mary we learn to trust even when all hope seems gone. From Mary we learn to love Christ, her Son and the Son of God. For Mary is not only the Mother of God, she is the Mother of the Church as well."

During Pope John Paul II's papacy, he made many journeys to Marian shrines. Whenever he was back in Poland, he visited the famous icon of the Virgin Mary located there, called Our Lady of Czestochowa. During his papacy, John Paul II was also responsible for creating an additional set of five mysteries, called the Mysteries of Light, which were added to the rosary.

Titles Associated with Mary

There are many titles associated with the Virgin Mary that have sometimes been used within the Catholic context as a way of understanding Mary. These terms are not considered formal dogma, but are suggestive of the unique nature of Mary's role in the world.

None of these terms are used universally, and they can be confusing when taken out of context. While some Catholics have pushed for these terms to be used more, or even to be proclaimed as dogma, there are still others who warn that terms like Mediatrix and Coredemptrix are likely to cause unnecessary confusion and should only be used with great caution, if at all.

Mediatrix

One of the most ancient of these terms is *Mediatrix*, which is the Latin feminine form of the word *Mediator*. This term is used to describe the mediating role the Virgin Mary has as the bridge between heaven and earth. This term is quite ancient and even shows up in the fourth-century writings of Saint Ephrem of Syria, who says, "With the mediator, you are the mediatrix of the entire world."

Applying the title Mediatrix to the Virgin Mary has been a source of controversy because, according to Scripture, there is only "one mediator between God and men, the man Christ Jesus" (1 Timothy 2:5). Many people feel that it is scandalous to confer a title on the Virgin Mary that seems to be reserved for Christ alone.

Those in the Roman Catholic Church who support the use of this title for the Virgin Mary feel that it is useful because it demonstrates the Virgin Mary's role, as she intercedes on behalf of humanity before the face of God. Some have even said that at the wedding at Cana when she pleaded with her son to turn water into wine, she was serving as a Mediatrix. This belief is expressed by Dwight Longenecker in the book he coauthored with David Gustafson, called *Mary: A Catholic Evangelical Debate*. Longenecker also makes the point that all Christians are called to a ministry of mediation and reconciliation.

As Christians pray before God for others and seek to bring knowledge of God into the world, they participate in a ministry that is something like Mary's. In this line of reasoning, Mary serves as the ultimate example of a ministry to which all Christians are called.

Advocate

The title Advocate is closely linked with the title Mediatrix. From a Biblical perspective, Jesus is the Advocate. His role as Advocate, however, does not diminish the idea that all Christians can have a ministry of advocacy.

This term implies that Mary, like a lawyer, stands up for people and makes a defense for them before God. This defense takes the form of fervent prayers. For some, this title is problematic because it hints of the notion that the Virgin Mary is compassionate while Jesus is merely a judge. Certainly, a balanced Biblical view of Jesus would see him as both compassionate advocate and judge, while Mary is never associated with judgment.

Coredemptrix

The term *Coredemptrix*, meaning that Mary participates in the redemption of humanity through her intercessions and cooperation with God, is perhaps the most controversial because Christians believe that Christ is the exclusive Redeemer. For those who embrace this term, however, calling the Virgin Mary Coredemptrix does not take away from Christ's redemptive work. Instead, the term highlights the fact that Mary, by being the first Christian and saying yes to God in such a way that redemption became possible, participated in God's plan of salvation.

Many Christians believe that Mary's openness and obedience to God continues, and that her participation in the salvation of the world is ongoing. Some interpret her apparitions as an expression of her continual desire to convince lost sheep of the importance of Jesus' message and to make her son known in this world.

From Title to Dogma

Some Catholics would like the titles of *Coredemptrix* and *Mediatrix* to be proclaimed as dogma. Supporters of these titles feel that they contribute to a more robust view of Mary, suggestive of her continual quest to reconcile humanity with God.

There are many, however, who don't want these titles to become dogma. In particular, Pope Benedict is opposed to Coredemptrix because he feels that it has the potential to create unnecessary confusion. These disagreements highlight the sometimes delicate process of articulating Christian teaching, as theologians attempt to bring clarity without confusion and fullness without excess in the Catholic Church.

CHAPTER 15

Mary in Popular Culture

Mary occupies a unique place in popular culture. She is an object of loyal devotion and of occasional artistic deprecation. In some cases, these strange manifestations seem to be largely harmless, while in others the Virgin Mary is exploited for commercial use in a way that is offensive to believers. This chapter dives into the more curious (and in some cases, disconcerting) manifestations of the Virgin Mary in popular culture, as well as the attempts of many of the faithful to protect her image when they feel it has been tainted.

The Power of Images

Who could forget the photographs taken during the terrorist attacks that occurred on September 11, 2001? Some of the most heartbreaking images were taken of people jumping from the windows of the smoldering Twin Towers, hands clasped as they fell to their deaths. These images express the reality of what happened that day in a way that words cannot, capturing the fear, desperation, and agony experienced by so many.

The images from September 11 were so powerful that many people sat before their televisions day after day in a sort of trance, repeatedly watching footage of the planes crashing into the World Trade Center towers, trying to piece together some semblance of order from all of these images. Even now, when people think of this day, they likely think not so much in words but in images. Long after the event, images remain crisp while words blur and become foggy in memory.

Images have also occupied a prominent place within many religions, including Christianity. Images of the Virgin Mary have been especially potent, not just for the way they express the traditional Christian teaching of the Incarnation, but also for the messages they convey about motherhood, femininity, and God.

symbolism

During the Christmas season of 1995, the U.S. Postal Service printed 700 million stamps bearing an image of the Virgin and Child created by Giotto di Bondone, a painter in Florence, Italy, in the fourteenth century. Although these stamps were scheduled to be replaced with angel stamps, they have been brought back due to popular demand.

In a more specific way, images are often viewed as synonymous with the Roman Catholic or Eastern Orthodox Churches. Sometimes, when people want to attack these churches or the ideas they represent, they vandalize statues or deface icons. This approach is not unlike burning flags to protest American policies.

Some critics believe that some pop-culture icons exploit images of the Virgin Mary in a way that is not only distasteful but also destructive. Some Christians might even believe that some cases of tainting Mary's image have a diabolical character because they only serve to distract people from more central Christian realities. You may discern for yourself how these images might be interpreted in light of larger cultural and spiritual realities.

Sacred or Profane?

Increasingly, we are assaulted by a barrage of images everywhere we go—billboards are plastered with scantily clad women, and the Nike and Starbucks logos are so widely recognizable that the companies don't even need words for promotion. Images are sometimes used to stir emotions and sell products. When the Virgin Mary is used as a marketing tool, this practice is sometimes viewed as disrespectful by religious people.

For this reason, the Christian response to these particular manifestations of Mary's image has often been one of skeptical wariness, if not outright condemnation. It's important to realize, however, that at least a few of the individuals who will be discussed in this chapter seem to be sincere. They don't necessarily recognize the negative impacts of their statements or art. Still, many of them have experienced a great backlash of criticism from those within and outside of Christianity who resent these depictions.

Mary in Modern Art

In an opening scene of a *Simpsons* episode, Bart writes on a chalkboard over and over, "I will not create art from dung." Bart's penance on the TV show was directly related to an exhibit that had opened at the Brooklyn Museum of Art in 1999. This exhibit was called "Sensations: Young British Artists from the Saatchi Collection" and featured the work of a variety of edgy artists. One of these, Chris Ofili, created a painting of the Virgin Mary that was dappled with elephant manure and encircled by pornographic images.

The Holy Virgin Mary was the most infamous and hotly contested piece in the exhibit, attracting over 300,000 people who needed to see this image for themselves. The image also generated a passionate response from the religious communities in New York City.

The Holy Virgin Mary

The Holy Virgin Mary contained a large Black Madonna who was surrounded with disembodied pornographic images. The painting was also created using elephant manure, a substance that the artist used frequently in his work. Supporters of Chris Ofili's art said that in the African culture from which Ofili drew his inspiration, dung and urine don't have the same negative connotation that Americans attach to them. These claims, however, did nothing to curb the backlash against the exhibit. New York's mayor at the time, Rudolph Giuliani, described it as "very sick stuff."

Even before the exhibit opened there were protests. One self-described artist stood in front of the museum, throwing manure at the museum's façade. When the police took him away, he explained that he was "expressing himself creatively," and that the painting of the Virgin Mary was just a form of Catholic-bashing.

discussion question

Was the reaction in New York to Chris Ofili's work unique?
No. The Tate Gallery in London garnered a similar response to the one experienced in New York City when it awarded Chris Ofili the prestigious Turner Prize in 1989. One protestor left a large heap of manure on the front steps of the museum, along with a sign that said, "Modern Art is a heap of . . . ."

Giuliani threatened to take away the city's funding of the museum for the month, and also expressed a desire to pull its lease. Like many of the opponents of the exhibit, he was particularity appalled by the image of the Virgin Mary. According to Giuliani, his position was not related to censorship but was primarily focused on concerns that public funds should be used appropriately. According to Giuliani, "art" that was deeply offensive to a large portion of the tax-paying public was not a proper use of funds. The case eventually went to court and the judge ruled in favor of the museum because of the First Amendment.

Neither the manure-slinging man nor Giuliani was successful in preventing the exhibit from opening. After the manure incident, the Brooklyn Museum of Art realized that more attacks were likely, so they covered the image with Plexiglass. The Plexiglass did not, however, deter a retired English teacher named Dennis Heiner who showed up at the exhibit with a tube of white paint. As he approached the image of the Virgin Mary, he leaned against a wall, pretending to be ill. He then snuck behind the Plexiglass and made a line of white paint all down the Virgin's face and body. He quickly spread the white paint with his hands all over the painting, effectively concealing the image.

When he was caught, he made no attempt to escape. When a security guard asked him why he had defaced the painting, he quietly responded, "It's blasphemous." Heiner was later charged with second-degree criminal mischief and a $250 fine. The verdict was seen as quite lenient by the arts community.

In the years since, Chris Ofili has toned down his work a bit. In an interview with *The New York Magazine*, Ofili told a reporter, "At the time, I felt quite vulnerable. I didn't really know what the American rules are. I didn't know how extreme things could get." When *The New York Times* interviewed Ofili, he refused to describe his inspiration or give any interpretation of the work, because he felt that viewers should interpret it for themselves.

Marian Kitsch

In recent years, there has been an overwhelming amount of products associated with the Virgin Mary. Some of these products are sold at tacky trinket stands in places like Lourdes where millions of pilgrims flock each year. At Lourdes, one can buy bright pink rosaries and velvet images of Christ. Online, one can purchase a variety of other items, from tasteful to tacky, and from reverent to flippant.

Printed Devotion

One of the more recent items associated with the Virgin Mary that is turning some heads and turning a significant profit is T-shirts that read "Mary is my homegirl." These T-shirts are being produced by Teenage Millionaire, a California-based clothing company. According to the company, these T-shirts are one of their bestsellers. Young Catholics and Protestants have been attracted to these T-shirts as a way to witness their love and admiration for Mary. There is, as one might imagine, a companion T-shirt that says "Jesus is my homeboy" on it.

Some skeptics have expressed concerns that these T-shirts (along with a the slew of other Mary products being marketed) are disrespectful because they present these spiritual figures in a way that is perhaps too lighthearted, or that is meant to be taken ironically. The "Mary is my homegirl" T-shirts, do, however, witness to increasingly widespread enthusiasm surrounding the Virgin Mary in our society. These T-shirts also garnered popular attention when they were mentioned on the hit TV show *Gilmore Girls*.

The "Holy" Sandwich

Sometimes Mary pops up in unusual places. In 1994, one of the most unusual Marian "manifestations" was claimed. This time, the face of the Virgin Mary appeared in the burn marks on a grilled cheese sandwich. According to Diana Duyser, a 52-year-old woman living in Hollywood, Florida, she had taken one bite of her grilled cheese sandwich, and then she noticed the face of the Virgin Mary staring back up at her. She was alarmed and called her husband into the room to see the image on the sandwich.

Duyser then put the sandwich in a clear plastic box and placed it beside her bed. She kept it for ten years, and she reports that it did not mold or crumble at all during the decade. According to Duyser, she sincerely believes that the image on her sandwich is that of Mary, the Mother of God. She was not, however, averse to making a profit off the sandwich. According to Duyser the sandwich brought her significant good luck and fortune, including winnings of $70,000 at several nearby casinos.

After ten years, Duyser decided that it was time to share her sandwich with the world and she posted an ad for it on eBay, with a starting bid of $3,000. While the sandwich was for sale, more than 1,700,000 people visited the site, and many of them placed joke bids, along with joke items that followed the theme of the sandwich. The price of the sandwich rose and rose to $99.9 million and then finally began to decrease, because so many of the bids were fake.

factum

eBay initially pulled the Virgin Mary sandwich from the site because they don't sell hoax items. Eventually, however, eBay allowed it to be sold because Duyser did intend to hand over the sandwich to the highest bidder. She wrote on online request that all hoax bids be stopped. She also cautioned potential buyers that the sandwich "was not for consumption."

In the end, an online casino called GoldenPalaceCasino.com purchased the sandwich for $28,000 The CEO of the online casino said that they intend to use the sandwich to raise money for charity. As to why they were so eager to acquire the sandwich, their spokesperson Monty Kerr was quoted in the *Miami Herald* saying, "It's a part of pop culture that is immediately and widely recognizable. We knew right away that we wanted to have it."

Mary in Popular Music

The pop star Madonna won her fame, in part, by exploiting the connections between her birth name, which is Madonna (given to her by her Italian immigrant parents), and the actual Virgin Mary.

Madonna was raised in a large, devout Catholic family located in a suburb of Detroit. For much of her childhood, she attended Catholic schools. Her mother died of breast cancer when Madonna was only five years old. Some have speculated that the trauma of Madonna's childhood loss permeates her music through her use of Mary imagery. Many of her videos also use religious imagery such as rosaries and crosses. These potent Catholic symbols are very likely drawn from Madonna's childhood experience in a devout family as well as her years in parochial schools.

symbolism

> The Virgin Mary has not only been the subject of songs by Madonna. She has also been the subject of a dazzling number of more reverent songs such as the Beatles' ballad "Let It Be."

Madonna must have sensed early on that her name was powerful. During the course of her career, she has often drawn on Christian and Marian themes and used them to shock and attract crowds. Madonna's use of religious imagery, however, has not always worked to improve her image. In the eighties, she lost a Pepsi sponsorship when she released the controversial hit song "Like a Prayer" in which she drew connections between prayer and sexuality. The music video for the song, which featured burning crosses and Madonna wearing provocative clothing, added to the controversy.

Madonna might have gained popularity in part because society is so full of conflicted feelings about the Virgin Mary and about sexuality. Madonna tapped into the public's general interest in the Virgin Mary when she named her 1990 album *The Immaculate Collection*. The album's colors of blue and gold resonate with some of the colors used in traditional images of the Virgin Mary. Madonna also named her daughter Lourdes, after the apparition site in France.

Mary in Literature

The Virgin Mary continually surfaces in contemporary literature. The Virgin Mary has inspired the poetry of Gerald Manley Hopkins and Rainer Maria Rilke, and she has even been indirectly referred to in Garrison Keillor's fictional *Lake Wobegon*, in which the town's Catholic church is named Our Lady of Perpetual Responsibility. The Virgin Mary has also taken a prominent role in the writings of Canadian poet and novelist Margaret Atwood.

Sue Monk Kidd

Perhaps one of the most gripping and vivid contemporary depictions of the Virgin Mary in literature appears in Sue Monk Kidd's *The Secret Life of Bees*. Although the Mariology expressed in Kidd's book might be seen as excessive, Kidd powerfully expresses the universal longing for a mother that so often motivates Marian devotion. Kidd's main character, Lilly, accidentally caused her mother's death when she was a small child, and this loss shaped her life. Ultimately Lilly finds solace in the Virgin Mary.

After Lilly runs away from her abusive father in search of the truth about her mother, she finds her way to the bright pink home of the Calendar sisters. The Calendar sisters are three African American beekeeping sisters named May, June, and August, who expose Lilly to their folk religion, which finds its heart in devotion to the Black Madonna. The women venerate a large black wooden statue of a woman who was once part of a boat's masthead. The statue is adorned in chains, and Lilly is startled by this until one of the Calendar sister explains to her that the Virgin Mary is adorned with chains not because she wears them, but because she breaks them.

In *The Secret Life of Bees* the Virgin Mary is clearly associated with the universal longing for a mother as well as the widely held belief that the Virgin Mary identifies with the oppressed, crossing racial and social lines as Lily did when she went to live with the Calendar sisters during the era of the civil rights movement in the South. Sue Monk Kidd writes in *The Secret Life of Bees:*

"She is a muscle of love, this Mary. I feel her in unexpected moments, her Assumption into heaven happening in places inside me. She will suddenly rise, and when she does, she does not go up, up into the sky but further and further inside me. August said she goes into the holes life has gauged for us."

Margaret Atwood

For Margaret Atwood and many contemporary women, Mary is increasingly considered an empowered woman who actively engages the questions of life, while being wearied (as contemporary women so often are) by the demands that love puts upon her. Sally Cunneen offers fascinating insights into Atwood's writing in Cunneen's book *In Search of Mary*.

Cunneen describes one scene from Atwood's book *Cat's Eye*, in which the author depicts a strikingly contemporary image of Mary. Atwood describes a painting of the Virgin Mary with the head of a lioness, dressed in the traditional blue and white. She is dressed in an overcoat and is carrying heavy bags of groceries from which several items have fallen.

This depiction captures a fierce side of Mary that seems somewhat unusual to most people. It also captures a weary Mary that seems very believable considering the depth of her active love and the ways in which she was called by God to suffer for it. The lioness image is based on some traditional images that have portrayed Christ as a lion. This image of Christ as a lion parallels C. S. Lewis's *Chronicles of Narnia* where Aslan the lion is a Christ figure.

factum

The Virgin Mary has been the subject of the poetry of Gerard Manley Hopkins. In his poem "The Blessed Virgin Compared to the Air We Breathe," he writes, "She, wild web, wondrous robe, Mantles the guilty globe . . . Men are meant to share her life as life does air."

According to the narrator in the Atwood story, "My Virgin Mary is fierce, alert to danger, wild. She stares levelly out at the viewer with her yellow lion's eyes. A gnawed bone lies at her feet." One can easily imagine why a less-tame, but still accessible, Mary would appeal to contemporary women.

Chicago Oil Spot

In 2005, a young woman named Obdulia Delgado was driving on one of Chicago's major freeways when she saw what she believed to be a figure of the Virgin Mary in an oil spot in an underpass. She was so astonished that she could barely drive, and many frustrated people honked at her as she slowed down to examine the figure. Delgado reported that she had been praying to the Virgin for assistance, which was in part why she found this figure so astonishing.

Word spread quickly, and many came to view the mysterious oil spot. Some left candles and flowers and prayed the rosary there, while others were skeptical, saying that the oil spot looked more like a pawn in a chess game than the Virgin Mary.

The city decided to treat the oil spot as they would any roadside memorial. They barricaded the area so that the image (which was accompanied by the phrase "Go Cubs" written in a graffiti tag beside it) would remain protected. Some people drew parallels between the event that was occurring in Chicago that day and the event that was occurring that same day in Rome, as the new pope was being selected.

Most people in society don't know quite how to feel about bizarre manifestations like the Virgin Mary oil spot or the face on the grilled cheese sandwich. There are many skeptics, but it is also striking that those who experience these manifestations directly often seem to be genuine in their responses.

All of these manifestations of the Virgin Mary offer different glimpses into the way that society views her. Just beneath the surface, emotions about Mary run deep. Some individuals are willing be arrested as they protest art that they perceive as disrespectful, while others will gather at a freeway underpass, light votive candles, and pray the rosary before an oil spot that loosely resembles Mary. Still others have found effective ways to tap into the passion surrounding Mary, to mingle the sacred and profane in ways that attract crowds and turn profits.

The Marian manifestations in popular culture witness to the reality that emotions surrounding Mary run deep. Images of her continue to be powerful, both for those who create them through art and literature, and for those who encounter them. In an age in which people are bombarded with images and often experience sensory overload, it is interesting to see how powerful images of Mary remain. Just as images spoke to those in the early church and to those in the medieval villages, images of Mary continue to resonate in our day.

CHAPTER 16

Praying with Mary

Some of the most ancient icons of Mary show her with her arms raised in prayer. According to the book of Acts, Mary prayed with the disciples while waiting for the Holy Spirit to come (Acts 1:14–2:1). These images express Mary's role as intercessor. This chapter will explore ways in which Christians have prayed with Mary through the centuries, as well as offering some practical suggestions for making space for Mary within our own homes.

The Meaning of Marian Prayers

Some of the controversies and questions surrounding Marian prayers were explored in Chapter 10. The most important thing to remember in relation to Marian prayers, however, is that all prayers to Mary find their end in Christ. Mary is never meant to be the end, but a means to an end.

The tradition of asking Mary to intercede for Christians is ancient, dating back to at least the fourth century. The idea of asking for the intercessions of those who have gone before is closely related to the belief in the Resurrection of the dead. Christians believe that Christ died and rose again, and that those who believe in him also continue to live, even after they have died. Because of this belief in the ongoing life of those who have died in the earthly sense, many Christians have embraced the idea that the departed in Christ can continue to pray for those on earth.

factum

Mahatma Gandhi, on observing Marian devotion, said: "The feeling has since then been growing on me, that all this kneeling and prayer could not be mere superstition; the devout souls kneeling before the Virgin could not be worshiping mere marble. I had the impression that I felt then that by this worship they were not detracting from, but adding to, the glory of God."

The intercessions of Mary are closely connected to this belief. Just as Mary was the link between heaven and earth when she lived on this earth, Christians have historically believed that Mary continues to help us. Mary's prayers have been invoked by millions of people around the world who seek her assistance in every kind of difficulty.

Mary's prayers have been requested by sailors at sea, couples struggling with infertility, soldiers heading into battle, farmers sowing their fields, and parents who grieve the loss of a child. Just as little children run to their mother when they are afraid, for centuries, Christians have invoked Mary's prayers. Some have even felt that Mary was more available and accessible than Christ, although the idea of seeking the intercessions of Mary instead of the intercessions of Christ was officially censured at Vatican II in which the pope said, "Mary is not happy when she is placed above her son."

Though the intercessions of Mary are never supposed to replace intercessions to Christ or God the Father, but only to be one piece of the entire fabric of a life of prayer, many ascribe miraculous events in their own lives directly to her, and have found comfort, solace, and strength in Mary's witness and her continual prayers.

Ancient Prayers

Marian devotion is quite ancient—one of the oldest frescos in the Catacombs is of the Virgin Mary and dates back to about the second century. The oldest known prayer to Mary, the Sub Tuum Praesidium, dates back to the third or early fourth century. By the fifth century, Christians described special Marian "graces." One such Christian was the historian Sozomen, who described the apparently miraculous events that occurred in the famous Anastasia Chapel in Constantinople (present-day Istanbul).

Sozomen described a divine power that seemed to manifest itself in this church. This power helped cure illnesses and brought relief from afflictions to members of this community. Sozomen wrote, "The power was attributed to Mary, the Mother of God, the Holy Virgin, for she does manifest herself in this way."

Sozomen's statement suggests that the events that occurred at this church were not entirely unique but were related to a broader phenomenon that he may have already been familiar with. His statement seems to parallel the reports of healings and transformed lives that are associated with apparition sites.

Saint Gregory of Nazianzus

It seems appropriate that the events described by Sozomen would occur at the Anastasia Chapel in Constantinople, because Saint Gregory of Nazianzus preached in this chapel.

discussion question

Was Saint Gregory open about his Marian devotion?
Yes. Saint Gregory was quite bold in his devotion to the Virgin Mary. In A.D. 379, he said, "If anyone does not accept the holy Mary as Theotokos, he is without the Godhead."

Saint Gregory was devoted to the Virgin Mary, and he did not shy away from mentioning her in his sermons, even early on in his career. During Saint Gregory's first year preaching in Constantinople in A.D. 379, he publicly called the Virgin Mary Theotokos, long before the Council at Ephesus had officially used this title to describe her. Saint Gregory also believed fervently that Mary responded to prayers and that healings could be attributed to her.

The conviction that Mary continually prays for those who seek her intercessions has been passed on from century to century, crossing ethnic and cultural lines, and finding different expressions within a variety of communities around the world.

Making Space for Mary

Saint John of the Cross said, "If you meet the Virgin on the road, invite her into your house. She bears the word of God." Increasingly, people are seeking ways to bring Mary into their lives and into their homes. There are many small ways to create space for Mary in one's home.

House Blessings

The Catholic, Eastern Orthodox, and many Protestant Churches have retained the ancient tradition of house blessings. House blessings are usually done by a parish priest who walks through a house with the family, sprinkling holy water throughout while praying for those who live in the house as well as for all of the family's loved ones.

The ancient ritual of house blessing is based on the idea that physical spaces can be transformed by prayer, meaning that a house of brick or wood can become a holy space through the prayer-infused sprinkling of water. Christians have also found intentional ways of inviting Mary to dwell in their homes.

Prayer Corners

In Eastern Orthodox communities, the most common way to create space for the saints inside of the home is by creating a prayer corner. Prayer corners do not always have to be literally located in corners, although many families do place them in a corner of their home. Traditionally, icon corners have been placed on a wall that faces east because Christians have historically prayed facing eastward—in the direction of the rising sun. Praying eastward is one more way in which the Church has integrated the natural rhythms of the earth into its prayers.

Icon corners vary from home to home. Some families will have an entire wall of images that are significant to them, while others will have very basic icon corners. The most basic family icon corners include icons of Christ, the Virgin Mary, and the saints for which each of the family members are named.

Prayer corners are often lit by small oil lamps called lampadas. Traditionally, these lamps are filled with olive oil because olive oil burns clean and is frequently used for liturgical purposes in the Church—baptisms, Chrismations (or Confirmations in the West), as well as anointing for healing.

Many Orthodox families keep their lampadas burning at all times as a way of remembering that God is always present, along with the unseen communion of saints, and that we are called to keep watch for the coming of the Lord. The lampadas that burn in the homes of many Orthodox bring to mind the ten virgins from Matthew 25:7, who must keep their wicks trimmed and their lamps full of oil in anticipation of the coming of the Bridegroom. These simple lampadas require only a minimal amount of care, but the very act of trimming the wicks and keeping the oil full can serve as a physical reminder of the continual sense of watchfulness that permeates a Christian's life of faith.

By creating icon corners, families are able to set aside a small sanctuary within their home. Many families place the icon corners in their dining rooms, saying prayer before meals while facing the icons. The icon corner serves as a constant reminder of unchanging heavenly realities, helping to transform the home from a mere dwelling place to a place of holiness, hospitality, and peace.

Mary Gardens

After inviting Mary into our homes, we might also consider inviting her into our yards. Gardens are particularly appropriate places for remembering God because according to the book of Genesis, the world began in a garden.

The Garden of Eden was originally a place of peace and harmony between man and woman, animals, and every type of plant. Many gardeners say that working in the soil is a spiritual experience for them. By helping to nurture and order the natural world, we are able to participate in the living memory of that very first garden.

symbolism

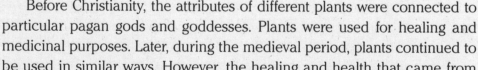

The early Church Fathers made a connection between Eden and Mary. Saint John Chrysostom wrote about a parallel between the soil of Eden, which blossomed without any seed, and Mary, who gave birth without the seed of man. According to Saint John Chrysostom, in Hebrew Eden means "Virgin Soil."

Before Christianity, the attributes of different plants were connected to particular pagan gods and goddesses. Plants were used for healing and medicinal purposes. Later, during the medieval period, plants continued to be used in similar ways. However, the healing and health that came from them became separated from their earlier associations with pagan deities, and came to be increasingly associated with the Virgin Mary.

Renaming the Flowers

When devotion to Mary was widespread, hundreds of flowers were renamed for her, each calling to mind a particular event, story, or characteristic. Marigolds were known as Mary's Gold, periwinkles were called Virgin Flower, forget-me-nots were called eyes of Mary, and bluebells of Scotland were called Our Lady's Thimble. During the Reformation many of these flowers lost their Marian folk names. Currently, flowers like "lady's slipper" are rooted in Marian devotion, but the flowers have become separated from their history.

One flower has a particularly interesting reason for its name. It is called milk thistle because of a legend that the white spots on its leaves were caused when the Virgin Mary dripped a little of her breast milk upon the plant. The naming of this flower suggests that Christians weren't afraid of Mary's earthiness.

According to the English writer Hepworth Dixon, the connection between Mary and flowers is quite strong. He writes, "We have made her the patroness of all our flowers. The Virgin is our Rose of Sharon, our Lily of the Valley. The poetry no less than the piety of Europe has ascribed to her the whole bloom and coloring of the fields and hedges."

Mary as a Garden

The Virgin Mary is not only historically and spiritually connected to individual breeds of flowers, she is also occasionally thought of as a garden. A particularly strong association was made between her and the garden mentioned in the Song of Solomon, "A garden enclosed is my sister, my spouse; a spring shut up a fountain enclosed" (Song of Solomon 4:12).

This garden imagery referred to Mary's ever-virginity. According to Roman Catholic and Eastern Orthodox tradition, her womb opened only once to bring Christ into the world. Because of this, medieval artistic renderings of the Virgin Mary show her in enclosed gardens, surrounded by many of the flowers that were associated with her attributes.

According to another legend, when the three magi came to the cave bearing gifts for the infant Christ, they discovered chrysanthemums blooming just beside the cave's opening. They picked a bouquet of them and presented them to the new mother with their gold, frankincense, and myrrh.

The tradition of Mary gardens is quite ancient. In the fourth century, Saint Benedict had a rosary, or a monastic rose garden. A few centuries later, in the seventh century, the Irish patron saint of gardening, Saint Fiacre, cared for a Marian garden dedicated to Mary that surrounded the small chapel and hospice for the poor and infirm. From the ninth century we have detailed records of "Assumption bundles," which were assorted flowers and plants that were taken to the church on the Feast of Assumption to be blessed, and then brought home.

The First Mary Garden

The first record of a garden that was actually referred to by the title "Mary Garden" is located in a fifteenth-century monastic accounting record from Norwich priory, England, which details the purchase of plants for a Mary Garden.

discussion question

What was the first flower named for Mary?
The earliest record of a flower named after Mary is Seint Mary Gouldes, or marigold, which was included in a recipe of a plant-based medication used for treating illness.

The connection between the Virgin Mary and flowers seemed to grow with time. According to records from the thirteenth century, Saint Francis of Assisi was extremely careful when walking because he didn't want to step on any flowers—for him, each of them represented the Virgin Mary, and he couldn't bear to stomp on her image.

By the fifteenth century, the Flemish and French *Book of Hours* included images of symbolic flowers associated with the Virgin Mary. Medieval artistic depictions of Mary show her surrounded by plants and animals, as well as many of the flowers that were symbolically associated with her.

In the twelfth and thirteenth centuries, the Christian mystic Hildegard of Bingen wrote beautifully about the Virgin Mary and flowers, "O Branch, God foresaw your flowering on the first day of his creation. You are the shining lily. You point before all creation where God fixes his gaze."

Mary Gardens Today

In recent years, some Americans have sought to revive the tradition of creating Mary Gardens. In 1951 John Stokes Jr. and the late Edward A. G. McTague were inspired to start a nonprofit organization called Mary's Gardens of Philadelphia after reading an article about a Mary Garden at Saint Joseph's Church in Woods Hole, Cape Cod, Massachusetts, which was originally planted in 1932 by Frances Crane Lillie around a statue of the Virgin Mary.

factum

Traditional paintings of the Annunciation from Florence often show the angel Gabriel presenting a lily to the Virgin Mary. Paintings from Siena do not use the lily imagery because Siena was historically the rival of Florence. In paintings from Siena, the angel Gabriel offers Mary an olive branch instead.

Mary's Gardens of Philadelphia, Pennsylvania, has been operating since its inception. This organization is dedicated to researching the vast, international varieties of plants with Marian associations, as well as helping to distribute information about the history of Mary Gardens. It is also committed to providing a wealth of practical information for those seeking to create their own Mary Gardens. Visit Mary's Gardens of Philadelphia online at *www.mgardens.org*.

Creating Your Own Mary Garden

Mary gardens are extremely versatile. They can be created in yards, on porches in small planters, or on windowsills. They are usually made up of at least a few varieties of flowers that have historical associations with the Virgin Mary, and in most cases, the flowers surround a small stone, wood, or ceramic statue of Mary. Some Mary gardens incorporate fragrant herbs that would have been used in medieval monastic gardens, while others incorporate small pools.

symbolism

Those who pray the rosary in their Mary Gardens use the white flowers for meditating upon the joyful mysteries, the purple and red flowers for meditating upon the sorrowful mysteries, and the gold and yellow flowers for meditating upon the glorious mysteries.

Three ideal flowers to incorporate into a Mary garden are roses, lilies, and irises. Each of these has symbolic ties to the Virgin Mary. Of all flowers, roses are the most closely linked to the Virgin Mary. She has dozens of titles directly linked to roses, and the image on the Tilma of Guadalupe was reportedly created through the Virgin Mary's careful arrangement of Castilian roses on Juan Diego's cloak.

These gardens offer a quiet place for peaceful reflection and prayer. Those who tend Mary Gardens feel that the work of nurturing the gardens helps them to remain attentive to the mysteries of faith. Some people even pray the rosary using the flowers in their gardens instead of rosary beads.

There are Mary Gardens located at the National Shrine of the Immaculate Conception in Washington, D.C., as well as at the University of Dayton in Ohio. There are also Mary Gardens located at some monasteries in America, as well as at several Catholic parishes. They provide a wonderful opportunity for education and spiritual growth within a community.

Mary and the Hour of Death

Many prayers make a connection between the Virgin Mary and death. The Gospel of John places the Virgin Mary at the cross with Mary (the wife of Cleopas) and Mary Magdalene. Mary's placement at the cross where her son died has also been a common theme in Western art, especially much-loved images of the Pieta, which show the Virgin Mary with a look of anguished sorrow on her face while holding Christ in her arms just after he died.

A Unique Experience of Grief

Because many believe that the Virgin Mary witnessed her son's death on the cross, it has been widely believed that her experience gave her unique insights into the experience of grief, loss, and death. Her presence at the cross has given Christians reason to turn to her both when facing the loss of a loved one and at their own final hour. This is especially true for parents who have lost a child, who have sometimes found strength and solace in the example of the Virgin Mary.

The famous philosopher Søren Kierkegaard wrote about the Virgin Mary in his journal. In one passage he described how both Christ and Mary had to suffer in Christ's death. According to Kierkegaard, the sword that was to pierce Mary's heart in the Gospels was not just related to her experience of watching her son die, but was also related to her son's experience of feeling abandoned by God when he was on the cross. According to Kierkegaard, the sword could be connected to the words Christ said from the cross, "My God, My God why have you forsaken me" (Matthew 27:46).

This feeling of being utterly abandoned by God was clearly experienced by Christ, and may have been experienced by his mother as well. Certainly this feeling is common among those who grieve the loss of a loved one.

Nightfall

According to Church tradition, there is a connection between Mary, Saint Simeon (who, as noted in Chapter 8, prophesied to Mary that a sword would pierce her heart), and the hour of death. Evening prayers in both Eastern and Western churches often quote the words Simeon spoke just after the infant Christ was brought to the Temple for dedication, "Lord you have now set your servant free to go in peace as you have promised, for my eyes have seen the Savior of the world a light to the gentiles and the glory of your people, Israel." This statement was not connected to Simeon leaving the temple so much as it was to Simeon leaving this world. According to a prophecy he would not die until his own eyes had seen the Savior. The placement of this passage in the Western Compline services and the Eastern Orthodox Vespers service draws a connection between nightfall and death.

factum

The ancient Christians believed that every night was a trial run for their own deaths, and that the darkness of night represented the fearfulness of the unknown and death.

Christians have held the belief that each night is a practice run for the final laying down of arms, in which we die in this world and wake in the next. Christians have also often referred to faithfully departed as those who "have fallen asleep."

This idea serves as a reminder that death is more like sleep than a final condition. Within the Eastern Church, the feast of the Dormition, the Virgin Mary's "falling asleep," is celebrated on August 15. (This is another name for the feast more commonly called the Assumption in the West.)

The Rosary and the Hour of Death

The connection between Mary and the hour of death is also made explicit through the rosary. The last line of the rosary prayer is, "Holy Virgin Mary, Pray for us sinners, now and at the Hour of our deaths." This section of the rosary was added later to the original, Scriptural portion of prayer. This change probably occurred during the eleventh century, a time when infant mortality was high and lives were shorter. Death was an ever-present reality, and the need to incorporate petitions related to that unavoidable reality would have been great.

Even in our day, when death seems more far off, these words allow a person who prays the rosary to retain a continual attitude of prayer and to remember that life can end at any moment. As this awareness grows, so does one's sense of needing mercy. The Virgin Mary has been closely associated with mercy through the ages, and this association is particularly clear at the hour of death.

CHAPTER 17

Special Devotions

For many Christians, the idea of praying to Mary might sound inappropriate at best, and idolatrous at worst. However, for millions of Christians around the world, prayers to and with Mary have been an integral part of faith. Some Christians believe that honoring Mary is an essential component of honoring Christ. This chapter will explore the ways that Christians have integrated Marian prayers into their own lives, as well as discuss some of the dilemmas that surround these types of prayers.

To Christ Through Mary

One of the guiding principles of Marian prayers is that they must always find their end in Christ. The Virgin Mary was never intended to be an end herself, but only a path to God. From time to time, concerns have been expressed that some faithful members of the Church have become too focused in praying to Mary and neglected the larger, spiritual picture. The entire context of worship, which is profoundly focused on the person of Christ and his role in the Trinity, in both the Roman Catholic and Eastern Orthodox Churches can help direct the focus of believers and clarify any confusion surrounding Marian prayer.

Complicated Prayer

One of the difficulties some have with idea of praying to Mary is related to the word *pray*. In contemporary usage, the word *pray* is almost always related to intercessions before God. However, if you've ever read Shakespeare, you've probably noticed that *pray* was once used differently as a synonym for *ask*. Similarly, some of the older texts can also be confusing in their use of the word *worship*. An example of this can be found in the marriage service in the old 1692 *Anglican Book of Common Prayer*. After the bride and groom exchanged their vows and as the rings were exchanged, the man would say, "With my body I thee worship." This statement expressed a pledge of honor and love rather than the kind of adoration which is due to God alone.

factum

Writer Jack Kerouac expressed his faith in Mary's prayers in a letter sent in 1963. "I had some stunning thoughts last night . . . as a result of praying to Saint Mary to intercede for me to make me stop being a maniacal drunkard," Kerouac wrote. "So far, every prayer addressed to the Holy Mother has been answered."

All Marian prayer finds its end in Christ. Throughout the centuries, there have been times when Marian prayer became especially pronounced because of historical circumstances. For example, Marian devotion was emphasized within the Roman Catholic Church during the seventeenth century when a distortion about Christ (that he was harsh and impossible to please) caused people to be afraid to pray to him.

One priest, Saint Louis de Mountfort, wanted to help his people learn to pray again, and he encouraged them to pray to Christ through Mary. At this time, especially, Mary seemed more accessible to some people than God. Rather than entirely halting their prayers, these people prayed through Mary to Christ.

Contemporary Devotion

Recently the Virgin Mary has become a subject of popular discussion. With the ever-increasing phenomenon of apparitions of Mary, many modern-day Christians have begun to reconsider her role in their own spirituality. Those who have developed a devotion to Mary testify that this devotion helps deepen, rather than distract from, their own relationship with Christ.

There has always been an important distinction (made in both the Roman Catholic and Eastern Orthodox Churches) between the type of honor given to Mary and the saints, and the honor that is reserved for God alone. In Greek, there are different words for the different types of honor:

- *Latria*
- *Dulia*
- *Hyperdulia*

Latria is the type of worship reserved for God alone, whereas *dulia* implies merely service and reverence. *Hyperdulia*, which is reserved for Mary, is an intensified form of *dulia*, which is commonly used to refer to all the saints.

The following methods of praying to and with Mary must be understood within these contexts. As the Protestant reformer Martin Luther said, "Mary doesn't ask that we come to her, but through her, to Jesus."

Pilgrimages

When Americans think of the term *pilgrim* they may think of the Mayflower and the Puritans. But historically, pilgrimages were not so much about escaping one's present circumstance as they were about growing spiritually and drawing closer to the past events that continue to shape the lives of the faithful. The pilgrimage concept is prominent in almost every world religion, including Christianity, Judaism, Islam, Hinduism, and Buddhism. Recently, as a response to readers' desires to travel in a more spiritually meaningful way, the online multi-faith publication *Beliefnet* began offering sacred tours to many different parts of the world.

One of the most popular pilgrimage sites continues to be the Holy Land, especially for Jews, Christians, and Muslims. This region has been much loved by pilgrims for millennia. Rich and poor, young and old, and healthy and sick have traveled great distances to walk in the footsteps of their spiritual ancestors.

fallacy

It is fallacy to believe that pilgrimages have only become popular in recent times. Pilgrimages to the Holy Land have been so common historically that by the fourth century, Saint Jerome wrote that so many pilgrims were pouring into the Holy Land that it felt almost as if the entire world were visiting.

In some cases, pilgrimages were very strenuous. The hardships along the way, however, only bolstered the spiritual value of the pilgrimage in the minds of the faithful. Some believed that by taking a difficult earthly journey to a faraway holy site, they were helping ease their transition into the next world. Three of the most popular ancient pilgrimage sites were Jerusalem, Rome, and Santiago de Compostela in Spain (because this city was believed to house the tomb of Saint James the apostle).

Pilgrimages continued to be popular through the eighteenth century, although during the Reformation some of the important European shrines, such as the House of Nazareth in Walsingham, were destroyed. When Catholics were again allowed to worship in England in 1827, much of Walsingham was restored, and an Anglican chapel was built on the site. Walsingham is now considered one of Europe's great ecumenical centers, and it continues to draw pilgrims.

Pilgrimages Today

Recently, pilgrimages have become increasingly common, and much of the current popularity is related to the widespread reports about apparitions of the Virgin Mary and healings associated with the places where she is reported to have appeared.

Marian shrines are visited by people of a wide variety of religious traditions. In some countries, such as Turkey (for a discussion of Mary's House at Ephesus, see Chapter 18) and India, shrines to Mary serve as a bridge between diverse cultures and religions that honor Mary. There are also special organizations that plan "interfaith" pilgrimages for those who would like to come into contact with Marian devotion outside of the boundaries of their own religion.

Seeking Mary

The increasing amount of media attention devoted to the apparitions of the Virgin Mary has helped the global community become aware of some of the most significant Marian shrines. Lourdes, France; Fatima, Portugal; and Vailankanni, India, continue to be popular Marian pilgrimage sites.

Appendix C contains a listing of many popular Marian pilgrimage sites. Also included is guidance about how to plan for a pilgrimage, times of year to visit, and general tips for those who are making a pilgrimage for the first time. If you are intrigued by a pilgrimage site that is not listed in the appendix, consider doing a simple search on the Internet. Most Marian pilgrimage sites have a wealth of online information devoted to them.

Dedications

Many Protestant denominations do not baptize infants. Some of these churches, however, devote services to the "dedication" of infants from the community to God. This idea echoes the Biblical story of Christ being dedicated in the temple as an infant (Luke 2:22–23). Within Christian tradition, it is also believed that the Virgin Mary was brought to the temple and dedicated as an infant.

factum

Even kings went on pilgrimages as a way to prepare for battle or to repent after they had ordered killings. After Thomas Becket, Archbishop of Canterbury, was murdered in Great Britain, Henry II took a pilgrimage as a penance.

This basic premise is helpful when we consider the practice that has been widespread in the Roman Catholic and Eastern Orthodox Churches of dedicating churches and monasteries to the prayers and memories of holy people.

The earliest examples of these dedications are shrines set up over the tombs of martyrs in the times when the imperial Roman authorities persecuted Christians. Even to this day, churches are often dedicated to a saint whose relics are placed within it.

That said, there was always a clear distinction made between the dedication of the church and the one to whom sacrifice was being made in the temple—sacrifice the Eucharist may be offered on behalf of many people, but it is offered only to God and never to a saint. Many times, people, and even whole nations, have been consecrated to the Virgin Mary. Correctly understood, all consecrations have their end in Jesus. Dedicating people or countries to Mary was seen as a way of placing them in the hands of God.

The Rosary

Saying the rosary is primarily a Catholic practice, although some Anglicans, Methodists, and Lutherans have been known to use the rosary as a way of integrating Marian prayer into their lives and contemplating different events from the life of Jesus. Although the practice of praying with beads or stones is quite ancient and is present in many religions, it has a unique role within Christianity.

Early Marian Prayer

Within Christianity, prayers to Mary have existed since at least the second century, and many of the earliest churches were dedicated to the Virgin Mary. The oldest known Marian prayer dates back to at least the fourth century and is still often sung in conjunction with bedtime prayer (the Compline service) in the Eastern Orthodox Church. This prayer is preserved in Greek on a piece of papyrus. The words of this prayer are: "Beneath your compassion, we take refuge, Mother of God. Do not reject our prayer in our necessities, but deliver us from harm, O pure and blessed One."

The rosary may be loosely related to the ancient Jesus Prayer, which is still used widely in the Eastern Orthodox Church. This kind of prayer became popular in early desert monasticism, and was explicitly mentioned by the fifth century when Diodochos of Photiki taught that repeating this prayer could lead to inner stillness.

In its most popular form, the words of the Jesus Prayer are: "Lord Jesus Christ, Son of God, have mercy on me, a sinner." Especially within monastic practice, a small prayer bracelet has been used for keeping count of prayers. This simple prayer is intended to be repeated over and over until it permeates all of life's decisions, thoughts, and actions.

The Origins of the Rosary

According to one legend, the rosary in its present form may have originated with Saint Dominic de Guzman (1170–1221), the founder of the Dominican Order. This legend states that Saint Dominic's devotion to the rosary began as the result of a series of revelations from the Virgin Mary in which she revealed the rosary to him.

This pious legend, however, seems to have little basis in historical fact. The story originated with a Dominican named Alain de la Roche abound two hundred years after Saint Dominic's death. Although the practice of saying the rosary dates back to at least the ninth century, the present form of the rosary dates back to the fifteenth century. In 1562, Pope Pius V issued an official statement about the rosary, in which he detailed the fifteen mysteries that are to meditated upon as a person repeats the prayers of the rosary.

symbolism

According to one medieval legend, as a young monk said Hail Marys, the Virgin Mary was seen taking rosebuds from his lips. She then arranged the rosebuds into a garland and placed them upon her head. *Rosary* means garland or bouquet of roses.

Many believe that saying the rosary will bring them special protection. When the atomic bomb exploded in Hiroshima, Japan, there was a house located just eight blocks (one kilometer) from the spot where the bomb exploded. All of the other houses and buildings in the area were obliterated, and the church that was attached to the house was destroyed. The house, however, survived, along with the eight German Jesuit priests who lived there and prayed the rosary each day. Many scientists continue to be puzzled by the fact that not only did these men survive with only minor injuries, but they all lived many more years without developing radiation sickness or loss of hearing as a result of the exposure.

How the Rosary Works

The rosary is a chain, much like a necklace, of about fifty beads with a crucifix on the end. The beads are broken into sections of ten beads each that are called decades. The decades are separated by larger beads. Each decade corresponds to a different event in the life of Christ, which is taken from the Gospel accounts. Many Roman Catholics believe that the rosary helps them to draw close to Christ and Mary and to enter into the central events in the life of Christ—to effectively integrate these pivotal moments into their own lives.

factum

The expression "knock on wood" can be traced back to some of the more ancient, primitive rosaries, which used wooden beads. During anxious times, Christians would knock their wooden beads together. Many cultures have "worry beads," which are typically used for non-religious purposes, as a way to keep the hands occupied in times of anxiety.

Saying the Rosary

The first step in saying the rosary is to say the Apostles' Creed, a statement of faith that originated as a baptismal formula in ancient times. Then, for each special bead separating the decades, the Lord's Prayer is said, followed by ten recitations of the Hail Mary (one for each bead in the decade). Then, at the end of each decade, the mystery from the life of Christ is meditated upon. There are four different sets of mysteries that have been prescribed by popes to correspond with different days of the week. Each mystery corresponds to a different phase of Jesus' life. The first set of mysteries is related to the very beginning of Jesus' earthly life. It includes:

- The Annunciation
- The Visitation of Mary with Elizabeth
- The Nativity of Jesus
- The Presentation of Christ in the Temple
- The Finding of Jesus in the Temple

The second set of mysteries is related to Jesus' public ministry. This set includes:

- Jesus' Baptism
- Jesus' First Miracle at Cana

- Jesus' Teaching Related to Repentance and the Kingdom
- The Transfiguration
- The Last Supper

The third set of mysteries is called the Sorrowful Mysteries. It includes:

- Jesus' Agony in the Gethsemane
- The Scourging of Jesus
- The Crowning of Jesus with Thorns
- Jesus' Carrying of the Cross
- The Crucifixion and Death of Jesus

The fourth set is referred to as the Glorious Mysteries. It includes:

- Jesus' Resurrection
- Jesus' Ascension
- The Coming of the Holy Spirit at Pentecost
- Mary's Assumption into Heaven
- The Coronation of Mary and Glory of All the Saints

In 2002, Pope John Paul II proposed an additional, fifth set of "Luminous Mysteries" for the rosary. This set includes:

- The Baptism of the Lord
- The Wedding at Cana
- The Proclamation of the Kingdom of God
- The Transfiguration
- The Institution of the Eucharist

Of these mysteries, some who pray the rosary may simplify their daily prayer by just selecting five mysteries for meditation. Different sets of mysteries may also be prescribed for different days.

discussion question

What is the Hail Mary based on?
The Hail Mary is based on the words from the Annunciation (Luke 1:26–38): "Hail Mary, full of grace, the Lord is with you. Blessed art thou among women, and blessed is the fruit of thy womb, Jesus. Holy Mary, Mother of God, pray for us sinners now and at the hour of our death."

According to Roman Catholic teaching, it is extremely important to pray the rosary in a way that is consistent, intentional, prayerful, and meditative. According to Pope Paul IV, if Catholics do not take time to ponder each mystery with awe, the rosary loses much of its power. It becomes "a body without a soul" and "a mechanical repetition of formulas, counter to the warning of Christ, who said, 'in praying do not heap up empty phrases as the Gentiles do; for they think that they will win a hearing by their many words'" (Pope Paul IV, *Marialis Cultus* 47, citing Matthew 6:7).

Scapulars

Scapulars originated as aprons worn by medieval monks. They were basically large swaths of cloth with a hole for the head, used to protect the monastic habit while the monk was doing manual labor. While scapulars originally had a largely practical function, over time various spiritual meanings became attached to them. In some Roman Catholic orders, they are now considered the most spiritually significant part of the monastic habit.

Saint Simon Stock

One of the traditions associated with the brown scapular of Our Lady of Mount Carmel involves a thirteenth-century saint, Saint Simon Stock, who asked for the Virgin Mary to intercede for his order. According to the story, the Virgin Mary appeared to him in Cambridge, England, on July 16, 1251, with the scapular and offered these words, "Take, beloved son, this scapular of thy order as a badge of my confraternity and for thee and all Carmelites a special sign of grace; whoever dies in this garment will not suffer everlasting fire. It is a sign of salvation, a safeguard in dangers, a pledge of peace of the covenant."

Power and Use of Scapulars

It is a fallacy to ascribe magical powers to scapulars, rosaries, or any other sacred object. Likewise, it is against official Roman Catholic Church doctrine to believe that wearing a brown scapular is a "ticket to heaven." Instead, the scapular is considered a way of dedicating oneself to Jesus and Mary and asking for the ongoing prayers of the Virgin Mary while wearing the scapular. There is an important distinction between magical and sacramental—a sacramental object possesses no power of its own, but is effective through participation in the mystery of Christ.

Scapulars are no longer reserved exclusively for monastic use. Catholics can now obtain smaller versions of the original scapulars. These modified versions look like two strips of cloth that hang over the shoulders with a small square pendant attached on each end. Scapulars are generally connected to specific monastic orders, with lay use being restricted to those associated with that order in a formal way. Those who wear them should be sensitive to the particular intentions of the community in which the particular scapular evolved.

The Use of Scapulars

In lay use, scapulars are to be warn inconspicuously under one's clothing and are often (but not always) made of wool. Laypeople must have their scapulars blessed by their priest, who will pray over the scapular and over the person who is to wear it. This service of dedication is known as the investment. Over time, scapulars wear out and can eventually be replaced with a silver pendant that has the face of Christ on one side and the face of the Virgin Mary on the other.

The scapular plays a significant role in the life of the person who wears it. If an unmarried person wears a scapular, they are expected to remain chaste. Of course, this is the case for all unmarried Catholics, but those who wear a scapular have a special level of accountability because of what they are wearing. The scapular serves as a reminder to continually strive to live a faithful life and to persevere until the end. Many who wear the scapular believe that it is a helpful reminder of God's loving care and protection, as well as a concrete way to remember that the Virgin Mary continually intercedes for them.

A Word for Protestants

Many of these devotional practices may seem foreign if you are not from a Roman Catholic or Orthodox background. Although Mary is an integral part of the worship and prayer life of these churches, the intercessions of the saints make up a small (but significant) portion of the whole spiritual life.

Especially for those who are not raised in these churches but come to them later in life, the veneration of Mary can be a great struggle. As prominent Roman Catholic writer Fr. Richard John Neuhaus wrote in a forward to the book *Mary: A Catholic-Evangelical Debate*, "For many of us who entered into full communion with the Catholic Church later in life, Marian doctrine and devotion was at one time a problem. I daresay that for most of us, and certainly for me, Marian doctrine and devotion has become an exciting and never-ending discovery of deeper dimensions of Christian fidelity."

Many who find their way into the Roman Catholic and Eastern Orthodox Churches later in life find that encountering Mary is a long process that continually calls them to leave behind their own contemporary assumptions about her and to grow and transform as they come to know Mary as she has been loved through the ages.

Pope Paul IV wrote, "When the liturgy turns its gaze either to the primitive Church or to the Church of our day it always finds Mary. In the primitive Church she is seen praying with the apostles; in our own day, she is actively present and the Church desires to live the mystery of Christ with her" (from his statement, *Marialis Cultus*, 1974).

This ancient Christian belief that Mary is present in the Church both yesterday and today is demonstrated through the ongoing devotional practices associated with her. Contemporary Christians, however, may be tempted to dismiss many of these more ancient practices as superfluous, belonging to another place and time. But it is best to retain a respectful silence until one has the opportunity to grasp the deeper idea behind the practice. C. S. Lewis described the temptation to dismiss the beliefs and practices from other times as "chronological snobbery."

Especially within the ever-evolving Christian world, we may be inclined to think in terms of an ongoing revelation where the faithful are always growing closer to the truth. We may imagine that from our place in history we know more than those who went before us. But according to Lewis, this kind of thinking is a grave error. While it can be equally dangerous to believe the opposite fallacy—that all that is ancient is somehow right or superior—it is certainly wise to listen to the voices of those who have gone before us and to see if their experiences might speak to and enrich our own spiritual lives. This is especially important when we think about how Christians in earlier times expressed their faith and their devotion to the saints.

CHAPTER 18

Mary and Islam

Some people are surprised to discover that the Virgin Mary is esteemed within Islam. One of the longest chapters of the Muslim Holy Book, the Koran, is devoted to Mary (Miriam, or *Maryam* in Arabic). For centuries, Muslims have visited Marian shrines, witnessed apparitions, and named their female children after Maryam, who, according to the Koran, achieved a level of perfection that no other woman attained.

Common Ground

In our day it is increasingly important to find common ground on which people from a variety of religious traditions can communicate. This is a particularly urgent concern in light of the current tensions between Christianity and Islam. It is often a struggle to find a common language and terminology between the two religions, but many scholars believe that the common ground can be found through Mary, who is loved and venerated within both religions, although many aspects of devotion to Mary in Islam do not parallel the way she is venerated within Christianity.

factum

There are currently about one billion professed Muslims in the world who adhere to the teachings and ritual observances set forth in their sacred book, the Koran, and elucidated by their prophet, Muhammad. They refer to God as Allah and reject the Christian understanding of the Trinity.

Islam was founded on the Arabian Peninsula during the seventh century and is based on the revelations of Allah to Muhammad. The Prophet Muhammad taught that Islam was the final religion, building upon and perfecting the teachings of the prophets who went before: Abraham, Moses, and Jesus.

This common story begins to diverge when Abraham becomes the father of two sons, Ishmael and Isaac. One of the most heartbreaking and beautiful stories in the Jewish and Christian tradition is the story of Abraham, who (according to the Old Testament) was told to sacrifice his son Isaac, whom he dearly loved. In the Old Testament account, Abraham and Isaac travel to Moriah for the sacrifice.

Isaac carries wood on his back and notes with some concern that they've got the wood, they've got the fire, but "where is the lamb for the offering?" You can almost hear Abraham sigh when he replies, "God himself will provide a lamb." In the end, God does just as Abraham has promised, but not in the way that Abraham had imagined—he prevents Abraham from killing Isaac and he provides a ram caught in a nearby thicket instead.

The Koran does not explicitly state which son was to be sacrificed, but according to most Islamic commentators, it is Ishmael, Abraham's son by Hagar, who is chosen for the sacrifice. Just as Abraham lowers the dagger to sacrifice Ishmael, the dagger turns to wax in his hand, and God prevents the sacrifice. Like the Old Testament account, God provides a ram in Ishmael's stead.

According to Islamic belief, Ishmael went on to become "the Father of all Arabs," the first Prophet to preach and write of the one true God, and the first to practice his prayers in a worthy manner. Ishmael's prominent status within Islam is especially interesting because the Old Testament account doesn't offer too many details about what ultimately happened to Ishmael after he and Hagar were sent away.

discussion question

What ultimately happened to Ishmael?
According to Genesis 21:18 when Sarah mistreats Hagar and Hagar departs for the first time, God tells Hagar that Ishmael will be the father of a great nation. When Abraham dies, Ishmael returns and reports that he has become the father of twelve sons who reside east and north of Egypt. This geographical location is in present-day Saudi Arabia.

While most countries have a significant Muslim presence, many of the countries of Western Europe have been experiencing particularly rapid growth in their Muslim populations. Muslims make up a majority of the population of the Middle East, North Africa, and Indonesia. Because of the increasingly large Muslim population worldwide, it is helpful to have at least a working understanding of this global religion.

Mary in the Koran

According to Islamic belief, the Koran is the word of God, revealed to Muhammad through a series of visitations from the Angel Jibreel (or Gabriel), which took place over a period of twenty-three years. Muhammad memorized many of these revelations and they were subsequently written down by his successors: Abu Bakr, Omar, and Othman. Islamic teachers have taught that the complete Koran existed in heaven before the Angel Jibreel revealed it to Muhammad. The Koran was completed by A.D. 656.

Even the original story of how Islam was founded holds within it some fascinating parallels between the Virgin Mary and Muhammad. According to Islamic thought, both Muhammad and the Virgin Mary were visited by the Angel Gabriel. Both were told that they would become bearers of the word of God, responsible for bringing messages of great significance into the world. Within Islam, Christ is viewed as both prophet and messenger, but not as the Son of God.

symbolism

The word *Islam* means "submission," and Muslims are those who submit to God. Mary is praised within the Koran for her obedience to God. It may be through Mary's perfect obedience that she is seen as a model of submission.

One of the most significant differences between Christian and Islamic teachings on the persons of Mary and Jesus are related to the Christian title Theotokos, or Mother of God, which is a term never used in Islam because Muslims do not believe that Jesus was God incarnate. Another significant difference is that Muslims do not believe that Jesus was actually crucified, only that he appeared to be crucified. Islam also objects to the use of religious imagery, so the portrayal of the Virgin Mary in icons has been rejected by Islamic teachers.

This initial parallel between the two accounts may help clarify why Mary holds a significant position within Islam. Many scholars have noted that the portrait of Mary in the Koran is more vibrant and detailed than the portraits in the Gospels. No other woman in the Koran has an entire chapter named after her, not even two extremely significant women—Eve, who is considered within Islam, Judaism, and Christianity to be "the mother of all living"

(Genesis 3:20), or Hagar, the mother of Ishmael, who was to become "the Father of all Arabs." The Virgin Mary offers a pivotal position in the text, and many references are made about her and her life.

According to the Koran, Mary's perfection began from the moment of her conception. Although this idea seems to echo the Roman Catholic Dogma of the Immaculate Conception, it should be noted that Muslims to do not believe in the Immaculate Conception. They do not ascribe to the same perspective on Original Sin, although they, like the Catholics and Eastern Orthodox do believe that Mary's special grace began at her conception.

The Koran also supports the idea of the virgin birth of Christ, and offers some details about Mary's early life that are not mentioned in the Gospels but clearly parallel some of the details given in some of the extra-Biblical texts.

Some Christian scholars have said that the contrast between the Gospels and the Koran is that the Koran seems to exalt Mary, while the New Testament is generally restrained in its attitude toward Mary. This may be reflective of the intention of the Gospel writers to emphasize the life and teachings of Jesus.

According to Christian belief, the central moment in the life of Mary occurred at the Annunciation, when she said "yes" to God. This moment is significant enough that it also occupies a prominent space in the Koran, which offers many parallel events with variations on the details from Luke's Gospel.

The Annunciation in the Koran

The Koran, like the Gospel of Luke, portrays Mary as fearful when the angel initially comes to her. Both accounts show the angel offering comfort and reassurance. In the Koran the angel says, "I am but a messenger, come from thy Lord to give thee a boy most pure" (19:19).

Like the Gospel accounts of the Annunciation, Mary responds with uncertainty, "How shall I have a son whom no mortal has touched, neither have I been unchaste?"

The angel's response both parallels and diverges from the Gospel accounts. "Even so thy Lord has said: Easy it is for me; and that we may appoint him as a sign unto men and a mercy from us; it is a thing decreed" (19:21).

The angel's response is especially interesting, because it shows where Muslim and Christian thought diverge in relation to Jesus. In Luke's Gospel, Mary is told that the Holy Spirit will overshadow her and she shall conceive the son of God. This statement is never made in the Koran. This significant omission speaks to the different views between Islam and Christianity about the person of Jesus.

The House of Imran

The House of Imran is a traditional title for one of the surahs, or books, of the Koran. It is named after Mary's father, Imran, whose name can be translated into English as John. This might be a little confusing for English speakers who are used to referring to Mary's father as Joachim, if they speak of him at all.

This chapter offers some fascinating ideas about Mary's conception and early childhood. Some Christian scholars have suggested that it may have been influenced by some of the extra-Biblical stories of Jesus' life that were common at the time. There is some evidence that suggests Muhammad had contact with Christians who would have been familiar with this kind of material. Like the Koran, many of these accounts give an exuberant, detailed account of Mary's conception and early childhood.

factum

> Muslims sometimes refer to Christians and Jews as "People of the Book." This statement affirms the common heritage of these three faiths, which all claim fidelity to the God who spoke to Abraham and Moses.

In this surah, when Mary's mother Anna conceived a child, Anna responded with great joy. When she dedicated her child to Allah, she must have imagined that he was to be a boy and that he had a bright future ahead of him as a religious teacher or scholar. But when the child was born, she was shocked to see that she had given birth to a baby girl. Anna expresses her disappointment but then goes on to say that "Allah knows best," and commends her child, as well as her child's future offspring to Allah's protection.

According to the Koran, Allah honors Anna's unusual request, and allows Mary to be raised in the temple and fed by angels. Mary is given to the care of Zachariah. Zachariah is also mentioned in the Gospels as the husband of Elizabeth, and as a priest.

As Mary matures in age, she also matures in virtue. When Zachariah comes to visit her in the temple, he is consistently surprised to see that food has been miraculously provided for Mary. This miraculous provision possibly echoes Old Testament stories about "manna from heaven" and further sets Mary apart as one who is special in the eyes of Allah.

Mary among the Shiites

The Shiite branch of Islam is the second largest. According to the Shiites, Mary is more than a holy woman. Shiite belief has created some interesting parallels between Mary and Fatima (who was the daughter of the Prophet Muhammad). Although the Koran denies that Jesus was crucified, Fatima's two sons were assassinated. Both Mary and Fatima are considered "suffering mothers." Also, just as Islamic belief puts forth the idea that Jesus was born of a virgin, within the Koran, Fatima, the wife of Ali, is also a virgin when she conceives her two sons. Another interesting parallel between Fatima and Mary is that within this tradition, Fatima comes over time to be viewed as "the protector of the persecuted."

Mary among the Sufis

Sufism is commonly considered the "mystical path" of Islam. Within Sufism, there is strong emphasis both on contemplation and action. One of the accounts of Mary from the Koran offers a text that seems to express something valuable about Sufism. In this text, Mary goes to a far-off place to give birth. While she is lamenting her condition, Allah instructs her to shake a palm tree so that ripe figs will fall to the ground for her.

Some have interpreted this passage to mean that not only must we pray, but we must be active as well. This idea is very much relevant to Sufism. Within Sufism, Mary is a model of the contemplative and active life. As George H. Tavard wrote in *The Thousand Faces of the Virgin Mary*, this passage is "an invitation to work actively rather than just wait for Allah to do something. Thus Miriam [which is Mary's name in the Koran] is a model of obedience and action in the service of Allah, no less than of faith, prayer and contemplation." According to Tavard, in Mary, the Sufis find inspiration, because her life was a clear expression of both obedience and action.

Healing Fountains

Another area of common ground between historical Judaism, Christianity and Islam is the ways in which all three religions "of the Book" relate to water. All three share a sensitivity to the theological significance of water, and water has been present in many significant rituals belonging to each of these religions.

They all teach that water was one of the principal elements in the creation of the world. All three understood that both life and death come through water and that we are inextricably dependant upon God (or Allah) to provide water for us.

Water in Judaism

Within Judaism, water is present in many rituals, most notably the purifying ritual bath called the mikvah, which is prescribed for women seven days after menstruation. The waters used in the mikvah must come from a natural, free-flowing source and must not have been carried by human hands. Women immerse themselves in the Mikvah not only to become ritually pure, but also as way of being spiritually renewed and cleansed before they return to their husbands, following a period of about two weeks of abstinence.

Within Judaism, hands are ritually washed as part of preparation for the Shabbat, or "Sabbath" meal, which begins at sundown on Friday. Within

Christianity, water plays an equally profound role. Christians are initiated into the faith by immersing themselves (or being sprinkled by) the waters of baptism, which also offer cleansing and renewal. Clergy in the Roman Catholic, Eastern Orthodox, and Anglican Churches ritually wash their hands before they consecrate the Eucharist.

symbolism

Within Christianity, water is deeply connected with Christ, who walked on water, promised to the woman at the well that he contained "the living waters," and when, according to Christian teaching, he was stretched upon the cross and a sword pierced his side, both blood and water flowed from him.

Water in Islam

Within Islam, water is also of central importance—offering life, sustenance, and purification. According to the Koran, water existed before heaven or earth (this belief brings to mind the Genesis account where the Spirit of God hovers over the water at the creation of the world).

The Koran recognizes the essential value of water for life and the way our relationship to water reminds us of our utter dependence upon the mercy of God. According to the Koran, "He sends down saving rain, for them, when they have lost all hope and spreads abroad his mercy" (Al-Furqan 25:48).

Ritual Cleansing

Within Islam, water is not only considered a principal element of life but is also an essential aspect of ritual purity. Within observant Islam, the faithful pray at five appointed times daily. Each call to prayer begins with a ritual washing, as described in the Koran, "O you who believe, when you rise to pray, wash your faces and your hands as far as the elbow, wipe your heads, and your feet to the ankle. If you are polluted cleanse yourselves . . . God does not wish to burden you but desires to purify you" (Al-Mai'dah 5:6).

Within Islam, a person who does not cleanse himself before prayer will have their prayers rejected. Like the Jewish prescription of a very specific natural source of water for the mikvah, Muslim teaching is specific about what water is acceptable for use in pre-prayer cleansing.

factum

Suitable water for cleansing before Muslim prayer must be pure (meaning that it can not be mixed with any other substances). Water from both moving sources such as rain, taps, streams, rivers, and still sources like lakes and ponds, may be used for ritual cleansing.

Because water holds such a significant place in all three religions, it is not surprising that within Islam, there is a connection between the Virgin Mary (or Miriam as she is referred to in the Koran) and water. According to the Koran, while Mary was in labor she took refuge under a palm tree and said, "Ah! Would that I had died before this! Would that I had been a thing forgotten and out of sight!" but a voice called to her from beneath the palm tree, "Do not anguish, for the Lord your God has created a rivulet beneath you, and shake toward yourself the trunk of the palm tree. It will let fall ripe dates upon you" (19:23–25).

This passage, which states that there will be a "rivulet" beneath her, is interesting in light of the role of water in stories about Mary. In another place in the Koran, it says that Jesus is born from the "waters of Mary." This is an allusion to the central role of water in birth.

According to the Christian tradition, Mary was at a well when the angel appeared to her. Also notable is the fact that many Marian shrines around the world contain water or wells that many believe contain healing properties. Because Mary holds a special place within Islam, Muslims often visit Marian shrines and drink of the wells. This is especially the case at the House of Mary in Ephesus, Turkey, a site that is arguably more often visited by Muslims than Christians.

The House of Mary

In Ephesus, Turkey, there is a small stone structure set high on a hill. This small structure is believed to be the place where Mary lived her final earthly days with the Apostle John. This tradition is partially based on the account from the Gospels when Jesus calls out to John from the cross to ask him to care for his mother. Christian tradition has taken these words to mean that John quite literally took Mary into his own home and cared for her until her dying day.

According to Christian tradition, John traveled to Ephesus after the death of Christ. It was very likely in this place that he made his home. Also, some say that the first known church dedicated to the Virgin Mary was located in Ephesus, and during the first few centuries of Christianity, churches were only named after saints in cities where that saint had personally resided. It is also notable that the most significant church council related to the title of the Virgin Mary was held at Ephesus in 431, where the name Theotokos was formally recognized as a proper way to refer to the Virgin Mary and to preserve the practice of venerating her.

Rediscovering the House of Mary

Another interesting story related to this house is that some Roman Catholic priests were led to this very site (which was then in ruins) through the revelations of a German Roman Catholic nun, Sister Catherine Anne Emmerich, who both experienced the stigmata and reported having visions of the Virgin Mary in which the exact location of the house at Ephesus was described. When the priests followed the directions set forth by the Roman Catholic nun, they quickly discovered a small stone building in the exact location and formation she had described.

This house has been preserved and is currently under the care of the Franciscans, a Roman Catholic order, and it receives more than a half a million visitors annually. Many of these visitors are Muslim, who come to the shrine to pray and to drink from the well there, which many believe contains healing properties.

Christian and Muslim Pilgrimage

Pilgrims often like to leave something of themselves behind at holy pilgrimage sites to show that they have visited a place personally. In many cases, pilgrims will leave behind a small swath of cloth. At the House of Mary, though, there is no place to attach pieces of cloth, so thousands of pieces of chewing gum have been left behind by those who have prayed at the well.

The House of Mary in Ephesus is a very tangible reminder that Mary plays an important role in both Christianity and Islam. Not only do more Muslims visit this holy site than any other religious group, there is also a small chapel that is part of the house and is reserved for Muslim prayer.

The image of Christians and Muslims praying beside each other at this holy site has profound implications for those who only see the areas where Islam and Christianity diverge, who focus on the very real tensions between the two religions without taking note of the authentic common ground. If there is any common ground within Christianity and Islam, a place of peace and prayer amid the tensions of our modern world it is most likely to be found in Ephesus, in the house where the Virgin Mary lived as a faithful model for both religions.

Important Distinctions

Although much has been made of similarities between Marian thought within Christianity and Islam, it is important to note that there are significant differences. Earlier in this chapter it was mentioned that the Muslims do not believe in the Immaculate Conception. This difference means that Muslims have a radically different view of the fall that occurred in the Garden of Eden. They do not share the Roman Catholic perspective that sin was passed on to all through conception but that the Virgin Mary was the exception to this rule. Likewise, within Islam, the Virgin Mary was never viewed as "a second Eve" as she often is in the writings of the church fathers.

It is also important to realize that although the Koran does teach that the Virgin Mary was a virgin, her virginal conception is viewed as just one of the miracles associated with her. There is no special spiritual significance attached to the fact that she was a virgin.

factum

Because of the idea of total dedication to God, celibacy has often been understood as a "foretaste of the kingdom" within Christian tradition. Islam (and most forms of Judaism as well) does not share this perspective and has no special theology surrounding celibacy.

It is also important to realize that the Virgin Mary is just one among many models of female holiness within Islam. Most of the models of female holiness were not celibate but married, such as the Prophet Muhammad's first wife Khadija, his daughter Fatima, and Asiya (who was the wife of the pharaoh in the story of Moses). Of these women, only one of them was unmarried.

Although the Virgin Mary is seen as a model within Islam, Fatima, Muhammad's daughter, is sometimes viewed as "the greater Mary." Some Christian commentators, however, have noted with interest that some of the most significant apparitions of the Virgin Mary of all time occurred at Fatima, Portugal, a name that is especially significant to Muslims. Likewise, Fatima is sometimes referred to as the Mother of Sorrows, a name that has also been ascribed to the Virgin Mary within Catholicism, because she is viewed as the patron saint of all who grieve.

Although it is valuable to explore the common ground between Christianity and Islam, a respectful dialogue between the two religions requires an honest assessment of the distinctions between Christianity and Islam. Some important differences exist in the way Mary is venerated in each tradition. Nevertheless, a common respect for Mary may well be an important bridge between the world's two largest religions.

CHAPTER 19

Mary and the Goddess

Although the Virgin Mary was never considered a goddess in the Eastern or Western Churches, her image reflects many of the goddesses from ancient religions. If the Virgin Mary seems similar to these goddesses, it is because within Christianity there are elements borrowed from ancient religions. This chapter will explore the similarities, as well as the differences, between the Virgin Mary and a variety of goddesses from ancient religions.

Baptizing the Goddess?

Historically, there has been some tension between ancient pagan religions and Christianity, and this surfaces in certain legends about the Virgin Mary. These legends, whether they are historically accurate or not, offer an interesting glimpse into the mindset of the early Christians, who responded to the interplay between Mary and the goddesses with a good deal of caution. In most of these tales, Christianity proclaims itself to be the fulfillment of everything that was good about the earlier pagan beliefs.

Christian Parallels

Although Christianity was built on the foundation of Judaism, it was not isolated from ancient pagan beliefs or the ideas of the ancient philosophers. There are many parallels between Christianity and other, more ancient religions. One way these parallels come out is through iconography. Christian iconography has many stylistic parallels, both in Roman (pre-Christian) Egypt, in the neighboring religions of the Ancient Near East, and in Hinduism and Buddhism. The way Christianity adapted these and other forms of religious art, teaching, and practice is significant and speaks also to what is unique within Christianity.

Many historians have pointed to a resemblance between the Virgin Mary shown in Eastern Orthodox iconography and the ancient goddess Isis. Likewise, even today, some Greek churches have icons of the ancient philosophers just inside the front entrance of their churches. According to Greek belief, the teachings of these philosophers helped prepare the minds of the people to receive Christianity.

One of the ancient legends about the Virgin Mary vividly expresses the tension between pagan religion and Christian belief. This legend is related to the Greek peninsula called Mount Athos, or the Holy Mountain. Mount Athos is a secluded, forested place where over 3,000 monks reside in twenty large monasteries.

Although Mount Athos is now seen as a great Christian center of monasticism, it was not always specifically Christian, but it was historically viewed as a deeply spiritual place. One of the great authors of Greek mythology, Homer, mentioned this mountain in his writings as one of the dwelling places of the Greek gods Zeus and Apollo before they moved to Mount Olympus.

According to this legend, because of the sacred history associated with Mount Athos, pagan hermits once inhabited the local caves. In A.D. 49 the Virgin Mary was sailing to visit her friend Lazarus, when her boat lost course. She was divinely led to a safe bay of Mount Athos. As she approached the mountain she looked up and according to legend, said, "This mountain is holy ground. Let this be my portion. Let me here remain."

As she stepped onto shore, a thunderous crash shook the mountain and the statues from the old pagan shrines toppled over. One of the statues declared that he was a false idol. According to this legend, the Virgin Mary then baptized the pagan hermits living on the mountain. Thus began the Christian history of Mount Athos, although Mount Athos did not become a well-known monastic site until many centuries later.

The Holy Mountain has since become the greatest monastic center in the Eastern Christian world. According to legend, the Virgin Mary was the last woman to ever set foot on the mountain. To this day, women are not allowed to visit the monasteries on Mount Athos, although they are welcome to visit sister monasteries located nearby.

factum

Just as the story of Mount Athos describes a loud thundering sound that caused the statues to topple, there is a well-documented earthquake that took place in Northern Greece in A.D. 49, the same year that, according to legend, the Virgin Mary visited Athos.

Architecture and Integration

Monasteries, churches, and shrines to Mary are often built on sites that were once central within ancient religions. This desire to build on the literal foundations of other religions expresses the ways in which Christianity sought to integrate those elements of the more ancient religions that were compatible with Christianity.

By building churches, shrines, or monasteries on these ancient holy sites, the Church was able to "baptize" certain elements of these ancient religions, as well as provide a bridge and a sense of continuity between the two religions.

One of the most interesting examples of a Christian church being built on a site that was already viewed as sacred within the minds of the local people occurred in Mexico during the visitations of Our Lady of Guadalupe. According to reports of this apparition, when the Virgin Mary appeared to Juan Diego, she requested that a church be built on a hill that was viewed as one of the dwelling places of an ancient Aztec goddess.

Another place where a similar phenomenon occurred was in the ancient city of Ephesus, Turkey. Ephesus was one of the ancient centers of worship of the goddess Diana, but it ultimately became a significant city for Christianity as well.

The New Testament book of Ephesians was written as a letter to the Christians dwelling there. Christianity had had a rocky start in Ephesus, however, because of the prominence of the goddess Diana in that location. When Paul preached in Ephesus, the metal workers who created statues of Diana heckled him, because they feared that if he brought Christianity to Ephesus, they would lose their livelihoods. Ultimately, their worst fears were realized, as Ephesus eventually became home to many Christians.

The temple dedicated to Diana was destroyed in about A.D. 400. Soon afterward, a new church was built in Ephesus, which was the first church dedicated to the Virgin Mary. When the Council at Ephesus declared in A.D. 431 that it would be right and proper to call the Virgin Mary Theotokos, those in the streets responded with enthusiasm. Just as they had once marched through the streets singing the praises of Diana, they now shouted, "Praised be the Theotokos."

The title Theotokos, which can be translated as "God-bearer" or "The One Who Gave Birth to God" connected Mary to the divine in a unique way. Yet, it was also at this council that official statements were made about how Mary was supposed to be viewed—with great respect, love, and reverence, but not as an object of worship.

Parallels Between Mary and the Goddesses

Although she was not to be worshiped as a goddess, there are some strong parallels between Mary and some of the ancient goddesses. In many ways, the Virgin Mary fits the type of woman who is described in the tales of the ancient goddesses. Many of them are referred to as *parthenos*, which means "virgin." Many of these *parthenos* goddesses give birth to a child who is to suffer. Like Mary, they are impregnated by a divine being (or they become pregnant within themselves using their own supernatural powers). These goddesses are often shown holding this sacrificial child, an image that is certainly familiar to those who have seen icons or statues of the Virgin Mary holding her infant Christ, who is destined to suffer for the whole world.

One of the images of the ancient goddess Isis seems to express this particularly well. The poet Lucius Apuleius's fictional story *The Golden Ass* includes the story of an apparition of Isis. In this story, a young man in distress runs to the seashore, prays to Isis, and falls asleep. While he is sleeping, he sees a gloriously beautiful woman rising from the sea before him with stars and a moon on her cloak. The woman begins to speak to him, telling him that she is the mother of all, and the queen of the dead and the immortals. She says that she is known by many names but her true name is Queen Isis and that she has come in response to his prayers. In this passage, the parallels between the Virgin Mary and the goddess Isis are startling.

In many depictions of the Virgin Mary, she has stars on her cloak, is often called Our Lady of the Sea, and is invoked to protect sailors. In this passage, Isis comes in response to intercessions, just as Mary is reported to sometimes come to those who seek her support in times of distress. The symbolism of the moon on Isis's cloak also speaks to the parallels between Isis and Mary—as Mary is also associated with the moon. In the Tilma of Guadalupe and the image of the woman from Revelations 12, she is shown standing upon the moon; and at the apparitions that occurred at Fatima and Medjugorje, lunar miracles are reported to have occurred.

Archetype of the Eternal Feminine

The renowned psychologist Carl Jung often talked about the archetypes that appear in the collective unconscious. Some have applied his "archetype of the eternal feminine" to the Virgin Mary in light of the psychological parallels between her role within Christianity and the role goddesses played in other religious contexts.

The Virgin Mary brought a female face to the Christian discussion of the divine. Although she was not a goddess, her exalted role within Christianity may have helped those who worked closely with the earth or worshipped goddesses to feel more at home within Christianity.

Another connection between Christianity and paganism is related to the dating of the great Christian feasts—Christmas and Easter. These holy days were set on days that had a universal cosmological significance and would have held a special meaning for the ancient pagans.

Christmas is commemorated just after the winter solstice, which is the darkest day of the year. As the hours of daylight begin to increase again, so also the light that comes into the world in Jesus begins our shift out of darkness. Similarly, the ancient formula for determining the time of Easter is to celebrate it on the first Sunday after the first full moon following the vernal (spring) equinox. At this time, spring is in full bloom, and life comes to reign again upon the earth.

symbolism

These lines from an ancient Celtic folk prayer offer a glimpse into how Christian symbols are mingled with the natural world through Mary: "The Virgin most excellent of face, Jesus more surpassing white than the snow, She like the moon rising over the hills, He like the sun on the peaks of the mountains."

These Christian feasts follow the natural rhythms of the earth. They suggest an earthly element in Christianity that is often obscured in the modern, post-industrial world. This earthly element of spirituality also offers a hint of why the worship of feminine goddesses might have held such an appeal in the ancient world and in the modern world as well, as many begin to hunger for a closer connection to the earth.

Because women were able to give birth and their menstrual patterns followed the cycles of the moon, ancient cultures naturally drew connections between motherhood and the earth. The soil, especially, was often equated with fertility. Just as women were able to weather seasons and bring life into the world, the soil was valued because of its ability to nurture seeds and bring life to fruition.

Black Madonnas

Some of the images that most directly connect the Virgin Mary to the soil are the Black Madonna images. Sometimes when the term *Black Madonna* is used, people think of the famed Polish icon of the Virgin Mary (detailed in Chapter 12) that has become black through years of exposure to soot and the elements.

However the Black Madonna does not only describe a single icon but an entire school of imagery that encompasses many icons and statues of the Virgin Mary and child. All of them have dark skin.

While it used to be widely believed that these images had darkened (like the Polish icon) because of exposure to the elements, it now seems likely that many of the images were created dark to begin with for very specific reasons that would have expressed something unique about Mary.

factum

In the Middle Ages, many people came to revere the Black Madonna images for their miraculous powers. Some communities even decided to paint their statues black in the hopes that they could attract more miracles to their own communities.

The Black Madonna statues became especially prominent during the Middle Ages. Some of the most beautiful and poignant of them are located in France and can be viewed to this day.

Many of these statues have special legends associated with them. One of the most common is that they were often found in natural settings, sometimes in caves, sometimes near rivers where they might been seen as providing safety for those crossing over the waters. When Christians found these small statues, they would often attempt to carry them to suitable places for building a church. As soon as the Christians turned away from the statues of the Black Madonnas, however, the statues would disappear and would be later found back in their original locations. This disappearing act would be repeated multiple times until the Christians would finally resign themselves to the fact that statues could not be moved. Ultimately, these Christians were forced to build small chapels around the statues in their natural habitats.

discussion question

How are Black Madonna statues similar to Eastern icons?
Black Madonna statues share many qualities with Eastern icons. In them, the Virgin Mary holds the infant Christ and seems to be gazing out from behind him with a look of timeless compassion. She does not smile, but she does not weep, either. Like her image in icons, she seems to be beyond emotions and sentimentality. Her gaze is steady and unrelenting.

The Meaning of the Black Madonna

The darkness of the Virgin Mary's skin has had many different meanings attached to it throughout the years. While some say that the darkness of her skin is merely a result of exposure to the elements, others suggest that the darkness of her skin is suggestive of her ability to identify with many different ethnic groups—this belief would certainly echo many of the apparitions in which Mary was reported to have appeared in familiar guise, with a face and dress recognizable to the local people. This can be seen, for example, in the case in Guadalupe when she appeared to an Aztec as an Aztec.

Still others point to a relationship between the color of the Virgin Mary's skin and the color of the soil. This idea finds echoes in both Christian and pagan belief. The Virgin Mary was often linked to soil and gardens both in the Eastern Church and in the medieval period. The darker skin on some images of Mary may also reflect her Middle Eastern heritage.

In the fourth century, Saint Ephrem the Syrian said that Mary was the soil on which Christ the sun could shine on the world and humanity. This image expressed how she, rooted in the earth as all humans are, was illuminated by her encounter with Christ.

Mingling Legends

Increasingly, as devotion to Mary grew, some of the properties that people once ascribed to pagan goddesses began to be connected to the Virgin Mary. It is also likely that in cultures where pagan beliefs were deeply rooted in the local people, legends surrounding Mary may have mingled with pagan beliefs. This mingling was a continual source of concern for the Church, as it tried to cleanse the beliefs that were incompatible with Christianity while still meeting the needs of those who required a bridge between their pagan beliefs and Christianity.

symbolism

The Black Madonna imagery would have been easily understood within the pagan context, where black was connected to fertility and life while white was connected to death. This symbolic color scheme was an exact reversal of the symbolism widely held among medieval Christians, in which black symbolized death and white symbolized life.

As Christianity spread throughout Europe, petitions that would have once been directed at gods or goddesses sometimes were redirected toward the Virgin Mary. Myths and legends about gods and goddesses that would have once captivated the hearts of the local people were replaced by legends and stories about Mary and the saints.

One of these stories, in particular, would have helped draw a connection between Mary and the fecundity of the earth. This legend was connected to the story of Joseph, Mary, and Jesus' journey into Egypt.

According to the Biblical account, the Holy Family had to flee Bethlehem because of the "slaughter of the innocents" in which King Herod sought to kill Jesus by sending soldiers to kill every male child in the region who was two years old or under. The Holy Family fled in order to protect Jesus, but it was most likely a perilous, frightening journey for them.

According to one of the medieval tales related to this journey, as the Holy Family passed one Egyptian farmer's field, Mary made the entire crop grow instantly. She did this both to bless the farmer, but also to confuse the soldiers who might have been pursuing her. Should the soldiers come by the farmer's field and ask him if he'd seen the Holy Family pass by, he could report, quite honestly, that he'd only seen the Holy Family just when he'd planted his field.

Gnosticism and Femininity

Gnosticism was a term used to describe a popular teaching within some early Christian circles. According to this teaching, which was ultimately condemned by the church, spirit and matter were utterly separated from each other. The Gnostics viewed the body as evil and the spirit as good and pure.

Although the Christian Church officially condemned Gnosticism, it is interesting to consider certain tendencies within Gnosticism in relation to the ways the Gnostics viewed femininity. Like Saint Paul who said that within Christ there was "no separation of Male and Female," the Gnostics took this idea to dramatic extremes, believing that as women became holy they became "like men."

This idea was related to the overarching belief that gender did not matter. The Gnostics thought that men were naturally more tied to the spiritual world while women were more linked to the physical world because of their menstrual cycle and the ability to give birth. Within this context, both men and women had to abandon their physical selves in order to become fully spiritual beings.

These views are interesting to consider in light of the Virgin Mary, because she was so fully feminine. She is not glorified for being "like a man" but for doing the thing that only women can do—giving birth to a child. Her greatness was directly connected to her femininity.

What's Different about the Virgin Mary?

One of the ancient dilemmas associated with the Virgin Mary has to do with the ways in which some cultures may have viewed her as a goddess. While this view is not compatible with official Christian teaching, the parallels between the Virgin Mary and some of the ancient goddess are strong enough that one can easily imagine the ways in which people may have conflated the Virgin Mary with some of the ancient goddesses.

But Mary's life can easily be separated from that of a goddess because she was never viewed as powerful, apart from her relationship with Christ. All of her strength and goodness came from her loving obedience to God, the way in which she let herself become a vessel of grace.

Mary is also distinct from the goddesses because all of her life pointed to someone else—to helping the story of her son come to fruition in the world. Her life was deeply rooted in both earthly and heavenly realities. She struggled in the way that all humans do, while remaining chiefly concerned with the purposes of God on this earth.

The Virgin Mary's ability to embrace the divine allowed her to become more and more like God, to be transformed by grace, while still remaining rooted in this earth—still connected to the soil from which she was formed.

factum

The fourteenth-century Saint Catherine of Siena said, "God Speaks: You see the gentle loving word born in a stable while Mary was on a journey, to show you, a pilgrim, how you should be constantly reborn in the stable of self-knowledge. There, by grace, you will find me birthed within your own soul."

Mary's human life helps her to be a bridge between earth and heaven, helping all of humanity to see what is possible. The popular author Kathleen Norris has slowly grown in devotion to Mary. According to Norris, all humans are called, like Mary, "To give birth to God in the this world."

This process of giving birth to the word of God offers many opportunities for fear. Even Mary was afraid, according to the Annunciation account in Luke. Mary's fear, as well as the angel's need to offer her reassurances, shows how fully human she was. If Mary was like the soil that God could shine upon, she was like all of humanity, rooted in the earth, as vulnerable as all living creatures are.

The apocryphal texts are also wonderful sources of very human details about Mary. Even if many elements of these texts are of dubious historical accuracy, they serve to humanize the Virgin Mary, showing that even her humanity was exalted through her perfect obedience to God.

Many examples of this are seen in the Protoevangelium of James. One can see Mary's humanity in the story in which Joachim and Anna consider sending her to live in the temple when she turns two, but they reconsider because of their fears that Mary would be sad without them. Like any toddler, Mary would grieve the loss of her parents, even though she was called to a life of special holiness.

factum

Many people believe that Mary's strength as an intercessor is directly related to her experience of being fully human. As the popular writer Jack Kerouac wrote in a letter to a friend, " . . . every prayer addressed to the Holy Mother has been answered . . . But I do want to point out that the reason I think she intercedes so well for us, is because she too is a human being."

One can also see how fully human the Virgin Mary was in relation to the priest Zachariah, who realized when she turned twelve that he was going to have to send her out of the temple because she would soon begin to menstruate. The Virgin Mary was human in every way. What sets the Virgin Mary apart from the rest of humanity are the choices she made—choices to live fully for God in every situation, to say yes to God in such a fully surrendered way that she could become a fully human "God-bearer" for the rest of humanity.

CHAPTER 20

Mary as Bridge Builder

There is perhaps no person in the history of the world who has served as a bridge between more cultures, peoples, and faiths than Mary. Mary's ability to connect diverse peoples and cultures is rooted in her openness to the divine—it was in her womb that heaven and earth met, mingled, and produced the person of Christ. People from many cultures report that Mary has appeared to them, offering warnings, reassurance and guidance. And for millions, both within and outside of Christianity, Mary has become the ultimate example of a woman exalted, of a fresh beginning for a weary world.

Heaven and Earth

Visitors to Orthodox Churches are often struck by something that appears strange upon first glance. Many of them have a large fresco of the Virgin Mary above the altar. Some may wonder why the Virgin appears so large and central, occupying such a prominent place.

Mary's place in the iconographic scheme is significant, and her prominence has little to do with her personal merit. When one examines the painted wall more closely, one can see that above her is Christ. She stands with her arms raised in prayer as an image of the Church ready to receive God incarnate. She represents a bridge between heaven and earth.

Just as the marriage of two people contains the mysterious ability to create an entire new being through their shared love, in Mary's womb, heaven and earth were able to come together and create the person of Christ.

It was in this role, when Mary served as the bridge between heaven and earth, that she served in her most cosmic and transformative capacity, offering her earthly self in service to the Divine and giving birth to infinite possibility.

Old and New

Christianity grew out of Judaism, but from very early on, also understood itself as something different, something new—the fulfillment of what had come before. So the task of the first Christians was essentially to find a way to integrate the Old Testament Scriptures into their lives in light of the Resurrection and to differentiate themselves appropriately from those in the Jewish community, who did not believe that Jesus was the Messiah.

Scholar and historian Jaroslav Pelikan points to the role Mary played in this process. In his book *Mary Through the Ages*, he wrote: "Because Mary was . . . 'Of the House and lineage of David,' she represented an unbreakable link between Jewish and Christian history, between the First Covenant *within* which she was born and the Second Covenant *to* which she gave birth."

factum

In contemporary times, people often view obedience as a passive willingness to comply with another's wishes. But the roots of the word imply action, not passivity. The Latin root of the word is *ob audire*, which means "to hearken to." This a form of active listening that requires an alert, attentive response. This type of obedience typifies Mary.

Mary's role as bridge between the Old and New Testaments is also expressed in her lineage. It is widely believed that she, like her husband Joseph, was a descendant of King David. A recently published book called *Mary's Message to the World* offers an interesting anecdote. The book features a woman named Annie, who experienced multiple visions of the Virgin Mary. When she first encountered Mary she said, "You can't appear to me because I'm not Catholic." The Virgin Mary replied, "Nor am I."

It may not be something one thinks about everyday, but Mary was raised Jewish, not Christian. She was spiritually and culturally deeply connected to Judaism.

According to extra-Biblical accounts, Mary was raised in the temple and very much lived according to the laws of Judaism, or the Old Covenant. Yet she was chosen, in a sense, to give birth to the person who was to become the New Covenant. As much as her life, her lineage, and her spiritual witness expressed her heritage and past, her willingness to become Theotokos or to become "the one who gave birth to the one who was God," helped her to bridge the gap between the Old and New Covenants.

Rich and Poor

Mary is known and loved by rich and poor alike. For almost 2,000 years, both have traveled rocky paths to make pilgrimages to her. Statues and images of her have adorned the homes and gardens of both the rich and the poor, and in every class of humanity, people of great resources and those of few, have looked up to her as an example of a faithful, attentive, transfigured life.

Mary is also a bridge between the rich and the poor in light of the ways in which she has appeared through visions. While it is true that she most often appears to the poor, in some cases, she has appeared to both the rich and the poor, instructing them to work together to accomplish God's purpose.

It might be suggested that Mary has always recognized what each person might have to offer. In many cases with the wealthy, she has viewed them as capable for helping to erect churches or shrines or to donate property to the faithful (as occurred on the property that was graced by the Holy Family in Zeitun, Egypt). In those lacking material resources, she may have seen an openness that she couldn't always expect in the wealthy.

Mary's Role

The Virgin's role, as a poor peasant from Nazareth who was chosen by God to become the bearer of the divine and to be remembered with love and reverence in all of the subsequent ages, also serves to remind us of another way in which she brings together the rich and the poor, that is, by clearly asserting that through her, the earthly orders and classes are subject to reversal. All that is seen as great in our world may not be seen as so great in the next, just as Christ said that the first on this earth shall be last and the last on this earth shall be first (Mark 10:31).

It is through Mary that we can see how God reverses the world order—those of few resources receive the wealth of revelation, those who are poor in this world become teachers to the rich, and all of this is demonstrated by the first peasant who lives this reversal in her own life—becoming powerful through humility, and strong in her weakness.

symbolism

The Virgin Mary illustrates the reversal of the classes when she sings her song, the Magnificat, in which she says that God has put down the mighty from the thrones and exalted those of low degree, that he has filled the hungry with good things, and the rich he has sent empty away (Luke 1:53).

Guadalupe

The Virgin Mary's apparitions at Guadalupe also speak to her recognition of the infinite value of people who lack material resources and are seen as powerless in the eyes of the world. It was there that the Virgin Mary appeared to Juan Diego, a peasant who was from one of the lowest classes in Mexico, an Aztec living in an occupied country, in a position of powerlessness.

After he took her message that the Virgin Mary wanted a church to be built the local bishop and was turned away, he returned to the Virgin and told her that if she really wanted the church to be built, then she should select a more important person to deliver the message.

But at this, the Virgin Mary offered Juan Diego the ultimate affirmation, telling him that it was he she chose. Her complete belief in him despite his powerless position in his own society offers hints of the ways in which the kingdom of God reverses earthly orders—the powerless can become powerful, those of low status, like the Virgin Mary, can be exalted for generations to come.

The message of Guadalupe has become central to Mexican identity, not only because the Virgin Mary's appearances sparked the conversion of nine million Aztecs but also because of the person she selected. Her choice of Juan Diego conveys the important message to anyone who feels slighted by society that they, too, can have a profound influence, and that their life is of infinite value. They, too, can become bearers of the word through their loving, attentive, and active obedience to God.

Women in the Church

For many women throughout Christian history, Mary's presence in the church, represented by icons or statues, affirmed their own unique Christian vocation. These representations made clear that church is a place for men and women equally. Some say that women play an insignificant role in the Bible, but this is not the case.

Even in the Genesis account, it is Eve who first tastes the forbidden fruit and in so doing changes the world. In the New Testament, Mary is chosen as the gate to paradise, the anti-Eve. Christ's death is witnessed by women, and it is the myrrh-bearing women who go to the tomb to anoint Jesus' body while everyone else sleeps. It is these women who are the first to witness the miracle of the Resurrection, and these women who, like Mary, become bearers of the message.

Mary's significant placement in the liturgy of the Church also speaks to her role among believers. Every commemoration and image of her speaks to the ongoing memory of the Church that women shape the world in small and large ways.

Islam and Christianity

As discussed in Chapter 18, there has perhaps been no time in history when the bridge between Christianity and Islam has been more important, especially in light of ongoing conflict between historically Christian and Muslim nations. As the memories of the Cold War dissipate, many political commentators have warned about a "clash of civilizations" which could turn into the greatest conflict the world has ever known.

Added to these concerns is the frightening lack of knowledge the Western world has about Islam, a religion that many believe to be the fastest growing in the world, claiming nearly one billion members. Just as Islam was able to gain dominion over the great Christian city of Constantinople, Islam is also growing in popularity and prominence in the historically Christian countries in Western Europe. Over the last century, Islam has also gained many new members in the United States, particularly within some African American communities.

In light of these developments, it is increasingly important that Christians and Muslims seek out ways to better understand each other. The Virgin Mary provides one such helpful bridge between the two religions.

There is a beautiful Muslim saying by Abu al-Qasim ibn 'Asakir which captures Islamic love for Mary:

"Mary said, 'In those days I was pregnant with Jesus, whenever there was someone in my house speaking with me, I would hear Jesus praising God inside me. Whenever I was alone and there was no one with me, I would converse with him and he with me, while he was still in my womb."

Many of the Marian apparitions and miracles have been experienced by Muslims, who already have within their holy book, the Koran, as well as within the lived practice of their religion, a deep and abiding love for the Virgin Mary. According to some reports from the apparitions at Medjugorje, a few of the visionaries were shocked when they asked Mary who the holiest local person was and she named a local Muslim woman.

Religious Dialogue

For religious dialogue to be fruitful, it must be based on knowledge as well as upon a desire to see and affirm all that is good beyond one's own particular context. This is an increasingly manageable task when one recognizes similar elements between different religions, without minimizing genuine differences.

In the Bible, Mary says, "Henceforth all generations shall call me blessed." The Koran opens a section with the words, "Commemorate Mary in the Book." This statement speaks to Mary's very distinct position within Islam.

Within Islam, Mary has been viewed for centuries as one of the most perfect women. Like Christianity, Islam heartily affirms the value of submission and surrender to God. This is part of why the Virgin Mary is viewed as a model of faith.

symbolism

There is an ancient Persian expression that goes, "Paradise is at the feet of the mothers." This saying is a reminder of the value of motherhood in the Muslim context.

The role of the Virgin Mary in Islam is quite notable for its practical implications as well. Because both Christianity and Islam deeply revere the Virgin Mary, members of both religions flock to Marian shrines to pray. It is quite remarkable against the current backdrop of hostility between these two religions that at certain holy sites such as the House of Mary in Ephesus and the healing pond in India, Muslims and Christians flock to both sites and pray peacefully beside each other (although not with each other). This model of peaceful surrender to God, despite significant religious, historical, and cultural divisions, remains a way out of the danger of increasing conflict and war under the guise of religion.

Nations Around the World

Within the last decade, Western Europe has sought to unify diverse currencies and cultures through the use of the Euro. This unified currency has simplified the rather complicated situation that previously existed because of the way so many little countries were packed so closely together, all using different currencies.

If there was a universally recognizable symbol that could link diverse countries it would most likely be the Virgin Mary, who remains central to many cultures around the world, most notably Latin American cultures such as Mexico, Spain, and Portugal. Within these contexts, the Virgin Mary is as central to their identities as their own national flags. The widespread immigration of Latinos to the United States has also brought the Virgin Mary into the wider attention of the public sphere.

Because the experience of apparitions of the Virgin Mary is shared by almost all of the nations around the world, the Virgin Mary has become for many a unifying symbol. Just as through her person she was able to bring about a unity between heaven and earth, many see in her the hope of peace between nations because she is shared by so many countries around the world. In each context, her appearances have been culturally appropriate to the people who have witnessed her appearance, yet there have also been striking universal themes that have emerged from these visitations, most notably her warnings as well as her exhortation to pray and to work for peace. In one of her visitations she was reported to have said, "Do not pray for peace unless you work toward it in your own life."

The Virgin Mary's visitations at Guadalupe came against the backdrop of a particularly threatening context. The Spanish domination of the local Aztec population involved a fair amount of brutality and violence. Just before the Virgin Mary appeared to Juan Diego, the Aztecs had secretly planned to revolt against the Spaniards and to kill them all. This mass bloodshed may have been inevitable, considering the intense conflict between the two cultures, had not the Virgin Mary appeared to Juan Diego, offering him an important job to do to convey her ongoing love and presence among the locals. After her appearance, almost the entire Aztec population converted to Christianity, and the two cultures then found a way to coexist peacefully together.

Mary has also been likened to the bride in the Song of Solomon who said, "I am black, but I am comely" (or as some have translated the verse, "I am black *and* I am beautiful"). This image has been viewed as a precursor to the much-loved Black Madonna icons, as well as to Mary's prominent position among people of color. This image has been seen as a powerful antidote for the Western European art that often portrayed Mary as a pale, blue-eyed European, an image that had no real grounding in her actual historical, geographical, or cultural setting.

The Virgin Mary's role among the nations is one of peace, unity, and love. Not only is she shared by many nations, but within each context her visitations have conveyed her desire that the nations work toward peace and unity despite significant historical, political, and spiritual struggles between them.

According to author Sally Cunneen, Mary's ability to transcend culture has powerful implications: "As God-bearer, she reveals that God both comforts and challenges us to new creation at all times. Her very capacity to be translated into images of every culture shows that she is what [St.] Ephrem called her, 'The daughter of humanity.'"

This is perhaps Mary's ultimate role—as bridge between heaven and earth, between God and human beings. The old and the new, man and woman, Christianity and Islam, and between all of the diverse nations around the earth—in each role, Mary bridges the gaps between the cultures and peoples. The Virgin Mary offers the possibility of healing historical divides and rifts through her prayers, love, and example. In this significant work she becomes accessible and available to all.

Glossary

Akathist Hymn

An Eastern praise hymn devoted to the Virgin Mary and comprised of twenty-four stanzas. During Lent, the hymn often is spread over four Fridays, and then the entire hymn is sung on the fifth Friday.

Annunciation

In Catholicism, the revelation to Mary by the angel Gabriel that she would conceive and bear a holy child who would be the son of God.

Apparition

A ghostlike manifestation that appears unexpectedly. Apparitions of the Virgin Mary have been reported in almost every culture and era in the world.

Ascetic

Monastic disciplines such as fasting, abstinence, prayer, and giving to the poor.

Assumption

The Roman Catholic dogma (proclaimed in 1950) that teaches that the Virgin Mary was assumed into heaven. This feast is celebrated on August 15, which is the same day that the Eastern Orthodox Church celebrates the Dormition, or the "Falling Asleep" of the Mother of God.

Canonize

A rigorous process by which the Roman Catholic and Eastern Orthodox Churches pronounce that a deceased person is holy and worthy of veneration.

Church Fathers

Some of the earliest Christian teachers and writers who were viewed as extremely influential, although not always saintly, generally connected to the first five centuries of Christianity.

Coredemptrix

A Roman Catholic belief that the Virgin Mary continues to participate in the salvation of humanity in a unique way through an ongoing ministry of intercession and intervention.

Ecstasy

A trancelike state in which a person experiences a transcendent spiritual encounter. During ecstasy, visionaries are unaware of their surroundings, unresponsive to pain, and their bodies do not receive injuries. They tend to focus on a specific spot, and their faces may shine in reflection of what they are seeing. The word *ecstasy* is taken from the Greek term *exstatsis* which literally means "to stand outside of oneself."

Eucharist

The gifts of bread and wine that the Roman Catholic and Eastern Orthodox Churches believe are transformed into the body and blood of Christ. The word *Eucharist* is taken from the Greek word *Eukharistia*, which means "thanksgiving."

Hallucination

A strangely real perception of something that is not visible to others, usually seen by only one person, and most often a result of mental illness or drug use.

Immaculate Conception

A Roman Catholic dogma that the Virgin Mary was conceived without the stain of original sin, or the sin that has been passed down to all humanity since Adam and Eve. This dogma was officially proclaimed by Pope Pius IX in 1854.

Laity

A term used to denote a non-clergy person.

Mediatrix

The Roman Catholic belief that the Virgin Mary continues to mediate on behalf of humanity.

Novena

Novena is a Roman Catholic devotional practice related to saying a prayer for nine days straight in an attempt to win special favor. Novenas have often been devoted to the Virgin Mary.

Panagia

The Eastern Orthodox term for the Virgin Mary's complete and total purity and holiness.

Rosary

A string of beads used in prayer to the Virgin Mary, which is viewed as an opportunity to meditate on Scripture and to pray the Lord's Prayer and the Hail Mary Prayer. This is primarily a Roman Catholic devotional pratice.

Scapular

Two strips of cloth that cross at the chest, a remnant from ecclesiastic garb that is worn for protection.

Stigmata

A spiritual condition in which the hands of a holy person begin to bear the same marks that Jesus' did when he was crucified. This temporary gift may cause great pain, and the wounds sometimes bleed. Experienced by Saint Francis and others.

Theotokos

An Eastern term for the Virgin Mary that can literally be translated as "The One who gave birth to the one who was God."

Transubstantiation

A Roman Catholic doctrine that teaches that the bread and wine of communion is transformed into the body and blood of Christ during the consecration. Within the Eastern Orthodox Church, it is believed that the bread and wine become body and blood in a spiritual sense while remaining bread and wine in the physical sense.

Veneration

An expression of devotion and love toward a saint or a holy item.

Vision

A state in which a person sees a person who is not visible to all, in which they enter into an ecstatic state where they are not able to feel pain or receive injuries.

Visionary

A person who experiences visions. According to records from the accredited apparitions of the Virgin Mary, these visionaries are consistently shown to be of sound mental health, without tendencies toward suggestibility or altered perceptions of reality.

Timeline

c. 4 B.C.	The Annunciation and birth of Christ (commonly the year 0, that is, the beginning of the calendar, since A.D. means "*anno Domini*," "in the year of the Lord").
A.D. 30	The death and resurrection of Christ.
C. A.D. 40	The first reported apparition of the Virgin Mary, who was very likely still alive when she appeared to Saint James the Greater in Saragossa, Spain.
C. A.D. 81	St. John's vision at Patmos, Greece, which served as the basis for the Book of Revelation. (There are many parallels between the "Woman Clothed with the Sun," as described in Revelation 12, and the Virgin Mary.)
C. A.D. 238	The Virgin Mary is reported to have appeared to Saint Gregory the Wonderworker in Neocaesarea, Asia Minor (present-day Turkey).
C. A.D. 300	The date of the oldest known prayer to the Virgin Mary.
A.D. 352	The apparition of "Our Lady of the Snows" in Rome, Italy, connected to the creation of Saint Mary Major Church.

A.D. 431	Council of Ephesus in which the Virgin Mary was officially proclaimed as Theotokos, "the birth-giver of God."
A.D. 911	The Protection of the Virgin Mary apparition at Blachernae Palace Church in a suburb of Constantinople.
1054	The Pope of Rome and the Patriarch of Constantinople excommunicate each other.
1061	The apparition at Walsingham, creation of "House of Nazareth" replica.
1204	The Crusaders sack Constantinople (during the Fourth Crusade, 1202–1204).
1382	The apparition at Czestochowa, Italy, connected to the famed Black Madonna icon.
1517	Martin Luther posts his *95 Theses*.
1531	The apparition at Guadalupe, Mexico.
1560	The apparition of "Our Lady of Good Health" at Vailankanni, India.
1798	Apparition at Lavang, Vietnam.

1830	The apparition to Sister Catherine Laboure at Paris, France, that served as inspiration for the Miraculous Medal.
1854	The dogma of the Immaculate Conception proclaimed by Pope Pius IV.
1858	Apparitions at Lourdes, France, in which the Virgin Mary is reported to have said, "I am the Immaculate Conception."
1917	Apparitions at Fatima, Portugal.
1950	Pope Pius XII proclaims the Dogma of the Assumption.
1962–64	The Second Vatican Council.
1968	Apparitions at Zeitun, Egypt.
1973	Apparitions at Akita, Japan, associated with statue that wept 101 times and also shed blood and tears.
1981	Apparitions at Medjugorje, Yugoslavia, often viewed as the fulfillment of the apparitions at Fatima.
1982	Apparitions at Damascus, Syria, associated with a myrrh-weeping icon and concerns over divisions within Christianity.

Pilgrim's Guide

Tips:

- Pack lightly—you may have to walk a good deal.
- Go with an open mind and a flexible attitude—pilgrimages are never quite what you expect them to be.
- Consider traveling with a local church group or with an organization responsible for organizing pilgrimages.
- You are likely to get the best price, and have a better experience when you travel with experts than if you strike out on your own.

General Pilgrimage Planning Web Sites

Here is a listing of some Web sites that might be useful as you plan your pilgrimage.

www.thecatholicpilgrim.com
www.unitours.com
www.gocatholictravel.com

Popular Marian Pilgrimage Sites:

LOURDES
www.lourdes-france.com

MEDJUGORJE
www.medjugorje.org

FATIMA
www.fatima.org

Additional Resources

MARY AND THE CHURCH FATHERS

Gambero, Luigi. *Mary and the Fathers of the Church* (San Francisco, CA: Ignatius Press, 1999). This book is a wonderful resource for understanding the thoughts of the Church Fathers in relation to the Virgin Mary. This is one of the few resources in which you can interact with their ideas in their own words.

_____. *Mary in the Middle Ages: The Blessed Virgin Mary in the Thought of Medieval Latin Theologians* (San Francisco, CA: Ignatius Press, 2005). This volume offers an opportunity to understand the thoughts of medieval Latin theologians in relation to the Virgin Mary.

MARY IN ROMAN CATHOLIC TEACHING

Bunson, Margaret (compiler), *John Paul II's Book of Mary* (Huntington, IN: Our Sunday Visitor, 1996). This book offers numerous glimpses into Pope John Paul II's love for the Virgin Mary. This book would be useful for devotions.

Catechism of the Catholic Church, Second Edition (New York, NY: Doubleday, 2003). (Available from various publishers or online at *www.scborromeo.org/ccc.htm*). This book offers the most authoritative Roman Catholic perspective on the Virgin Mary and the teachings of the Church.

Varghese, Roy Abraham. *God-Sent: A History of the Accredited Apparitions of Mary* (New York, NY: Crossroad General Interest Co., 2000). This very detailed book offers an exhaustive Roman Catholic perspective on the apparitions.

MARY AND THE EASTERN ORTHODOX CHURCH

Maximovitch, St. John. *The Orthodox Veneration of Mary the Birthgiver of God* (Wildwood, CA: St. Xenia Skete Press, 1997). Provides a doctrinal overview of Eastern Orthodox teaching on Mary.

Schmemann, Fr. Alexander. "The Presence of Mary" (Mount Hermon, CA: Conciliar Press, 1988). These two brief pamphlets offer extremely helpful perspectives on devotion to Mary in the Eastern Orthodox context.

Ware, Kallistos. "Mary Theotokos in the Orthodox Tradition" (Wallington, UK: The Ecumenical Society of the Blessed Virgin Mary, 1997). Available from Ecumenical Society of the Blessed Virgin Mary (ESBVM), *www.esbvm.org.uk*.

MARY AND PROTESTANTS

Braaten, Carl E., and Jenson, Robert W., eds. *Mary, Mother of God* (Grand Rapids, MI: Eerdmanns, 2004).

Longenecker, Dwight, and Gustafson, David. *Mary: A Catholic-Evangelical Debate* (Grand Rapids, MI: Brazos Press, 2003). This book offers a fascinating glimpse into a debate between a Roman Catholic and an Evangelical. The book-length debate, respectful and honest, offers different perspectives on titles of Mary, the rosary, apparitions, as well as the role of Mary's intercessions in the lives of the faithful.

Williams, Rowan. *Ponder These Things: Praying with Icons of the Virgin* (Franklin, WI: Sheed & Ward, 2002). Written by the Archbishop of Canterbury, this book offers an Anglican perspective on the Orthodox tradition of iconography.

GENERAL WORKS

Cunneen, Sally. *In Search of Mary: The Woman and the Symbol* (New York, NY: Ballantine Books, 1996). This highly readable book offers a fascinating glimpse into many of the historical debates and evolutions surrounding the Virgin Mary.

Ford-Grabowsky, Mary. *Spiritual Writings on Mary: Annotated & Explained* (Woodstock, VT: Skylight Paths Publishing, 2005). This book is wonderful for devotional use. It's full of short quotations from an incredible variety of sources from many religions, regions, and historical periods.

Pelikan, Jaroslav. *Mary Through the Centuries: Her Place in the History of Culture* (New Haven, CT: Yale University Press, 1996). This academic book offers a helpful overview of Mary's place in time, culture, and the arts.

Tavard, George H. *The Thousand Faces of the Virgin Mary* (Collegeville, MN: The Liturgical Press, 1996). This scholarly book is useful for providing an overview of the theological evolutions surrounding Mary.

MARY IN LITERATURE

Kidd, Sue Monk. *The Secret Life of Bees* (New York, NY: Penguin Books, 2003). This beautifully written book is a work of fiction that captures some of the mood of Marian devotion—the experience of a "mother ache" that is fulfilled as one draws close to Mary.